CULTURE IN THE DOMAINS OF LAW

What does it mean for courts and other legal institutions to be culturally sensitive? What are the institutional implications and consequences of such an aspiration? To what extent is legal discourse capable of accommodating multiple cultural narratives without losing its claim to normative specificity? And how are we to understand meetings of law and culture in the context of formal and informal legal processes, when demands are made to accommodate cultural difference? The encounter of law and culture is a polycentric relation, but these questions draw our attention to law and legal institutions as one site of encounter warranting further investigation, to map out the place of culture in the domains of law by relying on the insights of law, anthropology, politics, and philosophy. *Culture in the Domains of Law* seeks to examine and answer these questions resulting in a richer outlook on both law and culture.

RENÉ PROVOST is Professor of Law at McGill University, Canada, where he was the founding director of the McGill Centre for Human Rights and Legal Pluralism. He has researched and published widely on international law and legal pluralism. In 2015, he was named a fellow of the Trudeau Foundation for his contribution to the advancement of knowledge in the humanities and social sciences.

CAMBRIDGE STUDIES IN LAW AND SOCIETY

Cambridge Studies in Law and Society aims to publish the best scholarly work on legal discourse and practice in its social and institutional contexts, combining theoretical insights and empirical research.

The fields that it covers are: studies of law in action; the sociology of law; the anthropology of law; cultural studies of law, including the role of legal discourses in social formations; law and economics; law and politics; and studies of governance. The books consider all forms of legal discourse across societies, rather than being limited to lawyers' discourses alone.

The series editors come from a range of disciplines: academic law; socio-legal studies; sociology; and anthropology. All have been actively involved in teaching and writing about law in context.

A list of books in the series can be found at the back of this book.

CULTURE IN THE DOMAINS OF LAW

Edited by

RENÉ PROVOST

McGill University

CAMBRIDGE
UNIVERSITY PRESS

CAMBRIDGE
UNIVERSITY PRESS

University Printing House, Cambridge CB2 8BS, United Kingdom

Cambridge University Press is part of the University of Cambridge.

It furthers the University's mission by disseminating knowledge in the pursuit of education, learning, and research at the highest international levels of excellence.

www.cambridge.org
Information on this title: www.cambridge.org/9781107163331

First published 2017

A catalogue record for this publication is available from the British Library.

Library of Congress Cataloging-in-Publication Data
Names: Provost, René, 1965– editor.
Title: Culture in the domains of law / edited by René Provost.
Description: Cambridge [UK] ; New York : Cambridge University Press, 2016. | Series: Cambridge studies in law and society | Includes bibliographical references and index.
Identifiers: LCCN 2016028915 | ISBN 9781107163331 (Hardback)
Subjects: LCSH: Culture and law. | Sociological jurisprudence. | BISAC: LAW / General.
Classification: LCC K487.C8 C88 2016 | DDC 340/.115–dc23 LC record available at https://lccn.loc.gov/2016028915

ISBN 978-1-107-16333-1 Hardback

To Patrick Glenn and Rod Macdonald,
without whom
we wouldn't have written this
quite
the same way

CONTENTS

ACKNOWLEDGMENTS

This volume is the outcome of a multi-year research project supported by the Canadian Social Sciences and Humanities Research Council, in which Kirsten Anker, David Howes, René Provost, and Eric Reiter were participants. The research agenda was developed over three years, and included a research seminar in which undergraduate students in Law at McGill University and graduate students in Anthropology at Concordia University carried out research as a team. The work of these students, Annelise Godber, Caylee Hong, Jessica McCaffrey, Karmjit Sidhu, and Maike Storks, helped to lay the foundation for both the overall project and individual papers. The specific contributions included in this volume were prepared over a period of one year in which initial ideas and drafts were circulated, culminating in a public conference held at the McGill Centre for Human Rights and Legal Pluralism in 2014. In addition to the contributing authors, thanks are due to David Howes (Anthropology, Concordia), Alison Dundes Renteln (Law and Anthropology, University of Southern California), Ronald Niezen (Law and Anthropology, McGill), Frédéric Bachand (Law, McGill), Annie Bunting (Law and Society, York), Kamari Maxine Clarke (Anthropology, Yale), and Genevieve Painter (Law and Social Policy, UC Berkeley), for their contribution to the conference. Finally, the research assistance of Rachel Zuroff and Anne-Sophie Ouellet in editing the chapters is gratefully acknowledged.

The volume is dedicated to the memory of my colleagues H. Patrick Glenn and Roderick A. Macdonald, both of whom passed away during 2015. They appear in the footnotes of many of the chapters, and stand to remain sources of inspiration and models of creativity for many years to come.

René Provost
McGill University

CONTRIBUTORS

KIRSTEN ANKER is an associate professor of law at McGill University, where she teaches in the areas of property, legal theory, and Aboriginal peoples and the law, and has research interests that combine these areas, as well as translation studies, anthropology, education, evidence, and alternative dispute resolution. Her new book, *Declarations of Interdependence: Indigenous Rights, Legal Pluralism and Postcolonial Jurisprudence* (2014) explores various aspects of claiming Aboriginal Title as a way to inspire a re-imagination of law.

LUCIA BELLUCCI is an assistant professor at the University of Milan, Law School. She is the co-founder and co-director of the Summer School in 'Law and Bilateral Trade: North America-Europe' (Université de Montréal-University of Milan). She has taught (Flying Faculty) at the College of Europe (Natolin, Warsaw) and the Oñati International Institute for the Sociology of Law. She has been a Visiting Professor at the Université de Montréal, Law School, CRDP and a Visiting Researcher at the Oxford Centre for Socio-Legal Studies. She holds a PhD in Sociology of Law from the University of Milan as well as a PhD in Law from the University of Paris 1-Panthéon Sorbonne. In addition she holds a post-graduate degree in Economics and Management of Cultural and Artistic Goods from Bocconi University-SDA, and a master's and bachelor's degree in law from the University of Bologna. She has lectured in Italian, English and French at Italian and Canadian Universities (Université de Montréal and McGill University). She has researched and published on Law and Anthropology, EU Law and Politics, International Economic Law and Politics, and Media Law and Policy.

MORGAN BRIGG is Senior lecturer in the School of Political Science and International Studies at The University of Queensland. His research examines questions of culture, governance and selfhood in conflict resolution, peacebuilding, and development studies. Morgan's books include

The New Politics of Conflict Resolution: Responding to Difference (2008), and *Mediating across Difference: Oceanic and Asian Approaches to Conflict Resolution* (2011) (co-edited with Roland Bleiker). He is a practicing mediator and facilitator, and has provided policy and practice advice in Australia and internationally.

THOMAS BURELLI is a professor of law at the University of Ottawa. He specialized in environmental law, intellectual property, indigenous rights and research ethics. The main focus of his research is on the relationships between scientists and indigenous people in research projects involving the use of traditional knowledge (in particular ethnobotany and ethnopharmacology projects). He has investigated and revealed several biopiracy cases in New Caledonia and French Guyana in 2014 and 2016. He has contested these cases and contributed to the development of new tools such as models of contracts for the Institut de Recherche pour le Développement (IRD) and the Code éthique du Centre de Recherches Insulaires et Observatoire de l'Environnement (Criobe) in French Polynesia. He has also conducted several field missions in the French territories abroad (New Caledonia, French Polynesia, and French Guiana). He is currently working with the Legal Research Chair in Food Diversity and Security held by Professor Geneviève Parent from the Université Laval and with the Canada Research Chair on Legal Diversity and Indigenous People.

DAVID CHANDLER is Professor of International Relations, Department of Politics and International Relations, University of Westminster, London. He is the founding editor of the *Journal of Intervention and Statebuilding* and currently the editor of *Resilience: International Policies, Practices and Discourses.* His most recent books are *The Neoliberal Subject: Resilience, Adaptation and Vulnerability* (with Julian Reid) (2016); *Resilience: The Governance of Complexity* (2014); *Freedom vs Necessity in International Relations* (2013); and *The Routledge Handbook of International Statebuilding* (co-edited with Tim Sisk) (2013).

ANTHONY J. CONNOLLY is an associate professor at the Law School of the Australian National University, specializing in legal philosophy, indigenous rights law, and public law. He is the author of *Cultural Difference on Trial: The Nature and Limits of Judicial Understanding* (2010) and the editor of *Indigenous Rights* (2009), *Public Law in the Age of Statutes* (2015), and *Cultural Heritage Rights* (2015). He has also published a number of book chapters and journal articles on topics in his areas of expertise.

KRISTIN DOUGHTY is Assistant Professor of Anthropology at University of Rochester. Her book, *Remediation in Rwanda: Grassroots Legal Forums* (2016, Ethnography of Political Violence Series) examines how Rwandans navigated the combination of harmony and punishment in grassroots courts purportedly designed to rebuild the social fabric in the wake of the 1994 genocide. It is based on eighteen months of ethnographic research with grassroots legal forums in Rwanda, including genocide courts (gacaca courts) in which suspects from the 1994 genocide were tried among their neighbors before locally elected judges, as well as mediation committees for ordinary disputes (comite y'abunzi), and a legal aid clinic. Her teaching includes courses on political and legal anthropology, transitional justice, Africa, and human rights.

PASCALE FOURNIER, LLB (Université Laval), LLM (Toronto), SJD (Harvard), is Full Professor and Research Chair in Legal Pluralism and Comparative Law at the Faculty of Law, University of Ottawa. Professor Fournier is passionate about issues of access to justice. In 2014, the National Assembly of Quebec appointed her as Commissioner to the Quebec Human Rights and Youth Rights Commission (CDPDJ). Her research focuses primarily on family law, criminal law, human rights and comparative constitutional law. The author of more than forty academic publications, she is recognized internationally for her significant contribution to the study of law and gender, especially in the context of religious divorce. Her book *Muslim Marriage in Western Courts: Lost in Transplantation* was published in 2010, and a French version followed in 2013. Professor Fournier was awarded the Raymond-Blais medal (2008) and the Gloire de l'Escolle medal (2016) from Laval University, the Quebec Bar Advocatus Emeritus (Ad. E.) distinction (2009), the University of Ottawa President's Award for Excellence in Media Relations (2011), the Canada-Arab Chamber of Commerce Award for 'Academic Excellence and Contribution to Humanity' (2014) and the Capital Educators' Award for teaching excellence (2016). In 2014, Professor Fournier was named Fellow of the International Women's Forum and, in 2015, she was named 'one of the Top 25 Most Influential Lawyers in Canada' by the Canadian Lawyer Magazine.

JENNIFER HENDRY is a lecturer in Jurisprudence at the University of Leeds School of Law. She has an LLB (Hons) from the University of Glasgow (2002), an LLM from the University of Edinburgh (2003), and a PhD in Law from the European University Institute (EUI) in Florence (2009). She has been a visiting scholar at the University of Sydney's Department of Philosophy (2011) and the University of Arizona's James E. Rogers College of Law (2015), and is a principal investigator on a World Universities Network-funded interdisciplinary international research network focusing on 'spaces of indigenous justice'. She is on the editorial board of the *German Law Journal* and the executive of the UK Socio-Legal Studies Association (SLSA).

RÉGIS LAFARGUE† was a Président de Chambre at the Cour d'Appel d'Angers (France). He was also a judge in New Caledonia for many years (from 1989 to 1994 and from 2010 to 2015). He has taught in several French universities (Université Française du Pacifique, Université de Saint-Denis de la Réunion, Université de Paris X – Nanterre, Université de Paris I Panthéon-Sorbonne). After a new period of 5 years and a half in New Caledonia as Judge of the court of appeal of Noumea (2010–2015), he was appointed as President of a division (President de Chambre) of the court of appeal of Angers in 2015.

RENÉ PROVOST, LLB (Université de Montréal), LLM (UC Berkeley), DPhil (Oxford) is Professor of Law at McGill University, where he served as Associate Dean (Academic) from 2001 to 2003. He was the founding director of the McGill Centre for Human Rights and Legal Pluralism from 2005 to 2010. He has written extensively on international human rights and humanitarian law, including *International Human Rights and Humanitarian Law* (2002), *State Responsibility in International Law* (2002), *International Law Chiefly as Applied and Interpreted in Canada*, 7th edn. (2006), *Confronting Genocide* (2011), *Dialogues on Human Rights and Legal Pluralism* (2013), and *Mapping the Legal Boundaries of Belonging: Law Between Religious Revival and Post-Multiculturalism* (2014). He was the principal investigator for an interdisciplinary team, the Centaur Jurisprudence Project, funded by the Social Sciences and Humanities Research Council of Canada examining the construction of culture by legal institutions in a variety of settings. In 2015, he was awarded a fellowship by the Pierre Elliott Trudeau Foundation for his contribution to the advancement of knowledge in the social sciences and humanities.

ERIC H. REITER is Associate Professor in the Department of History, Concordia University, Montreal, and a member of the Barreau du Québec. He has published recently on judicial mediation in Quebec, the uses of history in Aboriginal rights litigation, and the history of nuisance law in Quebec, among other topics.

JUSTIN B. RICHLAND is Associate Professor of Anthropology at the University of Chicago and Research Professor at the American Bar Foundation. His research explores the intersections of culture, language and law in contemporary Native American and US settler colonial governance. He is the author of two books, *Arguing with Tradition, The Language of Law in Hopi Tribal Court* (2008) and (with Sarah Deer) *Introduction to Tribal Legal Studies, 3rd Edition* (2015) as well as articles in various scholarly journals including *American Ethnologist, Annual Review of Anthropology, Discourse & Society, Law and Social Inquiry,* and *Law & Society Review*. In addition to his research, he also serves as Associate Justice of the Hopi Appellate Court, the highest court of the Hopi Nation. In 2016, he was named a John Simon Guggenheim Fellow.

1

Centaur Jurisprudence

Culture before the Law

RENÉ PROVOST

Many claims to justice ask law to be responsive to the lived experiences of those to and through whom it is applied. 'Culture' is one label attached to collective forms of this lived experience. But what does it mean for courts and other legal institutions to be culturally sensitive? What are the institutional implications and consequences of such an aspiration? To what extent is legal discourse capable of accommodating multiple cultural narratives without losing its claim to normative specificity? And how are we to understand meetings of law and culture in the context of formal legal processes, such as when a criminal defendant invokes the acceptability of domestic violence within his ethnic community, when oral traditions are presented as the basis for an Aboriginal land claim, or when the custom of 'bush marriage' is evoked as relevant to the prosecution of the war crime of rape?[1] The encounter of law and culture corresponds to a polycentric relation, but these specific questions draw our attention to law and legal institutions as one site of encounter warranting further investigation, to map out the place of culture in the domains of law.

The title to this introductory chapter marries two references to interrogate the troubled relation between a perspective rooted in the law and one rooted in culture. 'Centaur jurisprudence' echoes the question raised by Clifford Geertz in his landmark article on law and fact as local knowledge: what do law and anthropology have to learn from each other, and what is the desired outcome of the encounter of these two disciplinary perspectives? Geertz sought to demonstrate that the objective lies not in the creation of a 'centaur discipline', but rather in a more diffuse cross-pollination that sees law and anthropology remaining distinct worldviews

[1] *R.* v. *Humaid*, 81 O.R. (3d) 456 (2006); *Delgamuukw* v. *British Columbia*, [1997] 3 S.C.R. 1010; *Prosecutor* v. *Brima*, Special Court for Sierra Leone, Appeals Chamber (2008).

enriched by a sensitivity to the insights of the other.[2] The second reference is to Kafka's parable 'Before the Law', in which a man from the country spends an entire lifetime trying to pass the terrifying doorkeeper to gain admittance through the gates of the Law, eventually dying before getting any further.[3] As brilliantly analysed by Jacques Derrida, the title of the story can be taken to mean a range of different ideas.[4] These all equally apply to culture if, as I have done, we add that prefix to Kafka's title: culture before the law in a chronological or genealogical sense, signalling that the formation of culture precedes the creation of law; culture before the law in a spatial or geographical sense, as in an encounter that might turn into a confrontation; culture before the law in a juridical sense, whereby culture is brought to the law to be judged; and culture before the law in an ideological sense, as a rallying cry for the need to protect culture above and beyond any duty to respect the law. As the countryman lay dying at the end of Kafka's parable, he asks the doorkeeper how come no one else ever sought admission to the Law. The latter responds: 'No one else could ever be admitted here, since this gate was made only for you. I am now going to shut it'. One understanding of this ending suggests that law is not a monistic projection of state power but rather an invitation for every individual to imagine their own path to the law. As such, it reflects the ethos of legal pluralism as one approach to law that answers Geertz' call for mutually reinforcing legal and anthropological perspectives so as to capture the full complexity of the encounter between law and culture as conveyed in Kafka's parable.

Legal pluralism, in rejecting a narrow focus on formal law and state institutions, offers a vision of law as dynamic and inherently open to 'culture'. This volume explores the potential of legal pluralism to account for the varied and dynamic roles of culture within legal discourse: can legal pluralism create a richer model of legal knowledge, one that reflects plural cultural narratives, while still offering a normative foundation for formal legal processes? In short, can legal pluralism bring culture within the domains of law? The chapters in this book suggest that the *métissage* takes place not necessarily in the definition of a new mutant discipline, as

[2] Clifford Geertz, 'Local knowledge: Fact and law in comparative perspective' in *Local Knowledge: Further Essays in Interpretive Anthropology* (New York: Basic Books, 1983) 167 at 169; Franz von Benda-Beckmann, 'Riding or killing the centaur? Reflections on the identities of legal anthropology' (2008) 4:02 *International Journal of Law in Context* 85.

[3] Franz Kafka, *The Trial* (Knopf, 1992) at 234–236.

[4] Jacques Derrida, 'Before the law' in Derek Attridge ed., *Acts of Literature* (Routledge: London, 1992) 181.

feared by Geertz, but rather in the mapping of a middle space of encounter in which the vernacular of law and anthropology can intermingle in what could be called a centaur jurisprudence, not wedded to shaping a new discipline but rather to providing richer views from the plurality of sensibilities embodied in these disciplines.

The encounters of law and culture within legal institutions are complex and dynamic, intersecting at multiple sites. Three distinct sites, understood as normative sites in which legal knowledge is produced, can be identified. The volume critically interrogates each of these sites by combining legal and anthropological perspectives. The first site, *translation of cultures*, relates to the process of representing cultures as facts which fall into categories known to law. The second, *acculturation of justice*, centres on the ways in which legal institutions react and adapt in an attempt to be culturally sensitive. This includes experimenting with alternative modes of conflict resolution, where legal processes are adapted to local cultural exigencies. The third, *pluralized narratives of law and cultures*, touches on the impact within a given community of the narrative created by legal institutions in the process of applying legal norms. In this respect, the volume contributes to assessing the *rayonnement* of legal culture beyond the boundaries of legal institutions and, by the same process, explores the extent to which legal culture itself is shaped through these encounters. These three normative sites are neither insular nor neatly bounded, but rather three facets of the continuous interaction between legal and cultural perspectives.

Overall, through each of the three sites, the chapters in this book provide a better understanding of the productive and transformative nature of the encounter of law and culture, making this encounter the primary locus of inquiry.[5] More specifically, the volume seeks to offer a critical understanding of the production of legal and cultural narratives by the various interveners in the legal process, including parties, judges, experts and community leaders; to question a vision of the encounter of law and culture as necessarily asymmetrical, as the subjugation of a given culture by law's own culture; to assess the extent to which the production of cultural narratives through legal processes can endow them with greater legitimacy, in ways for which legal pluralism may have failed to fully account up to now[6]; and at a more general level, to critically address

[5] Nicholas Kasirer, 'Legal education as métissage' (2003) 78 *Tul L Rev* 481.

[6] Brian Z Tamanaha, 'Understanding legal pluralism: past to present, local to global' (2008) 30 *Sydney L Rev* 375.

the interactive process whereby legal and anthropological knowledge is created and labelled as belonging to distinct disciplines, something we hope to achieve without unquestioningly surrendering to the hegemony of either anthropological or legal hermeneutics.[7]

Many of the important works that have explored the interaction of law and culture, including Sarat and Kearns' influential *Law in the Domains of Culture* to which the title of this volume gives a nod, appear rooted in a cultural more than a legal outlook.[8] The chapters in this book seek to give very significant space to a legal perspective on this complex issue. Law, as with many other disciplines, tends to break down into sub-categories that develop their own variant of the disciplinary discourse. For law, this can be said to include not only the way in which issues are framed and arguments presented, but also more elusively in the way in which the relationship between law and other social practices are represented. To return to the three examples given in the opening paragraph, the interaction of law and culture is painted in quite distinct colours in criminal law (invoking a cultural trait as a defence), Aboriginal law (invoking a traditional practice as a basis for a land claim) and international criminal law (invoking a local custom as a necessary context to the application of international law). Legal analysis not only has tended to focus on the articulation of the 'right' answer that a court ought to give in any one of these or similar contexts, but the conversations mostly occur in silos within each of the sub-disciplines of law without significant transversal attention to a phenomenon that can reveal more systemic features of the interplay of law and culture.[9] Thus, one animating objective in gathering the authors of the various chapters in this book has been to cut cross the boundaries internal to law, to bring into contact analyses that hail from corners of the discipline that rarely, if ever, meet. Accordingly, the three sites of interaction of law and culture described earlier are explored through essays in four legal fields, providing the structure for the four sections of the volume: the general accommodation of 'minority

[7] James Clifford, 'Rearticulating anthropology' in Daniel Segal & Sylvia Yanagisako eds., *Unwrapping the Sacred Bundle Reflections on the Disciplining of Anthropology* (Durham: Duke University Press, 2005) 24; Annelise Riles, 'Representing in-between: law, anthropology, and the rhetoric of interdisciplinary' (1994) *U Ill L Rev* 597.

[8] Austin Sarat & Thomas R Kearns, 'The cultural lives of law' in Austin Sarat & Thomas R Kearns eds., *Law in the Domains of Culture* (Ann Arbor: University of Michigan Press, 2000) 1, at 7.

[9] See Paul W Kahn, *The Cultural Study of Law: Reconstructing Legal Scholarship* (Chicago: University of Chicago Press, 1999).

practices' (chapters by Connolly ('Legal Pluralism and the Interpretive Limits of Law', Chapter 2), Fournier ('Family Law, State Recognition and Intersecting Spheres/Spaces: Jewish and Muslim Women Divorcing in the UK', Chapter 3), Bellucci ('Customary Norms *vs* State Law. French Courts' Responses to the Traditional Practice of *Excision*', Chapter 4), Indigenous law (chapters by Anker ('Law, Culture, Fact in Indigenous Claims: Legal Pluralism as a Problem of Recognition', Chapter 5), Richland ('On Perpetuity: Tradition, Law, and the Pluralism of Hopi Jurisprudence', Chapter 6), Hendry ('Existing in the Hyphen: On Relational Legal Culture', Chapter 7), Burelli and Lafargue ('The Unexpected Effects of the Recognition of Indigenous Rights in New Caledonia: The Story of an Assimilation Measure Becoming the Trigger for the Acculturation of the French Legal System', Chapter 8)), alternative dispute resolution (chapters by Reiter ('Cultures of Conflict: Welcoming and Resisting "Non-Western" Influence in Alternative Dispute Resolution', Chapter 9), Brigg ('Rebalancing Power and Culture: The Case of Alternative Dispute Resolution', Chapter 10), Doughty ('Grassroots Law in Context: Moving Beyond the Cultural Justification', Chapter 11)), and law in conflicts (chapters by Provost ('Cannibal Laws', Chapter 12), Chandler ('Beyond the Paradox of Exporting the Rule of Law: Resilience and the War on Drugs in the Americas', Chapter 13)). I now move to more finely explore each site of normative interaction, using contributions from across these four legal fields to support the analysis.

1.1 Translation of Cultures

Turning to the first identified normative site, a first investigation of the deployment of the concept of culture within formal legal processes begins with the observation that *talking* about aspects of life as culture is first and foremost a linguistic practice or discourse whose shape and consequences can be analysed discursively. Culture, it is suggested, has been largely invoked in courts to describe a 'thing' rather than a process or a normative regime. In Aboriginal rights cases, for example, Indigenous culture is something that can be measured and empirically observed.[10] Kirsten Anker in her chapter (Chapter 5: 'Law, Culture, Fact in Indigenous Claims: Legal Pluralism as a Problem of Recognition') argues that it is the paradigm of recognition that treats Indigenous law as a social fact

[10] *R.* v. *Van der Peet*, [1996] 2 S.C.R. 507.

transplants': exogenous institutions and ways of approaching conflict cannot be 'fit' within the strictures of Western legal systems without some measure translating them into Western categories and ways of thinking. Exotics get framed so as to ease entry into the receiving culture, and this most often means framing them within the dispute resolution enterprise as contributing in an instrumental way to classically Western goals like efficiency or justice. Reiter acknowledges that these exotic imports or resurrections of ancient Western values may well help us achieve better results, or permit wider access to justice, or perhaps even transform Western cultures of disputing, but what we are importing or resurrecting are Westernized images of exotic institutions, domesticated in name and, more importantly, in substance to achieve decidedly Western purposes like efficiency, therapy or justice.

In suggesting that the 'factualization' of culture is necessarily reductive, rendering an essentialized version of culture which denies the constant intercultural exchanges and redefinition which are critical to the continued survival of any culture[17], do we present a concept of culture that is unmanageable by courts? For instance in *Marshall (No. 2)*, a 1999 decision of the Supreme Court of Canada dealing with Aboriginal rights, Justice Binnie writes:

> The law sees a finality of interpretation of historical events where finality, according to the professional historians, is not possible. The reality, of course, is that courts are handed disputes that require for their resolution the finding of certain historical facts. The litigating parties cannot await the possibility of a stable academic consensus. The judicial process must do as best it can.[18]

Applying the law is a process in which cultural, as well as historical, narratives are created for the immediate purpose of permitting a resolution.[19] As such, the legal representation of culture is normative and instrumental from the start, reflecting political and cultural assumptions embodied in law and legal practice, clearly serving the epistemic interest in power.[20] What seems critical is how that representation is itself

[17] Ronald Niezen, 'Culture and the judiciary: the meaning of the culture concept as a source of aboriginal rights in Canada' (2003) 18 *Can JL & Soc* 1.

[18] *R.* v. *Marshall (No. 2)*, [1999] 3 S.C.R. 507 para. 37.

[19] William Twining, 'Narrative and generalizations in argumentation about questions of fact' (1999) 40 *S Tex L Rev* 351.

[20] Seyla Benhabib, *The Claims of Culture: Equality and Diversity in the Global Era* (Princeton University Press, 2002).

represented to all the actors involved.[21] The problem invites us to be conscious not only of the fluid nature of culture and law and of the existence of diversity internal to any culture, diversity which is often critical to the protection of marginal groups, but also of the crucially creative character of the process of presenting culture to law.[22] Thus, Jen Hendry argues in her chapter (Chapter 7: '"Existing in the Hyphen": On Relational Legal Culture') that legal culture should be conceptualized in a relational sense, as an operation instead of a place, as a process and not as a unit. Understood as a process, legal culture can be said to exist in the interactive tension between legal rules and social norms. A spatially detached or non-embedded understanding of legal culture frees it from the confines of both jurisdiction and hierarchical (albeit oftentimes interpenetrating) levels of legal institutions and operations, while the inclusion of a temporal dimension provides for the radical openness necessary to a relational procedural conception of legal culture.

The anthropological perspective that '*les milieux* are all *mixtes*', as Geertz puts it, poses a challenge to the 'factualization' of culture before legal institutions.[23] Because the ineluctable instrumentalism of the legal process promotes the essentialization of a given culture in order to make it amenable to a final decision, a fundamental precept of legal culture is its ability to affirm its supremacy, leading it to cannibalize any 'other' culture it encounters.[24] In part, legal pluralism suggests that the normative regime encompassing the official law of the state includes more than the formal sources of law: the practice of official institutions as well as the informal understanding of legal norms by all social agents can lead to the emergence of expectations which, when they intersect, become part of the normative fabric that gives law its meaning.[25] In addition, legal pluralism sees normative regimes entirely dissociated from any state institution or approval as falling within a broad definition of law.[26] These

[21] See Geertz, *supra* note 2 at 174.

[22] Alison Dundes Renteln, *The Cultural Defense* (Oxford University Press, 2004).

[23] Clifford Geertz, *Available Light: Anthropological Reflections on Philosophical Topics* (Princeton University Press, 2000) 68.

[24] Stanley Diamond, 'The rule of law vs. the order of custom' (1971) 38 *Social Research* 42.

[25] Lon L Fuller, 'Human interaction and the law' (1969) 14 *Am J Juris* 1.

[26] S F Moore, 'Law and social change: the semi-autonomous social field as an appropriate subject of study' (1973) 7:4 *Law and Society Review* 719; Boaventura de Sousa Santos, 'Law: a map of misreading. Toward a postmodern conception of law' (1987) 14 *Journal of Law and Society* 279; Emmanuel Melissaris, *Ubiquitous Law: Legal Theory and the Space for Legal Pluralism* (Farham, Surrey: Ashgate Publishing, Ltd., 2009).

insights suggest an understanding of the encounter of law and culture before legal institutions whereby courts and other legal institutions stand at the confluence of multiple regimes.[27] Culture, in offering an account of a discursive practice, is taken to be inherently normative.[28] Formal law is not seen as a monolithic system being forced upon an 'other' culture, but rather a regime whose fabric is liable to be transformed by the encounter.[29] In its most extreme form the very individuals involved, judges, lawyers, experts, community representatives, become normative sites in which a polyvocal legal culture is created.[30] This is vividly illustrated in Lucia Bellucci's study of the way many social actors come into play during *excision* trials in France (Chapter 4: 'Customary Norms *vs* State Law. French Courts' Responses to the Traditional Practice of *Excision*'). Of particular importance are the President of the Court, the prosecutor, the experts, the interpreter, the defending counsel and the associations joining the proceedings as civil parties. Bellucci argues that the conflict between the customary rule of *excision* and the state legal system translates into the legal world the conflict between two normative universes, which are conceptually distant with regard to the priority given to the individual and the group. This conflict demonstrates the way in which some traditional practices that were ignored when perpetuated only in colonized areas came to be considered crimes once 'imported' to the West. This situation transposes in the realm of criminal law a situation of legal pluralism[31]: the populations that practice *excision* view it as a binding customary rule with the force of law and practice it

[27] Anne Griffiths, *In the Shadow of Marriage: Gender and Justice in an African Community* (University of Chicago Press, 1997).

[28] Sally Engle Merry, 'Human rights law and the demonization of culture (and anthropology along the way)' (2003) 26:1 *Polar: Political and Legal Anthropology Review* 55; Annelise Riles, 'Anthropology, human rights, and legal knowledge: culture in the iron cage' (2006) 108:1 *American Anthropologist* 52; René Provost, 'Magic and modernity in Tintin au Congo (1930) and the Sierra Leone special court' (2012) 16:1 *Law Text Culture* 183.

[29] Kirsten Anker, 'The truth in painting: cultural artefacts as proof of native title' (2005) 9 *Law Text Culture* 91; Benjamin L Berger, 'The cultural limits of legal tolerance' (2008) 21:2 *Canadian Journal of Law and Jurisprudence* 245.

[30] Bernard S Jackson, *Making Sense in Law: Linguistic, Psychological, and Semiotic Perspectives* (Deborah Charles, 1995); Martha-Marie Kleinhans & Roderick A Macdonald, 'What is a critical legal pluralism?' (1997) 12:02 *Canadian Journal of Law and Society* 25; J Webber, 'Legal pluralism and human agency'(2006) 44 *Osgoode Hall LJ* 167.

[31] Marie-Claire Foblets, 'Les délits culturels : de la répercussion des conflits de culture sur la conduite délinquante ; réflexions sur l'apport de l'anthropologie du droit à un débat contemporain' (1998) 35:1 *Droit et cultures* 195 at 200.

with no intention to harm. The conflict between the rule of *excision* and the criminal justice system is especially complicated because it implies different pressures and sanctions that are respectively exerted and inflicted by the customary and state normative orders.

Anthony Connolly (Chapter 1: 'Legal Pluralism and the Interpretive Limits of Law') examines this phenomenon by interrogating the idea of the *interpretive* limits of state law. In his chapter, he examines the question of whether state law can do what it takes to adequately understand Indigenous law without having to become something other than law. He finds that the answer to this question depends on the operative concept of law informing the inquiry: the more content the judge's conceptual scheme shares with that of the Indigenous claimants in relation to their law, the more conducive it will be to the successful interpretation of those agents and their law; likewise, successful interpretation across a legal system or set of systems will be rendered more difficult (though not necessarily impossible) if a sufficient enough set of counter-interpretive legal factors obtain systemically across all hearings in that legal system or set of systems. The chapter uses a Hartian conception of law as a case-study and finds that nothing inherent to a positivist system of state law prevents it from being structured such that it *could* come to or provide for an adequate understanding of Indigenous law without losing its identity as law.

1.2 Acculturation of Justice

The second normative site identified earlier was that of the acculturation of justice: even if it were posited that courts and other legal institutions ought to be culturally responsive, what does that imply for the way in which the law is actually applied? Claims of cultural specificity can lead to a culturally reflexive jurisprudence in which substantive legal norms are adapted to respond to such claims.[32] Thus whereas the first site considers the process by which culture is made to speak in terms cognizable to the legal system – whether as something 'similar' or something 'different' – the second site focuses on the way law appears to change in order to respond to claims of cultural specificity. The chapters in this book seek to assess both the process whereby such adjustments are made and the cultural narrative that is created. For

[32] David Howes, 'Introduction: culture in the domains of law' (2005) 20:1 *Canadian Journal of Law and Society* 9.

instance, the Supreme Court of Canada's decision in *Van der Peet* requires courts to take into account 'Aboriginal perspectives' on the meaning of the rights claimed.[33] In later cases this perspective is said to influence the concepts of rights, title and culture itself, with judges debating just what this 'reconciliation' of perspectives means in terms of evaluating.[34] In the international criminal law sphere, references have been made before the Sierra Leone Special Court to the fact that 'bush wives', cannibalism and the use of child soldiers hold particular meaning in the cultural context of that armed conflict, and that legal norms should reflect such a fact.[35] The so-called cultural defense raised in some criminal cases in the United States and Canada likewise evokes the possibility of altering the fabric of criminal law to reflect the accused's distinct cultural background.[36]

The acculturation of legal institutions can also lead to development of rules governing the process whereby a matter is brought before a judge or other third party. In Canada, an initial response to the perception that criminal justice is failing Aboriginal peoples was to call for justice processes sensitive to and incorporating unique aspects of Aboriginal culture.[37] A diverse range of programmes has been initiated, some of which attempt to build hybrid institutions or practices by grafting traditional ways of dealing with offending onto a modern context, including sentencing circles, elders' panels, potlatch and the use of totem symbols.[38] In Aboriginal land claims, the Supreme Court has held that '[t]he law of evidence must be adapted in order that this type of evidence

[33] *R.* v. *Van der Peet*, [1996] 2 S.C.R. 507.

[34] *Delgamuukw* v. *British Columbia*, [1997] 3 S.C.R. 1010; *R.* v. *Sappier; R.* v. *Gray*, [2006] 2 S.C.R. 686; *Tsilhqot'in Nation* v. *British Columbia*, [2014] 2 S.C.R. 256.

[35] *Prosecutor* v. *Brima*, Special Court for Sierra Leone, Appeals Chamber (2008); Karen Barnes, Peter Albrecht & Maria Olson, *Addressing Gender-based Violence in Sierra Leone: Mapping Challenges, Responses and Future Entry Points* (International Alert, 2007); Karine Bélair, 'Unearthing the customary law foundations of forced marriages during Sierra Leone's civil war: the possible impact of international criminal law on customary marriage and women's rights in post-conflict Sierra Leone' (2006) 15 *Colum J Gender & L* 551.

[36] *People* v. *Romero*, 69 Cal. App. 4th 846 (1999); *R.* v. *Lucien*, 8 AQ (1998) (Cour du Québec), *R.* v. *Lucien*, J.E. 2000–219 (C.A.); *R.* v. *Nahar*, 181 C.C.C. (3d) 449 (2004); *R.* v. *Humaid*, 81 O.R. (3d) 456 (2006); Homi K Bhabha, *The Location of Culture* (Psychology Press, 1994); Renteln, *supra* note 22.

[37] Canada Royal Commission on Aboriginal Peoples, *Bridging the Cultural Divide: A Report on Aboriginal People and Criminal Justice in Canada* (The Commission, 1996).

[38] *R.* v. *Moses*, 71 C.C.C. (3d) 347 (2004); Chris Andersen, 'Governing aboriginal justice in Canada: constructing responsible individuals and communities through "tradition"'

[aboriginal oral testimony] can be accommodated and placed on an equal footing with other types of historical evidence that courts are familiar with, which largely consists of historical documents'.[39] One undeveloped question, explored mainly by anthropologists and historians as a matter of expert witnessing, is to ask whether, and if so how, in pragmatic terms, courtroom process and practices have been altered by the changes to evidentiary law.[40] Thomas Burelli and Régis Lafargue note in their chapter (Chapter 8: 'The Unexpected Effects of the Recognition of Indigenous Rights in New Caledonia: The Story of an Assimilation Measure Becoming the Trigger for the Acculturation of the French Legal System') that despite the principle that France does not allow for much pluralism in its legal system, certain French territories are resisting this model of the unitary State, causing the legal system to adapt its system and institutions in order to maintain its legitimacy. For example, in order to recognize the specificities and rights of the Kanak people in New Caledonia, the local authorities have actively worked to adapt institutions and establish a recognized form of legal pluralism. As a result of the interactions between judges and the Kanak people, exchanges between their respective legal orders and a mutual acculturation can be observed, including the decision by certain judges to work with Indigenous assessors. By adapting courtroom procedure, judges recognize that they are not the only relevant normative order to deal with legal issues and recognize the role that Indigenous authorities should play in resolving disputes.

The very institutional design of legal mechanisms reflects cultural markers. The adoption of ADR processes, for instance, where the conflict resolution paradigm is itself said to be influenced by Indigenous, African or other customary practices, promises to give voice to the parties themselves and to open a greater space in which culturally reflexive

(1999) 31:4 *Crime, Law and Social Change* 303; Ross Gordon Green, *Justice in Aboriginal Communities: Sentencing Alternatives* (Purich Pub., 1998); Darlene Johnston, 'Connecting people to place: great lakes aboriginal history in cultural context' (2006) Ipperwash Inquiry, online: http://papers.ssrn.com/sol3/papers.cfm?abstract_id=1864900; Paulette Regan, *Unsettling the Settler within: Indian Residential Schools, Truth Telling, and Reconciliation in Canada* (Vancouver: UBC Press, 2010) 193; Ronald Niezen, *Truth and Indignation: Canada's Truth and Reconciliation Commission on Indian Residential Schools* (University of Toronto Press, 2013).

39 *Delgamuukw* v. *British Columbia*, [1997] 3 S.C.R. 1010.

40 Arthur J Ray, 'Native history on trial: Confessions of an expert witness' (2003) 84:2 *Canadian Historical Review* 253.

approaches may flourish.[41] The question is whether the shift from adjudication to ADR allows the development of new views of the legal subject as a site of cultural encounter, particularly as the values and techniques of ADR loop back into the formal justice system. The emerging practice of creating hybrid international criminal courts (Sierra Leone, Cambodia, Bosnia, Timor Leste, Lebanon, Central African Republic, Kosovo) allows consideration of whether these institutions differ in design in a way that is anchored to some degree in the specific culture of their location.[42] Kristin Doughty considers the particular case of Rwanda in her chapter (Chapter 11: 'Grassroots Law in Context: Moving Beyond the Cultural Justification'), examining the interaction among *gacaca* courts, mediation committees for low-level civil and criminal disputes (*comites y'abunzi*) and a university-led legal aid clinic. Looking at mediation discourse as cutting across *gacaca*, mediation committees, and legal aid clinics shifts the debate away from deciding whether or not mediation is in fact the culturally appropriate model for Rwanda, as claimed by the government. Instead, this approach articulates what is at stake in the process of cultural justification, and how this mode of power constitutes people as particular kinds of subjects within a carefully constructed community. Doughty shows that while there are in fact deep cultural roots to mediation in Rwanda, at the same time, these forums, and the mediation discourse at their heart, are related to broader, historically situated neoliberal logics of governance. Mediation discourse operated differently across various legal forums, and influenced people differently depending on their social positionality. Doughty argues that Rwanda's particular instantiation of the mediation discourse that legitimized it through culture was insidious, because combining the cultural justification with

41 Michal Alberstein, 'Forms of mediation and law: Cultures of dispute resolution' (2007) 22 *Ohio St J on Disp Resol* 321; Carrie Menkel-Meadow, 'From legal disputes to conflict resolution and human problem solving: legal dispute resolution in a multidisciplinary context' (2004) 54 *J Legal Educ* 7; Kevin Avruch, 'Culture as context, culture as communication: Considerations for humanitarian negotiators' (2004) 9 *Harv Negot L Rev* 391; Catherine Bell & David Kahane, *Intercultural Dispute Resolution in Aboriginal Contexts: Land Claims, Treaties, and Self-Government Agreements* (Vancouver: UBC Press, 2007); Morgan Brigg, 'Mediation, power, and cultural difference' (2003) 20:3 *Conflict Resolution Quarterly* 287; George Pavlich, 'The power of community mediation: Government and formation of self-identity' (1996) 30 *Law and Society Review* 707.

42 Roland Adjovi, 'Introduction - L'Afrique dans le développement de la justice pénale internationale' (2006) 14 *Afr YB Int'l L* 3; Cesare PR Romano, P A Nollkaemper & Jann K Kleffner, *Internationalized Criminal Courts and Tribunals. Sierra Leone, East-Timor, Kosovo and Cambodia* (Oxford University Press, 2004).

state-backed authority amounted to making the beliefs and values of collective unity mandatory in and of themselves.

In his chapter (Chapter 10: 'Rebalancing Power and Culture: The Case of Alternative Dispute Resolution'), Morgan Brigg analyses the relationship between formal power and informal culture through ADR, to ask if ADR can be a site of serious legal pluralism. He finds that despite links with – and apparent openness to – cultural difference, ADR policy and practice is substantially informed and governed by modes of reasoning about conflict and social life that reflect and reproduce dominant Western law and political systems. At the same time, the prospects for legal pluralism through ADR are not entirely closed: a more genuine exchange may become possible by turning more fully to the lived experience of people and their social forms in order to mitigate the influence of Western liberal modes of reasoning about conflict and social life, but for this to lead to serious legal pluralism it must attend to ontological frameworks and reference points rather than rest at the level of behaviours and practices.

1.3 Pluralized Narratives on Law and Cultures

The narrative that is created when culture is brought before the law for the resolution of a particular dispute is one that may not necessarily conform to those generated either by anthropologists or by people who identify with a given culture. At the same time, it is a narrative that will be legitimized by the endorsement legal institutions give. When selecting facts needed to determine the outcome of a dispute, courts will necessarily arbitrate cultural debates. They will do so, whether consciously or not, on the basis of their own thought-world, embedded as it is in the architecture of legal institutions.[43] The weight carried by these legalized narratives can thus go beyond the immediate outcome of the decision, and may, for instance, strengthen the in-culture inequality of vulnerable groups such as women or shift the balance of power as some actors are validated over others.[44]

[43] Mary Douglas, *How Institutions Think* (Syracuse University Press, 1986).

[44] Annie Bunting, 'Theorizing women's cultural diversity in feminist international human rights strategies' (1993) 20:1 *Journal of Law and Society* 6; Simon Correy, 'The reconstitution of aboriginal sociality through the identification of traditional owners in New South Wales' (2006) 17:3 *Australian Journal of Anthropology* 336; Ayelet Shachar, *Multicultural Jurisdictions: Cultural Differences and Women's Rights* (Cambridge University Press, 2001).

A pluralization of the notion of audience with which judges and other legal actors are engaged could allow a dialogue with the community whose culture has been invoked.[45] The ambitious outreach programme run by the Sierra Leone Special Court attempted this to ensure that its work was accessible and visible in even remote communities.[46] What then becomes of such a cultural narrative beyond the specific case with which it was associated? To what extent, for example, do First Nations in Canada – and particular members within them – co-opt the picture of their community produced in the extensive litigation of Aboriginal rights? How transformative is this encounter for a given culture? Can Indigenous accounts of court proceedings such as the Sissons-Morrow collection of Inuit sculptures be seen as a reverse cultural translation of the legal process, a contribution to the constitution of a legal order for that community[47]? One approach, following Weiner, is to see these encounters not in terms of misrecognition or co-optation of some otherwise pure cultural realm, but as 'elicitory mechanisms' for the expression and actualization of cultural differences.[48] For example, Pascale Fournier in her chapter (Chapter 3: 'Family Law, State Recognition and Intersecting Spheres/Spaces: Jewish and Muslim Women Divorcing in the UK') examines what it is that makes a given legal or religious institution empowering for women. She finds that the empowering effect of both systems is a function of their interaction: specifically, it would seem that religion is much more empowering when it evolves alongside the law and is influenced by it. While Jewish family law is recognized and acknowledged by state law in the countries that she examines, Muslim law is not, with a resulting estrangement from the civil sphere on the part of Muslim

45 Richard D Mohr, 'Some conditions for culturally diverse deliberation' (2005) 20:1 *Canadian Journal of Law and Society* 87; René Provost, 'Judging in splendid isolation' (2008) 56:1 *American Journal of Comparative Law* 125.

46 Sam Muller, 'The triple helix of culture, international law, and the development of international law', in Paul Meerts ed., *Culture and International Law* (Cambridge: Cambridge University Press, 2008); Susan Shepler, *Childhood Deployed: Remaking Child Soldiers in Sierra Leone* (NYU Press, 2014); Augustine SJ Park, 'Consolidating peace: rule of law institutions and local justice practices in Sierra Leone' (2008) 24:3 *South African Journal on Human Rights* 536.

47 Shulamit Almog, 'Images of justice or images of dissonance: the Sissons-Morrow collection', paper delivered at the McGill Faculty of Law, 7 October 2005; Justin Richland, *Arguing with Tradition: The Language of Law in Hopi Tribal Court* (Chicago, IL: University of Chicago Press, 2008).

48 James F Weiner, 'Culture in a sealed envelope: the concealment of Australian Aboriginal heritage and tradition in the Hindmarsh Island Bridge affair' (1999) 5:2 *Journal of the Royal Anthropological Institute* 193.

communities. This revealed a contrast between Jewish women navigating strategically the civil regulation of their religious practices and Muslim women's frustrated agency, often baffled by the State non-recognition of their religious practices which contributes to further isolate them from alternative avenues.

This third normative site directs us to consider one further aspect of the encounter of culture and law: the significance of the creation of pluralized narratives for legal culture itself. In offering a narrative about 'other' cultures, legal institutions by the same token create a narrative about their own identity.[49] The exchange goes in every direction. It might take the form of a reaffirmation of normality, difference and even exclusion, when other social norms are highlighted as clearly different from those embodied in formal law. On the other hand, it may lead to the co-option of components that were initially presented as distinct, but are later taken as a model suited to use beyond the boundaries of their culture of origin. I take up this question in my chapter (Chapter 12: 'Cannibal Laws') by way of a thought experiment around three variations on the theme of cannibal law: a first variation examines the manner in which formal law regulates cannibalism understood as a crime under international criminal law; a second asks whether it could at all be possible to read the practice of cannibalism as itself normative, a code created by cannibals themselves to regulate their practice; and finally a third variation, in which cannibalism stands as a metaphor for the way in which legal discourse relates to other, competing forms of social discourse. Ultimately, all three variations emerge as interacting strands of the social production of law and culture, demonstrating that neither type of discourse can operate in full autonomy or dominance vis-à-vis the other. Instead, legal and cultural narratives emerge as mutually constitutive across the whole span of formalism in their expression.

We can question whether legal pluralism truly offers a richer view of law as setting the conditions for social action and providing a repertoire for social interaction across cultural boundaries.[50] For David Chandler (Chapter 13: 'Beyond the Paradox of Exporting the Rule of Law: Resilience and the War on Drugs in the Americas') the attentiveness to the cultural context and the acknowledged need to vernacularize legal norms

[49] David Nelken, 'Using the concept of legal culture' (2004) 29 *Austl J Leg Phil* 1; Jeremy Webber, 'Culture, legal culture, and legal reasoning: a comment on Nelken' (2004) 29 *Austl J Leg Phil* 27.

[50] von Benda-Beckmann, *supra* note 2.

remain trapped in a general project of exporting the rule of law. Using the context of the 'war on drugs' in the Americas, he offers an alternative to the problematic consequences of exporting Western liberal legal frameworks by using resilience approaches and their suggestion that formal frameworks of law can no longer be understood to work to shape or direct social processes in a top-down or hierarchical manner. From this starting point, Chandler notes that for resilience approaches 'everyday life' is neither conceived of as a problem nor romanticized as 'resisting', but seen as providing a problem-solving resource of practices to be drawn upon. In focusing on how everyday practices can provide the resources to address daily challenges, problems and solutions are no longer debated in the formal framings of the export of liberal institutions, laws and rights; instead, resilience approaches are based on how practices work in a particular context. In a shift away from understanding sociocultural values as the problem or barrier to be overcome or be adapted to, resilience approaches understand local practices as the dynamic of positive transformation once there is an enabling context.

The cultural narrative created by legal institutions fosters within the legal community a specific narrative about the formal legal regime.[51] From the perspective of these communities, the encounter of culture and law is thus not merely self-reflective but stands for a meaningful engagement with formal law, perhaps towards a more intercultural legal tradition.[52]

What emerges from the volume as a whole is a richer version of legal pluralism, one that factors in cultural difference as a key vector in the normative process whereby law is created and applied. The suggestion is not that this is a new strand of legal pluralism, warranting a distinct label as 'cultural legal pluralism', but rather that this is a dimension of legal pluralism that has been under-emphasized in most accounts of that approach to legal discourse. Meaningfully integrating cultural difference in the analysis of interacting and intersecting legal orders adds significantly to the complexity of the endeavour, but many chapters in this volume suggest that this is a cost likely to be rewarded by a legal regime that is more broadly embraced by a wide range of legal agents and, as a

[51] Lawrence Rosen, *Law as Culture: An Invitation* (Princeton University Press, 2006); Nicolau, Pignarre & Lafargue, *supra* note 11.

[52] Etienne Le Roy, 'L'accès à l'universalisme par le dialogue interculturel' (1995) 26 *Revue générale de droit* 5; Adam Kuper, *Culture: The Anthropologists' Account* (Harvard University Press, 2009); Shachar, *supra* note 44.

result, is ultimately more effective. The chapters also stand as an invitation to legal pluralists not to turn their back on the state and its institutions, as a reflection of pluralism's rejection of the nation-state as the monopolistic jurisprudential framing of all interactions. The point is not to suggest reverting to positivism as a necessary framing legal perspective, but rather that legal pluralism has matured sufficiently to serve as a toolkit to better understand the ways in which state institutions and formal law interact with cultural and other social discourses, resulting in richer views of legal normativity.

PART I

Accommodation of Minority Cultural Practices

2

Legal Pluralism and the Interpretive Limits of Law

ANTHONY J. CONNOLLY

2.1 The Problematic – Recognition, Interpretation, and Identity as Law

Much of the literature on legal pluralism in relation to Indigenous peoples is concerned with the recognition phase of the encounter between non-Indigenous state law and Indigenous law.[1] By recognition, I mean the establishment of an ongoing relationship between the two kinds of legal system, together with their respective cultures and peoples.[2] An intriguing question raised in this literature concerns the extent to which state law can properly recognise Indigenous law *without losing its identity as law*.[3] For example, in her chapter in this collection, Kirsten Anker speaks of the legal pluralist instinct 'that there is *something distinctively legal* in the encounter between courts and Indigenous

[1] See, for example, the literature discussed by Sally Engle Merry, 'Legal Pluralism' (1988) 22:5 *Law Soc Rev* 869; Brian Tamanaha, 'Understanding Legal Pluralism: Past to Present, Local to Global' 30 *Syd L Rev* 375; Kirsten Anker, *Declarations of Interdependence: A Legal Pluralist Approach to Indigenous Rights* (Farnham: Ashgate Publishing, 2014).

[2] My simple definition here implicitly nests within a number of richer conceptions of recognition, some of which are at work in the legal pluralist literature. See, for example, Charles Taylor, 'The Politics of Recognition' in A Gutmann, ed, *Multiculturalism and the Politics of Recognition* (Princeton: Princeton University Press, 1992); Axel Honneth, *The Struggle for Recognition: The Moral Grammar of Social Conflicts* (Cambridge: Polity Press, 1995); James Tully, *Strange Multiplicity: Constitutionalism in an Age of Diversity* (Cambridge: Cambridge University Press, 1995); Nancy Fraser, 'Rethinking Recognition' (2000) 3 *New Left Rev* 107; Nancy Fraser, 'Recognition without Ethics?' (2001) 18:2–3 *Theory Cult Soc* 21; Lois McNay, *Against Recognition* (Cambridge: Polity Press, 2008).

[3] The use of the term 'properly' here is meant to connote a relationship which satisfies some context-relevant set of practical, ethical, or political criteria – for example, a relationship in which Indigenous law is accorded some parity of legitimacy with state law. The term 'law' in this context is generally used synonymously with the term 'legal system', but it is also used from time to time to refer to the legal dimension of a range of other phenomena. Where it matters in the discussion to follow, I will endeavour to distinguish the various meanings of the term as best I can.

claimants'[4] and asks 'if state law is relativized and the definition of law broadened, then what stops *what is particular to law* disappearing into culture or social life in general?'[5] In a similar vein, Provost's introduction to this collection asks, 'to what extent is legal discourse capable of accommodating multiple cultural narratives *without losing its claim to normative specificity*?' and 'can legal pluralism create a richer model of legal knowledge, one that reflects plural cultural narratives, *while still offering a normative foundation for formal legal processes*?'[6]

Implicit in these questions seems to be an assumption that law as a category of phenomena *has* a distinctive identity or nature.[7] One of the ways in which we might conceive of this identity is in terms of a set of category-individuating properties.[8] So, we might construe these questions as assuming that there is a set of properties that all instances of law

[4] See Anker, Chapter 5, this volume (emphasis added). This phrase, 'the encounter between courts and Indigenous claimants', hints at the kind of cross-cultural interpretive engagement I am concerned with in this chapter.

[5] See Anker, Chapter 5, this volume (emphasis added). This concern with law disappearing into culture or social life more generally (and becoming just one more cultural field) also hints at a systemic understanding of the term 'law' – that is, law as 'legal system'.

[6] See Provost, Chapter 1, this volume (emphasis added). I take these latter two questions to be concerned with the same issue as Anker's. It is worth noting that a related question within this theoretical problematic (and one Anker is alive to) concerns the extent to which Indigenous law can be properly recognised by state law, without losing *its* identity as law. We could also flip the terms of this problematic around and raise the questions of the extent to which Indigenous law can properly recognise state law without losing its identity as (Indigenous) law and the extent to which state law can be recognised by Indigenous law without losing its identity as (state) law. Following the lead of the literature on this, I will in this chapter maintain my focus on the question of the identity of state law as law. However, virtually all of what I have to say could be applied to the other just-mentioned aspects of this problematic.

[7] That it does is a common assumption in much of the wider jurisprudential literature – particularly, that of the analytic tradition. See, for example, Joseph Raz, 'Two Views of the Nature of the Theory of Law: A Partial Comparison' in J Coleman, ed, *Hart's Postscript: Essays on the Postscript to the Concept of Law* (Oxford: Oxford University Press, 2001) 249; Joseph Raz 'Can There be a Theory of Law' in *Between Authority and Interpretation* (Oxford: Oxford University Press, 2009); Julie Dickson, *Evaluation and Legal Theory* (Oxford: Hart Publishing, 2001); T Endicott, 'The Generality of Law' in L Duarte D'Almeida & et al, eds, *Reading HLA Hart's 'Concept of Law'* (Oxford: Hart Publishing, 2013).

[8] There are a number of ways we can make sense of the role played here by these category-individuating properties. They may be construed in a metaphysically robust sense as comprising some discursively transcendent *essence* of the category in question (e.g. Dickson, *supra* note 7; Raz, *supra* note 7; T. Endicott, *supra* note 7.) or they may be construed in a more socially constructivist, discursive, and metaphysically more contingent sense as conventionally ascribed by some relevant conceptual community (e.g. Ian P Farrell, 'HLA Hart and the Methodology of Jurisprudence' (2006) 84 *Tex Law Rev*

(all members of the category of law) possess and which any given phenomenon must possess in order to be law – at least, by the lights of some or other community of agents.[9] Latent here also is the view that if a given instance of state law changes (for example, in response to its encounter with Indigenous law) in a manner that renders it no longer sufficiently possessed of these category-individuating properties, then it is no longer law (or is no longer identifiable as law by the relevant community of agents).

We can make sense of such a set of category-individuating properties in terms of the content of a theory of *what law is* – or, in Hart's terms, a *concept of law*.[10] In seeking to determine the extent to which state law can maintain a proper ongoing relationship with Indigenous law without losing its identity as law, much depends on the content of the operative concept of law which informs the inquiry. This is to say that much depends on the identity of the set of properties the participants in the inquiry believe characterises law as a category.[11] As any survey of the

983; Brian Leiter, *Naturalizing Jurisprudence: Essays on American Legal Realism and Naturalism in Legal Philosophy* (Oxford: Oxford University Press, 2007).

9 What we might term a conceptual community or a community of inquirers.

10 H L A Hart, *The Concept of Law*, 2nd ed (Oxford: Oxford University Press, 1994) at 239–40. See also F C Keil, *Concepts, Kinds, and Cognitive Development* (MIT Press, Cambridge, MA, 1989); Henry M Wellman & Susan Gelman, 'Cognitive Development: Foundational Theories of Core Domains' (1992) 43 *Annu Rev Psychol* 337; Alison Gopnik & Andrew N Meltzoff, *Words, Thoughts, and Theories* (Cambridge MA: MIT Press, 1997); Eric Margolis & Stephen Laurence, eds, *Concepts: Core Readings* (Cambridge: MIT Press, 1999); Susan Carey, *The Origin of Concepts* (Oxford University Press, 2009) on conceptual content as theoretical in nature.

11 It should be noted here that the relevant set of properties might be conceived of in classical definitionalist fashion as a fixed, finite and determinable set of necessary conditions all of which are required in order for there to be a metaphysical sufficiency or, alternatively, as a wider set of properties, one of a number of subsets (or combinations) of which must be instantiated in order for there to be metaphysical sufficiency (law as a so-called cluster concept). See Margolis & Laurence, *supra* note 10 at 8–27; G L Murphy, *The Big Book of Concepts* (MIT Press, Cambridge, MA, 2002) at 11–40; Jesse J Prinz, *Furnishing the Mind: Concepts and their Perceptual Basis.* (MIT Press, 2002) at 32–48 on definitionalism. See John R Searle, 'Proper Names' (1958) 67:266 *Mind* 166; P F Strawson, *Individuals: An Essay in Descriptive Metaphysics* (London, Methuen, 1959); Michael Devitt & Kim Sterelny, *Language and Reality: An Introduction to the Philosophy of Language* (MIT Press, 1999) at especially 43–6 on cluster concepts. Alternatively, we might see the category as one whose membership is not determined objectively by the possession of some set of necessary properties but, rather, is determined solely as a function of the categorising norms and practices of a relevant conceptual community, with no clear overlap of properties between members of the category. See Prinz, *supra* note at especially 18–22 on Wittgenstein's views on this.

jurisprudence on this will demonstrate, there are many concepts of law to choose from. There are many communities of jurisprudential inquirers maintaining different concepts of law – positivist, naturalist, realist, critical, and so on.[12] Different concepts of law may generate different accounts of the extent to which a given instance of state law (or the set of state legal systems as a whole) can refashion itself in response to the claims of Indigenous law, whilst maintaining its identity as law. Relative to different concepts of law, certain modes of recognition by state law of Indigenous law will fall within the realm of conceptual possibility and certain modes will not.

An example of this may be seen in the claim by certain legal positivists that it is a necessary property of law that it be sovereign in some politically exclusive and hierarchical sense.[13] If it were the case that the proper recognition of Indigenous law by state law entailed an ongoing relationship in which state law was *not sovereign* in these terms, then on this positivistic conception of law, state law would not be able to properly recognise Indigenous 'law' without losing its own identity as law.[14] A necessary condition of it being law would be lost by virtue of it entering into a recognitional relationship with Indigenous law which did not involve it being sovereign in this positivistic sense. This is not to say that it could not *as a matter of fact* fashion itself so as to properly recognise Indigenous law, but, rather, that it could not do so without taking itself outside the category of law as determined by the relevant conceptual community here. The necessity at work in this example is a conceptual one and not a natural (or factual) one.[15]

[12] For a survey of these see any introductory jurisprudence text – eg Dennis Patterson, ed, *A Companion to Philosophy of Law and Legal Theory* (Oxford: Blackwell Publishing, 1996); Jules L Coleman & Scott Shapiro, *The Oxford Handbook of Jurisprudence and Philosophy of Law* (2002), online: http://philpapers.org/rec/COLTOH; M Freeman, *Lloyd's Introduction to Jurisprudence*, 8th edn (London: Sweet & Maxwell, 2008).

[13] John Austin is a key progenitor of this approach to sovereignty. See John L Austin, *The Province of Jurisprudence Determined* (Cambridge: Cambridge University Press, 1995); Hart, *supra* note 10 at chapter 4.

[14] Of course, if sovereignty were to be conceived of in such exclusive terms, an Indigenous normative system operating within the territorial boundaries of the state could not be conceptualised as law at all on this approach (except, perhaps, in some attenuated 'factual' sense per Kirsten Anker, 'The Law of the Other: Exploring the Paradox of Legal Pluralism in Australian Native Title' (2008), online: http://papers.ssrn.com/sol3/papers.cfm?abstract_id=1606967. Hence, my use of the scare quotes in this sentence.

[15] Natural necessity may be thought of as grounded in the way the world naturally is – how it is as a matter of natural fact – independently of how we might conceptualise things. More technically, the term 'natural' here refers to those possible worlds governed by the

All of this is to say that the question of state law's capacity to properly recognise Indigenous law without losing its identity as law depends upon the concept of law which informs the inquiry. Rather than pursue this issue in the context of the *recognition* of Indigenous law by state law, however, I want to explore it in the context of a relatively under-theorised *prior phase* in the encounter between the two kinds of legal system – the *interpretive* phase.[16] In order for state law to properly recognise Indigenous law, it must (through its relevant agents) *understand*, to some practically adequate degree,[17] the nature of that Indigenous law. There is no proper recognition of a cultural phenomenon (such as a legal system) without a practically adequate degree of understanding of the nature and discursive content (meaning) of that phenomenon.[18] The agents of state law – like all agents – come to such an understanding through an active process of interpretation – for example, by means of the judicial interpretation of evidence about Indigenous law presented at a trial.[19]

laws of nature, as distinct from those governed by some conceptual truth. On the conceptual/natural necessity distinction, see Saul A Kripke, *Naming and Necessity* (Cambridge: Harvard University Press, 1972); Jeffrey Poland, *Physicalism: The Philosophical Foundations* (New York: Oxford University Press, 1994) at chapter 5; Andrew Melnyk, *A Physicalist Manifesto: Thoroughly Modern Materialism* (Cambridge: Cambridge University Press, 2003) at chapter 2.

16 In doing so, I draw on earlier research I have done on cross-cultural understanding within a legal context (Anthony J Connolly, *Cultural Difference on Trial: The Nature and Limits of Judicial Understanding* (Farnham: Ashgate Publishing, 2010); Anthony J Connolly, 'Naturalising Cultural Difference and Law: Author's Introduction' (2012) 37 *Austl J Leg Phil* 280; Anthony J Connolly, 'Cultures, Disciplines, and Differences: Author's Response to Commentators' (2012) 37 *Austl J Leg Phil* 323.

17 Practical adequacy here is a relative notion, informed by the nature and objectives of the actual encounter between the two systems. Practically adequate understanding is not an absolute or fixed state of affairs, but is relative always to some set of interpersonally or conventionally established theoretical and practical ends. David K Henderson, *Interpretation and Explanation in the Human Sciences* (Albany: SUNY Press, 1993); Connolly (2010), *supra* note 16.

18 See Connolly (2010), *supra* note 16 at chapter 3 on this. See also, more generally, Clifford Geertz, *The Interpretation of Cultures* (New York: Basic Books, 1973); Clifford Geertz, *Local Knowledge: Further Essays in Interpretive Anthropology* (New York: Basic Books, 1983); Jürgen Habermas, *The Theory of Communicative Action: Volume 1: Reason and the Rationalization of Society* (Cambridge: Polity Press, 1984); Jurgen Habermas, *The Theory of Communicative Action: Volume 2: Lifeworld and System: A Critique of Functionalist Reason* (Cambridge: Polity Press, 1987); Henderson, *supra* note 17.

19 Connolly (2010), *supra* note 16 at chapter 3. Of course, there have been a number of theorists who have claimed that *by its very nature* law cannot understand the Indigenous

The question I am concerned with in this chapter, then, picks up on the problematic identified in the legal pluralist literature on recognition. It concerns the extent to which state law can come to a practically adequate *understanding* of Indigenous law, *without losing its identity as law.*[20] This is to say that I am directly concerned here not with the *recognitional* limits of state law, qua law, but with the *interpretive* limits of state law, qua law.[21] Put bluntly, can state law do what it takes to adequately understand Indigenous law without having to become something other than law? The answer to this question, like the recognitional question, will again depend on the operative concept of law informing the inquiry. Because there are so many operative concepts of law out there in the legal theoretical literature, it would be impracticable for me in this chapter to seek to address the question with reference to all or even any significant set of them. I propose, therefore, to focus on what is widely considered to be the most influential approach to the question of 'what law is'[22] in Anglophonic legal theory and practice – the legal positivist approach.[23] However, even in relation to legal positivism there are a range of different concepts at work. Further, each of these is comprised of a significant number of constituent properties or elements. Analysing in its entirety any one of the major positivist concepts of law would be an onerous task and one well beyond the scope of a work such as this.

'Other' to any or any practically adequate degree. These include Drucilla Cornell, *The Philosophy of the Limit* (London: Routledge, 1992); Jacques Derrida, 'Force of Law: the Mystical Foundation of Authority' in M Rosenfeld, D G Carlson & D Cornell, eds, *Deconstruction and the Possibility of Justice* (New York: Routledge, 1992); Kenneth B Nunn, 'Law as a Eurocentric Enterprise' (1997) 15 *Law Inequal* 323; Penny Pether, 'Principles or Skeletons-Mabo and the Discursive Constitution of the Australian Nation' (1998) 4:1 *Law Text Cult* 115. In Connolly (2010), *supra* note 16 at chapter 6, I critique such radically incommensurabilist views of law's interpretive capacity.

[20] With reference to one of the comments made in Provost's introductory chapter in this volume (n.6), my question might be reframed as 'to what extent is law capable of *interpreting Indigenous culture* without losing its claim to normative specificity?'

[21] Of course, to the extent that a practically adequate understanding is a precondition of proper recognition, I am *indirectly* concerned with the recognitional limits of law. Independently of this connection, though, much of what I have to say in the discussion to follow about the limits of interpretation will resonate more broadly within the recognitional context.

[22] This is Hart's view of what a theory or concept of law ought to describe. Hart, *supra* note 10 at 239.

[23] I also focus on legal positivism and its concept of law because it seems to be the theory and concept of law of most concern to legal pluralists (see, for example, Kirsten Anker, *supra* note 1). This may be because of its dominance within much contemporary legal thought and practice.

What I propose to do, then, in order to keep the discussion manageable is to focus on a few key elements of a relatively generic legal positivist concept of law informed by the work of the most influential positivist of the past century, H.L.A Hart. My aim in this chapter is not to provide a detailed and comprehensive analysis of the interpretive limits of a positivistic (or any other) conception of law, but, rather, merely to provide a *sense* of what such an analysis might look like. Notwithstanding my circumscribing of the discussion in this way, I believe there will be some value in it for those interested in the interpretive limits of law. Many of the key issues associated with this topic will be implicated. Further though, by virtue of the analogy between the interpretive and the recognitional limits of law, it is my hope that the discussion to follow will be of value to those interested in the latter topic and will, therefore, comprise a modest contribution to the existing recognition-focused legal pluralist literature.

One further point of introduction: clearly, it is somewhat artificial (metaphorical, even) to speak of the capacity of state law, as a large-scale and complexly systemic phenomenon, to interpret and understand evidence of Indigenous law. Interpretation and understanding are actions and states of affairs which are carried out and achieved by human agents.[24] To speak of state law's capacity to interpret and understand is, in fact, to speak of the capacity of state law's *agents* – its judges, its bureaucrats, its other officials – to interpret and understand, in their roles as legal agents.[25] In the interpretive context we are concerned with, then, the question at stake may not so much be the abstract one of the extent to which state *law* can come to an understanding of Indigenous law without losing its identity as law, but, rather, one concerning the extent to which the state's relevant *legal agents* can do so without losing their identity as legal agents – or, better, without losing their identity as instances of the particular *kind* of legal agent they are (as judges, for example).[26] In this context, the capacity and limits of interpretation may depend not so much on an abstract concept of law as on a more localised operative

[24] Donald Davidson, *Inquiries into Truth and Interpretation* (Oxford: Clarendon Press, 1984); Daniel C Dennett, *The Intentional Stance* (Cambridge: MIT Press, 1987); Henderson, *supra* note 17; Connolly (2010), *supra* note 16.

[25] This is explored in depth by Thomas Burelli and Régis Lafrague in Chapter 8 of this volume, in the context of the recognition of Kanak law by French courts.

[26] In actual situations of cross-cultural interpretation, it is, I think, this latter question which is more likely to trouble a legal agent and, consequently, frame their practice. I have more to say on this later.

notion of what it is to be a judge or tribunal member or bureaucrat. In relation to a cross-cultural interpretive encounter at an Indigenous rights hearing, for example, the question we would most likely be concerned with is the extent to which a presiding judge could come to an understanding of evidence of Indigenous law without losing her identity *as judge*.[27] Again, here, the answer to the question would be determined – most directly, at least – with reference to some operative concept of judge, rather than law.

Of course, as the jurisprudential literature on this readily attests, the two concepts at work here are not unrelated.[28] Within the discursive framework of any credible legal theory, its concept of judge (as well as the cognate concept of adjudication) will be found to semantically subsist within its overarching concept of law. A legal positivist concept of judge, for example, will (as we shall see) necessarily be informed by an associated legal positivist concept of law.[29] The upshot of this is that as a result of the conceptual relation between the question of the interpretive capacity of law and that of a judge, we may in the discussion ahead encounter some slippage between operative concepts of law and operative concepts of judge and adjudication. I will be using all of these terms in the discussion to follow. If we keep in mind the point I have just made, this should not present too much of a problem. In any event, I will do my best to avoid confusion as we make our way through the issues.[30]

The chapter proceeds as follows. In the next part, I briefly set up a working model of cross-cultural interpretation in a legal context. This model derives from prior research I have done on this topic.[31] The key aim of this part is to identify those aspects of legal process and adjudication which have the potential to interfere with the effective interpretation and appropriate understanding of Indigenous law by a judge. In the following section, I explore whether, how, and to what extent any such

[27] Or without her practice losing its identity as a practice of adjudication.

[28] Hart, *supra* note 10; Ronald Dworkin, *Law's Empire* (Oxford: Hart Publishing, 1986); William Lucy, *Understanding and Explaining Adjudication* (Oxford: Oxford University Press, 1999).

[29] The necessity here is a conceptual necessity.

[30] I acknowledge that engaging with the concepts of judge and adjudication risks taking me further away from the original legal system-based recognitional problematic I started with (and, therefore, from the core concern of the legal pluralist literature), but not irredeemably so if we are able to keep in mind the semantic relationship mentioned here between the various concepts.

[31] Primarily, Connolly (2010), *supra* note 16.

counter-interpretive factors figure in a Hartian-style positivist concept of law and adjudication, limiting the capacity of judges and their legal systems to effectively interpret Indigenous law (or any other culturally different set of phenomena) without abdicating their very identity as judges and legal systems – at least, as far as Hartian positivists are concerned. My early finding on this front is that no such factors appear to inform Hartian concepts of law and adjudication. This is not to say, of course, that they do not inform the concepts of these things maintained by non-Hartian positivism or by other non-positivistic schools of jurisprudence. That is an analysis for another day. In the final part of the chapter, I reflect briefly on why it might matter what positivists think the interpretive limits of law and adjudication are, as well as what our response to it mattering might be.

2.2 Cross-cultural Interpretation and Understanding in Legal Settings

In order to set up the jurisprudential discussion which forms the core of this chapter, let me briefly outline a working model of the interpretive architecture of a recognitional encounter between state law and a culturally different system of Indigenous law.[32] In doing so, I will focus on a paradigm instance of such an encounter – namely, a judicial hearing into an Indigenous rights claim.[33] My model is premised on the proposition that cross-cultural interpretation in a legal context is a species of cross-cultural interpretation in general.[34] Any inquiry into the interpretive limits of a specifically legal process of interpretation must be informed by a sound theory of the general nature and limits of interpretation. Legal interpretation is that species of general interpretation which is characterised by the conditioning of the interpretive process by certain identifiably legal factors.[35]

[32] See Connolly (2010), *supra* note 16 at chapter 3 for a more detailed discussion of this model.

[33] The features of this particular mode of inter-legal encounter can be analogised to other common modes.

[34] Connolly (2010), *supra* note 16.

[35] According to some operative concept of 'legal'. In this context, we can construe the discussion to follow as concerned with the extent to which such factors form part of the set of properties definitive of law or adjudication, according to whatever concept of law or adjudication informs the inquiry.

One of the ways in which cultural difference may be usefully theorised is in terms of *conceptual* difference.[36] That is, the members of different cultures may be taken to possess different (sets of) concepts bearing some semantic relation to those phenomena which figure in their respective worldviews.[37] By virtue of their cultural difference, the conceptual schemes of these groups differ to some degree.[38] In light of this, one of the ways we can make sense of the process of cross-cultural interpretation and understanding is in terms of a process of *concept acquisition* on the part of interpreting members of a culturally different group. On this approach, an interpretive agent comes to an understanding of aspects of another culture by acquiring some set of the concepts informing that other culture and possessed by members of that other culture. In the paradigm legal context this chapter is concerned with, the interpretation of Indigenous law by a non-Indigenous judge may be construed as involving the acquisition by that judge (to some practically adequate degree) of some set of the Indigenous concepts which inform the Indigenous legal system in question.[39] This is to say that in this context we can theorise the interpretation of Indigenous law by state law as a process of *judicial concept acquisition*.

Within this framing of things, the success of any given cross-cultural interpretive attempt depends *as a general matter* upon two key factors – the content of the interpreting agent's pre-existing conceptual scheme at the commencement of the interpretive encounter[40] and the epistemic conditions which prevail over the course of the encounter.[41] If both of

[36] I argue for this in Connolly (2010), *supra* note 16 at chapter 4. See also Roy G d'Andrade, *The Development of Cognitive Anthropology* (Cambridge: Cambridge University Press, 1995); Scott Atran & Douglas Medin, *The Native Mind and the Cultural Construction of Nature.* (MIT Press, 2008).

[37] Or – for more radically inclined cultural difference theorists – in relation to those phenomena which figure in their respective *worlds*. See Donald Davidson, *supra* note 24 at essay 13 on Whorf and Kuhn.

[38] Or vice versa: by virtue of their conceptual difference, the cultures of these groups differ to some degree.

[39] As I have mentioned, practical adequacy here is relative to some set of interpretive and other practical ends informing the encounter.

[40] Particularly, in relation to that of the agents and culture under interpretation.

[41] By epistemic conditions in this general sense, I mean 'internal' factors such as the perceptual, cognitive, motivational, empathetic, and behavioural capacities (interpretive skills) of the interpreting agent, together with 'external' factors such as the availability and quality of evidence relating to the concepts to be acquired, the time available to engage interpretively, the prevailing environmental conditions (light, background noise, and so on), and the availability and effectiveness of external aids to interpretation. I will avoid

these factors are sufficiently favourable, interpretation will succeed. If either or both of these are not sufficiently favourable, then it will not.[42] So, to take a rather simplistic, but useful enough, example in relation to the first of these factors, if an undergraduate law student is seeking to understand the ramblings of their Indigenous Rights lecturer about (what for the student is) the conceptually alien legal topic of native title, the process by which that student acquires the alien legal *concept* of native title will be facilitated by her coming to the lecture 'equipped' with the conceptual repertoire she previously learned in her prior courses on property and public law (including, for example, the primary legal concepts of title and sovereignty), rather than by her coming lacking such a repertoire.[43] Her chances of adequately interpreting and understanding the alien legal discourse in question (and of acquiring the alien concepts informing that discourse) will be improved by her coming to the interpretive encounter with a conducive conceptual scheme (given the epistemic conditions that prevail over that encounter).

Likewise, even if the student maintains an adequate enough pre-existing conceptual scheme, if the lecturer is a particularly bad communicator, or if the student fails to pay attention in class, or if the sound system in the lecture hall is malfunctioning, the student may be unable to adequately interpret and understand the lecturer and the subject matter – that is, be unable to acquire the alien concepts implicated in that subject matter – at least, on that interpretive occasion. The epistemic conditions prevailing over the course of the interpretive encounter in question may not be conducive to adequate concept acquisition and understanding.

engaging at this point with the internalism/externalism debate in the philosophy of mind – nothing hinges on it here. Works on the nature of concept acquisition as a general matter include Gopnik & Meltzoff, *supra* note 10; Margolis & Laurence, *supra* note 10; Murphy, *supra* note 11; Carey, *supra* note 10. See Connolly (2010), *supra* note 16 at chapters 4 and 5 for a more detailed discussion of and set of references on the nature of concept acquisition.

42 It is a necessary condition of successful interpretation (understanding) that *both* of these be sufficiently favourable (or conducive). In Connolly (2010), *supra* note 16 at chapter 6, I set out to rebut the radical incommensurabilist view that law is *necessarily* non-conducive to cross-cultural interpretation – that is, that it is impossible for a legal agent to come to an understanding of the Indigenous Other. My conclusions there are that practically adequate understanding is not impossible in any metaphysically robust sense – at least, not on a scientifically informed and philosophically naturalistic approach to the question – but that it may not occur or it may be very difficult if certain contingent conditions obtain.

43 This explains to some degree the value of prescribing prerequisites for enrolment in certain courses in Law School.

In a cross-cultural interpretive encounter at trial, the capacity of a judge to acquire a set of Indigenous concepts sufficient for her to understand relevant aspects of Indigenous law (within the context of some or other set of legal-practical ends)[44] will also be contingent upon the nature of her conceptual scheme at the commencement of the judicial hearing[45] and upon the legal epistemic conditions which obtain over the course of the hearing. The more content the judge's conceptual scheme shares with that of the Indigenous claimants in relation to their law, the more conducive it will be to the successful interpretation of those agents and their law. Likewise, the more favourable legal epistemic conditions are, the more conducive things will be to interpretation. Legal epistemic conditions here include what I previously referred to as 'internal' factors, such as the cognitive capacities and interpretive skills of the judge and the judge's own concepts of law and the judicial role, as well as 'external' factors such as the mode of fact-finding operative within the hearing,[46] the rules regulating epistemic access to evidence of Indigenous law,[47] the actual availability and quality of evidence about Indigenous law, the availability and quality of extrinsic aids to judicial interpretation,[48] prevailing time constraints, and the physical environment in which the hearing take place.[49] These, individually and as a set, may be more or less conducive to the successful interpretation of Indigenous law and culture at hearing. A culturally insensitive mode of fact finding – involving aggressive cross-examination, for example – will be less conducive to cross-cultural understanding on the part of a judge than a non-adversarial, less intimidating, and more interpersonally sensitive mode.[50]

Interpretation will not succeed in a specific hearing context if the judge's conceptual scheme at the commencement of the hearing is not

[44] For example, determining the resemblance of contemporary claimant kinship relations to pre-colonisation relations in order to determine a native title claim.

[45] In particular, upon the degree to which the judge's conceptual scheme resembles or differs from the Indigenous conceptual scheme in question at a hearing. I explore in detail the question of conceptual difference and the degree to which two agents may conceptually differ (the degree to which the concepts of the one might be alien to the other) in Connolly (2010), *supra* note 16 at chapters 2, 4, and 6.

[46] For example, the adversarial mode of fact finding.

[47] Including the rules of evidence.

[48] Including translators, for example.

[49] Connolly (2010), *supra* note 16 at chapter 7.

[50] Michael Walsh, 'Interactional Styles in the Courtroom: An Example from Northern Australia' in J Gibbons, ed, *Language and the Law* (London: Longman, 1994); Diana Eades, *Language in Evidence: Issues Confronting Aboriginal and Multicultural Australia* (Sydney: UNSW Press, 1995); Diana Eades, *Sociolinguistics and the Legal Process* (Bristol: Multilingual Matters, 2010).

conducive to successful interpretation (given the epistemic conditions that prevail) or if the epistemic conditions obtaining over the course of the hearing are not conducive (given the nature of the judge's conceptual scheme). Another way of framing this is that it will not succeed if sufficient unfavourable or non-conducive factors – what I will term, *counter-interpretive legal factors* – obtain over the course of that hearing. Likewise, successful interpretation will be rendered difficult (though not necessarily impossible) if some lesser, though still obstructive, set of counter-interpretive legal factors obtain over the course of the hearing. The more counter-interpretive factors which figure over the course of a hearing, the harder it will be for a judge to acquire relevant Indigenous concepts and adequately interpret evidence of Indigenous law; the more interpretive work they will have to do to succeed. And at a certain point there may be so many of these factors that interpretive success is just not possible over the course of the hearing.

We might make sense of all of this by the use of two contrasting hypothetical examples. Imagine two native title hearings involving the same claimant group and relevant facts in which it is necessary for the judge to come to an understanding of the nature of the complex kinship relations which bind the group in order to be satisfied that they are individuated enough as a group to be able to collectively and effectively hold native title. In the one scenario – let's call it Case A – the judge comes to the hearing equipped with twenty years of judicial experience in hearing native title cases and actively engaging with expert evidence on Indigenous kinship relations. She has what we might term a working knowledge of the nature of kinship relations across a range of Indigenous groups. She has already acquired a number of Indigenous kinship concepts.[51] In the other scenario – Case B – the judge has been brought in at the last minute from the commercial division of the court and has no experience in native title hearings and no pre-existing knowledge of the nature of Indigenous kinship structures, general or specific. Further, in Case A the judge is evidentially assisted in making sense of the nature of the kinship relations in question by a suite of eminently qualified and communicatively effective Indigenous and expert anthropological

[51] This scenario is increasingly common in Australia since the birth of the contemporary native title jurisdiction in 1992. A number of Federal Court of Australia judges have gained extensive experience in hearing native title claims over the past ten years or so, as demonstrated by perusing the cases determined over that time.

witnesses, who are able to give their evidence on country.[52] In Case B, the legal aid resources provided to the claimant lawyers extend only to the engagement of a solitary and relatively inexperienced and inarticulate anthropologist, coupled with a small number of Indigenous witnesses who are uncomfortable speaking about their country and people within the alien and intimidating space of a metropolitan courtroom, thousands of kilometres away from their country.

At the risk of oversimplifying things here, it should be apparent that – all other things being equal – the judge in Case A might be expected to carry out her judicial role equipped with a conceptual scheme more conducive to understanding the evidence and deciding the case than the judge in Case B might. Likewise, the epistemic conditions which obtain in Case A – the quality of the witnesses, the nature of the hearing environment, and so on – are more conducive to both cross-cultural understanding and an appropriate determination of native title than the epistemic conditions which obtain in Case B. We might plausibly suppose that relatively fewer counter-interpretive factors obtain in Case A than in Case B and that an adequate enough degree of judicial understanding of the nature of Indigenous culture is more likely in Case A than it is in Case B.[53] Further, it is possible that the counter-interpretive factors at work in Case B either make it more difficult for the judge there to understand what they need to understand in order to properly decide the case or are sufficient to render that judge utterly unable to do so.[54]

Given the systemic orientation of the legal pluralist problematic we are concerned with in this paper, however, it is not *individual* hearings and judges which matter as much as a state-based *system* of hearings and judges. That is, we are primarily concerned in this context with the interpretive capacity and limits of state legal systems through their judiciaries. In light of this, we can construe the preceding comments as entailing that interpretation will not succeed in *any hearing* within a state system or across all state systems if the conceptual schemes of all relevant judges at the commencement of all hearings in those systems are not conducive to successful interpretation (given the epistemic conditions

[52] This is to say, outside of the metropolitan courtroom and physically present at relevant locations in the claimant territory.

[53] Again, for sake of our thought experiment, all other things being equal.

[54] That is, the counter-interpretive factors may be sufficient to render interpretive success impossible over the course of that hearing.

that generally prevail across those systems) or if the epistemic conditions obtaining across those systems are not conducive (given the general nature of their judiciaries' conceptual schemes). Likewise, successful interpretation across a legal system or set of systems will be rendered more difficult (though not necessarily impossible) if a sufficient enough set of counter-interpretive legal factors obtain systemically across all hearings in that legal system or set of systems.

Counter-interpretive legal factors *at the systemic level* might include a judicial selection culture which favours the engagement of judges whose conceptual schemes are significantly different in content from that of Indigenous claimants; a racist judicial ideology that renders judges unwilling to engage in interpretively optimal practice in relation to Indigenous witnesses and evidence of Indigenous law, more generally; an aggressively adversarial mode of fact finding which systematically interferes with the capacity of Indigenous witnesses to give oral evidence about their law; rules of evidence which demand that Indigenous modes of truth-telling be systematically disregarded as unreliable; unreasonably short time frames for the hearing of evidence about Indigenous law; and so on. If a sufficient number of these things operate to a sufficient degree as a systemic phenomenon throughout all cross-cultural encounters in a state's courts, then adequate judicial concept acquisition and understanding will either not obtain or will be more difficult to obtain across that legal system. State law either will not be able or will find it more difficult to adequately understand Indigenous law.[55]

To paraphrase all of this in the terms of the problematic we are concerned with here, state law will not be able to properly interpret and understand Indigenous law *and* maintain its own identity as law if sufficient counter-interpretive legal factors comprise part of the operative concept of law which figures in the inquiry. The more these factors comprise part of the inquiry's operative concept of law,[56] the more difficult it will be for state law to interpret and understand Indigenous law whilst maintaining its own status as law (according to that operative concept). If enough of these factors do so, it will not be possible at all for state law to adequately interpret Indigenous law and remain recognisably law by these lights.

[55] I argue in Connolly (2010), *supra* note 16 at chapter 6 that no natural necessity demands that such features figure in a legal system. Whether these features do or do not figure in a legal system is a naturally contingent matter.

[56] And, therefore, *indirectly* its cognate operative concepts of judge, adjudication, and so on.

2.3 The Interpretive Limits of Law – a Legal Positivist Case Study

So, does a set of counter-interpretive legal factors sufficient to disable or impede an adequate interpretation of Indigenous law comprise part of the generic legal positivist (Hartian) concept of law and those cognates I have chosen to focus on here? Before turning my mind to the challenging question of sufficiency, let me address the simpler and (as it happens) theoretically prior task of determining whether such concepts implicate *any* counter-interpretive factors. If they do, then I should be obliged to go on to determine the sufficiency of these factors for interpretive failure or difficulty. However, if our operative positivist concepts do not implicate *any* counter-interpretive factors, then there will not be a problem with sufficiency – or interpretive failure or difficulty, for that matter – in this context and our key question will be answered in the negative. That is, if Hartian concepts of law and adjudication do not implicate any counter-interpretive factors, then it will not be the case that law or adjudication is necessarily counter-interpretive as far as Hartian positivism is concerned. By the lights of such positivism, a legal system could be set up so as to enable a judge to interpret Indigenous law (to whatever extent is naturally possible,[57] of course) without threatening that system's identity as law and that judge's identity as judge.

Let me turn to the Hartian picture now.[58] As I said earlier, the relatively brief and somewhat impressionistic discussion to follow is designed merely to give a sense of what a more comprehensive and detailed analysis would be like. For Hart and for many subsequent positivists, law is most fundamentally a matter of rules.[59] A legal system is a system of rules,[60] and a judge is (for the most part, at least) an agent engaged in the application of legal rules to relevant facts.[61] Rules for Hart

[57] By 'natural' here, I mean to whatever extent is consistent with the laws of nature or, alternatively, with the way the world is as described by the natural sciences. See my comments on this in note 15. See also Connolly (2010), *supra* note 16 at chapter 1.

[58] Subsequent positivists of a Hartian stripe include Joseph Raz, Frederick Schauer, Scott Shapiro and Julie Dickson.

[59] Hart, *supra* note 10.

[60] Hart's most important definition of law is as 'a union of primary and secondary rules'. *Ibid* at 99.

[61] The complicating phenomena of legal indeterminacy and judicial discretion (as well as Hart's discussion of these in *The Concept of Law*) do not affect the plausibility of the discussion to follow in any significant way. Nothing distinctively counter-interpretive lurks in either of these phenomena, as far as Hart is concerned – or, at least, nothing more counter-interpretive than lurks in the process of interpretation as a general matter.

are collective social phenomena – social facts, in Hart's terms – comprised of the thoughts and actions of the members of some rule-constituting community.[62] A variety of kinds of rule – laws, moral norms, rules of etiquette, and so on – may operate within human communities. Legal rules are a distinctively systemic species of rule, individuated as law within a given community of agents by reference to a secondary (higher level) rule of recognition which (according to Hart) every legal system necessarily possesses.[63]

These well-known propositions are all conceptual truths about law within the Hartian schema. They constitute some (and only some) of the elements of Hart's theory or concept of law. They describe some of the more significant features a phenomenon or class of phenomena must possess in order to be law for Hartian positivists. What is notable about the various elements of Hart's concept of law as a system of rules (and I have only scraped the surface of that concept here) is that if we reflect upon them, it is not clear that any counter-interpretive factors either feature amongst them or are entailed by them.

First, there appears to be nothing inherently counter-interpretive in the general nature of rules. For Hart, rules are complexes of collective thought and action, the propositional contents and behavioural manifestations of which are contingent and infinitely variable.[64] A set of rules may be directed at and regulate any of a vast array of practices or situations – cross-cultural understanding being one of them. And they may regulate them in a manner that can subsequently be evaluated as positive or negative, good or bad, effective or ineffective, in light of some set of facts, beliefs, and values.[65] The only constraints at work here are

[62] Hart, *supra* note 10 at 9–12, 55–61.

[63] *Ibid* at 94–5. A legal system's rule of recognition is maintained by that system's class of legal officials and is normally articulable in terms of a set of procedural conditions which a putative legal rule must meet in order to attain the status of legality (or validity, in Hart's terms).

[64] This is not to say that they can have any content whatsoever (the limits of natural possibility operate here), but that the variety of natural content *they can have* is not limited.

[65] Jeremy Waldron, 'All We Like Sheep' (1999) 12 *Can JL Jurisprud* 169. Hart says at one point that 'it is in no sense a necessary truth that laws reproduce or satisfy certain demands of morality'. Hart, *supra* note 10 at 185–6. We could gloss that statement in this context to read 'it is in no sense a necessary truth that laws reproduce or satisfy certain demands of cross-cultural interpretation or understanding (or cross-cultural misinterpretation or misunderstanding, for that matter).'

natural ones.[66] One of the most compelling reasons for thinking this lies in the fact that within all of the world's cultures, concept acquisition and cultural learning *on the part of members themselves* takes place within rule-based contexts, including linguistic, educational, ethical, and religious contexts.[67] Indeed, the most important regulatory context in this regard is that comprising those rules which constitute and regulate the very practice of interpretation.[68] Interpretation is a rule-based activity, whether it be intra-cultural or intercultural.[69] Were the mere property of being a set of rules a source of interpretive difficulty we might wonder how this could be the case.

Further though, there appears to be nothing counter-interpretive in the peculiarly systemic nature of *legal* rules – the fact that legal rules always implicate a procedural relation between sets of primary and secondary forms of such rules. That law necessarily implicates secondary rules of recognition, change, and adjudication[70] operating in a procedural relation with an array of primary (largely) conduct-regulating rules, again, entails no obvious counter-interpretive consequences. That the secondary rules of a legal system are those primarily maintained by a class of agents recognised as legal *officials* also implicates no counter-interpretive factors. It does not appear to be the case that merely being the kind of agent that other kinds of agents recognise as having legal validity-determining status (the authority to determine which rules are legal and which are not) should render an agent interpretively incapacitated or impaired. Nor does it appear to be the case that a system of rules which necessarily includes such a kind of agent is rendered so. Whether a kind of legal agent or a system of rules is interpretively incapacitated or impaired is a contingent matter, not one inherent in their very identity as such.[71]

This is to say that the mere legality of legal rules – which is to say, their distinctive systematicity and (related) officiality – is not a source of interpretive constraint. On the Hartian picture, a given set of legal rules

[66] By which I mean constraints arising out of the status of human agents as phenomena subject to the laws of nature.

[67] D'Andrade *supra* note 36; Atran and Medin *supra* note 36; Margolis and Laurence *supra* note 10; Carey *supra* note 10.

[68] Geertz, *supra* note 18; Geertz, *supra* note 18; Habermas, *supra* note 18; d'Andrade, *supra* note 36; Henderson, *supra* note 17.

[69] Geertz, *supra* note 18; Geertz, *supra* note 18; Habermas, *supra* note 18; d'Andrade, *supra* note 36; Henderson, *supra* note 17.

[70] Hart's three categories of secondary rule. Hart, *supra* note 10 at 94–7.

[71] This, again, I would argue is consistent with Hart's view of the nature of law.

may, as a contingent matter of fact, operate so as to impede cross-cultural understanding on the part of legal agents, but this is not *necessitated* by the very nature of rules or legal rules. Nor is any interference with cross-cultural understanding necessitated by the fact that the interpreting agents in question are themselves *legal* agents or officials constituted by legal rules and acting qua legal agents or officials under the governance of legal rules. Indeed, it is quite consistent with the Hartian notion of law that a given set of legal rules might just as equally operate to better *facilitate* processes of cross-cultural understanding (than would otherwise be the case) by providing a social space in which some or all of those factors which a sound general theory of understanding identifies as conducive to understanding may operate. A legal system *might* provide for the presence of interpreting agents familiar with much of the conceptual scheme of culturally different interpretees and well skilled in the practice of interpretation, for example, or it might establish a communicative environment in which Indigenous people are able to effectively articulate the nature of their law and culture to such interpreters, and so on. It might. Nothing in the very nature of law prevents this, Hart would argue. What might prevent it are the contingent choices made by those responsible for the *content* of the rules and for the design and maintenance of the system of rules – legislators, judges, and bureaucrats.[72] It is not legality *as a general matter* which stands in the way of cultural understanding here, but the contingent counter-interpretive orientation of actual systems of legal rules in the world, as envisaged and constituted by actual agents. This is the level where those concerned with cross-cultural understanding should direct their theoretical and practical energies, then, not at the conceptual level.[73]

The point here is not that law on this conception *necessarily* facilitates cross-cultural communication – it does not – but that it *might contingently do so* without losing its identity as law, as a distinctive system of rules. It would appear that there is nothing in the Hartian notion of law as a 'union of primary and secondary rules' which necessitates *either* successful or unsuccessful cross-cultural understanding on the part of law's agents and other culturally different agents.[74] And so, going back to

[72] And, indirectly, the constituencies of these agents (the people, etc).

[73] This is one of Waldron's points in his 1999 analysis of Hart.

[74] I acknowledge at this point that a lot more analysis and argument would be called for to properly establish this claim in relation to the Hartian concept of law. Such will be a project for another day.

our original question it would seem that on a Hartian positivist conception of law, a system of state law might be structured such that it *could* come to or provide for an adequate understanding of Indigenous law without losing its identity as law.

Of course, one of the reasons why a positivist concept of *law* might not entail counter-interpretive consequences is that the very notion of law as a potentially large-scale, but always institutionally embodied system of rules, just does not intersect with the exigencies of cross-cultural understanding which, as I noted earlier, might be seen as a fundamentally *interpersonal* and, therefore, *sub-systemic* phenomenon. It might be argued that the general category and associated concept of law operates on the positivist model at too great a level of semantic and social abstraction to be capable of having any bearing on issues of interpersonal interpretation in law or anywhere else. That is, that in our search for counter-interpretive commitments of legal positivism we are looking in the wrong place, and that we need to shift to a semantic and social level far more proximate to the ground level reality of cross-cultural understanding in a legal context. It might be that a better focus for our inquiry here is a concept of adjudication or judge. What might a positivist – and, specifically, a Hartian – concept of these look like in this context?

As mentioned earlier, the positivist concepts of adjudication and its cognate judge derive from the positivist concept of law. Hart has relatively little to say about the conceptually necessary properties of either of these.[75] Adjudication comprises one kind of official practice within a legal system, constituted and broadly regulated by a distinctive category of secondary rules he terms rules of adjudication.[76] Adjudication and its agents (judges, for example) are thought by Hart to perform a number of roles necessary for a legal system to exist within the relatively large-scale societies he is concerned about. One key role relates to the problem of uncertainty within a society as to 'what the [legal] rules are or as to the precise scope of some rule'.[77] The process of adjudication plays a necessary role in determining what the legal rules are and what their scope is.[78] Without this role being performed, Hart believes, there could be no

[75] Most of Hart's discussion of these in *The Concept of Law* concerns the role of judges in the face of the 'open texture' (semantic indeterminacy) of rules. Hart, *supra* note 10 at chapter 7.

[76] *Ibid* at 96–8. [77] *Ibid* at 92.

[78] This role is performed in part with reference to the legal system's rule of recognition. *Ibid* at 94.

law.[79] Another adjudicatory role is to address what Hart terms the problem of inefficiency within a society in relation to the day-to-day maintenance of legal rules.[80] Diffuse social pressure on the part of the members of a society at large is not enough to maintain effective law. Some agency needs to be available to step in and resolve problems surrounding the operation of law within the society – particularly, where disputes arise as to its operation. 'Disputes as to whether an admitted rule has or has not been violated will always occur and will, in any but the smallest societies, continue interminably, if there is no agency empowered to ascertain finally, and authoritatively, *the fact of violation*.'[81] The judiciary is the agency empowered 'to make authoritative determinations of the question whether, on a particular occasion, a primary rule has been broken'.[82]

On this Hartian conception of things we might elaborate the concept of judge, then, as describing that category of official agents of a legal system whose role is to engage in the peculiarly legal activity of adjudicating – formally and authoritatively identifying relevant legal rules and facts and rationally[83] applying those legal rules to those facts in order to reach a decision about relevant legal rights and duties, under conditions of dispute about these things. Once more, though, on the face of it, it does not appear that any counter-interpretive factors are implicated in this conception. First, there seems no obvious reason to think that the mere activity of identifying rules and facts and applying one to the other in the

[79] The slippage in Hart's thinking here between the conceptual and the functional-empirical has been much discussed. Of late, see, for example, the papers by D'Almeida, LD & et al, eds, *Reading HLA Hart's 'The Concept of Law'* (Oxford: Hart Publishing).

[80] Hart, *supra* note 10 at 93–4.

[81] *Ibid* at 93 (emphasis added). I should note here that a role for adjudicatory officials may also be found in relation to the third of Hart's key rationales for the existence of secondary rules and, hence, legal systems – namely, that of enabling effective *change* of the legal rules in response to changing circumstances. *Ibid* at 95–6. I do not intend to discuss this arguably less fundamental aspect of adjudication here other than to note that no counter-interpretive consequences appear to be entailed by it.

[82] Hart, *supra* note 10 at 96. Hart goes on (p.97) '[t]he minimal form of adjudication consists in such determinations, and we shall call the secondary rules which confer the power to make them "rules of adjudication". Besides identifying the individuals who are to adjudicate, such rules also define the procedure to be followed. . .they do not impose duties but confer judicial powers and a special status on judicial declarations about the breach of obligations. Again, these rules. . .define a group of important legal concepts: in this case the concepts of judge or court, jurisdiction and judgment.' *Ibid* at 97.

[83] The term 'rationally' here is used to connote notions of logicality and conformity by the judge with relevant legal norms about the very process of adjudication itself.

manner described need be counter-interpretive. Again, it would appear that all depends on the way this general activity is actually regulated and carried out in a given legal system or adjudicatory context. If counter-interpretive factors happen to obtain in the activity of identifying and reasoning on the basis of rules and facts, whether locally within a given hearing or hearing type, or more widely within a given legal system or set of systems, or even across all hearings and all legal systems, they would appear to be contingent factors operating independently of any conceptual demands.

Further, the fact that the carrying out of the adjudicative role is done formally and authoritatively also does not appear to entail detrimental consequences for cross-cultural understanding. Formality here merely connotes legal rule-boundedness, and we have seen that legal rule-boundedness is not necessarily counter-interpretive. Authoritativeness, too, need not in itself import any counter-interpretive factors into the process of adjudication.[84] First, the notion of judicial authority implicates most fundamentally circumstances surrounding the making of a *final* decision or determination (about the application of the rules to the facts, as well as the associated distribution of rights and duties), rather than circumstances relating to the in-hearing *interpretation* of cultural difference. This is to say that for Hart the authority of judges lies primarily in their social role in resolving disputes in a manner that has the effect (at least in the majority of cases) of ending – or at least partly neutralising – their pernicious social effects, particularly in the public sphere. This judicial function constitutes the prime conceptual necessity for him here. In this sense, authority most importantly plays out for Hart *after* all the interpretive and fact finding work has been done by a judge. As a result, *in this sense* judicial authority has little opportunity to affect – positively or negatively – the judicial interpretive process.

However, even if we read into Hart's concept of law an alternative notion of judicial authority, construed in terms of the exercise of judicial power to regulate the conduct of a legal hearing – and, therefore, the conduct of a process of cross-cultural interpretation on the part of a judge – it is still not clear that Hartian authority entails counter-interpretive factors as a conceptual necessity. There is nothing in this alternative procedural construal of the Hartian notion of judicial authority which necessitates the *counter-interpretive* exercise of judicial power

[84] Though, as I will discuss shortly, some non-Hartian versions of it may import *counter-recognitional* factors.

at hearing. It is just as consistent with Hartian authority in this second sense that a judge uses her power at hearings to *facilitate* cross-cultural understanding (through constraining unreasonably aggressive examining counsel or taking the hearing onto the claimant territory, for example) as it is that she uses it to obstruct such understanding.[85] The authoritative exercise of judicial power here does not *entail* any counter-interpretive consequences over the course of a hearing.[86] Again, Hartian adjudication and the exercise of judicial authority may be as counter-interpretive as those who constitute, regulate, and practise these things decide.

2.4 A Legal Pluralist Intervention – Indigenous Law as Fact

On a related issue, Anker and others have argued that the treating of Indigenous law as *fact and not law* in colonial, positivistically inclined legal systems such as those in Australia and Canada is significantly counter-recognitional.[87] Doing so constitutes a denial of the status of Indigenous peoples and their cultures as politically (if not ethically) equal to the dominant non-indigenous people and culture in these societies. I agree. However, that Indigenous law is treated by judges in those jurisdictions in this manner is not a function of a Hartian *concept* of law or adjudication. It is not a necessary feature of either law or adjudication on Hart's conception that judges (or other officials) treat Indigenous law as fact in their dealings with it. Their doing so is, from a Hartian point of view, a *contingent* feature of the legal systems in question.

The source of their doing so is to be found in a (conceptually contingent) commitment on the part of those legal systems to the notion that law is necessarily sovereign in the exclusivist and hierarchical sense articulated by (amongst others) John Austin's *pre-Hartian* concept of law.[88] On this Austinian view of things, Indigenous law is not and cannot (as a conceptual necessity) be law for two reasons. First, to the extent that

[85] In Connolly (2010), *supra* note 16 at chapter 7, I describe some of the ways in which judicial power can be and has been exercised by judges in the Australian native title sphere to facilitate their understanding of claimant law and culture.

[86] It is an interesting question, however, whether a role defined by the rational application of rules to facts entails some commitment to optimally finding out what the facts actually are and, therefore, entails, as a conceptual matter, certain *pro-interpretive* factors. Following this question through is a project for another occasion, however.

[87] Anker, *supra* note 14; Anker, *supra* note 1.

[88] Austin, *supra* note 13.That is, judges in these legal systems as a contingent matter of fact adopt an Austinian view of the nature of legal sovereignty.

the Indigenous law in question is not itself exclusivist, hierarchical, and, therefore, sovereign in the Austinian sense, *it just isn't law* according to the Austinian concept. It doesn't take the form of law as conceived within the Austinian frame of things. Second, according to the Austinian concept of law, there can be, as a matter of conceptual necessity, only one sovereign – and, therefore, only one sovereign legal system – within a given territory. Whatever the actual form an Indigenous legal system might take within a colonial setting, a colonial legal system operating with an Austinian conception of law and sovereignty cannot (again as a matter of conceptual necessity) recognise that Indigenous legal system as law – that is, as an operative and co-equal legal system – within that setting. It can only recognise it as a set of normative *facts*, to be dealt with as all facts are dealt with by the colonial legal system.[89]

Hart, however, convincingly debunked the idea that this kind of sovereignty is part of the very concept of law.[90] A legal system and a

[89] This two-pronged Austinian approach was articulated by Chief Justice Gibbs of the High Court of Australia in *Coe v Commonwealth (No 1)* (1979) 24 ALR 118, who stated at 129 and 131, 'It is not possible to say...that the aboriginal people of Australia are organised as a "distinct political society separated from others" or that they have been uniformly treated as a state...The aboriginal people...have no legislative, executive, or judicial organs by which sovereignty might be exercised [the first prong]. If such organs existed, they would have no power, except such as the law of the Commonwealth, or of a State or Territory might confer on them [the second prong]. The contention that there is in Australia an aboriginal nation exercising sovereignty, even of a limited kind, is quite impossible in law to maintain...there is no aboriginal nation, if by that expression is meant a people organized as a separate state or exercising any degree of sovereignty' In *Members of the Yorta Yorta Aboriginal Community* v *Victoria* (2002) 214 CLR 422, Chief Justice Gleeson and Justices Gummow and Hayne of the High Court of Australia reiterated the second prong of the Austinian approach stating at 443–4, '...what the assertion of sovereignty by the British Crown necessarily entailed was that there could thereafter be no parallel law-making system in the territory over which it asserted sovereignty. To hold otherwise would be to deny the acquisition of sovereignty and as has been pointed out earlier, that is not permissible.'

[90] Hart, *supra* note 10, chapter 4. Justice Blackburn of the Northern Territory Supreme Court recognised this in the first significant land rights claim of the modern era in Australia, *Milirrpum* v *Nabalco Pty Ltd* (1971) 17 FLR 141. At 266 he stated 'The Solicitor General contended that before any legal system can be recognised by our law as a system of law, there must be not only a definable community to which it applies but also some recognised sovereignty giving the law a capacity to be enforced... Implicit in much of the Solicitor General's argument on this aspect of the case was, I think, an Austinian definition of law as the command of a sovereign.... I do not find myself much impressed by this line of argument. The inadequacy of the Austinian analysis of the nature of law is well known.... If a definition of law must be produced, I prefer a system of rules of conduct which is felt as obligatory upon them by the members of a definable group of people...The evidence shows a subtle and elaborate system highly adapted to the country

judiciary which maintain such a self-conception is certainly *possible* within the Hartian schema but it is not *necessitated* by that schema. By Hartian lights, a legal system and its judiciary need not hold to these Austinian notions about law and sovereignty in order to be a legal system and a judiciary. This is so, notwithstanding Hart's account of the role necessarily played in law by a rule of recognition. Let me explain why.

A rule of recognition is a means of identifying within a given geographic or social space those norms which are law within that space and those norms which are not. A variety of kinds of rules of recognition are able to perform this function and meet Hart's demands. An exclusivist sovereignty-based rule of recognition – according to which valid law in a given space is *exclusively* comprised of the norms promulgated by that non-indigenous legislative body (or set of bodies) recognised as validly empowered to do so by a non-indigenous corps of officials – is *one way* to make the distinction between law and non-law at stake here. But it is not the only way.

For example, to the extent that a rule-governed Indigenous community maintains, amongst other things, a socially based capacity for identifying the rules that govern the community, then that community may be said to maintain a rule of recognition. To the extent that it also maintains socially based law-making, enforcing, and adjudicating mechanisms, then it meets the Hartian requirements for possessing a legal system. No Austinian notion of a sovereign need figure here. Thus, an Indigenous legal system may be recognised as law on the Hartian approach even though its form is not Austinian.[91]

Further, though, Hart's model of a rule of recognition does not entail that the law of the colonists unilaterally prevail to the exclusion or subordination of the law of the Indigenous peoples in a colonial setting.[92] A rule of recognition which identified the procedural requirements for validity (broadly construed here, of course) within *both* the non-Indigenous and the Indigenous legal regimes, as well as the scope of application of valid laws, and which provided a mechanism for the distribution of adjudicative responsibilities and the resolution of

in which the people led their lives, which provided a stable order of society and was remarkably free from the vagaries of personal whim or influence. If ever a system could be called "a government of laws and not of men" it is that shown in the evidence before me.'

[91] Contra the first prong of the Austinian picture outlined earlier, see my discussion of this point in Connolly (2010), *supra* note 16 at chapter 3.

[92] Contra the second prong of the Austinian picture outlined earlier.

application conflicts between the two regimes should they arise, is not in any way ruled out by Hart's notion of a rule of recognition or his concept of law, more generally. Analogies of such an arrangement may be found within the contemporary system of international law, as well as within supranational and radically federal national legal regimes.[93] These offer alternative non-Austinian models of law consistent with both the Hartian approach and the legal recognition of Indigenous law as law and not fact.[94]

Such regimes may be seen as prototypes of a properly pluralistic legal system in which non-Indigenous law and its agents engage with Indigenous law and its agents *as law and as legal agents* and not merely as politically subordinate facts. Under such an arrangement, the judicial agents of the non-Indigenous legal system would be as capable of recognising Indigenous law as law and of engaging with it as law within such an arrangement as the judicial agents of international or supranational law are, at present, of recognising and engaging in a non-subordinating manner with the laws of member nations as law.[95] Hence, the obstacles to designing a legal system which does not misconstrue Indigenous law as fact lie not in the Hartian concept of law but in the contingent – though,

93 An example of a supranational legal regime which offers an analogy here is European Union law. See Mark L. Jones, 'The Legal Nature of the European Community: A Jurisprudential Analysis Using HLA Hart's Model of Law and a Legal System' (1984) 17(1) *Cornell Int'l L J* 1. See also Marcelo Neves, *Transconstitutionalism* (Oxford: Hart Publishing, 2013) on the human rights jurisdiction of European Union law. In reflecting on the nature of the federal US legal system, Kent Greenawalt refines the notion of a rule of recognition and the Hartian concept of law, more generally. Kent Greenawalt, 'The Rule of Recognition and the Constitution' (1987) 85 *Michigan L Rev* 621.

94 See Hart *supra* note 10, chapter 6 and, especially, chapter 10. Contrary to popular misconception, Hart did not deny that international law may be a mode of law. His view on this is complex and nuanced, as a careful reading of chapter 10 of *The Concept of Law* will attest. 'Austin, says Hart, neglected the very real modern possibility of a sovereign that not only created law, but was also bound by it. . .Contrary to Austin's picture, it is a characteristic of contemporary constitutional governance that the government as well as the governed are subject to law, and no account of modern law could be complete without taking this feature of legality into account. When we add the complications to the sovereignty picture that are provided by judge-made common law, *by federalism, by partial sovereignty*, by the separation of powers, *by a sometimes robust international law*, and *by numerous other complexities of the contemporary constitutional nation-state*, we see that an attempt to model all of law on the image of an absolute monarch imposing rules on a subservient citizenry is a poor picture of the nature of law in most of today's sophisticated legal systems.' Frederick Schauer, 'Was Austin Right After All? On the Role of Sanctions in a Theory of Law' (2010) 23(1) *Ratio Juris* 1 at 6 (emphasis added).

95 Neves, *supra* note 93 at 56–70, 96–105 and especially, 136–44.

admittedly, often historically conditioned – will of powerful legal and political interests, as well as in the limits of our current legal imagination.[96] These obstacles are not conceptually necessitated. They are practically and politically contingent.[97]

2.5 Concluding Remarks: Positivist Concepts and Judicial Practice

A more comprehensive and thorough analysis of the Hartian concepts of law and adjudication could be pursued at this point, analysing all the finer elements of those concepts and then evaluating whether they, in turn, entail any counter-interpretive factors.[98] A careful analysis of elements traditionally ascribed as conceptual necessities to Hart and other positivists such as sovereignty (in some soft, non-Austinian sense), rationality, efficiency, impartiality, and so on, might yield results different from those outlined here. I must say, though, that my initial work in relation to these elements does not indicate that to be the case. Even if these elements were conceptually necessary components of law or adjudication, it is not clear that any counter-interpretive factors are in their turn necessarily linked to these elements.[99]

[96] I should acknowledge here that if, contra my argument, Hart's concept of law *did* entail a sovereign exclusivity in Anker's sense, I would be faced with the challenge of determining whether such a feature of that concept was not only counter-*recognitional* but also counter-*interpretive* – and if so, how. Though treating Indigenous law as fact is clearly counter-recognitional, it is not entirely clear that it is counter-interpretive. Pursuing this intriguing question is a project for another occasion.

[97] One way to think about this issue in Hartian terms would be to ask whether we could imagine a legal system in which non-Indigenous judges either acknowledged the authority of Indigenous adjudicators to adjudicate in relation to certain kinds of matter or collaborated with those adjudicators in resolving certain kinds of matter, and in which the results of those adjudications were recognised as valid within the jurisdiction by reference to some set of criteria (a rule of recognition) accepted by some set of non-Indigenous and Indigenous persons we could classify as having authority to do so within the jurisdiction (in Hart's terms, officials).

[98] And, of course, I could do the same with the whole range of non-positivist concepts of these things were I minded to. But that is not my project in this chapter.

[99] For example, even if it could be established that judicial impartiality was a necessary feature of law and adjudication for Hart or some other positivist, it is not at all clear that the exercise of judicial impartiality entails any counter-interpretive consequences. A concept of judging which implicated impartiality would not be counter-interpretive on that account. Of course, someone like Iris Marion Young might disagree with me on this score. See Iris Marion Young, *Justice and the Politics of Difference* (Princeton: Princeton University Press, 1990) at chapter 4.

So where do we stand after all of this? Recall that our original question was the extent to which state law can come to a practically adequate understanding of Indigenous law, without losing its identity as law. Can state law do what it takes to adequately understand Indigenous law without having to become something other than law? Is there something inherently counter-interpretive about law as such? My initial point was that the answer to these questions depends on the concept of law one brings to the inquiry. Rather than argue for the superiority of one concept of law over another in this context, I chose to explore the issues through the lens of a common and influential positivist concept of law. From the point of view of that conceptual orientation, it turns out on my preliminary exploration that – for Hartian positivists, at least – state law *can* come to a practically adequate understanding of Indigenous law, without losing its identity as law. It *can* do what it takes to adequately understand Indigenous law without having to become something other than law. There is nothing inherently counter-interpretive about law as far as Hartian positivism is concerned.

In closing, I would like to pursue briefly one further related point. In response to the preceding discussion, those of a more practical and political bent might object, 'Who really cares what Hartian positivists think about this issue? This is all just a conceptual matter, an entirely abstract and academic affair with no actual consequences in the real world – which is to say, the world of day to day legal practice or the world of Indigenous people pursuing their concrete claims for justice before state law.' My response to this objection – and my final point in this chapter – is that the issue I have discussed here certainly *is* a conceptual, abstract, and academic one, but it is not *just* that. Indeed, it is an issue which is very much of consequence to the real world of Indigenous rights litigation and justice for Indigenous peoples. This is because the Hartian view on what is conceptually possible within law and adjudication is, arguably, the view held – often tacitly – by many, if not all judges, within the Anglophonic and many other contemporary jurisdictions.[100] That is, Hartian positivism is the ideology of law maintained

[100] This proposition has been argued for and evidenced by many on the critical wing of Anglophonic jurisprudence for many years. See, for example, Critical Legal Studies theorists such as James Boyle, 'The Politics of Reason: Critical Legal Theory and Local Social Thought'(1985) 133 *Univ Pa Law Rev* 685; Gary Peller, 'The Metaphysics of American Law' (1985) 73 *Calif Law Rev* 1151; Roberto Unger, *The Critical Legal Studies Movement* (Harvard: Harvard University Press, 1986); David Kairys, *The Politics of Law: A Progressive Critique* (New York: Pantheon Books, 1998); Duncan Kennedy, *Critique of*

by many legal systems and their agents.[101] More than this, though, judicial beliefs about what kinds of interpretive practices fall within the very notion of law or of adjudication might be expected to affect the willingness of judges to engage in interpretive practices that either contradict or fall outside of those beliefs – *even if* those practices are otherwise necessary for an adequate understanding of Indigenous law or any other culturally different phenomenon they might encounter over the course of a hearing.

As I have argued in previous work,[102] the thought and practice of a judge over the course of a hearing – including her capacity to interpret and understand evidence of a culturally different law and society – is affected by a range of factors, some internal and some external. These factors include the positive legal rules regulating judicial practice – the rules of evidence, and so on. But they also include the beliefs that judges have about the nature of law and about the nature of their own adjudicatory role. As mentioned, there are grounds for believing that in many legal systems some version of Hartian positivism serves as a largely implicit judicial ideology of law and the adjudicative role.[103] Judges in these jurisdictions tend to believe that law and adjudication, as a general matter, are pretty much as the Hartian conception would have it (though they may not be consciously aware of the detail or even existence of Hart's theory). Further, though, judges are motivated to think and act in a manner consistent with this conception of their own identity or role and the institutional context in which that identity or role subsists. Their concepts of law and adjudication serve a *normative function* in their practice, additional to that played by any positive rules overtly regulating that practice. Being a judge involves, for them, *doing what judges do*, according to their operative concept of judge. Within many Anglophonic

Adjudication (fin de siecle) (Harvard: Harvard University Press, 1997). Other critical theorists holding this view include Young, *supra* note 87; Martha Minnow, *Making All the Difference: Inclusion, Exclusion, and American Law* (Ithaca: Cornell University Press, 1990); Valerie Kerruish, *Jurisprudence as Ideology* (London: Routledge, 1991); Margaret Davies, *Asking the Law Question* (Sydney: Lawbook Co, 2008). For evidence of this in the Australian judicial context, see the decisions of Blackburn J in *Milirrpum* v *Nabalco Pty Ltd* (1971) 17 FLR 141, and Gleeson CJ, Gummow and Hayne JJ in *Members of the Yorta Yorta Aboriginal Community* v *Victoria* (2002) 214 *CLR* 422.

101 Where there is a widespread sharing of beliefs amongst and across generations of judges about the nature of these things, we might speak of a judicial *ideology* of law and adjudication. See Kerruish, *supra* note 100.

102 Connolly (2010), *supra* note 16.

103 See note 100.

jurisdictions, what judges think they *are* at the most fundamental level is what Hart said they are.[104]

Now, *if it were the case* that the Hartian concepts of law and adjudication included certain counter-interpretive factors as conceptual necessities, it would be expected that judges maintaining those concepts would be reluctant to think and act in ways inconsistent with those factors for fear of engaging in thought and practice that was no longer legal or judge-like as far as they were concerned – *even if that meant not coming to an adequate understanding of some culturally different aspect of Indigenous law relevant to the hearing.* Why? Because we may plausibly expect that as a general rule their commitment to properly maintaining their status as judges (as legitimate legal agents) would override their commitment to properly understanding evidence of culturally different Indigenous law. This is to say that if it were the case that the Hartian concepts of law and adjudication included counter-interpretive factors, those concepts would serve as a reason for such judges to engage in less than optimal interpretive practice. Importantly, this would be the case independently of any positive legal rules regulating that practice.[105]

Further, if it were the case that most or all judges in a legal system subscribed to such concepts – and I would argue that in some jurisdictions this is the case[106] – then there would be an increased *systemic risk* that cross-cultural understanding at law would fail as a result. Again, this would be the case independently of any positive rules or other aspects of the legal system which additionally obstructed judicial understanding. It is clear that such a risk could have significant consequences for Indigenous peoples before the courts and for their chances of having their claims effectively and justly heard. A failure of understanding of an Indigenous claim on the part of a judge enhances the risk of a failure of justice in relation to such a claim.[107]

I have argued that Hartian concepts of law and adjudication do not appear to implicate any counter-interpretive legal factors and that,

[104] I should stress here that I am not arguing that Hart's work was the sole cause or even the most significant cause of judges thinking this way – though it is clear from the case law that a number of judges have, in fact, subsequently been influenced by his work in relation to their concept of law. Even so, one could just as easily argue that Hart's theory of law *reflects* Anglophonic judicial ideology as much as it informs it.

[105] Of course, we might expect the legal rules regulating judicial practice in court to reflect the primacy of maintaining their status as judges.

[106] Australia is one such jurisdiction. See note 100.

[107] Connolly (2010), *supra* note 16 at chapter 1.

therefore, there appears to be no risk of a systemic failure of cross-cultural understanding *on account of judges holding such concepts*. There may, of course, be a risk of systemic interpretive failure on account of some other factors – including, for example, certain of the positive rules regulating judicial practice. But these are empirically contingent factors, not conceptually necessary ones. However, if I am wrong in my analysis of the Hartian concepts of law and adjudication, then the risk I have just mentioned would be a real one in those jurisdictions that maintain a Hartian judicial ideology of law and adjudication. If such were the case, it would be incumbent upon those concerned about the ethical and political consequences of such a risk to act against it. One strategy here would be to argue against the adoption by the judiciary of such counter-interpretive concepts of law and adjudication and to offer and argue for interpretively more conducive concepts of these things – non-Hartian concepts of some kind.[108] A range of arguments are available in the jurisprudential literature in this regard. I do not propose to rehearse them here.[109] Again, my analysis leads me to believe that the Hartian concept of law and adjudication is not counter-interpretive and that, therefore, there are no good grounds for a judge or judiciary of a Hartian stripe to interpretively constrain themselves for fear of compromising their identity as judge or judiciary or their legitimacy as an agent of the law. Nor is there any good reason for legal pluralists concerned about the interpretive and not merely the recognitional limits of law to think that state law could not adequately understand Indigenous law without losing its identity as law – at least, by the lights of the dominant positivistic concept of law at work in the Anglosphere.

[108] And, of course, if it were the case that alternative, though still counter-interpretive concepts of law and adjudication operated in the Anglosphere or elsewhere, then the same strategy might be taken in relation to those concepts.

[109] I have recently become intrigued by the possibilities offered by Brian Leiter's naturalised jurisprudence in this regard. See Leiter, *supra* note 8; A J Connolly, *Naturalised Jurisprudence as an Experimental Philosophy of Law: An Incursion into the Methodology Debate* (forthcoming 2017).

marriage contract through a declaration of the husband only.[8] Jewish women also experience gendered disadvantages under Jewish law. In order to be "halachically"[9] correct, a Jewish marriage may only end in the death of a spouse or the voluntary granting of a divorce (*get*) by the husband[10] and its simultaneous acceptance by the wife.[11] The husband thus has the exclusive power to deliver the *get*.[12] If a Jewish woman is entitled to a *get* and has not received one due to her husband's refusal, she is referred to as an *agunah* (pl. *agunot*);[13] literally, a "chained" or "anchored" woman.[14] If an *agunah* marries a man civilly, the relationship

just cause for more than six months, and failure to comply with the *nikahnama* terms and conditions. The Maliki school permits divorce on the basis of cruelty and ill-treatment.

8 El Alami & Hinchcliffe, *supra* note 6 at 22.

9 *Halacha* is the entire corpus of Jewish law, which draws on the Torah, rabbinical laws and customs. *Halakhah* (New York: Macmillan Co., 1971) at 1156–7.

10 *See* Irwin H Haut, *Divorce in Jewish Law and Life (Studies in Jewish Jurisprudence Volume 5)* (New York: Sepher-Hermon Press, 1983) at 18: ("It is a fundamental principle in Jewish law that only a husband can give a *get*").

11 Ayelet Blecher-Prigat & Benjamin Shmueli, "Interplay between Tort Law and Religious Family Law: The Israeli Case, The" (2009) 26 *Ariz J Intl Comp L* 279 at 281; Karin Carmit Yefet, "Unchaining the Agunot: Enlisting the Israeli Constitutional in the Service of Women's Marital Freedom" (2008) 20 *Yale JL Fem* 441 at 443–4.

12 The biblical foundation for this prerogative is found in Deuteronomy 24:1: "When a man has taken a wife and married her, and it comes to pass that she finds no favour in his eyes because he has found some unseemliness in her, then let him write her a bill of divorce and give it in her hand and send her out of his house." This passage was interpreted as bestowing upon the husband the exclusive privilege of initiating divorce. Yehiel S Kaplan, "Enforcement of Divorce Judgments by Imprisonment: Principles of Jewish Law" (2004) 15 *Jew Annu* 57 at 61.

13 The situation of the *agunah* is mentioned but once in the Bible, at Ruth 1:13. However, the Mishnah and Talmud both refer to it frequently, as does the subsequent literature in response. *See* Aviad Hacohen, in Blu Greenberg, ed., *Tears of the Oppressed: An Examination of the Agunah Problem: Background and Halakhic Sources* (Jersey City, NJ: KTAV Publishing House, Inc., 2004) at passim. Originally, this term was reserved for women whose husbands had disappeared. Unless a woman had proof of her husband's death, she could not remarry religiously. Michelle Greenberg-Kobrin, "Civil Enforceability of Religious Prenuptial Agreements" (1998) 32 *Colum JL Soc Probs* 359 at 359. However, the modern *agunah* problem has more to do with recalcitrant rather than missing husbands. Michael J Broyde, *Marriage, Divorce, and the Abandoned Wife in Jewish Law: A Conceptual Understanding of the Agunah Problems in America* (Hoboken, NJ: KTAV Publishing House, Inc., 2001) at 3, 8.

14 Although a wife can in theory refuse a *get* issued by her husband, in practice the consequences for the man are neither as serious nor as far-reaching as they are for an *agunah*. As put by Nichols, "A man who marries without a Jewish divorce has not committed adultery, but has only violated a rabbinical decree mandating monogamy; he is nonetheless considered married to his second wife, and his children are legitimate."

is considered adulterous under Jewish law.[15] Therefore, she is never permitted to marry that man religiously.[16] Moreover, any child born to a woman who has not received a *get* is labelled *mamzer* (pl. *mamzerin*).[17] Such children are "effectively excluded from organized Judaism,"[18] as they are illegitimate and may never marry anyone but another *mamzer*.

Recently, there has been a flurry of literature addressing the issue of the gendered impact of religious family law in Western states.[19] But beyond the words, what is the reality of women's experiences of a religious and/or civil divorce? To work toward a fuller and more truthful picture, I present portraits of women moving through civil and religious divorce as social agents[20] and outline that law and culture are *contested* social spaces, which can be, and indeed sometimes are, used by women to their advantage. Based on fieldwork and interviews done among Jewish and Muslim women in the United Kingdom, I present an account of legal pluralism in which culture and law are mutually constitutive and fashion the economic welfare and bargaining positions of parties. I outline how a *legalization* of religious law, whereby culture is rendered more contestable, flexible, and legalistic, sometimes occurs. The study of Jewish and

Joel A Nichols, "Multi-Tiered Marriage: Ideas and Influences from New York and Louisiana to the International Community" (2007) 40 *Vand J Transnatl L* 135 at 155.

15 *Ibid.*

16 Margit Cohn, "Women, Religious Law and Religious Courts in Israel–The Jewish Case" (2004) 27 *Retfaerd Scand J Soc Sci* 57 at 66.

17 *Ibid.*

18 Nichols, *supra* note 14.

19 Pascale Fournier, *Muslim Marriage in Western Courts: Lost in Transplantation* (Farnham: Ashgate Publishing, Ltd., 2010); Maleiha Malik, *Minority Legal Orders in the UK: Minorities, Pluralism and the Law* (London: The British Academy, 2012); Ayelet Shachar, *Multicultural Jurisdictions: Cultural Differences and Women's Rights* (Cambridge: Cambridge University Press, 2001); Ayelet Shachar, "Religion, State, and the Problem of Gender: New Modes of Citizenship and Governance in Diverse Societies" (2005) 50 *McGill LJ* 49 at 49–8; Ayelet Shachar, "Privatizing Diversity: A Cautionary Tale from Religious Arbitration in Family Law" (2008) 9 *Theor Inq Law* 573; Werner Menski, "Governance and Governability in South Asian Family Laws and in Diaspora" (2013) 45:1 *J Leg Plur Unoff Law* 42; Sherene Razack, *Casting Out: The Eviction of Muslims from Western Law and Politics* (Toronto: University of Toronto Press, 2007); Leah Bassel, "Intersectional Politics at the Boundaries of the Nation State" (2010) 10:2 *Ethnicities* 155; Lila Abu-Lughod, "Against Universals: The Dialects of (Women's) Human Rights and Human Capabilities" in Michelle Molina & Donald K Swearer, eds., *Rethinking the Human* (Cambridge MA: Center for the Study of World Religions, Harvard Divinity School, Harvard University Press, 2010).

20 On the topic of Muslim women's agency, *see* Anna C Korteweg, "The Sharia Debate in Ontario Gender, Islam, and Representations of Muslim Women's Agency" (2008) 22 *Gend Soc* 434 at 444 (developing a conception of "agency . . . embedded in religion").

Muslim women in the United Kingdom provided a means to test the hypothesis that the legalization of religious norms is enhanced when religion and civil law interact through state recognition and inter-normative legal dialogue.

In the United Kingdom, Jewish family law is to a large extent recognized by the state through the *Marriage Act 1949–96*, whereas Muslim family law is not. Consequently, Muslims must "marry twice" in order to benefit from state recognition: civilly according to the "secular" registration ceremony, and religiously and/or customarily by adhering to the rites of their communities.[21] This asymmetry gives a rich occasion to ascertain what the effects of legal recognition of culture might be on Jewish and Muslim women.

However, our perception of this problem is considerably obscured by the intellectual impetus to conceive the (religious) family and the market as two distinct spheres that do not overlap. I will refer to this as the family/market dichotomy, whereby the family is constructed as the opposite of the contractual market and as emotional, identity-based, coerced, and/or driven by status, not contract.[22] While the concept of the "relational contract" developed within literature on family law bridges the gap between strictly status or contract-based conceptions of marriage,[23] it often remains the case that religious family law is portrayed as derived from static notions of revealed religious doctrine infused with identity concerns. In other words, religious family law, the historical focal point of the family/market dichotomy, continues to be conceptualized as status and not contract.[24] Women then are typically characterized as lacking the agency associated with contracting and relegated to a

[21] Ashraf-ul Hoque & Prakash Shah, *Challenges Of Religious Accommodation In Family Law, Labour Law And Legal Regulation Of Public Space And Public Funding: United Kingdom Socio-Legal Research Report*, Religare Socio-Legal Report – UK (Leuven, Belgium: RELIGARE Project, 2012) at 34.

[22] *See* Janet Halley & Kerry Rittich, "Critical Directions in Comparative Family Law: Genealogies and Contemporary Studies of Family Law Exceptionalism" (2010) 58:4 *Am J Comp Law* 753.

[23] Lloyd Cohen, "Marriage, Divorce, and Quasi rents; or, 'I gave him the best years of my life'" (1987) 16:2 *J Leg Stud* 267; Robert Leckey, "Relational Contract and Other Models of Marriage" (2002) 40 *Osgoode Hall Law* J 1; Jennifer Nedelsky, *Law's Relations: A Relational Theory of Self, Autonomy, and Law* (New York: Oxford University Press, 2011).

[24] Fournier, *supra* note 19; Pascale Fournier, "Calculating Claims: Jewish and Muslim Women Navigating Religion, Economics and Law in Canada" (2012) 8:1 *Int J Law Context* 47.

subordinate or "dependent" status with respect to marriage. This misleading picture is shared both by secular feminists, who present religious law as irretrievably oppressive to women,[25] and by tenants of identity politics, who seek to shore up minority identities in the face of majority oppression by recognizing religious family law.[26] This chapter attempts to move past static hierarchical binaries and examines the interaction and intersection between these two phenomena.

In Section 3.2, I situate the chapter within the theoretical literature on legal pluralism. Throughout, I adopt the "critical legal pluralist" methodology of decentering the concept of law to account for its impact on subject-constitution and its constant openness to transformation at the hands of legal subjects. In addition, I infuse this research with a concern for the distributive role of law *and* culture and conceptualize both state law and cultural norms as background rules of socio-economic bargaining. In Section 3.3, I present the findings from the fieldwork and elaborate the hypothesis that state recognition of Jewish marriage (and likewise the non-recognition of Muslim marriage) has consequences both on religious women's subjectivity and on the distributive impact of law. The fieldwork allows me to explore the hypothesis that state recognition

[25] Susan Moller Okin, in Joshua Cohen, Matthew Howard & Martha C. Nussbaum, eds., *Is Multiculturalism Bad for Women?* (Princeton: Princeton University Press, 1999); On Jewish women, *see* Carmel Shalev, "Women in Israel: Fighting Tradition" in Julie Peters & Andrea Wolper, eds., *Women's Rights. Human Rights: International Feminist Perspectives* (New York: Routledge, 1995) at 89, 92 ("[S]ubstantive Jewish laws of marriage and divorce are pervaded by a double standard that is patently discriminatory"); Gila Stopler, "The Free Exercise of Discrimination: Religious Liberty, Civic Community and Women's Equality" (2004) 10 *William Mary J Women Law* 459 at 462 ("The close ties between religion and the state in Israel clearly violate women's rights to equality"). On Muslim women, *see* Margot Badran, *Feminists, Islam, and Nation: Gender and the Making of Modern Egypt* (Princeton University Press, 1996) at 124 (denouncing Islamic family law as perpetuating the "[p]atriarchal domination remain[ing] most entrenched in the family"); Homa Hoodfar, "Circumventing Legal Limitation: Mahr and Marriage Negotiation in Egyptian Low-Income Communities" in Homa Hoodfar, ed., *Shifting Boundaries Marriage Divorce Muslim Communities* (Gabels, France: Women Living Under Muslim Laws, 1996) at 121, 124 (portraying Islamic marriage as a "fundamentally unequal social institution").

[26] Leti Volpp, "Feminism versus Multiculturalism" (2001) 101 *Columbia Law Rev* 1181; Sherene H Razack, "The 'Sharia Law Debate' in Ontario: The Modernity/Premodernity Distinction in Legal Efforts to Protect Women From Culture" (2007) 15:1 *Fem Leg Stud* 3; Natasha Bakht, "Religious Arbitration in Canada: Protecting Women by Protecting them from Religion" (2007) 19 *Can J Women L* 119; Lila Abu-Lughod, "Do Muslim Women Really Need Saving? Anthropological Reflections on Cultural Relativism and its Others" (2002) 104:3 *Am Anthropol* 783.

of religious law accentuates the legal dimension of religion. This translates in a view of religion/culture as receptive to strategies, recourses, and individualist bargaining of the sort normally associated with civil law. Inversely, non-recognition and confinement of religious norms to a private, non-legal sphere seem to reinforce the (misleading) idea of religion as status, submission, and fixed identity, a phenomenon fraught with unfavorable distributive consequences for women. I consider the repercussions of this phenomenon on subjective perceptions of religion, on the concrete strategies adopted by women, both with regards to substantive legal arguments and interpersonal relationships among religious communities, on the decisions of religious authorities, for example whether they consider civil outcomes and enforce religious financial provisions, and finally on the economic outcomes produced by the interplay of culture and law.

3.2 A New Approach to the Study of Law and Culture

This chapter uses critical legal pluralism as a methodological and theoretical framework to emphasize the subjective construction of law by legal subjects.[27] To grasp religious women's complex interactions with "culture," the insights of legal pluralism are most useful. In recent decades, a deepened legal pluralism was developed, one which goes beyond pluralizing normativity and directly questions the very notion of positivity. Roderick A. Macdonald, the flag-bearer of critical legal pluralism, has headed the Canadian manifestation of this movement. Critical legal pluralism understands the law as encompassing "how legal subjects understand themselves and the law."[28] For critical legal pluralists, "law arises from, belongs to, and responds to everyone,"[29] and one cannot only understand law through the ontological tools of "legal evangelicalism,"

[27] For a genealogy of legal pluralism, *see* John Griffiths, "What Is Legal Pluralism?" (1986) 24 *J Leg Plur* 1 at passim; Sally Engle Merry, "Legal Pluralism" (1988) 22:5 *Law Soc Rev* 869 at passim; Franz von Benda-Beckmannn & Keebet von Benda-Beckmannn, "The Dynamics of Change and Continuity in Plural Legal Orders" (2006) 53 *J Leg Plur Unoff Law* 1 at passim. *See also* Angela Campbell, "Wives' Tales: Reflecting on Research in Bountiful" (2008) 23 *Can J Law Soc* 121 at 130–2.

[28] Martha-Marie Kleinhans & Roderick A Macdonald, "What Is a Critical Legal Pluralism" (1997) 12 *Can JL Soc* 25 at 36.

[29] Roderick A Macdonald, *Lessons of Everyday Law* (Montreal: Mcgill-Queen's Press for the School of Policy Studies, Queen's University and the Law Commission of Canada, 2002) at 8.

which "breeds a reliance on the rituals, catechism, and creed of official institutions that focus on the word (especially on the definitive pronouncements of the curia that sits at the top of an institutional hierarchy)."[30] In this view, legal subjects shape and produce law as much as Parliament does, through their constructive creativity and normative interpersonal interactions.[31] As put by Kleinhans and MacDonald:

> Legal subjects are not wholly determined; they possess a transformative capacity that enables them to produce legal knowledge and to fashion the very structures of law that contribute to constituting their legal subjectivity. This transformative capacity is directly connected to their substantive particularity. It endows legal subjects with a responsibility to participate in the multiple normative communities by which they recognize and create their own legal subjectivity.[32]

This outlook led me to analyze religious law through the eyes of women of differing subject positionalities, ranging from autonomous individuality to those who refer to themselves through the continued relevance of kinship networks.[33] Indeed, our encounters underline "the relevance of first-person accounts [...] to the development of a fuller sense of the law."[34] My own perspective, however, departs from the critical legal pluralism ethos and methodology on the view it holds of "culture"/non-state law. In the work of several influential legal pluralists, the objective has been to demonstrate that contrary to positivist dogma, law is not separate from culture and is in fact part of the cultural fabric

30 Roderick A Macdonald, "Custom Made—For a Non-Chirographic Critical Legal Pluralism" (2011) 26 *Can J Law Soc* 301 at 306.

31 For an empirical study of norm-generating everyday interactions, *see* Susan S Silbey & Patricia Ewick, *The Common Place of Law: Stories from Everyday Life* (Chicago: University of Chicago Press, 1998). *See also* Austin Sarat & Thomas R Kearns, "Beyond the Great Divide: Forms of Legal Scholarship and Everyday Life" in Austin Sarat & Thomas R Kearns, eds., *Law Everyday Life* (Ann Arbor, MI: University of Michigan Press, 1993) at 21 passim; Sally Engle Merry, "Everyday Understandings of the Law in Working-Class America" (1986) 13 *Am Ethnol* 253 at passim; Austin Sarat, "Law Is All Over: Power, Resistance and the Legal Consciousness of the Welfare Poor, The" (1990) 2 *Yale JL Hum* 343 at 344–5.

32 Kleinhans & Macdonald, *supra* note 28 at 38.

33 This article borrows from the theory of agency developed by Deniz Kandiyoti, "Bargaining with Patriarchy" (1988) 2:3 *Gend Soc* 274, where she examines the coping strategies and lifestyle choices that women make under patriarchal constraints: "these patriarchal bargains exert a powerful influence on the shaping of women's gendered subjectivity and determine the nature of gender ideology in different contexts [and that they] influence both the potential for and specific forms of women's active or passive resistance." *Ibid* at 275.

34 Campbell, *supra* note 27 at 191.

of society.[35] Hence, law is susceptible to the constant semiotic redefinition identified by anthropologist Clifford Geertz in his landmark interpretive theory of culture.[36] In other words, law *is* culture. I aim, if not to contradict this approach, at least to emphasize another aspect of the law/culture intersection: the fact that cultural mechanisms, including the decentralized normative processes embraced by legal pluralists, also act as authoritative norms and socio-economic bargaining endowments, much in the way state law does. In the case of women facing religious family norms, this means that religious customs and meaning attribution processes also carry distributive implications in the legal structure of religious communities. In other words, if law is culture, it is also the case that *culture is law*. Thus, this chapter's approach places the emphasis on what agents do with culture and how the latter influences their subjectivity and bargaining possibilities. In this regard, I am inspired by scholarship in the vein of left law and economics.[37] The present work also draws much inspiration from the traditional law and economics analyses of family life[38] to picture the micro-level power relations that religious women must face.[39] So, although this chapter shifts the focus from state law to sovereign legal subjects, thereby borrowing from critical legal pluralism, the analysis remains on how law (and culture) structures contextual, micro power relations.

[35] *See e.g.*, Benjamin L Berger, "The Cultural Limits of Legal Tolerance" (2008) 21:2 *Can J Law Jurisprud* 245–277; Jeremy Webber, "Legal Pluralism and Human Agency" (2006) 1 *Osgoode Hall LJ* 44; Annelise Riles, "Anthropology, Human Rights, and Legal Knowledge: Culture in the Iron Cage" (2006) 1 *Am Anthropol* 108; Bernard S Jackson, *Making Sense in Law: Linguistic, Psychological and Semiotic Perspectives, Legal Semiotics Monographs* (Liverpool, UK: Deborah Charles Liverpool, 1995).

[36] Clifford Geertz, "Thick Description: Toward an Interpretive Theory of Culture" in *The Interpretation of Culture - Selected Essays* (New York: Basic Books, 1973) at 3–30.

[37] *See e.g.*, Duncan Kennedy, "Distributive and Paternalistic Motives in Contract and Tort Law, with Special Reference to Compulsory Terms and Unequal Bargaining Power" (1982) 41 *Md Law Rev*; Frances E Olsen, "The Family and the Market: A Study of Ideology and Legal Reform" (1983) 96 *Harv Law Rev* 1497.

[38] For economic analyses of family life, *see* Francine D Blau, Marianne A Ferber & Anne E Winkler, *The Economics of Women, Men, and Work*, 3rd edn (1988); Lloyd R Cohen, "Marriage: The Long-Term Contract" in Antony W Dnes & Robert Rowthorn, eds., *Law Econ Marriage Divorce* (2002) 10; Robert A Pollak, "Gary Becker's Contributions to Family and Household Economics" (2003) 1 *Rev Econ Househ* 111. For an analysis of legal realist-inspired law and economics and its relationship to feminist thought, *see* Prabha Kotiswaran, *Dangerous Sex, Invisible Labor: Sex Work and the Law in India* (Princeton: Princeton University Press, 2011) at 185–211.

[39] My conception of power and freedom owes much to Duncan Kennedy, "The Stakes of Law, or Hale and Foucault" (1991) 15 *Leg Stud F* 327.

The emphasis on culture's influence on the bargaining positions of legal agents should not be seen as a step back into the "social-scientific" positivity denounced by leading critical legal pluralists.[40] Rather, I argue it brings contextualization of legal subjects' agency and proper assessment of their concrete possibilities, however unstable and shifting they may be.[41] The analysis allows us to discuss the effects of both civil and religious laws on legal subjects. Moreover, it should be noted that the empirical work is not intended to bear sufficient objective representativeness and exhaustiveness to be labelled legal anthropology or ethnography. My goal is to better illustrate and emphasize how religious women and their husbands play out the secular/religious divide through a qualitative "story-telling" approach to socio-legal studies.[42] Our encounters with religious women can shed some light on the agency and resistance deployed by religious women navigating law and culture in diverse contexts.

3.3 Law and Culture as Intersecting Spaces: Legalizing Religion

This section presents the results of fieldwork research among Jewish and Muslim women in the United Kingdom. The bulk of this fieldwork occurred in the Greater London Area and comprised interviews with eight women who were in the process of or had already undergone

[40] *See* Kleinhans & Macdonald, *supra* note 28 at 35.

[41] As put by Duncan Kennedy:

> [W]e do not assume that the legal system as a whole deliberately decrees one thing or another [...] Rather, we conceptualize the network as providing background rules that constitute the actors, by granting them all kinds of powers under all kinds of limitations, and then regulating interaction between actors by banning and permitting, encouraging and discouraging particular tactics of particular actors in particular circumstances.

Duncan Kennedy, "Legal Economics of US Low Income Housing Markets in Light of Informality Analysis" (2002) 4 *JL Soc* 71 at 80.

[42] For examples of using a story-telling approach, *see* Campbell, *supra* note 27; Shauna Van Praagh, "Faith, Belonging, and the Protection of Our Children" (1999) 17 *Windsor YB Access Just* 154 (interweaving stories with legal argument); Shauna Van Praagh, "Education of Religious Children: Families, Communities and Constitutions, The" (1999) 47 *Buff L. Rev* 1343. *See also* Jane B Baron, "Resistance to Stories" (1994) 67 *Cal L. Rev* 255 at 282 (arguing that storytelling plays an important role in advancing legal studies by provoking dialogue among groups typically not heard in legal scholarship); Lucie E White, "Subordination, Rhetorical Survival Skills, and Sunday Shoes: Notes on the Hearing of Mrs. G." (1990) 38:1 *Buff L. Rev* 33 n.96 ("A feminist alternative to this monologic approach to scholarship would entail conversation and translation, rather than observation and pronouncement").

religious and/or civil divorce in the United Kingdom.[43] The women were contacted through religious officials, barristers, researchers, non-governmental organizations, and connections among religious communities.[44] The interviews lasted about an hour and a half each and focused on repudiation: the Jewish *get* and the Islamic *talaq*, religious divorces that can only be granted by the man according to Jewish and Islamic family law.[45] They also incorporated questions on religious beliefs and practices, religious and civil marriage and divorce, their impact on women's welfare, the intervention of the religious community, and the strategies adopted by women to influence religious and civil outcomes. The participants were educated and employed, both British-born and migrants, from the ages of twenty-nine to seventy-two, with a diverse range of personal socio-economic and family circumstances. Cultural diversity and identity varied greatly, encompassing a number of cultural and religious observance practices: Jewish participants belonged or used to belong to the Orthodox sect and were from the Ashkenazi and Sephardic communities. Muslim participants belonged to the Sunni sect and were of Bangladeshi, Austrian and Pakistani descent and/or origin.

Our fieldwork indicates that the socio-economic impact of religious and civil laws cannot be easily determined. No *a priori* evaluation seems to hold true in all circumstances. For some religious women, the civil sphere is *not* the liberating entity it is often made out to be by secularists. Fieldwork research in Europe,[46] Canada,[47] and the

[43] Given the size of our sample, we do not claim to have reached conclusions relevant from a quantitative point of view. As we discuss in this paper, our interviews reveal many phenomena unaccounted for in the mainstream discourse that should be further explored.

[44] This method was approved by the University of Ottawa's Office of Research Ethics and Integrity.

[45] Kaplan, *supra* note 12 at 61; El Alami & Hinchcliffe, *supra* note 6 at 27–8.

[46] John Bowen, *What is True and False about UK Sharia Councils* (London: Queen Mary University of London, 2012); Alison Dundes Renteln & Marie-Claire Foblets, *Multicultural Jurisprudence: Comparative Perspectives on the Cultural Defense* (Oxford and Portland, Oregon: Hart Publishing, 2009); Kim Lecoyer & Barbara Truffin, *Pathways to Family Dispute Resolution within Migrant Families in Belgium* (London: Queen Mary University of London, 2012); Anika Liversage, *Unregistered Marriages in Denmark* (London: Queen Mary University of London, 2012); Mathias Rohe, "On the Applicability of Islamic Rules in Germany and Europe" (2003) 3 *Eur Yearb Minor Issues* 181; Pascale Fournier, "Secular Portraits and Religious Shadows: An Empirical Study of Religious Women in France" in Jacques Berlinerblau, ed., *Secul Edge Contemp Church-State Relat U S Fr Isr* (New York: Palgrave Macmillan, 2014).

[47] Fournier, *supra* note 24; Farrah Ahmed, "Personal Autonomy and the Option of Religious Law" (2010) 24:2 *Int J Law Policy Fam* 222; Bakht, *supra* note 26; Fournier, *supra*

United Kingdom[48] reaches similar conclusions. In fact, some participants perceived the civil law as adversarial and costly, which translated itself into socio-economic disadvantage:

> **Participant 2**
> I wasn't in charge. I wasn't in command. I didn't really know what was going on. [. . .] And I really don't think that the [secular] lawyer did very well. I think he made too much of it. [. . .] What a ridiculous waste of money and time. And making more antagonism than there needed to be. I blame the [secular] lawyers very much for that.
>
> **Participant 4**
> Yeah, I didn't like the whole petition, and who is going to pay whose costs. [. . .] The whole court process takes forever. Every hearing, every this and that.

These complaints about the deficiencies of civil law echo the literature, which also attests to the lack of access to justice of women from religious and ethnic minorities in Europe.[49] Unsurprisingly, while it seems that women can sometimes be disadvantaged by civil law, religious law can also be a major source of disempowerment for women:

> **Participant 6**
> I was never very engaged with my religious community. I hated it. I hated – all my life I was battling with the male-dominated environment. [. . .] My culture needs to be educated. [. . .] I tell my friends this all the time. I have friends that went to school with me and now they are stuck in a rut, cooking and cleaning. I tell them to get out of it.

note 19; Korteweg, *supra* note 20; Sonia Lawrence, "Cultural (in) Sensitivity: The Dangers of a Simplistic Approach to Culture in the Courtroom" (2001) 13 *Can J Women L* 107; Razack, *supra* note 26.

48 Ahmed, *supra* note 47; Samia Bano, "Muslim Family Justice and Human Rights: The Experience of British Muslim Women" (2007) 2:2 *J Comp L* 1; Samia Bano, *Muslim Women and Shari'ah Councils: Transcending the Boundaries of Community and Law* (New York: Palgrave Macmillan, 2012); Lucy Carroll, "Muslim Women and 'Islamic Divorce' in England" (1997) 17:1 *J Muslim Minor Aff* 97; Gillian Douglas, *Religious Divorce in the Secular-State: A Case-Study Analysis* (London: Queen Mary University of London, 2012); Prakash Shah, "A Reflection on the Shari'a Debate in Britain" (2010) 13 *Stud Z Prawa Wyznaniowego (Studies Eccles Law)* 71; Prakash Shah, "Transforming to Accommodate? Reflections on the Shari'a Debate in Britain" in Grillo et al, eds., *Legal Practices and Cultural Diversity* (Aldershot: Ashgate, 2009) 73; Sonia Nourin Shah-Kazemi, "Cross-Cultural Mediation: A Critical View of the Dynamics of Culture in Family Disputes" (2000) 14:3 *Int J Law Policy Fam* 302.

49 Mavis Maclean & John Eekelaar, eds., *Managing Family Justice in Diverse Societies*, Oñati International Series in Law and Society (Oxford: Hart Publishing, 2013).

> **Participant 2**
> I did feel that I didn't like the way the secular system was working. I felt exactly the same about the religious system. With the religious law – oh gosh – there are so many changes they need to make [. . .] But with the actual procedure, and what needs to happen, there needs to be a reinterpretation of the law, because it's all in the hands of the men, it's only the husband, who can give the *get* and that has just got to be interpreted in another way.
>
> **Participant 1**
> [Pause] You can't change. That's it. The only thing that you could change is the way the actual issuing authority dealt with you on a personal basis, which would make enough of a difference[. . .] And that is training for the people at the *beth din*[. . .] I wish things could be changed, but I've given up hope of that. Because[. . .] the rabbis may have changed things many years ago and those changes became what is now accepted but nobody will make any changes now.
>
> **Participant 3**
> The general attitude and treatment of women by the London *Beth Din* is what needs changing. However, this change is not occurring. Members of the *Agunah Campaign* have tried to affect change by forging closer relationships with the London *Beth Din* however, this has proved to be ineffective, as it has made it more difficult to speak against or criticize the *beth din*.
>
> **Participant 5**
> I don't think it [the *get* ceremony] can be changed. You can't mess with religion[. . .] It's not flexible. It will not change. But I would like it to be less painful. It's hard enough, so if it could be more efficient, that could be nice.

For some of the participants, religion and civil law can both be disadvantageous. While this finding may serve to qualify simplistic views on the "liberating" effect of either system, it also begs the question: what is it that makes a given civil or religious institution empowering for women? In this article, I posit that the empowering effect of both systems may be a function of their interaction. Specifically, it would seem that religion is much more empowering when it evolves alongside the civil law and is influenced by it.[50] This hypothesis revealed itself through a comparative assessment of the Jewish and Muslim communities, whose

[50] The author is however aware that more empirical studies pertaining to the real and effective practices of religious authorities in both communities, and the justification for said practices, may be necessary to strengthen such assertion. For instance, interviews with rabbis and imams may confirm the reality of such ongoing empowerment.

legal norms are very differently positioned with regards to British civil law. While Jewish family law is recognized and acknowledged by state law, Muslim law is not, with a resulting estrangement from the civil sphere on the part of Muslim communities.

The *Marriage Act 1949–96*, which governs solemnization of marriages in England, outlines detailed rules concerning where the marriage may take place, who should conduct the ceremony, the time of day it may occur, and the nature of the celebration.[51] According to section 26(I), marriages *other than* those conducted according to the rites of the Church of England, the usages of the Society of Friends (i.e., Quakers), or "a marriage between two persons professing the Jewish religion according the usages of the Jews,"[52] must be performed in an office of the superintendent registrar or a registered building, between 8 am and 6 pm, in the presence of either a registrar or an "authorized person," with the couple exchanging vows according to a standard form of words prescribed by statute.[53] Amendments passed in the 1990s attempted to take into account the fact that people wish to marry in different ways. For instance, the *Marriage (Registration of Buildings) Act 1990* removed the requirement to have a separate building as a registered place of worship. The *Marriage Act 1994* allowed the registration of "approved premises" other than religious buildings or local authority registries but also stipulated that "[n]o religious service shall be used at a marriage on approved premises."[54] These amendments appear to accommodate increasingly secularized celebrations of marriage, but continue to disregard minority religious marriage practices.

Muslim marriages conducted in England and Wales are consequently regarded as legally valid if the marriage takes place in a mosque that is duly registered as a place of worship and for the solemnization of marriage. The marriage must also be attended and registered by a person

51 Sebastian Poulter, "Chapter 6: Muslims: The Claim to a Separate System of Personal Law" in *Ethnicity, Law and Human Rights: The English Experience* (Oxford: Oxford University Press, 1999) at 205.

52 *The Marriage Act 1994*, 1994 [*The Marriage Act 1994*] at s 26(1) a–e.

53 *Ibid.*

54 In the Guidelines issued by the Registrar General under the *Marriage Act 1994*, paragraph 7 stipulates: "Marriages on approved premises may be followed by a celebration, commemoration or blessing of the couple's choice, providing that it is not a religious marriage ceremony and is separate from the civil ceremony. However, if a religious blessing were to regularly follow marriage ceremonies on particular premises, or be considered part of the service being offered on the premises, there may well be a religious connection which would break the requirements and lead to the local authority having to consider revoking the approval."

authorized by the *Marriage Act 1949*. Since in Islamic law a marriage can be contracted merely in the presence of witnesses and requires no other formalities,[55] the consequences of this legislation are far-reaching. Various sources estimate that a significant and increasing number of Muslim marriages in the United Kingdom go unrecognized by civil law.[56] A prominent Muslim woman barrister reports: "The problem (of unregistered Muslim marriages) is a major trend - it is growing rapidly, especially amongst the under 30s. In my experience of clients, 80% of Muslim marriages are not registered and this percentage is growing."[57] Though Muslims comprised 2.78 percent of the UK population in 2001, a mere 163 legally recognized marriages took place in registered mosques.[58] These numbers appear very small, especially in comparison to Sikhs who comprised 0.59 percent of the population and had 1,008 legally registered marriages in the same time period.[59]

English family law regards Muslim women who do not have legally recognized marriages as if they are in a cohabiting relationship. They are therefore unable to benefit from the civil divorce procedure and many other legal protections and economic advantages of the civil law reserved for legally married spouses.[60] The situation is aggravated by recent

[55] Jamal J. Nasir, *The Islamic Law of Personal Status* 45 (2002); Ziba Mir~Hosseini, *Marriage on Trial. Islamic Family Law in. Iran and Morocco,* I.B.Tauris Publishers. London New York, p. 168.

[56] Khola Hasan is the spokesperson for the Islamic Sharia Council. The interview was conducted on 23 January 2012, ISC, East London. Khola Hasan, *Interview* (2012). The East London mosque affiliated with the Islamic Sharia Council reported that two marriages were performed in the five years the mosque has been a registered building that can perform solemnized marriages; Ministry of Justice, *Muslim Marriage: Report of Working Group – Submission* (Ministry of Justice, 2012) at 1; Aina Khan, *The Way Forward for Islam and English Law* (Russell Jones & Walker, London, UK, 2011). *See also* Bano, *supra* note 48; Shah-Kazemi, *supra* note 48.

[57] Aina Khan, "Aina Khan and Baroness Warsi Kickstart Muslim Marriage Project," *Online Duncan Lewis Solicit* (January 13, 2014), online: www.duncanlewis.co.uk/IslamicLaw_news/Aina_Khan_and_Baroness_Warsi_kickstart_Muslim_Marriage_Project_(14_January_2014).html.

[58] Office for National Statistics (ONS), *Focus on Religion* (2004); ONS, table 3.4: *Marriages (numbers and percentages): Type of Ceremony, Denomination and Day of Occurrence,* Marriages Series FM2 no 29 (England and Wales, 2001).

[59] Office for National Statistics (ONS), *supra* note 58.

[60] Legal protections and economic advantages of civil law include for example, capital and income provision on relationship breakdown, capital provision where there is a dependent child or children, intestate succession and family provision on death, and inheritance provisions. *See e.g., Married Women's Property Act 1882* [*Married Women's Property Act 1882*]; *Matrimonial Causes Act 1973* [*Matrimonial Causes Act 1973*]; *Fatal Accidents Act 1976* [*Fatal Accidents Act 1976*]; *Domestic Proceedings and Magistrates' Court Act 1978* [*Domestic Proceedings and Magistrates' Court Act 1978*]; *Inheritance Tax Act 1984*

changes to legal aid that no longer cover family law, including divorce and child residence.[61] The number of Muslim women approaching Islamic *sharia* councils for dissolution of their marriages may consequently increase without comparable levels of protections available under civil law.[62] However, legal status has not been given to any religious tribunal in the United Kingdom and therefore the authority of *sharia* councils extends only to those who choose to submit to them.[63] It is worth mentioning that legal recognition of marriage practices among minority religious communities such as Jews and Muslims have developed alongside the United Kingdom's Christian-based ethos and increasingly secularized society. At the current time, social tensions[64] are exacerbated by discrimination and disenfranchisement of Muslims from wider British society, the sustained relevance of transnational migration, connections to countries of origin and kinship networks, as well as

[*Inheritance Tax Act 1984*]; *Children Act 1989* [*Children Act 1989*]; *Family Law Act 1996* [*Family Law Act 1996*]; *Civil Partnership Act 2004* [*Civil Partnership Act 2004*]. *See also* Law Commission, "Cohabitation: The Financial Consequences of Relationship Breakdown" (2007) 307 *Law Com*, online: http://lawcommission.justice.gov.uk/docs/lc307_Cohabitation.pdf; Citizens Advice Bureau, *Ending a Relationship When You're Living Together*.

61 Polly Curtis, "Legal Aid Cuts Will Hit Women the Hardest, Says Justice Department," *The Guardian* (December 26, 2010), online: www.theguardian.com/law/2010/dec/26/legal-aid-cuts-hit-women-justice; *See also* Emily Dugan, "Courts Becoming Clogged as Legal Aid Cuts Affect Separating Couples Seeking Mediation," *The Independent* (January 13, 2014), online: www.independent.co.uk/news/uk/politics/courts-becoming-clogged-as-legal-aid-cuts-affect-separating-couples-seeking-mediation-9057133.html; "Government's Legal Aid Cuts Will Harm Women and Children, Say National Meeting of Family Barristers," *Fam Law Week* (September 19, 2011), online: www.familylawweek.co.uk/site.aspx?i=ed86242.

62 Gillian Felicity Douglas et al, *Social Cohesion and Civil Law: Marriage, Divorce and Religious Courts*, Report of a research study funded by the AHRC (Cardiff: Cardiff University, 2011) at 29: "Shariah councils serve as alternative forums for dispute resolution which apply Muslim legal and ethical principles as well as the cultural norms of local communities. Shariah Councils have three main functions: reconciliation and mediation; issuing Muslim divorce certificates; and producing expert opinion reports on Muslim family law and practice." *See also* Ministry of Justice, *supra* note 56 at 2.

63 Douglas et al, *supra* note 62 at 44.

64 For further details on social issues in Britain (including England), and how they are perceived by the British people, please refer to NatCen Social Research thematic reports, available online at: www.natcen.ac.uk. See *also* "British Social Attitudes 2012 Report," available online at: www.bsa-29.natcen.ac.uk/read-the-report/immigration/introduction.aspx; "British Social Attitudes 2013, Attitudes to Immigration," available online at: www.natcen.ac.uk/media/205573/immigration-bsa31.pdf. *See also* UK Home Office report, "Social and Public Service Impacts of International Migration at the Local Level," Migration Research and Analysis, July 3, 2013, available online at: www.gov.uk/government/publications/social-and-public-service-impacts-of-international-migration-at-the-local-level (last accessed April 10, 2014).

practices commonly associated with Muslims, such as arranged marriage,[65] forced marriage,[66] and polygamy,[67] which fly in the face of British sensibilities.

As far as divorce goes, no recognition is granted to religious divorce of any faith. Civil divorce is solely granted through a decree or order granted by an English court of civil jurisdiction on the grounds that the marriage has irretrievably broken down.[68] However, the Jewish community does have an element of "recognition," which is perhaps more aptly described as "consideration" of religious law on the part of civil courts: *The Divorce (Religious Marriages) Act 2002* (hereinafter *2002 Act*).[69] This law enables the civil courts to "order that a decree of divorce is not to be made absolute until a declaration made by both parties that they have taken such steps as are required to dissolve the marriage in accordance with '(i) the usages of the Jews, or (ii) any other prescribed religious usages' is produced to the court."[70] The *Act* specifically refers here to religious divorce and was meant to counter the *agunah* problem by providing civil courts with means to pressure the husband to give the *get* by suspending the civil divorce procedure.[71] Though the *2002 Act* is

[65] Pat Strickland, *Forced Marriage*, Home Affairs Section (House of Commons Library, 2013) at 1: (An arranged marriage occurs when "both parties fully and freely consent to the marriage, although their families take a leading role in the choice of partner.") *See* P R Jones & S Shah, "Arranged Marriages: A Sample Survey of the Asian Case" (1980) 8:3 *J Ethn Migr Stud* 339; Prakash Shah, "Inconvenient Marriages, or What Happens When Ethnic Minorities Marry Trans-Jurisdictionally According to their Self-Chosen Norms" (2010) 6:2 *Utrecht Rev* 17–32.

[66] Pat Strickland, *supra* note 65 at 1 (A forced marriage is defined as "one conducted without the valid consent of both people, where pressure or abuse is used.") *See Forced Marriage (Civil Protection) Act 2007* [*Forced Marriage (Civil Protection) Act 2007*]; *Forced Marriage*, Marriage, civil partnership and divorce (GOV.UK, 2013); Anne Phillips & Moira Dustin, "UK Initiatives on Forced Marriage: Regulation, Dialogue and Exit" (2004) 52:3 *Polit Stud* 531; Sundari Anitha & Aisha Gill, "Coercion, Consent and the Forced Marriage Debate in the UK" (2009) 17:2 *Fem Leg Stud* 165.

[67] *See e.g.*, Pearl & Menski, *supra* note 7 at 273; Sebastian Poulter, *English Law and Ethnic Minority Customs* (London: Butterworth, 1986) at 45; Federica Sona, "Polygamy in Britain" (2005) *Osservatorio delle Libertà ed Istituzioni Religiose Online*, online: www.Sona_Polygamy_in_Britain.pdf; Katharine Charsley & Anika Liversage, "Transforming Polygamy: Migration, Transnationalism and Multiple Marriages among Muslim Minorities" (2013) 13 *Glob Netw* 60; Catherine Fairbairn, *Polygamy*, Home Affairs Section (House of Commons Library: Parliament, 2012) at 1.

[68] Poulter, *supra* note 51 at 207–8.

[69] *Matrimonial Causes Act 1973*, *supra* note 60 at section 10A.

[70] *Ibid* at section 10A(2).

[71] Gillian Douglas, *supra* note 48 at 13–4. As Douglas makes clear, "this is not a case of the state recognizing the religious divorce: rather the state is delaying the divorce until the

open to other religions seeking inclusions within the terms of the provision, Jews have been the exclusive users so far.[72] Muslim abstention from the use of the *2002 Act* may also be explained by the fact that the *Act* addresses divorce refusal, a problem which seems less widespread in Muslim communities. Indeed, while a husband may refuse the *talaq* divorce, Muslim women may have recourse to the *khul* or fault-based *fashk* divorce, not to mention the fact that imams in Western Europe have been known to tend toward reforming divorce laws in the direction of granting women the right to obtain divorce unilaterally.[73] In any case, this asymmetrical relationship with the civil law seems to have an impact on religious women's subjectivity and constitutes the religious sphere in quite distinct ways for Jews and Muslims. In fact, in the case of Muslim women, a recurrent theme was that religion was a "cultural" sphere based on status and submission to revealed, sacred rules:

> **Participant 8**
> My understanding of both the religious marriage and divorce was nil. I knew that a *nikah* happened and there were witnesses to a *nikah*. But nobody talked about it – I was coming from a culture that is fairly conservative – and these things were not discussed with girls before they got married. [...] At the time of my marriage, I didn't know anything about it. I don't think I even saw my *nikahnama* [marriage contract].

> **Participant 6**
> For the marriage, we went to the mosque. I was dressed up, my family came, his family came. It was a really nice ceremony. There were 30 of us, I think. I didn't sign anything. I don't even remember saying yes. But I think I must have said '*kabul*' maybe. That was followed by the exchange of rings, we shared sweets, and that was it. [...] I have never seen my contract. I don't know what my contract looks like. I don't know what was in it. I don't even know my actual *mahr*. I left it up to my family because I thought this is where the culture kicked in. I thought that's the way to do it. You shouldn't question these things.

There thus seems to be some evidence that the non-recognition of Muslim marriage and the resulting estrangement of Muslim communities from the

party's position has been protected, in the same way that it may do so to ensure that arrangements for children, or the financial consequences, are satisfactorily resolved."

72 *Ibid* at 14.

73 Pascale Fournier, *supra* note 46; Pascale Fournier & Pascal McDougall, "False Jurisdictions: A Revisionist Take on Customary (Religious) Law in Germany" (2013) 48:3 *Tex Inter'l LJ* 435. On similar attempts by the Birmingham Sharia Council in the United Kingdom, *see* Gillian Douglas, *supra* note 48.

civil sphere reinforce the idea that religion is perceived as based on status and not contract. This constitutive effect is made all the more interesting by the fact that Jewish women who deal with the civil law in addition to religious law had quite a different view of religion. Our participants depicted religious norms as contestable, legalized, and open to recourses. They used the words "business contract" and "legalistic" to describe the same types of rules that Muslim women portrayed as "god-derived" and "cultural." Indeed, Muslims are asked to believe in what is "fated, decreed, destined, preordained,"[74] that is the written or *Maktub*, leaving little, if no, space to negotiation and bargaining and leading to some extent to intrinsic submission to God; this is *versus* the belief in a personal negotiation with God of the Jewish community, a belief whereby religious space becomes contractual and agency operates at full capacity. Women also described religious law as riven by legal "loopholes" which allowed for strategizing and litigating of the *get*:

> **Participant 1**
> The *ketubah* is a contract. It's about how the bride will bring to the marriage various household goods. [. . .] It is a business contract!
>
> **Participant 2**
> Judaism has quite a strong legalistic side to it, this thing called *Halakha*, the Jewish law.
>
> **Participant 3**
> The discussions with the London *Beth Din* (United Synagogue) through the *Agunot Campaign*[75] left me with the strongest impression. There was quite a lot of interaction between the London *Beth Din* and me and my husband when we were trying to resolve my *agunah* status. We explored various loopholes in rabbinical law and tried to accommodate each suggestion put forward by the *beth din*. Ultimately, each loophole was discounted, and I was disillusioned by the whole process. One example of a proposed loophole was whether my ex-husband actually bought the ring he gave me. If he hadn't, there was a chance the marriage could be annulled as rabbinical law states a man must buy the ring himself and not delegate this responsibility. I was in touch with my ex-father-in-law, and he was willing to support me by providing in writing or in person his

[74] Moshe Piamenta, *Islam in Everyday Arabic Speech* (Leiden: Brill Academic Pub, 1997) at 192.

[75] The *Agunot Campaign* is an organization dedicated to "remedy the injustice suffered by Jewish women whose husbands deny them a religious divorce (called a 'get') after their marriages have irretrievably broken down." *See*: www.agunot-campaign.org.uk.

> testimony that he gave my ex-husband the money to buy the ring so we could pursue this loophole. However, the rabbis changed their minds at the last moment and said this loophole option was not sufficient.

For these participants, religion cannot be reduced to status, but is instead ripe with contractual recourses and avenues for private ordering and negotiation. Consequently, they sometimes employed the strategy of giving religious norms the form of a civil contract binding the husband to perform certain religious duties such as the giving of the Jewish *get*. Other strategies included the use of *The Divorce (Religious Marriages) Act 2002*[76] to pressure the husband into granting the *get*. Our participants confirmed that this is an efficient bargaining tool for women.[77]

> **Participant 1**
> I don't know if you are aware of the great publicity there was in the UK because of the *agunah* [. . .] one became far more aware. In fact, I drew up a ten-point thing, an agreement, which made it absolutely categorically clear: I wanted the *get*. [. . .] When we had the hearing at the High Court, the judge asked him why he hadn't granted me the *get*. The judge made it a condition of the Decree Absolute. [. . .] The judge told him he'd better address that agreement quickly, and in fact, he did.

Another strategy was that of changing religious denomination (a strategy eased by the belief in a continuous personal negotiation with God) for instance from Orthodox to Reform Judaism, in order to mitigate the consequences of the *agunah* status. Participant 3 confesses: "I left the Orthodox sect to become a Reform Jew, and this meant I would no longer be an *agunah* and I could have my son without him being considered 'illegitimate'." In fact, traditional *halakha* is considered binding authority for Orthodox Jews and therefore a civil divorce is not recognized as equivalent to granting the *get*. Moreover, among the different branches of Judaism, the Orthodox Rabbinate does not recognize the validity of the measures introduced by any other denomination.[78] The Conservative branch of Judaism similarly adheres to

[76] *Matrimonial Causes Act 1973*, *supra* note 60 at (c.) 18 S. 10A.

[77] A note of caution is necessary, however. As mentioned by Douglas et al, *supra* note 62 at 48: "This remedy is ineffective if the husband does not himself wish to be able to remarry under civil law since he is indifferent to whether a civil divorce is granted or not. The London *Beth Din* considers, however, that the legislation has reduced the number of *agunot*."

[78] Judith Romney Wegner, "The Status of Women in Jewish and Islamic Marriage and Divorce Law" (1982) 5 *Harv Womens LJ* 32; Esther Rosenfeld, "Jewish Divorce Law"

traditional *halakhah* in matters of family law and is thus bound by the formality of the *get*; however, modern resolutions developed by the Conservative Rabbinate attempt to address the plight of the *agunah*. First, if a husband fails to give a wife the *get* within six months of a civil divorce, the marriage shall be considered *void ab initio*. Second, the *beit din* has the power to annul the original marriage of a woman whose husband has rescinded a *get* prior to its delivery.[79] As for the Reform branch of Judaism, the requirement of a *get* for the dissolution of marriage was abolished after a resolution was adopted at the Philadelphia Conference in 1869.[80] However, the Reform Rabbinate may urge congregants to secure a *get* in order for their divorce to be recognized by other branches of Judaism.[81]

In these scenarios, we see women treating culture and religion as permitting strategies and assertiveness. These women were willing to find innovative ways to resolve their religious disputes and challenge the religious outcomes in order to attain a better future for themselves and their children. This form of agency also translates into a willingness to use the support of religious authorities and the wider community as a bargaining chip. Such a view contrasts with the following depiction by Muslim participants:

> **Participant 6**
> I just wanted out. [. . .] I didn't even have a contract, I didn't even know where this guy is that conducted my *nikah*. The institutional Islam – the mosque – that exists, I don't agree with it and I just didn't know where to begin. I couldn't go to my family because to be honest, they weren't very supportive. [. . .] They would just push me back to my in-laws. I was on my own.

(1995) 1 *UCDavis JInt'l Pol'* 147; Yael Levy, "The Agunah and the Missing Husband: An American Solution to a Jewish Problem" (1993) 10:1 *J Law Relig* 49 at 62–6.

79 Wegner, *supra* note 78 at 31–2: "The most interesting Conservative innovation in the divorce laws is based on the single talmudic reference to a *bet din's* power to annul the original marriage of a woman whose husband has exercised his power to rescind a *get* prior to its delivery. This court action was motivated by the fear that the woman, having accepted the *get*, might remarry, not knowing that her husband had rescinded it. Recent Conservative practice has been to allow the *bet din* to grant *hafqa'at qiddushin* (annulment of marriage) to a woman whose husband unconscionably withholds a *get* after the parties have been civilly divorced"; Levy, *supra* note 78 at 64–5; David Cobin, "Jewish Divorce and the Recalcitrant Husband: Refusal to Give a 'Get' as Intentional Infliction of Emotional Distress" (1986) 4:2 *J Law Relig* 405 at 418–19.

80 *See* David J Bleich, "Jewish Divorce: Judicial Misconceptions and Possible Means of Civil Enforcement" (1983) 16 *Conn Rev* 232.

81 *See* Lisa Fishbayn, "Gender, Multiculturalism and Dialogue: The Case of Jewish Divorce" (2008) 21 *Can JL Jurisprud* 80.

Participant 8
Ninety percent of the time, it is considered to be the woman's fault. Even when people know the details, there is an expectation that the woman should have given in, done more, conformed, changed herself. I find that to be very cruel to women. [...] There is no acceptance of divorced women. They are perceived as pariahs, outcasts, or social deviants.

Khola Hasan[82]
I think the biggest barrier always is the cultural thing – "How dare you think about it [divorce]! Stay in an unhappy marriage; if he beats you fine, never mind." [...] And sometimes it's their own families, their own parents saying "don't bring shame on us." [...] So there is this perception that Islam does not approve of divorce [...].

Meanwhile, the Jewish participants depicted religious law as very often dependent on the actions of third parties. In their accounts, culture is constantly mediated by intricate family loyalties, community and kinship networks, ties of friendship, and what Michel Foucault called the "little tactics of the habitat."[83] In terms of outcomes, case-specific stakeholder strategizing has the potential to greatly alter the course of religious adjudication:

Participant 4
My aunty who lives here got very upset because of the way the community took up my divorce. People were calling her asking how I could cheat on him. I couldn't even walk down the streets.

[...]

The reason why I was quite fortunate was because my aunty knew the rabbi and the rabbi indirectly put it down to him and said: "Look if she really cheated on you, like you claim she did, you have to divorce her." So in a way, he put it the other way around and managed to get me out of it.

Participant 5
If you go to the *beth din*, give it 6 months. If you know someone you can escalate it faster. It took me two weeks. [...] I was lucky I had some connections, but it could have taken longer.

[82] Khola Hasan, *supra* note 56.
[83] Michel Foucault, *Power/Knowledge: Selected Interviews and Other Writings, 1972–1977* (New York: Random House, 1980) at 149.

The relevance of interpersonal networks for successful legal strategizing echoes the findings from my earlier fieldwork in Israel,[84] France,[85] Canada,[86] and Germany.[87] However, what is new in the case of the United Kingdom is that the disentanglement of religious and civil law (in the case of Muslim participants) seems to diminish the importance of this stakeholder strategizing. Inversely, the interplay between the civil and religious spheres seemed to produce among Jewish women a will to exploit these networks in order to influence the religious outcomes.

The respective spheres of influence of religious and civil law represent another point of strategizing and contestation. Some participants mentioned that religious authorities consider the religious impact of – or even require – the civil divorce to carry out religious adjudication. This can be analogized to a decision of private international law, whereby authorities in one legal system recognize and uphold the decisions of another system though a procedure called *exequatur*.[88] Participants also noted that religious authorities had an inconsistent practice when it came to the religious relevance of civil marriage, echoing the academic literature.[89] For instance, some participants indicated that religious authorities required a civil divorce before overseeing a religious one, while others simply had to explain to the authorities that civil procedures were underway. Interestingly, others indicated that there was no requirement, and that the authorities simply mentioned the need for civil procedures before going on with the religious procedure. This inconsistency is no doubt due in part to the diversity of the religious sources on which adjudicators rely to justify their decisions. This leaves many fertile bargaining avenues for women who wish to obtain a religious divorce more easily:

> **Participant 3**
> When I began divorce proceedings, I became aware that I needed a *get*. I made a call to the London *Beth Din* to inquire about the procedure in obtaining a *get* and was quite bluntly told I needed a civil divorce before I approached the *beth din* for any assistance.

[84] Pascale Fournier, "Halacha, The 'Jewish State' and The Canadian Agunah: Comparative Law at the Intersection of Religious and Secular Orders" (2012) 65 *J Leg Plur Unoff Law* 165.

[85] Fournier, *supra* note 46.

[86] Fournier, *supra* note 24 at 47–72.

[87] Fournier & McDougall, *supra* note 73 at 70.

[88] Xandra Ellen Kramer, "Harmonisation of Civil Procedure and the Interaction with Private International Law" in Cornelis H van Rhee & X E Kramer, eds., *Civil Litigation in a Globalized World* (The Hague: T.M.C. Asser Press, 2012) at 134 et seq.

[89] *Ibid*; Gillian Douglas, *supra* note 48; Douglas et al, *supra* note 62.

Participant 2

The *beth din* knows and understands obviously - that you have to have a civil divorce. If you live in the UK and want to re-marry, you can't re-marry simply on the strength of the religious divorce. [. . .] I think we did say things to the effect that the civil matter was progressing, and there might be a civil divorce in 'x' amount of time – that sort of thing.

Participant 4

The *beth din* doesn't care, in all honesty, about [the civil divorce]. The rabbi kind of mentioned that we need to start the procedure on the civil side as well. But, their main concern is that you actually get the *get*, so they were very helpful.

In addition to granting the religious divorce or supervising the process, religious courts often adjudicate financial religious entitlements. In fact, Muslim and Jewish family law provide for many financial obligations between spouses. For instance, *mahr*, meaning "reward" (*ajr*) or "nuptial gift" (*sadaqa*), is the expression used in Islamic family law to describe the "payment that the wife is entitled to receive from the husband in consideration of the marriage."[90] Another important issue is the enforcement of the financial provisions of the *ketubah*, the Jewish marriage contract so central to the marriage celebration.[91] The *ketubah* is often presented as a protection for the wife, as it proclaims that the husband will pay his wife a sum of money if he divorces her for no good reason or if he dies.[92] According to the literature, the rabbinical court may enforce the amount stated in the *ketubah*, while the civil court usually does not.[93] Here again, the shadow of the civil law influences how religious law is applied and conceptualized. It would seem that non-recognition and

[90] John L Esposito & Natana J DeLong-Bas, *Women in Muslim Family Law* (Syracuse, NY: Syracuse University Press, 2001) at 23.

[91] Linda S Kahan, "Note, Jewish Divorce and Secular Courts: The Promise of Avitzur" (1984) 73 *Geo LJ* 193 at 193 & n.2 (The financial provisions contained in the *ketubah* are enforceable in Israel but not in Western countries such as the United States); Jonathan Reiss & Michael J. Broyde, "Prenuptial Agreements in Talmudic, Medieval, and Modern Jewish Thought" in Michael J Broyde & Michael Ausubel, eds., *Marriage Sex and Family in Judaism* (Oxford: Rowman & Littlefield Publishers, 2005) 192 at 202–3.

[92] Susan Metzger Weiss, "Sign at Your Own Risk: The RCA Prenuptial May Prejudice the Fairness of Your Future Divorce Settlement" (1999) 6 *Cardozo Womens LJ* 49 at 54; Louis M Epstein, *The Jewish Marriage Contract: A Study in the Status of the Woman in Jewish law* (Clark, NJ: The Lawbook Exchange, Ltd., 2005) at 163.

[93] *See* Ruth Halperin-Kaddari, *Women in Israel: A State of Their Own* (Philadelphia: University of Pennsylvania Press, 2004) at 252.

estrangement from the civil sphere leads the financial religious rules to be unenforced. This can either be because they are not conceived as enforceable, or because women do not feel empowered to claim their enforcement before religious authorities:

> **Khola Hasan (Spokesperson for the Islamic Sharia Council)**
> For example, the *mahr*, a woman's right [. . .]. We cannot enforce it, we cannot police it, we cannot say to the police they should enforce it. [. . .] So we can only rely on the good will of the people.
>
> **Participant 6**
> All these things finally contributed to me saying to myself: "So what difference does it make if we get a divorce? He didn't accept the *nikah*, we didn't have a civil registration, so under the eyes of the law, I am single and cohabiting. Everything was separate. He made sure of that. Even when he bought the house, he used my money to put a deposit down but my name was never in the contract. I was so naïve. I let it be because I thought: "I need to trust him." I even gave him the gold I was getting as my *mahr* because he needed it. I cared for him so much.

Interestingly, some Jewish participants indicated that *beth dins* will enforce the *ketubah* and (more surprisingly) adjudicate financial claims ancillary to the divorce. Whether or not these participants were right about what the *beth din* would do and whether its orders are adequately enforced may be less important than the very existence of such perceptions among religious women for whom the realm of culture is pervasively legal and open to bargaining:

> **Participant 2**
> Q: So the *ketubah*, is it enforceable under Jewish Law?
>
> A: Well yes, because it is a proper document.
>
> **Participant 4**
> You can go to the rabbi and instead of sorting your case civilly, say for example, I want £20,000 out of the settlement, they will sit in front of the rabbi and they will agree to the terms and conditions and everything.

Such a difference in attitudes may lead to divergent outcomes. Predictably, the Muslim participants who expressed a less contractual view of the religious sphere obtained significantly less favorable outcomes than the Jewish participants who described the religious sphere as a legal entity. In addition to being completely excluded from the civil law benefits, religious Muslim women often have very little bargaining power in the religious sphere, prompting them to incur significant economic costs:

> **Participant 8**
> On my part, nobody negotiated, not even my parents. At one point, I did. I said to him on the phone: "I need some guarantees that you should behave yourself [. . .] As a guarantee, give me the house." And he just blew his top. I said: "Okay there are actually no guarantees that you will not misbehave again." So that was it. That was the only negotiation, and it was half-hearted. [. . .] My children have done well, and they have had my full support, my parents' full support. And he hasn't contributed anything. Neither financially, emotionally, or otherwise. They have his name and that's about it.

> **Khola Hasan (Spokesperson for the Islamic Sharia Council)**
> I was talking to another woman from Tower Hamlets and she was telling me about her divorce situation. Unfortunately in the end, when they had their religious divorce, there were problems with property, and she was not able to claim anything because she did not have the protection of civil law, and therefore, she couldn't arbitrate for those things. He was a nice person, and she had no ill will against him, but it came down to an inequality with respect to division of assets. And so unfortunately, she wasn't able to recoup any of that and had to walk away.

These narratives stand in sharp contrast to those shared by Jewish participants such as the following, who described how she views the economic gains brought to her by the civil law:

> **Participant 1**
> Well, [. . .] I got 46%, I think it was 46% because it was a long marriage. And I think that it's absolutely right that somebody who's been in a *long* marriage, has made a contribution, an equivalent contribution in raising a family, and all the other duties, even if she's not going out to work.

While the legalization of religious norms is enhanced in the case of Jewish participants seeking a religious divorce, the non-recognition of Muslim marriage has presented difficulties for divorcing Muslim women, especially if they had not undergone a civil marriage. As a matter of fact, the civil law regards them as if they are in a cohabiting relationship. Therefore, they must rely on a complex process of cultural and religious reformulation via *sharia* councils to assist them in religiously divorcing their husband in the event that he has not repudiated the marriage. After resolving to leave her husband, often times the woman's family or in-laws are involved as informal mediators where steps are taken to reconcile the couple. The *sharia* council thus becomes an extension of this reconciliatory effort:

> [I]t became apparent that the women had little alternative other than to approach a *Sharia* Council to obtain divorce when their husbands refused to grant them a unilateral divorce. It also became clear that they often had to struggle against the prevalence of conservative attitudes endemic within such bodies. They talked about the confusion generated by the different interpretations of Islamic divorce adopted by the Councils which led to difficult decisions regarding the validity of the divorce certificate.[94]

At each and every level, power dynamics contour the options available to the woman. Whereas both Jewish and Muslim women seek divorce through all accessible channels, the non-recognition of Muslim marriage combined with growing evidence of unregistered Muslim marriages[95] significantly differentiate Muslim women's experiences and bargaining capabilities in comparison to Jewish women. Moreover, the ability to contest cultural interpretations of religious law is directly affected by the amount of family and/or kinship support and the civil and religious bargaining power available. As demonstrated in this section, whether or not the woman has legal recognition contributes to afford or deny her a degree of strategizing in order to obtain the dissolution she seeks.

3.4 Conclusion

> SIMIN: So, what happens to me?
> JUDGE: Nothing. Go back to your life.
> SIMIN: If I could, I wouldn't file for a divorce.
>
> *A Separation*, Dir. Asghar Farhadi, Prod. Negar Eskandarfar, Asghar Farhadi, 2011

[94] Bano, *supra* note 48 at 16.

[95] *See* Gillian Douglas, *supra* note 48 at 14; Werner F Menski, "Angrezi Shariat: Glocalized Plural Arrangements by Migrants in Britain" (2008) 10 *Law Vis* 10; Prakash Shah, *Unregistered Marriages in the English Courts* (London: Queen Mary University of London, 2012); Malik, *supra* note 19. Similar findings have been acknowledged by the Ministry of Justice: "Evidence from community groups shows that such cases [of unregistered marriages] form a high proportion of their workload, and that the numbers are increasing." Ministry of Justice, *supra* note 56 at 1. In a 2007 study on British Pakistani Muslim women, it was reported that among participants who had a married partner in England, less than half had registered marriages; Bano, *supra* note 48 at 14.

The semiotic redefinition of law as culture is a constant, dynamic process. By no means an exhaustive analysis of this phenomenon, this article is an attempt to demonstrate how acknowledging and further exploring this process can have a beneficial impact on legal and cultural subjects. First, I presented a decentralized conception of law by examining socio-economic bargaining and its distributive aspects through the critical legal pluralist lens. This theoretical framework has allowed me to highlight the pervasive contractual and legal role of cultural and religious norms. This proposition, while of timely relevance, came as no surprise: the regulatory power of non-legal norms extends beyond religion and has in fact been studied in family law by generations of scholars drawing from American legal realism[96] and legal pluralism.[97] The family/market distinction, however, has proven particularly resilient in the realm of religion and culture, leading to lesser attention being paid to its intimate complexity. Thus, the second endeavor of this article was to contribute to useful fieldwork that could potentially disenchant the family/market distinction by empirical and sociological means. Our findings, although not quantitatively sufficient to support general inferences, allowed for a relevant qualitative appreciation of minority women's shared experiences and perceptions. They consistently reflected how women can instrumentalize all norms accessible to them in order to pursue autonomous interests. They revealed a contrast between Jewish women navigating strategically the civil regulation of their religious practices and Muslim women's frustrated agencies, often baffled by the State's non-recognition of their religious practices, which contributes to further isolate them from alternative avenues.

Of course, the argument that non-recognition and cultural estrangement leads some Muslim women in the United Kingdom to have a more acquiescent relationship to religion than other Jewish women does not imply that there is anything inherently more submissive about Islam itself. Indeed, fieldwork carried out among Muslim communities in France, Canada, and Germany suggests that the higher level of civil/religious interaction occurring in those countries has precisely led to the

[96] Robert L Hale, "Coercion and Distribution in a Supposedly Non-Coercive State" (1923) 38:3 *Polit Sci Q* 470; Robert H Mnookin & Lewis Kornhauser, "Bargaining in the Shadow of the Law: The Case of Divorce" (1979) 88 *Yale Law J* 950; Halley & Rittich, *supra* note 22.

[97] Griffiths, *supra* note 27; Robert Leckey, "What Is Left of Pelech?" (2008) 41 *Supreme Court Law Rev* 103; Fournier, *supra* note 84; Angela Campbell, *Sister Wives, Surrogates and Sex Workers: Outlaws by Choice?* (Farnham, UK: Ashgate, 2013).

kind of contractual and legal bargaining we have observed among Jewish communities in the United Kingdom.[98] Moreover, the religious doctrine surrounding both Islamic marriage and Jewish marriage has a deeply contractual nature: it is, from the outset, structured around negotiation, bargaining, and enforcement mechanisms.[99] Given that both religious doctrines hold great potential for contractual and legal bargaining, the asymmetry observed between Islam and Judaism in the United Kingdom appears as nothing more than a historical accident. This circumstance could very well become a thing of the past as religious women, activists, and lawyers fight conservative interpretations of religious law and reveal the crucial insight that culture is much more legal than many would have us believe. This present fieldwork on the workings of religious norms thus supports Susan Weiss's view that Jewish law "is not a collection of harsh and uniform rules, but rather embraces various and contradictory voices

[98] Fournier, *supra* note 46; Fournier, *supra* note 24; Fournier & McDougall, *supra* note 73. But again, the author is aware that more empirical studies pertaining to the real and effective practices of religious authorities in both communities, and the justification for said practices, may be necessary to strengthen such an assertion.

[99] *See* Fournier, *supra* note 24. Under Islamic family law, marriage establishes a reciprocity system in which each party is assigned a set of contractual rights and duties towards the other party. *See* Lama Abu-Odeh, "Modernizing Muslim Family Law: The Case of Egypt" (2004) 37 *Vand J Transnatl L* 1043 at 1063–4. An Islamic marriage contract can only be concluded through the principles of offer (*ijab*) and acceptance (*qabul*) by the two principals or their proxies. Jamal J Nasir, *The Islamic Law of Personal Status*, 3rd edn (New York: Springer, Arab and Islamic Law Series, 2002) at 45. Upon marriage, the husband acquires the right to his wife's obedience and the right to restrict her movements outside the matrimonial home. The wife acquires the right to her *mahr* and the right to maintenance. *Nafaqah* is the "husband's primary obligation" to his wife and "includes food, clothing, and lodging." Esposito & DeLong-Bas, supra note 90 at 25; Mohammad Afzal Wani, *The Islamic Law on Maintenance of Women, Children, Parents & Other Relatives: Classical Principles and Modern Legislations in India and Muslim Countries* (Upright Study Home, 1995) at 195. Like Muslim marriage, Jewish marriage is finalized according to contractual principles. The parties execute a marriage contract (a *ketubah*, pl.: *ketubot*), often written in Aramaic, which lists the duties of each spouse. Jodi M Solovy, "Comment, Civil Enforcement of Jewish Marriage and Divorce: Constitutional Accommodation of a Religious Mandate" (1996) 45 *DePaul L. Rev* 493 at 496. Unlike the Muslim marriage contract, which is negotiated between the parties and is therefore unique to them and their relationship, the *ketubah* is fairly standard. As put by Elliott N. Dorff and Arthur I. Rosett, "the parties may determine by contract only those elements of the relationship which the law permits them to decide." Elliot N Dorff & Arthur Rossett, *A Living Tree: The Roots and Growth of Jewish Law* (Albany, NY: SUNY Press, 1988) at 453. Based on the Torah's articulation of a husband's duties towards his wife, this contract includes requirements for adequate food, clothing, shelter and regular intercourse, as well as the payment of money by the husband to the wife in case of divorce or death. Epstein, *supra* note 92 at 163.

[and that the] outcome of a given case depends upon the rabbinical authority consulted, the 'facts' he deems worthy of emphasis, and the voices he chooses to heed."[100] We have sought to demonstrate that this analysis also applies to Muslim family law, a proposal which strongly supports the plea for its recognition within civil law. In fact, interactions between civil law and religion would only further the legal malleability so accurately depicted by Weiss, as it would enable women to actively *treat culture as law*. This is, I have argued, a fruitful and promising way to empower women within minority groups that also resonates with the growing mass of feminist scholarship reinterpreting the internal legal doctrines of Jewish law[101] and Islamic law.[102]

[100] Susan Weiss, "Israeli Divorce Law: The Maldistribution of Power, its Abuses, and the 'Status' of Jewish Women" in Rachel Elior, ed., *Men Women Gend Jud Democr* (Van Leer Jerusalem Institute: Urim Publications, 2004) 53 at 63. *See also* Philippa Strum, "Women and the Politics of Religion in Israel" (1989) 11:4 *Hum Rts Q* 483 at 496. ("The problem is not *halacha*, ... but who interprets it.") (internal quotation marks omitted).

[101] *See, e.g.*, Naomi Graetz, *Unlocking the Garden: A Feminist Jewish Look at the Bible, Midrash and God* (Piscataway, NJ: Gorgias Press LLC, 2005) at 4 ("[S]ince feminism is inseparable from our religious orientation and is viewed as part of our concepts of spirituality and holiness, its teachings must be integrated. We bring to the texts questions from our time and seek to uncover meanings ... that relate to these questions"); Tamar Ross, *Expanding the Palace of Torah: Orthodoxy and Feminism* (Lebanon, NH: Brandeis University Press, 2004) at xvi–xvii ("[F]eminism need not be seen as a threat to traditional Judaism ..."); Esther Fuchs, "Jewish Feminist Scholarship: A Critical Perspective" in Leonard J Greenspoon et al, eds., *14 Stud Jew Civiliz* (2003) 225 at 225 (describing feminist Jewish scholarship as being "a new field of study"); Judith Hauptman, "Feminist Perspectives on Rabbinic Texts" in Lynn Davidman & Shelly Tenenbaum, eds., *Feminist Perspectives on Jewish Studies* (New Haven: Yale University Press, 1994) 40 at 43 ("[T]here has been an explosion in the number of recently published popular works on feminism and Judaism"); N Joseph, "Jewish Law and Gender" in Rosemary Skinner Keller & Rosemary Radford Ruether, eds., *2 Encyclopedia of Women and Religion* (Bloomington, IN: Indiana University Press, 2005) 576 at 588 ("Since the legal system was established as a responsive one, much of [Jewish law's] content can be addressed in today's language and terms, using women's experience to pry it open"); *see also* Laura Levitt, *Jews and Feminism: The Ambivalent Search for Home* (New York: Routledge, 1997) at 128 (detailing the author's experience coming to terms with feminism and its liberation as a Jewish woman); Isaac Sassoon, *The Status of Women in Jewish Tradition* (New York: Cambridge University Press, 2011) ("[T]he presence of feminist research in religion has been intensified because there is more at stake than simple scholarly investigation").

[102] *See, e.g.*, Leila Ahmed, *Women and Gender in Islam: Historical Roots of a Modern Debate* (New Haven: Yale University Press, 1992) at 63 (arguing that the voice of Islam can be "stubbornly egalitarian"); Asma Barlas, *Believing Women in Islam: Unreading Patriarchal Interpretations of the Qur'an* (Austin: University of Texas Press, 2002) at 3 (arguing that "the Qur'an's epistemology is inherently antipatriarchal"); Amina Wadud, *Qur'an and Woman: Rereading the Sacred Text from a Woman's Perspective* (Oxford:

Beyond academic work, artistic contributions can also serve as useful tools for transforming conservative perceptions of religious negotiation settings. In fact, a recent convincing plea for a more nuanced conception of divorce in religious contexts came from Asghar Farhadi's 2011 critically acclaimed movie "A Separation." Although set in the singular and distinct context of Iran, its astute account of a middle-class couple's separation under Islamic law undoubtedly shattered some preconceived ideas in Western minds. Its fascinating opening scene in which Simin assertively argues for her right to pursue her daughter's interests despite her husband's pacific and resigned objection foreshadows the complex interaction between individual agency and kinship dynamics the movie goes on to depict. Simin, as she quietly refuses to let a judge tell her that hers "is only a small issue" embodies the film's essential proposition: the failure of all normative systems to arbitrate intersecting legal, religious, socioeconomic and class factors as well as the imperfect human nature. Farhadi incidentally demonstrates that it is both useless and delusive to think of these dimensions as watertight compartments. The idea that a certain sphere of one's life, a certain set of rules, offers more protection to prevail upon the intimate suffering of domestic collapse is, at best, wishful thinking. It seems to be that protection can only rise from enabling individual agency in all possible ways, through all possible channels. Hence, the value of recognizing culture and law as the malleable, empowering tools that they are, and allowing them to support conflicting conclusions.

Oxford University Press, 1999) at 79–80 (emphasizing that women can benefit from the "broader Qur'anic wisdom which aims at harmonious reconciliation"); Fatima Mernissi, *Beyond the Veil: Male-Female Dynamics in Modern Muslim Society* (Bloomington, IN: Indiana University Press, 1985) at 52 (arguing that the *talaq* is an Arabian tradition which the Prophet himself did not live by); *see also* Barbara Stowasser, "Gender Issues and Contemporary Qur'an Interpretations" in Yvonne Yazbeck Haddad & John L Esposito, eds., *Islam Gend Soc Change* (Oxford: Oxford University Press, 1998) at 34 (discussing the modernist school and its spirit of reformism).

4

Customary Norms *vs* State Law

French Courts' Responses to the Traditional Practice of *Excision*

LUCIA BELLUCCI

4.1 Introduction

Customary norms and state legal systems often reflect different narratives which creates normative conflicts. Some traditional practices that were ignored when perpetuated only in colonised areas came to be considered crimes once 'imported' to Europe and to 'Western countries'[1] more generally. These crimes transpose 'in the realm of criminal law a situation of legal pluralism'.[2] The study of the French legal system's treatment of female genital cutting (FGC, *excision*) confirms this remark.

FGC is an ancient practice that is widespread in many places, particularly Africa. It consists of the ablation, to varying degrees, of female genital organs. Because FGC violates fundamental rights such as the right to physical integrity, health and non-discrimination on the basis of gender/ethnicity/culture, the practice of *excision* creates a normative conflict between a customary norm and the state legal system. The written rules of the French Penal Code consider individuals as rights holders and value the right to physical integrity, health and non-discrimination. By contrast, *excision*, which is transmitted orally[3] but

[1] Not having found a more appropriate expression, I will use the expression 'Western countries', despite being fully aware that its use is entirely subjective given that the notion of East or West depends on one's point of reference. I continue in any case to prefer it to the expression 'country of immigration', because in the current usage this expression excludes, for example, African countries which receive a very large number of immigrants and refugees from neighbouring countries.

[2] Marie-Claire Foblets, 'Les délits culturels: de la répercussion des conflits de culture sur la conduite délinquante; réflexions sur l'apport de l'anthropologie du droit à un débat contemporain' (1998) 35:1 *Droit et Cultures* 195 at 200.

[3] Cf. Lucia Bellucci, *Consuetudine, diritti e immigrazione: La pratica tradizionale dell'escissione nell'esperienza francese* (Milano: Giuffrè, 2012) at 37–40.

inscribed on the bodies of women, implies a normative order where individuals are considered as part of a group, a group whose interests prevail over its members. In this context, the protection of individuals is usually linked to the maintenance of their ties to the group as well as to the respect of gender and status relations within it. Furthermore, in African traditions both the group and individuals have strong relationships with the ancestors (the dijin), and respect them to an extent unheard of in 'Western societies'. In African traditional conceptions customary norms draw their strength not only from the moral support of the living, but also from that of the group's members who have lived in the past. Moving away from tradition and questioning customary norms would be an affront to them and their role in legitimising the established order.[4] The ancestors watch over the living but, if they are not respected, they may retaliate against them, especially against the child, who is the link between them and the adults, and therefore particularly vulnerable.

In France, FGC is perpetuated mostly by West African immigrants. Inquiries conducted in this country examine the explanations these immigrants give to the practice and perpetuation of *excision*.[5] These explanations concern custom, family, marriage, religion, ritual cleanness/purity (*propreté*), aesthetics and sexuality.[6]

The most common explanation refers to custom: 'It is the custom. My grand-mother did it, my mother did it, I will do it'. Women coming from rural areas, with a low level of education limit their explanation to custom. They consider any explanation of the custom inconceivable because it is already the supreme justification for their behaviour. Even though one must be careful not to take statements about tradition too

[4] Cf. Jack Jerbert Driberg, 'The African Conception of Law' (1934) 16 *Journal of Comparative Legislation and International Law* 230 at 238.

[5] Cf. Anne Raulin, *Femme en cause: Mutilations sexuelles des fillettes africaines en France aujourd'hui* (Paris: Centre Fédéral (FEN), 1987); Isabelle Gillette, *La polygamie et l'excision dans l'immigration africaine en France analysées sous l'angle de la souffrance sociale des femmes* (Lille: Presses Universitaires du Septentrion, 1998); Sylvie Fainzang, 'L'excision, ici et maintenant: Étude ethnologique' in *Les mutilations du sexe des femmes aujourd'hui en France* (Paris: Tierce, 1984). By the same authors cf. also Isabelle Gillette-Frenoy, 'L'excision et sa présence en France' (1992) 88:2 *L'Ethnographie* 21; Isabelle Gillette-Frenoy, *L'excision et sa présence en France: Étude ethno-sociologique* (Paris: GAMS, 1992); Anne Raulin, 'Problèmes éthiques d'une recherche en sciences sociales: l'excision et sa présence en France' (1990) 88 *Cahiers internationaux de sociologie* 157; Sylvie Fainzang, 'Circoncision, excision et rapports de domination' (1985) 9:1 *Anthropologie et Sociétés* 117; Sylvie Fainzang, 'Excision et ordre social' (1990) 20 *Droit et Cultures* 177.

[6] On these topics, see extensively Bellucci, *supra* note 3 at 77–92.

literally,[7] it is widely known that in traditional cultures rationalising customary norms is secondary to honoring the ancestors' gestures and words.[8] Women coming from the cities seem also not to want to displease their families.

Most West African immigrants hope to go back to their countries of origin someday, even if this dream is in reality rarely realised. Therefore, they are afraid to diverge from the norms of their village and their families. They fear being marginalised both in their country of origin, thus preventing their return home, and in France. As underlined by Catherine Quiminal,[9] the ties among the members of African communities in France are strong. These communities tend to reproduce the social structure of the home village. Immigrants are afraid of feeling like aliens everywhere, among the Soninke or the Bambara as well as the French. The explanation referring to custom is often accompanied by other reasons. One of the arguments most frequently used by women to explain why they want FGC to be practiced on their daughters is that uncut women will not get married. Most West African immigrants wish their daughters to marry somebody from their community, either in their home country or in France. This hope of endogamy needs to be put in the context of the traditional African family, which is the extended family composed of grandparents, aunts, uncles, sisters, etc.[10] The extended family is a very powerful influence with regard to FGC. The decision to perpetuate this practice is in fact often made by grandparents, aunts or older sisters. Borrowing an expression from Jacqueline Rabain,[11] Anne Raulin remarks that the couple does not break away from the family group. It instead finds a place in the latter, 'manifesting the pledges of its inclusion, with the child playing a crucial role: [he] is less the couple's son

[7] Cf. Sally Falk Moore, *Law as Process: An Anthropological Approach* (London, Henley & Boston: Routledge & Kegan Paul, 1978) at 14.

[8] Cf. Norbert Rouland, 'La coutume et la pensée juridique sauvage: L'apport des sociétés Inuit' in J Gilissen, ed., *Coutume-Costume* (Brussels: De Boeck Université 1990) at 316.

[9] Cf. Catherine Quiminal, *Gens d'ici, gens d'ailleurs: Migrations Soninké et transformations villageoises* (Paris: C Bourgois, 1991).

[10] Max Gluckman had already pointed out the need to analyse family relationships in light of broader social relations, including the relationship of the woman with her husband's sister as well as the fact that in traditional African culture a wife's happiness depends more on her husband's relatives with whom she lives than on her husband himself. Cf. Max Gluckman, *Custom and Conflict in Africa* (Oxford & Cambridge: Blackwell, 1956) at 78 and 59.

[11] Cf. Jacqueline Rabain, *L'enfant du lignage: Du sevrage à la classe d'âge chez les Wolof du Sénégal* (Paris: Payot, 1979).

than the lineage's child'.[12] FGC could therefore be practised during the holidays in Africa without the parents' even knowing. Traditionally *excision* is practiced by women, the *exciseuses*, who belong to the blacksmith caste (*forgerons*) and how to perform the operation is handed down from generation to generation among the women of their family. Numerous West African societies rely on *forgeronnes* for *excisions*, in particular the Mandé (e.g. Bambara, Diakhanké, Malinké, Mandingue, Nyominka, Socé and Soninké) and Halpulaar peoples (Peul and Toucouleur).

Religion is another explanation of the practice. Some immigrants operate under the assumption that religion, in particular Islam, stipulates the custom. FGC is practised by some Muslims, Christians, Jews[13] and Animists, but no religion explicitly requires it. There is no mention of the practice in the Quran, the Hebrew Bible (and the Talmud) or the Christian Bible. The first written reference to *excision* goes back the Ptolemaic epoch, in particular the second century BC. The practice is mentioned in the fifteenth Greek papyrus kept in the British Museum that refers to an argument between a man and a woman whose daughter is old enough to undergo FGC ('to undergo the circumcision accordingly to the Egyptian tradition'[14]). Yet, the binomial *excision* – religion is difficult to analyse. The relationship is full of ambiguities because it implies an analysis of sacred texts separate from the study of their interpretations, and because it very much depends on the historical, cultural and social context.

Some immigrants believe that *excision* increases women's fertility and that it eases the birthing process. The latter explanation is not negligible if one considers that societies practicing FGC highly value motherhood. The need for women to be 'clean' is also among immigrants' explanations. While scholars have offered a range of interpretations of this concept, it remains ambiguous. Another explanation for the practice is aesthetics. If one entertains Edmund R. Leach's idea that to understand the ethical rules of a society one needs to study its aesthetics,[15] this should be considered an important argument, although according to Isabelle Gillette the valuing of aesthetics is falling into desuetude, if it is not already

[12] Raulin, *Femme en cause, supra* note 5 at 64. [13] The Fallasha of Ethiopia.

[14] Michel Erlich, *La femme blessée: Essai sur les mutilations sexuelles féminines* (Paris: L'Harmattan, 1986) at 39.

[15] Edmund Ronald Leach, *Political Systems of Highland Burma: A Study of Kachin Social Structure* (London: G Bell & Sons, 1964) at 12.

obsolete.[16] Some immigrants also explain that they practice *excision* to preserve morality and limit sexuality. Some men argue that they would not be able to satisfy their wives sexually in a polygamic marriage if the women were not excised. Their wives might otherwise go with other men. Some women cite the difficulties of raising well-behaved girls as a reason. Nevertheless, societies that practice FGC do not have homogenous attitudes towards premarital freedom or towards sexual behaviour within marriage. Furthermore, traditionally, polygamic societies do not always exclude the possibility of female adultery. Sometimes they recognise the husband as the father of his wife's primogeniture, and therefore allow him to 'regain' the children born from an extramarital union.

This chapter discusses how the French criminal justice system has dealt with the conflict between the state legal system and *excision.* It draws from the results of an ethnographic inquiry into the French criminal trials related to this practice and it is centered on the narratives of the prosecutors' conclusive arguments. Its theoretical framework is shaped by legal anthropology's contributions to the study of custom and customary law in traditional societies, mainly by Africanist perspectives.

Section 4.2 focuses on the methodology of the empirical research on the response of the French criminal justice system. Section 4.3 defines *excision* as a customary norm which has the force of law. Section 4.4 introduces the above-mentioned response and briefly mentions its premises. Section 4.5 discusses the state legal system's 'reasons' for criminal punishment of *excision* as they emerged from the prosecutors' closing arguments. Section 4.6 shows that not all the social actors of the trials who represent this system share common views on how it should respond to FGC. Section 4.7 discloses the contradictions related to the role of men in the perpetration of *excision.* Section 4.8 concludes the analysis.

4.2 Customary Norms *vs* State Law: An Ethnographic Inquiry on the Response of the French Criminal Justice System

The conflict between the customary norm of *excision* and the state legal system translates into the legal world the conflict between two normative universes, which are conceptually distant with regard to the priority given to the individual and the group. In almost all traditional societies, autonomy and individual freedom are valued when they are consistent

[16] Cf., on the topic, Gillette, *supra* note 5 at 123–4.

and therefore compatible with the preservation of relationships and harmony within the community. In African societies, where FGC is most widespread, marriage, for example, is traditionally conceived of as more an alliance between family groups than as a union between individuals.[17] The spouses' families are involved 'in the establishment, preservation and dissolution of their union'.[18]

The conflict between *excision* and the criminal justice system implies different pressures and sanctions that are respectively exerted and inflicted by the customary and state normative orders. To more deeply analyse this conflict, I carried out empirical research, conducting an ethnographic inquiry into the French criminal trials related to this practice. This inquiry analysed the judicial responses, disclosing the narratives of the trials and the dialectic between those normative universes. This empirical research has been carried out through a qualitative content analysis of documents and through in-depth interviews with some of the main social actors (judges, lawyers, doctors, anthropologists, interpreters, etc.) involved in the trials. The pairing of oral accounts obtained through in-depth interviews and written legal documents is a well-known method of conducting qualitative research within the scope of 'law and society' studies.[19] It is applied more specifically in legal anthropology. In a study on customary law in traditional African societies, Simon Roberts mentions, for example, court decisions and informers as a privileged binomial in field research.[20]

[17] Cf. Eugene Cotran, 'African Law' in R David, ed., *International Encyclopedia of Comparative Law*, Vol. II 'The Legal Systems of the World: Their Comparison and Unification' (Tübingen: JCB Mohr (Paul Siebeck) & The Hague, Paris: Mouton, 1974) at 163; Camille Kuyu, 'Les réformes des droits africains de la famille: un projet juridique visant une hégémonie culturelle' in C Kuyu, ed., *À la recherche du droit africain du XXIe siècle* (Paris: Connaissances et Savoirs, 2005) at 88; Gordon R. Woodman, 'African Legal Systems' in N J Smelser & P B Baltes, eds., *International Encyclopedia of the Social & Behavioral Sciences* (Oxford: Pergamon, 2001) at 229. With regard to the relationships born of the marriage and that influence women's positions and gender relations, see also Anne Hellum, 'Actor Perspectives on Gender and Legal Pluralism in Africa' in H Petersen & H Zahle, eds., *Legal Polycentricity: Consequences of Pluralism in Law* (Aldershot & Brookfield: Dartmouth, 1995) at 21.

[18] Anthony N Allott, 'African Law' in J Duncan & M Derrett, eds., *An Introduction to Legal Systems* (London: Sweet & Maxwell, 1968) at 154.

[19] See, by way of example only, Lucia Bellucci, 'National Support for Film Production in the EU: An Analysis of the Commission Decision-Making Practice' (2010) 16:2 *European Law Journal* 211.

[20] Cf. Simon Roberts, 'The Recording of Customary Law: Some Problems of Method' in A Dundes Renteln & A Dundes, eds., *Folk Law: Essays in the Theory and Practice of Lex* Non Scripta (New York & London: Garland, 1994) at 332–4.

To reconstruct the cases and the trials, I considered it necessary to consult different sources. My research coupled written sources, comprised of legal (rulings) and non-legal sources (newspapers, periodicals, academic journals and grey literature), with oral accounts.

I aim to give a principal role to documents as narration, effectively taking readers to a criminal court. I was able to reconstruct nineteen cases which I believe form a representative sample of the complexity of the conflict between the two normative orders in question. They are all the cases in relation to which I was able to obtain enough documentation to reconstruct the proceedings. It is in fact my belief that it is not possible to construct a legal anthropological work based solely on the text of the judgment, particularly with regard to the very brief rulings handed down by the French *Cour d'Assises*. Only since 2012 have these courts been required to give reasons for their rulings, including a *motivation*,[21] as provided for by Article 365–1 of the Criminal Procedure Code. This change in French criminal procedure followed certain European Court of Human Rights' rulings and aimed to reduce the risk of arbitrary judgements and facilitate the accused in understanding the judgments, as provided for under Article 6 of the European Convention on Human Rights (ECHR). Mentioning the most recent rulings on FGC, without reconstructing the cases through an empirical research, would have been relevant in a work on positive criminal law, but it would have been even dangerous in an ethnographic inquiry. Preventing a deeper reconstruction and understanding of the cases, it would have given limited and even misleading information. The absence of reference to the most recent cases concerning *excision* is therefore not the result of forgetfulness or laziness, but a precise methodological choice.

The first case that I was able to reconstruct was tried in 1979.[22] If the aim is to provide a big-picture view of the proceedings, one needs to spend a long time on the field in order to access law and media libraries

[21] See Article 365–1 of the Criminal Procedure Code, introduced by Article 12 of the Law n. 2011–939 of 10 August 2011 'sur la participation des citoyens au fonctionnement de la justice pénale et le jugement des mineurs'.

[22] Doua, a three months old baby, had died after her *excision*. The *exciseuse* was accused of manslaughter before the XVI *Chambre correctionnel* of the *Tribunal* of Paris, which ordered her to serve a one-year suspended sentence. Cf., on this case, Gillette, *supra* note 5 at 17; Commission nationale consultative des droits de l'homme (CNCDH), *Étude et propositions sur la pratique des mutilations sexuelles féminines en France* 2004 at 70, available at www.cncdh.fr/sites/default/files/cncdh-_etude_msf.pdf, accessed on 9 September 2014.

as well as archives and conduct in-depth interviews. I was able to do that until 2003 and therefore to reconstruct trials until then.[23] Thus, the empirical research covers twenty-four years.

The in-depth interviews have not only helped shed light on French institutional and political models, such as the model of immigrants' social inclusion, but they have also served as a useful tool in the analysis of the documents and, thus, of the proceedings. I interviewed judges, lawyers, anthropologists who were heard as experts or who have written about and witnessed *excision* proceedings, French and African NGO members fighting for the elimination of FGC, NGO members joined to the civil proceedings, interpreters, and doctors of centers for maternal and child protection (*centre de Protection Maternelle et Infantile*, PMI). I conducted exactly twelve in-depth interviews: a small number in absolute terms, but a substantial number if one considers the complexity of the practice of *excision* and the taboo surrounding the issue. Out of respect for the privacy of the interviewees, I have omitted their names and other identifiable information.

While excised women were among those interviewed, I only interviewed excised women who had been directly involved in the proceedings. The answers provided by the immigrant women as to why they subjected their daughters to *excision* constitute second-hand data obtained from inquiries conducted in France by French academics. To the data gathered from these interviews were added data received from conversations with other individuals knowledgeable about the topic; these informal conversations did not have the methodological rigor of the in-depth interviews.

The fact that I was not able to pursue empirical research in France on *excision* trials after 2003, due to limited funding and the onset of other commitments, is probably the biggest shortcoming of the work. And yet, although I was forced to interrupt my fieldwork after 2003, I needed, and in fact welcomed, the break. First of all, it helped me put some distance between myself and my work. After her research on *excision* the scholar Anne Raulin wrote an article demonstrating how a researcher who has dealt for a long period of time with this subject-matter often feels the need to reflect on the actual work.[24] When studying *excision* it is in fact

[23] I first plunged in the empirical research in France in 1997 for six months and then continued it during my stay in this country from 2000 to 2003.

[24] Cf. Raulin, 'Problèmes éthiques d'une recherche en sciences sociales: l'excision et sa présence en France', *supra* note 5 at 157–72.

easy to succumb to the temptation to provide solutions, rather than try to understand how the practice spreads, how it is perpetrated and lived, and what sort of power it has on individuals. As you try to avoid the daily temptation of quitting your academic role, time and study at the table become very important. They enable you to remove yourself from the emotional side of the issue and foster scientific reflection. Emotional detachment is essential in order to process with a clear mind the deep involvement that empirical research on *excision* implies for a woman. The interruption of my research also gave me ample time to elaborate a theoretical framework and analyse data.

4.3 *Excision* as a Customary Norm with the Force of Law

People who perpetrate *excision* perceive this ancient practice as a customary norm which is as binding as law. It is their law and they consider it as more binding than state legal norms banning *excision*. Considering a customary norm as the way a social group behaves for a relatively long time,[25] as a behaviour that the members of the group perceive as binding, *excision* can be defined as a customary norm which has the force of law. This operational definition of *excision* both influenced the analysis of the results of my empirical research and was shaped by them. Since wording choices reflect conceptual categories, in an anthropological work they are not made *a priori*, but in the field and by successive approximations.

It is clear that the acceptance of a customary norm can be tightly linked to the fear of the sanction,[26] as the study of the practice of *excision* demonstrates. However, it is important to provide a minimum definition that includes a broader number of cases. This would not be possible if compliance with the customary norm were univocally bound to the fear of the sanction by the group of origin. I use John Gilissen's expression 'a relatively long time' because it duly summarises the idea of continuity over time and is appropriately vague. How much time is required to give rise to a customary norm has been the object of long debates among anthropologists of law.[27] Legal anthropologists have come to refute that a

[25] Cf. J Gilissen, 'Essai de synthèse générale' in J Gilissen, ed., *Coutume-Costume* (Brussels: De Boeck Université, 1990) at 434.

[26] Cf. Charles Ntampaka, 'La coutume dans les droits africains après la réception des droits romanistes: L'exemple des pays d'Afrique centrale, le Rwanda et le Zaïre' in J Gilissen, ed., *Coutume-Costume* (Brussels: De Boeck Université, 1990) at 185.

[27] Within these debates, authors refer to the far more widespread term 'custom'.

time defined as 'immemorial' is necessary to constitute a customary norm. This norm clearly evokes the idea of continuity for a considerable amount of time, but indicating an exact amount would be misleading and inaccurate.[28] I do not embrace the expression 'customary law'[29] which has been criticised in legal anthropology,[30] since it refers to laws born during the colonial period and often presented as autochthonous.

The argument that *excision* is a 'customary norm which has the force of law' (hereafter 'customary norm'), because it has the same binding nature for the populations who practice it as law does in 'Western societies'[31] is not without implications. It entails taking a position in the debate on what should be considered as customary norm,[32] a debate which arose within legal anthropology and comparative law and developed especially in Africanist literature. This argument implies not limiting the concept of customary norm in traditional societies only to behaviours recognised as such by the courts,[33] but espousing a wider view that goes beyond the idea of control by the courts.[34]

Traditional societies, in fact, take on differing and complex legal forms and adopt various practices that are on the border between legal, social and ethical norms, which are perceived as binding by the population,[35] as

[28] See, on the matter, Annie Rouhette, *Coutumier (Droit)* in *Encyclopedia Universalis* (Paris: Encyclopedia Universalis France, 2008) at 5.

[29] For a different option, see the excellent writing of Lyda Favali and Roy Pateman. The authors address female genital mutilation within the context of customary law and traditional law. They use the two expressions interchangeably (and draw from the definition given to the terms 'tradition/custom' by L Pospisil. See Lyda Favali & Roy Pateman, *Blood, Land and Sex: Legal and Political Pluralism in Eritrea* (Bloomington & Indianapolis: Indiana University Press, 2003) at 14–15; Leopold J Pospisil, *Anthropology of Law: A Comparative Theory* (New York: Harper & Row, 1971) at 196.

[30] For details and bibliographic references on this topic see Bellucci, *supra* note 3 at 25–9.

[31] See note 1.

[32] Within this debate, authors refer to the expressions 'custom' and 'customary law'.

[33] For statements on this position, see, on the contrary, Anthony N Allott, 'Methods of Legal Research into Customary Law' in A Dundes Renteln & A Dundes, eds., *Folk Law: Essays in the Theory and Practice of Lex* Non Scripta (New York & London: Garland, 1994) at 246; Alan Watson, 'An Approach to Customary Law' in A Dundes Renteln & A Dundes, eds., *Folk Law: Essays in the Theory and Practice of Lex* Non Scripta (New York & London: Garland, 1994) at 143 and 154.

[34] Cf. R David, ed., *International Encyclopedia of Comparative Law.* Vol II 'The Legal Systems of the World: Their Comparison and Unification' (Tübingen: JCB Mohr (Paul Siebeck) & The Hague, Boston, London: Martinus Nijhoff, 1984) at 97.

[35] Cf., on this topic, Étienne Le Roy, 'Norme (en anthropologie du droit)' in A-J Arnaud, ed., *Dictionnaire encyclopédique de théorie et de sociologie du droit* (Paris: Libr. générale de droit et de jurisprudence, 1993) at 402; Étienne Le Roy, 'L'esprit de la coutume et

shown from empirical research, for example on *excision*. Even though, in the study of traditional practices such as *excision*, perceived as mandatory and imported into so called 'modern' state legal systems, some scholars have felt the need to refer to it as an example of normative, rather than legal, pluralism,[36] the leading assumption that the anthropologist can 'consider as law even norms imposed by a generic social pressure [and that law. . .] is a notion that does not have an exact correspondent in all cultures'[37] has not been questioned.

Field research confirms that the most fruitful path in the anthropological study of customary norms is not that of defining law, but of ascertaining the binding nature of traditional practices, having previously accepted that highly complex legal systems exist in traditional societies that can hardly be analysed through 'Western' conceptual categories. Anthropologists of law have abandoned the long and exhausting debate over the definition of law. The debate dominated the discipline for several years, despite the fact that in 1954 Hoebel had already declared that 'to seek a definition of the legal is like the quest for the Holy Grail'.[38]

l'idéologie de la loi à travers quelques exemples sénégalais contemporains' in J Vanderlinden, ed., *La connaissance du Droit en Afrique* (Bruxelles: Arsom, 1984) at 210 & 221; Étienne Le Roy & Mamadou Wane, 'La Formation des droits "non étatiques"' in P-F Gonidec & M A Glele, eds., 'Encyclopedie juridique de l'Afrique'. Vol. I. *L'État et le droit* (Dakar: Les Nouvelles Editions Africaines, 1982) at 359; Jeffrey Richstone, 'The Inuit and Customary Law: Constitutional Perspectives' in B W Morse & G R Woodman, eds., *Indigenous Law and the State* (Dordrecht: Foris, 1987) at 245; Michel Alliot, 'L'évolution de la notion de droit en Afrique' in G Conac, ed., *Dynamiques et finalités des droits africains: Actes du Colloque de la Sorbonne 'La vie du droit en Afrique'* (Paris: Economica, 1980) at 105–6; Michel Alliot, 'La coutume dans les droits originellement africains' (1985) 7-8 *Bulletin de liaison du LAJP* 79 at 87, also available at, www.dhdi.free.fr/recherches/theoriedroit/articles/alliotcoutume.doc accessed on 9 September 2014. According to Alliot, since customary norms have a cohesive function within the group, in the event of conflict, invoking them is often avoided to keep the conflict from escalating into open confrontation. If no other option is available, a solution is sought, on a case by case basis, in accordance with what is thought to be in the interest of the group. In this way, customary norms are stable only to the extent required by their cohesive function.

36 Alessandra Facchi expressed this need. Among her books see, for example, Alessandra Facchi, *I diritti nell'Europa multiculturale: Pluralismo normativo e immigrazione* (Roma & Bari: Laterza, 2001) at 405–12.

37 Rodolfo Sacco, *Antropologia giuridica* (Bologna: Il Mulino, 2007) at 18–19.

38 Cf. Edward Adamson Hoebel, *The Law of Primitive Man: A Study in Comparative Legal Dynamics* (Cambridge: Harvard University Press, 1967) at 18. Perplexities as to the usefulness of defining law in legal anthropology have been expressed by Keebet von Benda-Beckmann. See Keebet von Benda-Beckmann, 'Dispute sans fin sur la méthode de l'anthropologie juridique' (1991) 21 *Droit et Cultures* 73 at 82.

At a certain point, it became clear that this debate, just as the debate on the definition of culture within the context of cultural anthropology, was going in circles. By the 1970s, it had become increasingly sterile and was therefore mainly abandoned.[39] Only recently has the debate received limited new attention in certain interdisciplinary works.[40] What one can learn from this is that in the study of traditional societies, empirical research proves to be a more fruitful tool than *a priori* theoretical elaboration when determining whether or not a norm is binding. In confirmation of this statement, Peter Ørebech argues that to determine if (and to what extent) a customary norm carries the popular perception of valid legal obligation, empirical research is often necessary,[41] as the research on *excision* cases seems to confirm.

4.4 The Response of the French Criminal Justice System and its Premises

Studying the response of the French criminal justice system is particularly interesting because France is the country with the most extensive jurisprudence on the matter of FGC. It is the only country where cases of FGC are systematically brought to court. It is also one of the few countries, among the 'Western countries' sanctioning this practice, that

[39] Cf. Sally Engle Merry, 'Law: Anthropological Aspects' in N J Smelser & P B Baltes, eds., *International Encyclopedia of the Social & Behavioral Sciences* (Oxford: Pergamon, 2001) at 8489; P Bohannan & R French, 'Legal Anthropology' in D Levinson & M Ember, eds., *Encyclopedia of Cultural Anthropology* (New York: Henry Holt, 1996) at 699. On the abandonment of the spasmodic attempts to define law within the context of 'other' cultures, see also Eve Darian-Smith, 'Ethnographies of Law' in A Sarat, ed., *The Blackwell Companion to Law and Society* (Malden, Oxford & Carlton: Blackwell, 2004) at 547.

[40] See, for example, the contributions contained in Alison Dundes Renteln & Alan Dundes, eds., *Folk Law: Essays in the Theory and Practice of Lex* Non Scripta (New York & London: Garland, 1994), in particular: Gordon R Woodman, 'Some Realism About Customary Law–The West African Experience' in A Dundes Renteln & A Dundes, eds., *Folk Law: Essays in the Theory and Practice of Lex* Non Scripta (New York & London: Garland, 1994) at 83–110; JPB de Josselin de Jong, 'Customary Law: A Confusing Fiction' in A Dundes Renteln & A Dundes, eds., *Folk Law: Essays in the Theory and Practice of Lex* Non Scripta (New York & London: Garland, 1994) at 111–17; Alan Watson, 'An Approach to Customary Law' in A Dundes Renteln & A Dundes, eds., *Folk Law: Essays in the Theory and Practice of Lex* Non Scripta (New York & London: Garland, 1994) at 141–57.

[41] Cf. Peter Ørebech, 'The Linkage between Sustainable Development and Customary Law' in P. Ørebech, F. Bosselman, J. Bjarup, D. Callies, M. Chanock & H. Petersen, eds., The *Role of Customary Law in Sustainable Development* (Cambridge: Cambridge University Press, 2005) at 17 and 19.

did not adopt (through an act or an article in the Penal Code) *ad hoc* provisions to prohibit it.[42]

In France, the practice of *excision* was strongly debated after a few young girls died from the haemorrhaging caused by FGC. It returned to the spotlight when it was no longer classified as a *délit* but as a *crime*, with the consequent transfer of FGC cases from the jurisdiction of the *Tribunal Correctionnel*, which is part of the *Tribunal de Grande Instance* (hereafter *Tribunal*), to that of the *Cour d'Assises*.

Between the end of the 1970s and 1980s, the *Tribunal Correctionnel* had jurisdiction over cases of FGC. Since the late eighties, the *Cour d'Assises* has had jurisdiction over these cases. This change was crucial to the treatment of *excision* cases because the earlier-mentioned courts have jurisdiction on different offences and a different composition. The *Tribunal Correctionnel* has jurisdiction over offences that may be sanctioned with less harsh punishments, which in the French system are called 'délits'. It is composed solely of professional judges (three for most of the crimes), assisted by a clerk; one of the three judges presides over the court. The *Cour d'Assises* has jurisdiction over offences that may be sanctioned with the harshest punishments, which in the French system are called 'crimes'. It is composed of three professional judges, one of whom is the President of the Court, and a popular jury formed by French citizens randomly selected by lot, in particular six of them in the courts of first instance and nine in the courts of appeal. Since 1980s, verdicts have been therefore rendered by a popular jury after a long and complex procedure. Often the trial attracts a lot of media attention. The change of jurisdiction was based on a case concerning a Breton woman who cut off her daughter's clitoris in a moment of insanity. In this case the court argued that 'the clitoris and labia are female erectile organs; [...] their absence as a result of acts of violence constitutes a mutilation within the meaning of Article 312–3 of the Penal Code'.[43] The case did not have anything in common with traditional *excision* apart from the end result and therefore prompted heated debate. Some thought that choosing this case proved that the classification of FGC as a *crime* was not

[42] For the adoption of *ad hoc* provisions in Australia, Belgium, Canada, Cyprus, Denmark, Great Britain, Italy, Norway, New Zealand, Spain, Sweden, Switzerland and United States, see Center for Reproductive Rights, *Female Genital Mutilation (FGM): Legal Prohibitions Worldwide*, available at http://reproductiverights.org/en/document/female-genital-mutilation-fgm-legal-prohibitions-worldwide, accessed on 9 September 2014.

[43] *Cour de Cassation, Chambre criminelle* (1983) 229 *Bulletin criminel* 582 at 583.

discriminatory, including NGOs working for the abandonment of FGC, while others emphasised that a moment of insanity could not be compared to a traditional practice.

The transfer of jurisdiction occurred during the *Coulibaly* case, which was first tried before the XV *Chambre correctionnelle* of the *Tribunal* of Paris.[44] In this case Linda Weil-Curiel and Catherine Sviloff, who joined the proceedings as a civil party, respectively on behalf of SOS Femmes Alternatives and Enfance et Partage,[45] pleaded a lack of jurisdiction of this court. Linda Weil-Curiel argued that *excision* is recognised as a voluntary mutilation by the entire medical profession and therefore the accused must appeared before the *Cour d'Assises.*[46]

The *Tribunal Correctionnel* of Paris declined jurisdiction and the deputy public prosecutor appealed its decision. The *Cour d'Appel* declined jurisdiction,[47] on the basis of the decision of the *Chambre criminelle* of the *Cour de Cassation* of 20 August 1983,[48] concerning the earlier mentioned case of a Breton woman who cut off her daughter's clitoris in a moment of insanity. The *Chambre criminelle* of the *Cour de Cassation* confirmed the criminal qualifications of the facts only on 9 May 1990.[49] In the meantime other three cases before the *Cour d'Assises* were judged.[50]

Pressure for the change came from civil society activists. It is worth mentioning that Linda Weil-Curiel joined the proceedings as a civil party. Initially she did so on behalf of SOS Femmes Alternatives and

44 Cf. Catherine Nisak, 'L'excision une pratique en recul?' (1986) June *Enfant d'abord* 33 at 44; Lucia Bellucci, 'Escissione e diritto nell'esperienza francese' (1999) 25 *d/D il Diritto delle donne*, Commissione Pari Opportunità della Regione Emilia-Romagna at 20–1.

45 Cf. Michelle Majorelle 'L'excision des six filles Coulibaly' (1986) 26–7 April *Libération* 15; Nisak, *supra* note 44 at 44.

46 Cf. Nisak, *supra* note 44 at 44. On this topic see also Sylvie Briet & Sandrine Cabut, 'La France est un des seuls pays à faire des procès pour excision', (2005) 5 February *Libération*, available at www.liberation.fr/week-end/2005/02/05/la-france-est-un-des-seuls-pays-a-faire-des-proces-pour-excision_508632, accessed on 9 September 2014.

47 Cf. Georges Levasseur, 'Violences entraînant mutilation. Excision' (1989) 1 *Revue de science criminelle et de droit pénal comparé* 107 at 109; Georges Levasseur, *Coups et blessures* – Paris, 10 July 1987, in *Receuil Dalloz Sirey*, 1987, 33° cahier – informations rapides 197.

48 Cf. *Cour de Cassation*, *supra* note 43; Georges Levasseur, *'Violences à enfant de moins de quinze ans entraînant une mutilation'* (1984) 1 *Revue de science criminelle et de droit pénal comparé* 73 at 73–4.

49 Cf. 'Coups ou violences volontaires' in (1990) November *Editions Techniques. Droit pénal* 3.

50 The *Baradji* case of 1988, the *Fofana Traore* case of 1989 and the *Soumare* case of 1990.

the Ligue du Droit International des Femmes, and then she joined the proceedings on behalf of the Commission pour l'abolition des mutilations sexuelles (CAMS), of which Weil-Curiel is president. Weil-Curiel fought for the change and kept joining the proceedings as a civil party even when other non-profit organisations had stopped. The fact that *excision* cases are tried before the *Cour d'Assises* and *excision* trials continue to occur in France is very much due to her commitment.

The change needs to be placed in a precise historical moment and cultural context. The international political climate and the French model of immigrants' social inclusion (*modèle français/républicain d'intégration*) can be considered as the premises for the French normative response to FGC.

It is plausible that the French choice to intervene openly in FGC cases by bringing them to court was spurred by a change in the international political climate – specifically, growing international attention to the damages caused by the traditional practices that affect the bodies of women and girls. Although the World Health Organisation (WHO) had previously considered FGC to be beyond its competence, in 1979 started to consider it as a practice harmful to women and girls. Since then, the WHO has organised several seminars. In 1979, the Convention on the Elimination of All Forms of Discrimination against Women (CEDAW) was adopted. Its Article 2, letter f) provides that state parties agree to 'take all appropriate measures, including legislation, to modify or abolish existing laws, regulations, customs and practices which constitute discrimination against women'. This convention was signed by a number of African countries where FGC is widespread.[51] Furthermore, in 1984, the Inter-African Committee on Traditional Practices Affecting the Health of Women and Children (IAC) was founded at the Dakar seminar (organised by the WHO and the United Nations Children's Fund-UNICEF).

It is evident that the decision to sanction FGC according to the existing rules of the Penal Code was influenced by the French model of immigrants' social inclusion. Although in France this choice was both supported[52] and

[51] See Benin, Burkina Faso, Central African Republic, Chad, Djibouti, Egypt, Ethiopia, Eritrea, Gambia, Ghana, Guinea, Kenya, Ivory Coast, Liberia, Mali, Nigeria, Tanzania.

[52] NGO members working in France for the abandonment of *excision* considered that making an exception to this model only with regard to *excision* would expose their work to the accusation of racism and further stigmatise the concerned populations. Even Linda Weil-Curiel supported this choice, in line with the French model of immigrants' social inclusion as she reaffirmed in Natacha Henry & Linda Weil-Curiel, *Exciseuse. Entretien*

criticised,[53] no one has questioned that it has ties to the French model of immigrants' social inclusion, known as the 'modèle français d'intégration'. According to this model, immigrants should not be considered as members of a community/an ethnic minority group, but only as individuals. The law should not recognise specific rights based on geographical and cultural origins. Therefore, the French legal system does not provide for rules specifically aimed at protecting ethnic minority groups.

NGOs working in France for the abandonment of FGC positively welcomed the transition to the jurisdiction of the *Cour d'Assises*, while among legal professionals (lawyers and judges in particular) opinions were divided. Most criticisms were raised by academics.[54] To summarise,

avec Hawa Gréou (Saint-Victor-d'Epine: City Editions, 2007) at 106. Cf. also Nisak, *supra* note 44 at 46.

[53] Among these was the lawyer Xavier-Jean Keïta, the Senegalese *exciseuse* defending counsel in the Coulibaly case before the *Cour d'Assises* of Bobigny. He would have liked that *excision* was mentioned in clear and explicit terms by French law in a specific piece of legislation, following a parliamentary debate. Cf. also Xavier-Jean Keïta, *Rapport France-Afrique. Le droit au respect de l'integrité physique et la coutume: la pratique de l'excision en France* (Créteil: Publications du Barreau du Val de Marne, 1995) at 16–19. Those who have criticised the choice include Judge Corneloup. He would have preferred that the courts use *ad hoc* provisions clearly stating that *excision* in France is prohibited, rather than rules designed to sanction behaviours that intend to harm the child. Cf. also Yves Corneloup, *L'excision*, contribution presented to the *Académie de sciences d'outre mer*, 17 February 1995, 108 at 112.

[54] In the academic context, criticisms were raised in particular by the journals *Droit et Cultures*, *Revue du MAUSS* and *Nouvelle Revue d'Ethnopsychiatrie*. On the criminalisation of *excision* see for example Raymond Verdier, 'Chercher remède à l'excision: une nécessaire concertation' (1990) 20 *Droit et Cultures* 147; Geneviève Giudicelli-Delage, 'Excision et droit pénal' (1990) 20 *Droit et Cultures* 201; Catherine Quiminal, 'Les Soninké en France et au Mali: le débat sur les mutilations sexuelles' (1990) 20 *Droit et Cultures* 183; Michel Erlich, 'Notions de mutilation et criminalization de l'excision en France' (1990) 20 *Droit et Cultures* 151; Jean-Thierry Maertens, 'Les mutilations rituelles en corps et toujours' (1990) 20 *Droit et Cultures* 163; Pierre Maligne, 'L'excision des enfants africains: Politique du Parquet Général de Paris' (1993) 25 *Droit et Cultures* 139; Robert Pageard, 'A propos des procès d'excision en France' (1993) 25 *Droit et Cultures* 141; Martine Lefeuvre, 'Le devoir d'excision' (1988)1 *Revue du MAUSS* 65; Olivier Mongin, 'L'excision en procès' (1989) 4 *Revue du MAUSS* 137; Alain Caillé, 'Notes sur les problèmes soulevés par l'excision' (1989) 4 *Revue du MAUSS* 116; Alain Caillé, 'Breve réponse à Olivier Mongin' (1989) 4 *Revue du MAUSS* 149; Anne Biquard, 'Bouturage, l'initiation des femmes' (1991) 18 *Nouvelle Revue d'Ethnopsychiatrie* 153; Michel Erlich, 'Circoncision, excision et racisme' (1991) 18 *Nouvelle Revue d'Ethnopsychiatrie* 125; Christian Kottler, 'L'excision en France est-elle une affaire judiciaire'? (1991) 18 *Nouvelle Revue d'Ethnopsychiatrie* 51. In addition to these journals, see Jean Dubois, 'Une violence sacralisée, la judiciarisation de l'excision' in E Le Roy & T Von Trotha, eds., *La violence et l'État: Formes et évolution d'un monopole* (Paris: L'Harmattan, 1993) at 114; Jean Dubois, 'Les impensables de la judiciarisation de l'excision' in E Rude-Antoine, ed., *L'immigration*

their criticisms centred around the arguments that an ancient practice perpetuated within a cultural context and without any intention to harm could not be considered a crime, that women were themselves victims of the tradition, and that law should not separate families nor incite them against one another.

4.5 The 'Reasons' for Punishment in the Prosecutors' Closing Arguments

A content analysis of both legal and non-legal documents confirms that *excision* is a binding norm, it is a valid legal obligation. Nevertheless, the analysed documents do not equally reflect the two poles of the conflict between two normative orders, which focus respectively on individual fundamental rights and on group interests. On the one hand, documents either mention that the accused refused to speak in court or they very briefly list the explanations that the accused gave for the perpetuation of *excision*. They shortly refer to custom, marriage and family. On the other hand, documents extensively discuss the 'reasons' given in favour of punishing FGC through penal sanctions.

These reasons are rooted in the fact that *excision* violates the right to physical integrity, health and non-discrimination on the basis of gender/ethnicity/culture. In the analysed cases the charges pursued by French courts include personal injuries, manslaughter and failure to render assistance to a person in danger. Documents make reference to *excision* as mutilation and violence. In most cases *excision* literally qualified as 'intentional acts of violence (*violences volontaires)* [or personal injuries (*coups et blessures*)] that have caused mutilation (*ayant entraîné une mutilation*), perpetrated on a minor aged less than 15 years'.[55] The term 'violence' is the most glaring example of a contrast between the legal expressions used in the French legal system and the 'reasons' given by immigrants mentioned in the introductory chapter, since parents who have their daughters excised in truth have no intent to harm. In some of the cases, the mothers charged were in fact expressly found to take good

face aux lois de la République (Paris: Karthala, 1992) at 162–3; Marie-José Bourdin, 'Tu ne couperas point. L'excision ou l'impossible compromis' (1992) 70 *Migrations-Santé* 5; Marie-José Bourdin, 'Les Blancs ont dit c'est pas bon pour les filles' (1994) 195 *Accueillir* 34.

[55] See Articles 222–9 and 222–10 of the new French Penal Code and Article 312–3 of the former French Penal Code.

leads to 'better integration—that is to say in judicial terms, a sort of imposed and accepted general education which might open the path to literacy, to health education, to intercultural dialogue and—who knows, maybe one day—to the assimilation of the values to which we are so deeply attached. Without an accompanying mechanism of oversight, a simple suspended sentence is nothing but a slap on the wrist. Not a cure, it is simply a placebo'. Since this sentence does not exist, properly speaking, in French law, Commaret invited the jurors to begin to draw up its first legal contours by sentencing the Coulibaly to a three-year suspended prison term with probation. A judge would have them under his authority, beginning from the end of the trial and throughout the time period set by the jury, and would be supported by all the public associative instruments able to foster dialogue. Pursuant to Article R. 58-3 of the Penal Code of Procedure, the Coulibaly could, for example, be submitted to 'educational instruction'. The verdict, then, would have a double function: it would show both firmness and imagination. 'Is it not thus [. . .] that the law can make progress?'[62] After a three-day trial, the *Cour d'Assises* of Paris ordered the Coulibaly to serve a five-year suspended sentence and two years' probation.[63] Keita, the *exciseuse*, was sentenced to five years' imprisonment.[64]

In the *Traore, Doucoure* case of 1993 the prosecutor, Mr. Jean-Claude Thin, argued that if the relationship between the law and a customary norm was the matter, only repression could induce the latter to recede. Mrs. Taky Soucko, married to Traore, and Mrs. Oura Yattabare, married to Doucoure (or Doukouré, depending on the source), were accused before the *Cour d'Assises* of Paris of being accomplices to 'personal injuries on a child aged less than 15 years that have caused mutilation'. *Excisions* had been performed on two minors, their respective daughters.

[62] 'Réquisitoire de Mme Commaret' (1991) 21 *Droit et Cultures* 193. The English translation is mine. Another English version can be found in 'The Summation of Prosecutor Commaret' *Passages* (Ann Arbor: MPublishing, University of Michigan Library, 1992) available at http://quod.lib.umich.edu/p/passages/4761530.0003.004/–summation-of-prosecutor-commaret?rgn=main;view=fulltext, accessed on 9 September 2014.

[63] Cf. Commission nationale consultative des droits de l'homme (CNCDH), *supra* note 22 at 71; Edwige Rude-Antoine, *Des vies et des familles: Les immigrés, la loi et la coutume* (Paris: Odile Jacob, 1997) at 233. Another source mentions instead five years' imprisonment, including three in jail and a two-year suspended sentence. Cf. Levasseur, *supra* note 61 at 565.

[64] Cf. also Rude-Antoine, *supra* note 63 at 233.

According to the prosecutor, the husband (he seemed to refer to Mr. Traore)[65] understood the universal concept of prohibition, which is the same in Mali and therefore in the villages around Keyes. The prosecutor went on to state that during the trial it was noted that *excision* was perpetrated even in the West at the beginning of the twentieth century and was witnessed by colonial administrators, who watched it in the sixties: obscurantism, thus, has no borders and exists both in France and Africa. Nevertheless, not to apply existing penal norms would be anti-educational, Thin argued – 'Educating and Punishing [are in fact] complementary'. There may be reference points, such as religion, but rules to be followed are set by the law. Penal law, in particular, constitutes the lowest common denominator among individuals and the right to difference does not change this fact. Thin continued by saying that the law needs to be applied to all citizens of the state. The rights to dignity and physical integrity exist, as well as the particular rights protecting the weakest members of society, that is children. Thin then read Article 24 of the Convention on the Rights of the Child,[66] which recognises 'the right of the child to the enjoyment of the highest attainable standard of health [. . .]' (paragraph 1) and that 'States Parties shall take all effective and appropriate measures with a view to abolishing traditional practices prejudicial to the health of children' (paragraph 3).

Debates over culture have nothing to do with *excision*, the prosecutor continued. What counts is the protection of the child, which the state is obliged to pursue. With regard to this issue Africa and France are moving in the same direction. Thin then reminded the jurors that one's freedom ends where another's begins and that the rights of the child, a more vulnerable being, need to be unequivocally respected. Thin concluded by saying that information and repressive efforts to discourage *excision* needed to be coordinated. Not enforcing the law would mean considering Malian people unequal to French before the law. The accused themselves were victims, but if punishment was not applied, the customary norm of *excision* would ever be suppressed. The prosecutor asked for a five-year imprisonment and requested that at least part of the sentence, though minimal, be served in jail, citing as grounds for his request the fact that the convicted, irrespective of their origin, often do not fully understand

[65] It emerged during this trial that the fathers had told their wives that *excision* was against the law. Mr. Traore specified that he had told his wife only once. According to the prosecutor, Mr. Traore said this to protect her.

[66] Adopted by the United Nations General Assembly in 1989.

the meaning of a suspended sentence.[67] The *Cour d'Assises* of Paris ordered Traore and Doucoure to serve a five-year suspended sentence.

Even in the *Ba* case of 1996 the prosecutor denied in his closing argument the efficacy of suspended sentences. This case was tried before the *Cour d'Assises* of Bobigny. The accused was Mrs. Hadidja Ba, married to Marega (or Maréga according to the sources). *Excisions* had been performed on her five daughters. The prosecutor argued that the state has the right to intervene in the issue of *excision* because French law is applied in France. He argued that *excision* is a form of violence against children, illegal under French law. In this case both the children and their father were French citizens, their father since 1968. The prosecutor went on to claim that the notion of bodily integrity is universal and the role of the jury-citizen is to judge both the accused and the principles at work. Prevention, he continued, is not enough to eradicate this practice: suppression is needed as well, considering that the babies in question had their mother's breast as their only reference and that Dr. Breaux (or Breaud, the source is contradictory on this point), who belonged to the Pantin' s PMI, has informed on *excision* since 1987. The prosecutor asked for a punitive sanction that would serve as an example: five-year imprisonment with at least one year to be served in jail.[68] Ba was sentenced to three years' imprisonment of which one in jail and a two-year suspended sentence.

The prosecutor, Philippe Bilger, argued in the *Gréou* case of 1999: 'This trial of large amplitude could have been a disaster; it could have oscillated between the trial of *excision* and that of those who have committed it. It could have fallen into paternalism or neo-colonialism. These two alternatives have been avoided. You have to treat these women [the excised girls] like everybody else, these girls that wanted to be like

[67] Cf. 'Procès de Mesdames Taky Traoré et Oura Doukouré Cour d'Assises de Paris (Ière section) (8–9 février 1993): Réquisitoire de Monsieur l'Avocat général Jean-Claude Thin' (1993) 25 *Droit et Cultures* 135. On this case cf. also Martine Lefeuvre-Déotte, *L'excision en procès: un différend culturel?* (Paris: L'Harmattan, 1997) at 72, 75 and 76; Commission nationale consultative des droits de l'homme (CNCDH), *supra* note 22 at 72.

[68] Information on this case comes from Luce Syrkis' notes which she took during the trial as a member of GAMS. This NGO working for the abandonment of FGC is strongly engaged in prevention. It was first called *Groupe femmes pour l'Abolition des Mutilations Sexuelles*, then *Groupe pour l'Abolition des Mutilations Sexuelles*. It is now part of the *Fédération nationale GAMS* (Groupe pour l'Abolition des Mutilations Sexuelles, des Mariages Forcés et autres pratiques traditionnelles néfastes à la santé des femmes et des enfants). GAMS was born as the French section of the IAC. It consists of African and French members. On this case cf. also Commission nationale consultative des droits de l'homme (CNCDH), *supra* note 22 at 74.

everybody else'.[69] Mrs. Hawa Gréou (Greou or Graou, depending on the source) was accused before the *Cour d'Assises* of Paris of 'intentional acts of violence committed on minors aged less than 15 years that have caused mutilation'[70] for forty-eight *excisions* performed. Twenty-six parents were charged as accomplices to this offence. Because of the number of people involved, the trial was highly publicised. The *exciseuse* had previously been ordered to serve a one-year suspended sentence in 1994,[71] yet had continued to practice *excision*.

The *Gréou* case of 1999 is the second trial[72], among the analysed cases, in which the complaint came from one of the excised girls, the daughter of one of the accused, who had reached the age of majority. Previously entrusted to another family due to her parents' financial problems, she underwent *excision* at the age of eight, a month after she returned to live with her family of origin, whose culture and language she did not know. She waited until the age of eighteen to leave her family and denounce her *excision*, bringing the *exciseuse* that performed it to court.

The prosecutor continued by saying that one can no longer claim ignorance of the ban on *excision* with respect to the period between 1982 and 1999, because news about various trials had spread widely within the communities which were directly concerned. Even the media devoted attention to it, informing the public of the criminal sanction on *excision*. Furthermore, in

[69] Documentation on this trial, particularly on the hearing of Friday, 12 February 1999, received through GAMS. It was given to its members by Marie-France Casalis, Prefecture d'Ile de France, Secrétariat Général-Délégation Régionale aux Droits des Femmes et à l'Egalité. On this case cf. also Thomas Hirenée Atenga, 'Droits de l'homme: Une exciseuse malienne condamnée à huit ans de prison', available at www.ips.org/fr/droits-de-lhomme-une-exciseuse-malienne-condamnee-a-huit-ans-de-prison/, accessed on 9 September 2014; Commission nationale consultative des droits de l'homme (CNCDH), *supra* note 22 at 74.

[70] Blandine Grosjean, 'Excision: une victime dénonce. Mariatou est la première à avoir porté plainte. Des dizaines d'accusés sont jugés aux assises' (1999) 2 February *Libération*, available at www.liberation.fr/societe/1999/02/02/excision-une-victime-denonce-mariatou-est-la-premiere-a-avoir-porte-plainte-des-dizaines-d-accuses-s_263875#, accessed on 9 September 2014.

[71] In the *Diarra, Traore, Greou* (Gréou or Grau as well as Traoré, depending on the source) case of 1994 before the *Cour d'Assises*, wherein the presiding judge was Yves Corneloup. Cf. Maurice Peyrot, 'Deux parents africains acquittés dans un procès d'excision' (1994) 17 September *Le Monde* 15. On this case see also Keïta, *supra* note 53 at 14; Pascale Gerin, 'L'exciseuse dénoncée par une de ses victimes' (1994) 17 May *Libération* 12.

[72] The first trial among the analysed cases in which the *exciseuse* was reported by one of the excised girls who was nineteen years old at the time of the trial was the already mentioned *Diarra, Traore, Greou* case.

this particular case, the presumption of ignorance was eliminated by the fact that the *exciseuse* had already been convicted in the past.

The *exciseuse* was sentenced to eight years' imprisonment. Among the analysed cases this is the harshest punishment inflicted on an *exciseuse*. The *Gréou* case is the fourth trial in which an *exciseuse* was convicted. It is also the only example of recidivism involving an *exciseuse*, although it should be remembered that, among the analysed cases, only two *exciseuses* have been tried before the *Cour d'Assises*[73]. It is not easy to identify the *exciseuses* because they are often protected by the parents. The mother of the girl who filed the complaint against Gréou was sentenced to two years' imprisonment. Three fathers and twenty-three mothers were ordered to serve a five-year suspended sentence. Mrs. Diénéba Cissé, married to Koïta, the mother of Mariatou, the girl who has filed a complaint, was sentenced to two years imprisonment. Among the other twenty-five parents, twenty-two were ordered to serve a five-year suspended sentence, while three were ordered to serve a three-year suspended sentence. Gréou was also ordered to pay a sum to each of the forty-eight girls in compensation for damages and interests.

4.6 State Legal System *vs* Customary Norm? A More Complex Polarisation of the Conflict

The previous paragraphs should not make the reader think that one of the two poles of the conflict between normative orders is monolithic. Nor should we assume that the social actors of the trials who represent the French legal system all hold the same positions and beliefs. Not all prosecutors and judges were convinced that an intervention through legal means was suitable and/or that *excision* cases should be tried before the *Cour d'Assises*.

Numerous cases shed light on these differing opinions, including the *Traore* case of 1984. After the death of Bobo, their three-month old daughter[74], Mr. Décé Traore and Mrs. Bougoury Coulibaly were accused

[73] Aramata Keita (in the *Coulibaly* cases before the *Cours d'Assises* of Paris and Bobigny) and Hawa Graou (in the *Diarra, Traoré, Greou* case and *Graou* case. In these cases the *exciseuse*'s name is spelled differently but it makes reference to the same woman).

[74] The expert's report, written by Dr. Bailly, concludes in this way: 'It appears from the autopsy that the death of Bobo, aged of three months, is the result of an external haemorrhage for clitoral excision. It was a complete excision of the clitoris'. Ligue du Droit International des Femmes, 'L'embarras de la justice' in *Les mutilations du sexe des femmes aujourdhui en France* (Paris: Tierce, 1984) at 68.

initially before the XIV *Chambre correctionnel* of the *Tribunal* of Créteil[75] of failure to render assistance to a person in danger. During the trial they told the press that they were planning to perform *excision* on another daughter in Mali. The civil society organisations joining the proceedings as a civil party asked for all child protection measures to be taken for this baby and recommended an order be given not to remove the child from France,[76] which they considered the only means to preserve the eight-month old baby's health and physical integrity. The judge of the *Tribunal pour enfants*[77] (hereafter juvenile court judge) of Créteil, Antoine Garapon, decided that no 'educational assistance measure' (*mesure d'assistance éducative*) would be taken. He then published an article were he discussed the issues that arose in his decision.[78]

Garapon argued that the principal means at his disposal in the Traore case, the Educational Assistance in an Open Environment measure (*Assistance Educative en Milieu Ouvert*, AEMO)[79] and the custody order, would have been either powerless or too powerful. The Civil Code does not include the order not to remove a child from France among its judicial protection measures. The aim of this order could be reached only through an interim

[75] After a long and complex course of proceedings the case was judged by the *Cour d'Appel* of Amiens which ordered Mrs. and Mr. Traore to serve a one-year suspended sentence. Cf. on this case Georges Levasseur: 'Violences volontaires à enfant' (1986) 4 *Revue de science criminelle et de droit pénal comparé* 849 at 851; Levasseur, 'Violences entraînant mutilation. Excision' *supra* note 47 at 108–9; Georges Levasseur, 'Abstention de porter secours à l'occasion d'une excision' (1989) 1 *Revue de science criminelle et de droit pénal comparé* 107 at 112–13; Cour de Cassation, Chambre criminelle (1986) 136 *Bulletin criminel* 346; Cour de Cassation, Chambre criminelle (1988) 188 *Bulletin criminel* 484.

[76] Cf. Ligue du Droit International des Femmes, *supra* note 74 at 69.

[77] The *Tribunal pour enfants* is in charge of children's protection. It may order placement in a foster home and arrange visits with parents. It has also jurisdiction over young offenders. Nevertheless, the *Cour d'Assises de Mineurs* has jurisdiction over crimes committed by a minor older than 16. Cf. *Tribunal pour enfants*, available at www.justice.gouv.fr/organisation-de-la-justice-10031/lordre-judiciaire-10033/tribunal-pour-enfants-19650.html, accessed on 9 September 2014.

[78] Cf. Antoine Garapon 'La culture dangereuse' (1987) 114:1 *Le groupe familial* 78.

[79] The Educational Assistance in an Open Environment (*Assistance Éducative en Milieu Ouvert*, AEMO) is a judicial measure, ordered by the juvenile court judge for a fixed term (Article 375 and following of the Civil Code, concerning the protection of children), whose aim it is to accompany minors who have been the subject of reports because of educational, emotional, moral and psychological issues that compromise their safety, morality and development. Cf. *Action Éducative en Milieu Ouvert (AEMO) et Aide Éducative à Domicile (AED)*, available at www.sauvegarde93.fr/action-educative-en-milieu-ouvert-aemo-et-aide-educative-a-domicile-aed-18, accessed on 9 September 2014. This measure is implemented through educators, social workers, psychologists, etc. It allows the judge to help families without separating a child from his or her parents.

custody order (*ordonnance de garde provisoire*). However, to give absolute assurance, the measure should be permanent and prolonged until the age of majority, but even at that age the risk would not cease. It is known that *excision* could still be practiced after a girls' return to the village of her family's origin regardless of her age. Furthermore, the judge argued: 'Isn't it exaggerated, even intolerable, to ask a stranger to give up his cultural identity and practices even in his own country? It may turn out that the mere removal of the child is more respectful to the freedom of the family than getting it to deny its culture. Is it possible for the French judge to escape from a moral and ethnocentric appreciation of excision'? Garapon continued by saying that the principle of removing the child from the family does not automatically follow that of recognising the integrity of the child. In the context of judicial proceedings everything must be discussed and willingness to go deeply into the decision does not prevent the juvenile court judge to recognise that *excision* is mutilation and it is against French public order.

Garapon asserted that the juvenile court judge should avoid any decision based on principle. In his view, the appreciation of danger in the abstract is limited to a very general consideration of the child's right to physical integrity, which only allows medical interventions that bring a physical improvement. A concrete appreciation of danger, together with a consideration of the particular family context and the personality of the child, should guide the search for the measures to effectively end risks to a child wellbeing. Garapon concluded by asking 'which decision will prove to be more traumatic [in the present case] and in the long-term more dangerous for the child: being excised in the context of the traditional life of her parents, like her mother, her sisters, her aunts and all of her ancestors or being definitively removed from her natural environment until the age of majority with the risks of abandonment and *déculturation* that this represents? In deciding, the juvenile court judge favoured family, as is encouraged by Article 375–2 of the Civil Code which states that the child should remain in his or her current environment whenever possible. The risk, however real, that the child runs is shared by all his people'.

Other examples also shed light on the conflict in question. In the previously mentioned Coulibaly case before the XV *Chambre correctionnel* of the *Tribunal* of Paris[80] the deputy public prosecutor, Mrs. Martine Vezant,[81] asked the court to give the mother, Mrs. Coulibaly, a one-year

[80] Cf. Nisak, *supra* note 44 at 44. [81] Cf. Majorelle, *supra* note 45.

suspended sentence and to drop the charges against the father, Mr. Coulibaly, considering that *excision* is a women's issue and that the father was not aware of it. She asked for a moderate punishment, taking into account the cultural *tiraillements* in which the accused are trapped. In this case only the parents were accused because the *exciseuse* could not been found. They were both accused of being accomplices, the mother to 'intentional personal injuries on a minor aged less than 15 years' and the father to 'supply of means' (*fourniture de moyens*). As already mentioned in paragraph 4.4, the *Tribunal Correctionnel* of Paris declined jurisdiction and the deputy public prosecutor appealed its decision. She argued that there was no intention to mutilate. In her view it was a matter of a 'ritual excision practiced at the request of the Malian parents, who are subject to the imprint of their ancestral culture. The application of a foreign customary norm does not remove wilfulness [and] suppressive measures are to be desired, but it does not seem appropriate to submit to the jury of a *Cour d'Assises* the appreciation of facts whose legal classification is not unanimous either in doctrine or in case law'.[82]

In some cases before the *Cour d'Assises*, the President of the Court allowed careful and wide-ranging debate on the facts, on the practice of *excision* and on the individuals involved in the specific case. In these cases the documents reflect an attempt to shed light on and understand the issue by all sides, and to consider FGC in its context. The President of the Court can also decide whether or not to allow the testimony of experts, of various backgrounds (anthropology, sociology, psychiatry, or other medical fields) and beliefs. He or she may also admit the screening of films in the court room. We can imagine that the effect films have on jurors depends greatly on whether or not they contain explicit images of *excision*. For example, *La Duperie*, produced by the IAC, is a very explicit film while *Le Pari de Bintou*[83], by Kirsten Johnson, produced by CAMS, or *L'Afrique accusé?*, by Jean-Pierre Zirn, are not so. The first two films were both been produced as educational tools by NGOs working for the abandonment of *excision*, but they are very different. *Le Pari de Bintou* takes place in Paris and only depicts family life. Bintou questions tradition and refuses *excision* for her daughter against the will of part of her family. *La Duperie* is a documentary shot in South Nigeria and shows graphically the *excision* of a young girl. In the already mentioned *Graou*

[82] Levasseur, 'Violences entraînant mutilation. Excision' (1989) *supra* note 47 at 109.

[83] The film is available at www.youtube.com/watch?v=oCC9pPU7fpk, accessed on 9 September 2014.

case the defense challenged the projection of this film in court. In the *Wagué, Diawara* case of 2002 in which Mr. and Mrs. Wagué as well as Mr. Diawara and his two wives who were both mothers, were accused before the *Cour d'Assises* of Bobigny of 'intentional acts of violence that have caused permanent mutilation'[84] the defense lawyers opposed the projection of *La Duperie*, as well as *Le Pari de Bintou*. They argued that these films were shown with the sole purpose of influencing the jurors, with no aim to depict the truth about *excision*. The next day the civil party withdrew its request to project the films, since excerpts of the films had been aired on television the night before.

In the *Coulibaly* case before the *Cour d'Asssies* of Bobigny[85], the presiding judge was Yves Corneloup. The trial lasted ten days, during which time the Court heard a number of the accused, experts and testimony. Anthropologists, ethnologists and sociologists explained the practice in question and its cultural framework[86]. The film *L'Afrique accusé?* was shown. Judge Corneloup's choices of testimony and film seem to be in line with his paper of 1995. In this paper, whose content has been confirmed by my in-depth interviews, he deemed that it was possible, as an alternative to a trial before the *Cour d'Assises*, to request temporary or permanent exclusion from French territory, which would affect not only the parents and *exciseuse*, but also the inhabitants of their home village, who rely on migrant remittances.[87]

In this case the choices made during the trials were accompanied and maybe supported by the presiding judge's conviction that *excision* cases

[84] In this case the court ordered Mrs. and Mr. Wagué to serve a two-year suspended sentence and Mr. Diawara and his two wives to serve a three-year suspended sentence. The court also ordered all the accused to pay each organisation joining the proceedings as a civil party a sum in compensation for damages and interests. Cf. on this case 'Procès de l'excision: prison avec sursis pour les cinq Maliens' (2002) 15 March *Le Monde.fr*, available at http://denisoturet.fr/eurodroit/islam-excision.html, accessed on 9 September 2014; Émilie Rive, 'Le procès de l'excision à Bobigny' (2002) 14 March *L'Humanité*, available at www.humanite.fr/node/261877, accessed on 9 September 2014; Commission nationale consultative des droits de l'homme (CNCDH), *supra* note 22 at 75. I also received information on this case through GAMS.

[85] Even though the case concerned the *excision* of sixteen young girls, one of whom died, the punishments handed down in this closed hearing trial were not as harsh as those in the trial in Paris. The *exciseuse* was sentenced to four years' imprisonment, with three in jail and a one-year suspended sentence, while three parents were released and the others ordered to serve a one-year suspended sentence.

[86] Unfortunately, the analysed documents do not give detailed information on the content of experts' testimony.

[87] Cf. Corneloup, *supra* note 53 at 113.

should not be tried by the *Cours d'Assises*. This example allows us to hypothesise that presiding judges' convictions on the criminalisation of FGC contribute to shape the structure of hearings, therefore influencing the course of the trials and sentencing. Nevertheless, in order to test the strength and veracity of this hypothesis, further empirical research is needed.

In the Coulibaly case before the *Cour d'Asssies* of Bobigny the summation given by the prosecutor was very different than that given by Commaret. It pointed out the characteristics of *excision* and the fact that there was no intention to harm the children.[88] In the prosecutor's closing argument *excision* was not depicted as a lucrative activity, but described as an obligation which parents are essentially unable to escape; at the time when the *excision* was carried out, in 1982–3, there was widespread ignorance of the prohibition against this practice. This ignorance was compounded, according to prosecutor, by the isolation of women and the weight of taboos and custom.[89]

4.7 The Complex Role of Men in the Perpetration of *Excision*

The complex issue of the role of men in the perpetration of FGC has also emerged from an analysis of prosecutors' statements, testimonies and questioning in the trials under examination. With the exception of the *Doucara* case of 1984 before the *Tribunal Correctionnel* of Paris[90] in which the father, Mr. Fousseyni Doucara (or Doukara according to the sources),[91] confessed to having practised *excision* on Bintou,[92] his three-month-old daughter, and the *Soumare* case of 1990 before the *Cour d'Assises* of Bobigny[93] in which the father, Mr.

[88] The source available does not quote the exact words of the prosecutor's closing argument.

[89] Cf. Raymond Verdier, 'Une exciseuse en Cour d'Assises: Le procès de Soko Aramata Keita' (1991) 21 *Droit et Cultures* 184; Rude-Antoine, *supra* note 63; Raymond Verdier, 'Le double procès de Mme Kéita (Paris-Bobigny, mars-juin 1991)' in E Rude-Antoine, ed., *L'immigration face aux lois de la République* (Paris: Karthala Karthala, 1992) at 149–56.

[90] Cf. Dominique Vernier, 'Le traitement pénal de l'excision en France: historique' (1990) 20 *Droit et Cultures* 193 at 195 and 197; Nisak, *supra* note 44 at 43; Ligue du Droit International des Femmes, *supra* note 74 at 68, 71, 72 and 73; Commission nationale consultative des droits de l'homme (CNCDH), *supra* note 22 at 70.

[91] He was accused of 'intentional personal injuries on a child aged less than 15 years'. The court ordered Mr. Doucara to serve a one-year suspended sentence.

[92] It is impossible to know if his confession corresponded to reality or if it aimed to protect his wife.

[93] Cf. F. Aubenas, 'Procès de l'excision: "qui fait pleurer les femmes"', (1990) 21 June *Libération* 35; 'Excision et répression sur le territoire français: Création d'un groupe de réflexion (octobre 1989)' (1990) 20 *Droit et Cultures* 146.

Saloum Soumare,[94] had asked that *excision* be carried out on Kadidia, his one-year-old daughter, without his wife's knowledge,[95] the analysed trials did not disclose men's direct involvement in the operation or organisation of *excision*.

Except for the already mentioned *Traore, Doucoure* case, in which the prosecutor showed that the father of the excised children had told their wives that *excision* was against the law, the testimonies and questioning also revealed that, generally speaking, women tend to keep their *excision* a secret. It is a taboo subject that is not discussed between the mother and daughter and least of all between men and women. In the *Fofana Traore* case of 1989 in which Mrs. Dalla Fofana, married to Traore, was accused before the *Cour d'Assises* of Paris,[96] Mr. Traore, the father of the excised baby, declared that he would have stopped the plan to practice *excision* if he knew about it, because he was aware of the fact that *excision* is forbidden in France.[97] Even during the *Graou* case it emerged that people do not discuss about their own *excision*, even mothers and daughters. Besides confirming this finding, the already mentioned *Wagué, Diawara* case revealed additionally that talking about this practice among men is considered a shameful behaviour.

In this sense, an analysis of the trials confirms that the secrecy surrounding the traditional transmission of the customary norm allows the members of a group to prevent any dividing effect.[98] The transmission

[94] He was accused of 'being an accomplice to mutilation on a minor'. The court ordered him to serve a five-year suspended sentence.

[95] Among the analysed trials, it is the only case in which the mother was of French origin. Christiane Soumare in fact was from Poitiers. She became her husband's wife after he married, in Africa, the cousin who had been promised to him at birth.

[96] She was accused of being an accomplice to 'intentional personal injuries that cause mutilation'. Cf. Commission nationale consultative des droits de l'homme (CNCDH), *supra* note 22 at 71. The court ordered Mrs. Traore to serve a three-year suspended sentence. It was the first case wherein a *Cour d'Assises* was called upon to rule on an *excision* that did not result in the death of a child and the first one that was tried before the *Cour d'Assises* of Paris.

[97] Cf. on this case Alessandra Facchi, 'L'escissione un caso giudiziario' in M Barisone, L Graziano: F Prina, eds., *Contributi in tema di pluralismo giuridico* (Torino: Università degli Studi di Torino, 1992) at 36–53; Alessandra Facchi, 'L'escissione: un caso giudiziario' (1992) 19:1 *Sociologia del diritto* 111; Martine Lefeuvre, 'Le procès de Dalla Fofana' (1989) 4 *Revue du MAUSS* 124; Martine Lefeuvre, 'Le devoir d'excision' (1988) 1 *Revue du MAUSS* 65.

[98] Cf. Alliot, 'L'évolution de la notion de droit en Afrique', *supra* note 35 at 105; N Rouland, 'La coutume et la pensée juridique sauvage: L'apport des sociétés Inuit' in J Gilissen, ed., *Coutume-Costume* (Brussels: De Boeck Université, 1990) at 316.

tool of *excision*, orality, should therefore not be misleading here. Words are the vehicle for the perpetuation of the binding norm. They are used and regulated because this norm has to be followed.[99] Nevertheless, they do not take the form of a dialogue on *excision*, either between age groups,[100] or between different sexes. 'Verbal interactions are [...] the main learning contexts of an oral culture',[101] but in the case of *excision* as in that of other traditional practices, they do not open spaces for debate and dissent, privileging the continuity of transmission and community cohesion. Particularly appropriate in this regard is Jacques Vanderlinden's reflection, that a customary norm is non-written as well as non-oral. It is first of all gesture and is neither an oral nor a written source.[102]

The results of the empirical research also confirm that in Africa feminine and masculine collectivities are traditionally separate. They do not mix. The crucial stages of men and women's lives are determined and organised by people of the same sex. Men and women do not share their respective secrets (examples for women include childbirth and *excision*). Inquiries on *excision* conducted in France[103] frequently show the attitude: 'Men have nothing to do with it; it is a women's issue (*c'est une affaire de femmes*)', which supports these results.

Nevertheless, ethnologists have revealed that, despite the separation of the sexes, in African traditions men play a role in *excision*. Even though the general trend is to lower its age and limit its rituals, scholars have detected a considerable diversity in the practice of *excision*. 'Where excision is part of a long lasting and collective initiation ritual, the fiancé and his family sustain ceremony expenses and the girl's livelihood during the period of seclusion. It seems that in all societies concerned by this

[99] For the idea that speech (as well as memory) is the informal, though often highly disciplined, tool for the teaching of the past, see H Patrick Glenn, *Legal Traditions of the World: Sustainable Diversity in Law* (Oxford: Oxford University Press, 2007) at 61.

[100] The topic of age groups is very complex and would require an extensive treatment. In a nutshell it can be said that the expression 'age group' refers to a social group in which the recruitment is based on the similar age (not necessarily corresponding to the years of the individual) of its members. It is an institution that can cross as a unit varying degrees of age. With regard to women, in traditional societies, the link between biological and social age is generally centered on the phases of life related to the reproductive cycle: puberty, marriage, first child, etc.

[101] 'Orale/Scritto' in U Fabietti & F Remotti, eds., *Dizionario di antropologia* (Bologna: Zanichelli, 2001) at 537.

[102] Cf. Jacques Vanderlinden, *Anthropologie Juridique* (Paris: Dalloz, 1996) at 49.

[103] See note 5.

ritual financial contribution is quite substantial, enough in any case to make these rituals impossible during some years (for example among the Oubi because of poor collections of coffee, in 1954–1955)'.[104] According to Michel Cartry the *excision* ceremony carries substantial costs, which are met mainly by the groom's family.[105] Among some groups, for example the Minyanka, traditionally expenses are high even though *excision* is performed individually. These are necessary for the *exciseuse*'s services but even more so for the sacrifices made on the occasion: *excision* marks a girl's separation from the relatives and ancestors of the family. Until a fiancé can pay he cannot get married.[106] Nevertheless, when the fiancé is particularly poor, the future in-laws sometimes allow him to sleep with the promised girl not yet excised, waiting for him to be able to pay the costs of the operation.[107] Similar sacrifices are also made when the *excision* is performed collectively. According to Cartry among the Gourmantché, a given number of animals can be found at the altar of *excision*, in particular sheat-fishes (silurus) and goats that are brought by the grooms' families, more precisely by the oldest living members. Every family must provide four sheat-fishes and a goat.[108]

A contradictory role of men in the perpetration of this practice also emerged from a deeper analysis of the trial documents. The prosecutors' words underlined men's involvement in financing *excisions* practiced by immigrants residing in France. It is possible to link this involvement also to the fact that the majority of West African female immigrants in France cannot count on personal incomes as they usually did in Africa thanks to the cultivation of land or small businesses. Immigration implies a considerable loss of autonomy for these women. In France they generally become housewives and their husbands provide for the maintenance of the family.

In the previously mentioned *Coulibaly* case before the *Cour d'Assises* of Paris the prosecutor highlighted the contradictory statements of the accused with regard to the type of compensation given to the *exciseuse* and the role that husbands/fathers play in the practice of *excision*. How is

[104] Raulin, *Femme en cause*, *supra* note 5 at 71; Bohumil Holas, 'L'évolution du schéma initiatique chez les femmes Oubi (Région de Taï, Côte d'Ivoire)' (1957) 27:3 *Africa: Journal of the International African Institute* 241 at 245.

[105] Cf. Michel Cartry, 'La calebasse de l'excision en pays gourmantché' (1968) 38:2 *Journal de la Société des Africanistes* 189 at 189 note 2.

[106] Cf. Danielle Jonckers, 'Chez les Minyanka: Mali' (1984) 29:1 *Cahiers du* GRIF 22 at 28 and 27.

[107] Cf. Bohumil Théophile Holas, *Les Sénoufo, y compris les Minianka* (Paris: Presses Universitaires de France, 1957) at 114–15.

[108] Cf. Cartry, *supra* note 105 at 209–10.

it possible to imagine, even if *excision* is apparently a women's matter, asked the prosecutor, 'that Sory Coulibaly, the father of these children, the only means of support in the household, would not have been consulted, then solicited to finance the operations before they were performed'? Considering the sum of money at stake, a hefty sum for a person responsible for a large family and who sends money to his village, how was it possible that he did not inquire about how the money was to be used? All of the reports on *excision* have proved 'the necessary complicity on the part of the heads of families in perpetuating these practices. Not only because they finance them but equally because they are, in reality, the only beneficiaries – assuring in this way the fidelity and submission of their wives and the marriageability of their daughters, thereby ensuring receipt of the bridewealth. Aminata Diop, the young Malian woman who fled her family and country to escape excision, told you how involved the fathers were and how much they intervened in this domain. [. . .] Sory Coulibaly is complicit through financial assistance and through instructions he gave, in the ethnic mutilations performed on his daughters even if he did not physically participate. To my mind, it would be a real injustice, a sort of deception, to cast the weight of this act solely on women who are its first victims'.

In the *Teneng Jahate* case of 1993, the mother, Mrs. Fofana Teneng, married to Jahate, was accused before the *Cour d'Assises* of Paris of being an accomplice to 'intentional acts of violence or *voies de fait* on a child aged less than 15 years that have caused mutilation'.[109] *Excisions* had been practised on her two daughters in 1987, aged one and two years old.

The prosecutor, Jacques Mouton,[110], argued in his closing argument that 'we must be aware of [...] and repeat [that *excision*] is essentially practiced by patriarchal societies for the benefit of men'. His closing argument also mentioned an article by Françoise Gaillard on FGC, published on 23 December 1988 in the journal *Actualités Sociales Hebdomadaires*, in which the author recalled Assitan Diallo's[111] educational and sensitisation work in Mali, before quoting one of her statements: '[W]e need to convince men because they are those who decide'. The

[109] The offence she was accused of is mentioned in Cour de Cassation, Chambre criminelle, 29 September 1993, n. 93–80.370, unpublished, available at www.legifrance.gouv.fr/affichJuriJudi.do?idTexte=JURITEXT000007561532, accessed 9 September 2014.

[110] For his closing argument cf. 'Procès Teneng Fofana épouse Jahate Cour d'Assises de Paris (7 et 8 janvier 1993): Réquisitoire de Monsieur l'Avocat général Jacques Mouton' (1993) 25 *Droit et Cultures* 130.

[111] Malian researcher and international consultant engaged in the eradication of FGC.

prosecutor went on to say that, despite this, only Fofana was prosecuted as an accomplice for the *excision* of her daughters, while her husband was left out of the case: Mrs. Fofana had asked a third person to come to her house to perform the operation and took part in it. The prosecutor continued by underlining that the report of the PMI showed that the husband declared to the social worker to have turned to an 'angel maker' (*faiseuse d'anges*) to carry out these mutilations, even though the day before, during the trial, he had denied both this statement and having seen a social worker. Given that the topic was not pursued either by the police or by the investigating judge, the prosecutor admitted that he could only have his suspicions towards the husband, who was not one of the defendants.

The prosecutor's reference to the PMI offers the opportunity to note that most complaints of *excisions* were filed by doctors working in the hospitals where the young girls had been admitted or in the PMI centres where mothers took their daughters for routine check-ups. These doctors followed the Recommendations of the National Medicine Academy (*Académie nationale de Médecine*), aimed at the eradication of FGC[112] and different articles of the law. PMI doctors, who are functionaries, are in fact obliged to report any evidence of bodily harm to a child under Article 40 of the French Criminal Procedure Code. Doctors working in hospitals who, with the exception of academic doctors, are not considered functionaries, can violate their professional secrecy in order to report cases of *excision*, under Article 226–14 of the French Penal Code.

According to Mouton, regardless of what Mr. Jahate had said the day before, contradicting himself with what appeared in the statements made to the investigating judge, it had emerged from the investigation on the personality that the family budget was managed by Jahate, who paid for all purchases, given that his wife, the accused, as recognised by the court, could not count. Where, then, did the 300 or 350 francs used to pay the *exciseuse* come from, if it is true that the husband knew nothing about it and that the wife would not have been able to acquire such a sum without addressing him? 'In any case, when Mr. Jahate told the investigating

[112] See 'Recommandations de l'Académie nationale de médecine visant à l'éradication des mutilations sexuelles féminines (MSF)' (2004) 188:6 *Supplément au Bulletin de l'Académie Nationale de Médicine* 122. See also Emmanuelle Piet & Bernard Topuz, *Note à l'attention des Médecins de Protection Maternelle Infantile et de Planification Familiale. Objet: Conduite à tenir pour lutter contre les Mutilations Sexuelles Féminines* (Bobigny: Seine-Saint-Denis. Conseil Général. Direction de l'Enfance et de la Famille. Service de la Protection Maternelle et Infantile, 2006).

judge that he did not know if his wife had paid anything for the operation, we know that he lied, on the one hand because it is he who manages the budget, on the other hand, because this is contrary to the tradition, since it is known that the exciseuses are paid in cash or with gifts, they are important and respected people'. Furthermore, according to the prosecutor, while claiming that *excision* was a women's issue of which people do not speak, the husband said to know that it can be dangerous.

The prosecutor argued that around a three- or four-year sentence would be reasonable and left the details up to the court's judgment. He asked that at least a part of the sentence be served in jail so that the accused would feel the full weight of the punishment ('*le coup de bâton tombe*'). Teneng was sentenced to five years' imprisonment, serving one year in jail and a four-year suspended sentence. Among the analysed cases, she is the first mother who did not receive a fully suspended sentence.[113]

In the *Aïdara* case of 1997 Chiekhna Aïdara (or Haïdara, depending on the source) and his wife, Fatou Badiaga, are accused before the *Cour d'Assises* of Bobigny of being accomplices to 'intentional acts of violence that have caused mutilation on a child aged less than 15 years'. Their two daughters, who are French citizens residing in France, were excised and partially infibulated.

At first the father said that he had given his consent to *excision*, but later retracted this statement. At a different time, the mother said that during a meeting between women of her country during which *excision* was discussed, one of them claimed to be able to perform it. The description given by Badiaga suggested that she had this conversation in the subway. She made an appointment with the earlier mentioned woman, who came to her house two or three days afterwards. Aïdara, her husband, gave his wife money for the operation. During the first hearing, assisted by an interpreter, he retracted the statement he had made to the police and said he had not been informed of the plan to excise his young daughters and its later execution. He claimed that he did not know where, when, or by whom the *excisions* were performed. They happened between the first and second year of the girls' lives, but each time he was not there, because he was on holiday in Senegal, where he regularly

[113] On this case cf. also 'L'action civile' in (1993) 2nd sem. *Gazette du Palais* 574; Georges Levasseur, 'Coups et blessures volontaires. Excision' (1994) 2 *Revue de science criminelle et de droit pénal comparé* 328 at 329–30.

returned each year for a period of between forty days to two months. He argued that he had stated to be aware of his wife's request only because, after the PMI visit, she had told him that she would have been in trouble if he had not declared this. Aïdara claimed that in Africa men are never apprised of these problems and that women are wholly responsible for taking care of them.

Aïdara was sentenced to five years' imprisonment, with one year served in jail and four years of suspended sentence. The court ordered Badiaga to serve a five-year suspended sentence.[114]

4.8 Conclusion

'The vision of simpler societies dominated by integrated traditions of ancient origin gave scholars license to differentiate with exaggerated sharpness between'[115] the norms of traditional societies and those of modern states.[116] The characteristics of homogeneity and unitarity of African societies prior to colonial rule were often uncritically accentuated.[117] Anthropological literature has often disproportionally depicted their communal nature. The opposition between communitarian and individualistic societies should not, on the contrary, be overemphasised. On the one hand, 'Western societies' are less homogeneous than one might think in shaping the concepts of community and individual: they generate tensions between principles aimed at protecting individuals and principles aimed at protecting collectivities, which take precedence over each other depending on the time and contexts.[118] On the other hand, if the oral and communal nature of the transmission of traditional norms strongly spurs consensus, dissent has historically emerged even irretrievably and traditions have been modified by people who rejected, in whole

[114] Cf. Marie-France Casalis, Prefecture d'Ile de France, Secrétariat Général-Délégation Régionale aux Droits des Femmes et à l'Egalité, *Affaire Aïdara. Procès à la Cour d'Assises de Bobigny: Audience du vendredi 7 février 1997*, 17 February 1997 at 1–5; Commission nationale consultative des droits de l'homme (CNCDH), *supra* note 22 at 74.

[115] Falk Moore, *supra* note 7 at 14. On the impossibility of drawing a clear line between 'early law' and modern state law cf. Arthur L. Goodhart, 'Foreword' in Max Gluckman, *The Judicial Process among the Barotse of Northern Rhodesia* (Manchester: Manchester University Press, 1967) at XIII.

[116] Sally Falk Moore literally refers to the customs of 'such "early" societies' and the statutes of 'self-conscious modern states'. Cf. Falk Moore, *supra* note 7 at 14.

[117] See, for example, Alexander Nekam, 'Aspects of African Customary Law' (1967) 62:1 *Northwestern University Law Review* at 47.

[118] Cf. Allot, *supra* note 18 at 149.

or in part, their own society. Even the traditions in which the transmission of information is severely limited cannot avoid the flourishing of opinions.[119]

This does not preclude the fact, however, that in traditional societies the violation of unwritten norms is punished by sanctions that may amount to ostracism or may push the dissenting party to voluntary exile and that the substance of the belief often seems so essential that it survives as a tradition despite all dissent and defection.[120] It is also true that the organisation of traditional societies has historically emphasised the corporate and collective dimensions to the detriment of the individual, both in social relations and in legal forms. These considerations help to explain the continuing practice of FGC.

FGC collides with the individual fundamental rights recognised by modern states and its perpetuation generates a conflict between this customary norm and the state legal system. This conflict has played out multiple times before French courts which have developed the richest jurisprudence on *excision*. Court involvement was likely encouraged by the increasing international attention given to the damage caused by FGC.

The response of the French criminal system to FGC is not based on *ad hoc* provisions, which were not adopted in France. Rather, *excision* is sanctioned by the already existing rules of the Penal Code. This choice has evident ties with the *modèle français/républicain d'intégration*, which does not recognise ethnic minority groups' rights.

Only in France are *excision* cases regularly brought to court. They were initially tried before the *Tribunal Correctionnel*, then before the *Cour d'Asssises*. Because *excision* cases have indeed been concluded with sanctions and the Penal Code previously provided for a maximum penalty of life in prison (replaced following a reform with twenty years' imprisonment),[121] the transfer of jurisdiction might have led to harsh penalties. Nevertheless, in the analysed cases, the accused tried before the *Cour d'Assises* received moderate punishments. The harshest punishment inflicted on an *exciseuse* was eight years' imprisonment without suspended sentence, but this was a case of recidivism[122] in which forty-eight *excisions* were carried out. The most severe punishments imposed on mothers were five years' imprisonment, with one year in jail and a

[119] Cf. Glenn, *supra* note 99 at 62, text and note 14.

[120] Cf. Glenn, *supra* note 99 at 63.

[121] See Article 222-8 of the Penal Code.

[122] In the *Graou* case tried before the *Cour d'Assises* of Paris.

four-year suspended sentence,[123] and two years' imprisonment.[124] The harshest sentence imposed on a father was five years' imprisonment, of which one was to be served in jail and four were suspended.[125]

Just as the associations joining the proceedings as civil parties, the prosecutors have often requested that at least a part of the sentences given be served in jail, citing as grounds for their request the fact that the convicted, no matter their origin, do not fully understand the meaning of a suspended sentence. And yet, the sentences were almost all suspended. As a result it seems there have not been cases of 'exemplary' punishments.[126]

The analysed trials extensively depict one pole of the conflict between two normative orders. They broadly refer to the prosecutors' concluding arguments, which mostly ask the courts to condemn *excision* because it violates the rights to physical integrity, health and non-discrimination on the basis of gender/ethnicity/culture. The prosecutors' summations and the legal expressions used during the trials link *excision* to violence and mutilation, although it seems clear that while FGC is dangerous for girls and women's health and has in some cases caused the death of children, it is practiced with no intention to harm.

An analysis of the trials shows that the pole of the conflict representing the state legal system was not homogenous in France. Prosecutors and judges did not speak with one voice about the effectiveness of the legal instruments available and the criminalisation of *excision.* Some of them did not consider trials before the *Cour d'Assises* as an appropriate response to FGC. In one case a juvenile court judge preferred not to act to prevent the risk of *excision* in order to avoid having to adopt measures that would prevent the child from growing up in her family and cultural environment.

An analysis of the trials also reveals that, with regard to FGC, the relations between the sexes are complex and difficult to unveil. It reveals that *excision* is a taboo subject between men and women but that at the same time men are involved in the expenses that it entails, which suggests that they are aware of its practice. The above-mentioned relations and the role of men are even more difficult to discern because the explanations of the accused only partially emerge from the analysed documents,

[123] In the *Teneng Jahate* case. [124] See note 122.

[125] In the *Aïdara* case. Even though I could not reconstruct the trial, I know that until 2003 in just one case (the Keïta case of 1993 tried before the *Cour d'Assises* of Bobigny) the husband of an *exciseuse* was convicted as an accomplice and sentenced to five years' imprisonment and a four and a half-year suspended sentence.

[126] In this sense, see also Lucia Bellucci, 'Immigrazione, escissione e diritto in Francia' (2006) 33:3 *Sociologia del diritto* 195 at 195–8.

as well as because *excision* is a subject that women generally do not discuss, but rather are accustomed to keep shrouded in silence. The empirical research shows that *excision* is a binding customary norm. It is strongly rooted in the populations that practice it and is handed down through the generations. It is therefore difficult to break away from it, even when certain aspects related to its perpetration come under discussion. However, the documents only briefly refer to custom, marriage and family. Inquiries conducted in France and mentioned in the introductory paragraph consequently become crucial to explain this practice.

The prosecutors' closing arguments cannot be considered an exhaustive source with which to interpret tradition. This is even more true since the views on the relations between sexes expressed in these documents could be influenced by the fact that prosecutors represent before the courts the legal systems' principles and norms. Nevertheless, even with regard to African traditions, ethnologists have shown that a separation between the sexes exists side-by-side with the involvement of grooms and fiancés, and their families in the costs of *excision*.

Besides these costs, it seems that while FGC is perpetuated and practised by women, the collective imagination which encourages its continued existence is shaped by the thinking of men. According to the Bambara tradition, for example, the clitoris could kill the man during penetration, so should be removed. Despite the fact that, traditionally, the last word on *excision* has been given to different groups of women (age groups, families, etc.), depending on the context and epoch, what is good for women seems to be decided based on what is good for men. Beyond any feminist consideration, one can argue that this is not surprising, since it has historically happened in every society, shaping the roles of women according to socio-economic changes and needs, as is particularly evident in the transition from rural to industrial societies occurred in our modern 'Western societies'.

In the case of marriage interests as the reason for the perpetration of *excision*, the most crucial consideration with regard to the relations between the sexes and men's involvement in it seems to be that men belonging to ethnic groups practising FCG in general refuse to marry a woman who is not excised; or rather, since not all ethnic groups consider *excision* a *conditio sine qua non* for marriage because among some people it can be done later,[127] one can argue that men refuse, in general, to be the husbands of women who are not excised.

[127] Cf. Erlich, *supra* note 14 at 32–5; Gillette, *supra* note 5 at 90–6; Nicole Sindzingre, 'Le plus et le moins: à propos de l'excision' (1977) 17:1 *Cahiers d'études africaines* 65 at 69.

Excision is not just a women's issue. Its organisation and perpetration are entrusted to women but men play a key role in its perpetuation, a role to be taken into account in undertaking any action on the matter. Nevertheless, in order to fully understand this role, one needs to contextualise the relations between the sexes in light of respectful and non-ethnocentric interpretations of men and women's powers and social roles. Further empirical research on traditional practices, including legal anthropological analyses of the most recent *excision* trials in Western countries and Africa as well as comparative studies of different responses to FGC, would help shed light on the complexities of these relations and the conflict between normative orders.

PART II

Aboriginal Law

5

Law, Culture, and Fact in Indigenous Claims

Legal Pluralism as a Problem of Recognition

KIRSTEN ANKER

5.1 Introduction

The "Centaur Jurisprudence" of the volume title arises from positioning legal pluralism as an awkward hybrid of two seemingly exclusive disciplinary perspectives on the responses of legal institutions to cultural claims. On the one hand, there is the orthodox legal approach that takes culture to be part of the world of fact from which law is separate and to which law is applied. On the other, there is the cultural anthropological approach that sees everything – courts and their law included – as culture.[1] Legal pluralists would rather see cultural recognition and accommodation as the interplay of different legal orders, discourses or forms of normativity, going beyond a definition of law as the formal rules for decisions by state actors. The question that has plagued legal pluralist theories is that if state law is relativized and the definition of law broadened, then what stops what is particular to law disappearing into culture or social life in general?[2] This is an analytical and conceptual issue, but it is also a normative one: can an understanding of diverse forms and sources of law be taken on board by state actors charged with providing authoritative decisions about cultural claims?

It may be that the idea of the centaur simply represents the fact that although social scientists and jurists are both talking about "law," they are engaged in different enterprises. Social scientists are largely interested in reflexive description and analysis of human social life, while jurists are pre-occupied with normative questions of how law should respond to

[1] Annelise Riles, "Anthropology, Human Rights, and Legal Knowledge" (2006) 108:1 *Am Anthropol* 52 at 53.

[2] Sally Engle Merry, "Legal Pluralism" (1988) 22 *Law Soc Rev* 869 at 878.

concrete problems.[3] However, the centaur-like mix of conceptual and normative issue appears not at all misplaced in the context of Indigenous claims. It has been widely argued that the fact of "cultural difference" alone can neither explain, nor satisfy, the need for recognition or acknowledgment of Indigenous rights by the courts, and that recognition must include as its object Indigenous sovereignty and the normativity of Indigenous law.[4] Consequently, the legal pluralist instinct that there is something distinctively legal in the encounter between courts and Indigenous claimants is important in order to understand the character of Indigenous claims. However, the problem is not simply in having "culture" rather than "law" as the object of recognition. As I will show, many of the issues raised by the recognition of culture by courts risk being reproduced in other ways even when judges are called on to take Indigenous traditions as a source of *law*. My argument will be that the problem lies with the paradigm of recognition itself that treats Indigenous law as a social fact rather than as a normative or authoritative discourse.

Critiques of recognition from within political theory have attempted to show that, to the extent that approaches to recognition treat culture or identity as a pre-existing fact, they are irreconcilable with the roots of the idea of political recognition, coming to us from W. G. F. Hegel via Charles Taylor and others, as a mutually constitutive dialogic relation. Patchen Markell, in particular, has argued that in its cognitive/factual mode, the struggle for recognition is a wrong-headed attempt at mastery – either over oneself or over others – that denies this dependent relation.[5] In trying to untangle the web of law, culture and fact in the example of Indigenous rights in Canada, this chapter will connect these critical theories of recognition with contemporary legal pluralist theories that, although coming at the problem from a different direction and focusing on "law" rather than "culture" or "identity," likewise frame claims for legal recognition in terms of dialogue or discursive relations. Both veins of theory, I will argue, lead to understanding recognition

[3] Franz von Benda-Beckmann, "Riding or Killing the Centaur: Reflections on the Identities of Legal Anthropology" (2008) 4 *Int J Law Context* 85 at 94–5. But see also Annelise Riles, who notes the interdependence of the reflexive and normative as "modes" of thinking: "Representing In-between: Law, Anthropology, and the Rhetoric of Interdisciplinarity" (1994) *U Illinois LR* 597 at 643–50.

[4] See also: Morgan Brigg, Chapter 10, this volume; Thomas Burelli & Régis Lafargue, Chapter 8, this volume; and Eric Reiter, Chapter 9, this volume.

[5] Patchen Markell, *Bound by Recognition* (Princeton: Princeton University Press, 2003) at 10–16, 39–43.

institutions as sites of productive translation of life as law, and legal pluralism as an account of our "constitutive vulnerability" to others. The question remains whether this discursive legal pluralism offers a normative foundation for formal legal processes. In aspiring to post-colonial justice, is legal pluralism something that judges can "apply"? I will suggest below that understanding law as rules applied by legitimate authority already sells short any aspirations to adopt a legally pluralist frame for Indigenous claims, and that we should instead understand law as the discursive practices of communities.

5.2 The Legal Recognition of Indigenous Rights

In Canada, the official legal recognition of Indigenous rights turns around s.35 of the Constitution through which "Aboriginal and treaty rights are hereby recognized and affirmed." Aboriginal rights have been defined in terms of "the distinctive culture of the aboriginal group"[6] that pre-dates contact with Europeans.[7] Claims are framed as the right to engage in a particular activity (frequently one that is being proscribed by state regulatory laws): to fish a particular species in a given area, to bring goods across the border for the purposes of trade, or to cut timber for domestic purposes, for example. At trial, evidence is brought as to the way in which this activity is continuous with the group's pre-contact culture, understood as a way of life.[8] It is demonstrated through archeological, historical, and anthropological research, and assessed by the court as to its persuasiveness on the balance of probabilities.[9] The Supreme Court has stipulated that the kinds of practices that merit protection are those that form an integral part of the distinctive Aboriginal culture in question, are a "defining feature"[10] of that culture or of central significance to it,[11] or lie "at the core of the peoples' identity."[12] Where the claim concerns possessory title to land based on exclusive occupation (Aboriginal title), it is assumed that the resulting connection with a particular territory is of central significance to the group's distinctive culture.[13] Proof then turns around establishing the extent of past

[6] *R* v *Van Der Peet*, [1996] 2 Sup. Ct Rep. 507 at 46. [7] *Ibid* at 165.
[8] *R* v *Sappier; R* v *Gray*, [2006] 2 Sup. Ct Rep. 686 at 24.
[9] *Mitchell* v *MNR*, [2001] 1 Sup. Ct Rep. 911 at 39.
[10] *R* v *Van Der Peet*, *supra* note 6 at 59. [11] *Ibid* at 55.
[12] *Mitchell* v *MNR*, *supra* note 9 at 12.
[13] *Delgamuukw* v *British Columbia*, [1997] 3 Sup. Ct Rep. 1010 at 128.

occupation, for which Aboriginal laws relating to land may be relevant. In keeping with the *sui generis* or unique character and historical roots of Aboriginal rights and title, and the reconciliatory purpose of s.35, questions of proof and the nature of rights should consider both the "Aboriginal" and the "common law" perspective.[14]

Two brief examples will illustrate the Court's approach to recognition. In *R* v *Van Der Peet* [1996], a member of the Sto:lo First Nation sought to defend a charge under provincial laws prohibiting the sale of fish caught under an Indian food fish licence by arguing that the regulations infringed her Aboriginal rights.[15] To succeed, the appellant had to demonstrate facts supporting a right characterized in terms commensurate with both the nature of the regulation, and the action for which she was charged, namely, a one-off sale of ten salmon [para. 76–8]. Having first reasoned that the purpose of s.35 was to acknowledge the distinctive *cultures* that pre-dated colonization and reconcile them with Crown sovereignty [para. 30–1], the Court (per Lamer CJ) held that the appellant would have to show that it was the *practice* of exchanging fish for money or other goods that was integral to her distinctive culture in order to succeed [para. 80]. However, rather than characterize the right according to its significance to the Sto:lo – for instance, the right to fish to "provide for a moderate livelihood" [para. 79], which may have extended to commercial exchange – the Court stated that only "the actual practices, customs and traditions related to the fishery" that had been proven as historical fact could form the basis of the right [para. 79].

In the result, the Court held that while proof of the significance of fisheries as livelihood might help demonstrate that fishing per se was integral to Sto:lo culture, there was insufficient evidence that a *trade* in fish was itself integral prior to contact with Europeans and the salmon market established by European traders. According to the Court, the evidence established that the occasional trade that did appear to have occurred was "incidental to fishing for food purposes" rather than part of a "regularised system," and was "primarily linked to the kinship and family relationships" as part of a reciprocal system of gift-giving and hospitality [para. 84]. Consequently, Van Der Peet was unable to establish that she had an Aboriginal right relevant to her offense.

The test for Aboriginal rights established in the *Van Der Peet* majority decision thus defines rights in terms of practices rather than in terms of

[14] *Ibid* at 50 and 149; *R* v *Van Der Peet*, *supra* note 6 at 42.
[15] *R* v *Van Der Peet*, *supra* note 6.

cultural meaning or significance, and requires an ability to distinguish between "core" and "peripheral" cultural practices. In addition, it requires that the "integral" test be directed toward Aboriginal societies that existed prior to contact with Europeans; current practices must be "rooted in the pre-contact societies" in order to constitute an Aboriginal right [para. 62]. In contrast, L'Heureux-Dubé J's dissent places emphasis on the distinctive culture as a whole – in terms of the significance of activities to the people – rather than a "catalogue of individualised practices" [para. 157]. Her approach would also allow these to evolve so as to maintain relevance to contemporary Aboriginal societies, provided that any activity in question has been significant "for a substantial continuous period of time" [para. 175]. The Court in subsequent cases appears to back away from the "centrality" requirement, as Russel Barsh and Sákéj Henderson note, holding in *R* v *Adams* and *R* v *Cote* that fishing was an "important" source of sustenance rather than central per se.[16] Nevertheless, and in contrast to l'Heureux-Dubé's dissent, a key part of recognising Aboriginal rights still involves characterising elements of culture in terms of a specific practice – and usually, in terms of a regulated contemporary activity.[17]

The role of translation in characterising Aboriginal rights became an explicit part of the interpretation of the term "recognition" in s.35 in *R* v *Marshall; R* v *Bernard* [2006], a pair of cases in which several Mi'kmaq respondents were seeking to defend charges of logging without a licence on the basis that the Mi'kmaq held Aboriginal title to the land on which the cutting sites were located.[18] In order to answer the question of the degree of land use that was required to establish the element of exclusive occupation in the test for Aboriginal title, McLachlin CJ wrote for the Court that the "task in evaluating a claim for an aboriginal right is to examine the pre-sovereignty aboriginal practice and translate that practice, as faithfully and objectively as it can, into a modern legal right" [para. 48]. Thus evidence would be required of use "sufficiently regular and exclusive to comport with title at common law" [para. 58] the core of which is "the intention and capacity to retain exclusive control" [para. 57]. Since the respondents were unable to provide evidence that the specific cutting sites had been subject to "regular occupancy or use"

[16] Russel Barsh & James Henderson, "The Supreme Court's Van der Peet Trilogy: Naive Imperialism and Ropes of Sand" (1997) 42 *McGill Law J* 993 at 1005.

[17] See also *Mitchell* v *MNR, supra* note 9 at 15.

[18] *R* v *Marshall; R* v *Bernard*, [2006] 2 Sup. Ct Rep. 220.

as one of (a lack of) Indigenous participation: the goal of s.35 jurisprudence so far has been to define the content of Aboriginal rights in terms of European understandings of culture, not to "begin a cross cultural conversation about the meaning of sovereignty or political legitimacy."[29] Thus the problem is not just with the definition of culture being used, but with the question of "who possesses classificatory authority."[30] The upshot of these criticisms, even when their proponents argue for a more sophisticated cultural basis for Aboriginal rights, is that the focus of Aboriginal rights should be on the recognition of Indigenous self-government or sovereignty (including the capacity to evolve to meet the needs of the community), the recognition of frameworks (like languages, values and traditions) that provide normative content to material practices, and the recognition of the unique status within Canada of polities having never ceded their right to self-govern.[31]

These critiques of Aboriginal rights jurisprudence are reflective of three sets of problems identified more broadly in the politics of recognition. The first set of problems, reification and essentialism, arises via the cognitive sense of recognition as backward-looking identification of a pre-existing "thing," and the tendency for identity claims to focus only on one discrete aspect of identity (culture, gender or race, for example), to set it up in opposition to a dominant identity, and to ignore differences within the group. The idea of something being "integral" or "central" to Aboriginal culture in the previous section is an example of essentialization, but so is the tendency to think of culture as a set of traits or practices. In legal processes, reification/essentialism is caught up in the archetypal activity of "applying law to facts" in which, instead of taking recognition as constitutive of identity, law recognizes by attaching legal labels and consequences to a pre-existing object (fact) of recognition, whether that be pre-contact practices (as in Canada), tribal identity (as in the US) or property under traditional laws and customs (as in Australia). Where the terms of recognition become criteria for the allocation of

J Can Stud 182; Ronald Niezen, "Culture and the Judiciary: The Meaning of the Culture Concept as a Source of Aboriginal Rights in Canada" (2003) 18:2 *Can JL Soc* 1.

29 Dale Turner, *This Is Not a Peace Pipe* (Toronto: University of Toronto Press, 2006) at 83.

30 Dick, *supra* note 21 at 962.

31 John Borrows, *Recovering Canada: The Resurgence of Indigenous Law* (Toronto: University of Toronto Press, 2002) at 64; Patrick Macklem, *Indigenous Difference and the Constitution of Canada* (Toronto: University of Toronto Press, 2001) at 61; Michael Murphy, "Culture and the Courts: A New Direction in Canadian Jurisprudence on Aboriginal Rights?" (2001) 34:1 *Can J Polit Sci Can Sci Polit* 109 at 123.

benefits, there is pressure to mobilize around one aspect of group identity to the exclusion of more nuanced, hybrid or context-dependent accounts of identity, effectively disciplining group members into a particular reified self-understanding.[32]

The second set of problems is the ethnocentricity of the labels used and the assimilative effect of this, since the differences, the uniqueness, of the other can only ever be identified in terms of the self. Stewart Motha argues that in any liberal humanist attempt to recognize difference, "a universal is being smuggled in."[33] Even when the stopping point is nothing smaller than humanity, others are always being reduced to the terms of the self: they are human, like us. Difference is erased "by the very gesture that purports to recognise it."[34] Aboriginal rights jurisprudence has not attempted to pursue the universal frame of recognition very far, choosing possession and use of land and resources as its stopping point. Even if the will were there to go further, the problem of the ethnocentric universal seems to pose itself as a cognitive problem, as Kelly Oliver puts it, of being unable to re-cognize that of which we have no cognition.[35] In the Mik'maq cases discussed earlier, the ethic of sharing professed in the case was seen as incompatible with the "exclusive possession" requirement of common law title to land and so unrecognizable. However, even in an alternative translation that tries to get closer to the Mi'kmaq rather than the common law legal sensibility – Sákéj Henderson, for example, describes the Mi'kmaq concept *netukulimk* as an "obligation to protect the ecological order and right to share nature's resources" with the Mawi'omi (Grand Council) as "'trustee' of the sacred order and territory"[36] – each of these terms can be argued to be only an approximation or reduction to the familiar English terms.

In the politics of recognition, Taylor's famous turn to dialog and the "fusion of horizons" of value can be seen to address both reification/essentialism and ethnocentrism/assimilation. He argues that the terms of recognition cannot be taken for granted or known in advance (for

32 Anthony Appiah, "Identity, Authenticity, Survival: Multicultural Societies and Social Reproduction" in Amy Gutmann, ed., *Multiculturalism: Examining the Politics of Recognition* (Princeton: Princeton University Press, 1994) at 163.

33 Stewart Motha,"MABO – Encountering the Epistemic Limit of the Recognition of Difference" (1998) 7:1 *Griffith Rev* 79 at 79, 85.

34 *Ibid* at 86.

35 Kelly Oliver, *Witnessing: Beyond Recognition* (Minneapolis: University of Minnesota Press, 2001) at 2.

36 Henderson, *supra* note 19 at 20–1.

instance, so as to locate them only in the culture or language of the recognizer), but must develop via a mutual engagement over the set of criteria by which we evaluate (our horizon of value develops out of a dialogic process).[37] While we may not – and cannot – wholly adopt the perspective of others, our understanding of our own criteria will be necessarily affected by having made a genuine attempt to come to terms with a different set of criteria. A genuine attempt to understand *netukulimk*, for example, might bring non-Indigenous peoples to a different sense of what it is to be trustee for a territory, or what territory itself is. There is some evidence of openness to the dialogic approach to Aboriginal rights, at times named "an intersocietal law,"[38] because of the way that its principles have emerged over a long period of engagement between Aboriginal peoples and colonists about normative standards and practices that should guide their conduct with respect to each other.[39] It is this intersocietal engagement that gives rise to what the courts call the *sui generis* character of Aboriginal rights.[40] In the contemporary context, the Supreme Court of Canada's commitment to take Aboriginal perspectives into account alongside common law perspectives, and the definition of Aboriginal rights as being sourced partly in Aboriginal law, suggest some kind of contemporary dialogue, although there is very little evidence of judges actually doing this. LeBel J's judgment in *Marshall* and *Bernard* [para. 129] held that Aboriginal title should be taken as shaped by both common law concepts and Aboriginal standards of occupation in an ongoing and case-by-case manner.

For Markell, in that these first two problems raise critiques of the terms of recognition with respect to a "true" version of culture or identity, they expose incoherence in the politics of recognition due to the tension between the ideal of authenticity and the dialogic nature of identity formation.[41] How can I make a demand for recognition on the basis of an authentic identity when that identity is the result of exchanges of recognition with others?[42] This critique joins with poststructuralist attacks

[37] Taylor, *supra* note 23 at 66–73. [38] *R* v *Van Der Peet, supra* note 6 at 42.

[39] For an approach to Aboriginal rights based on Taylor's intercultural dialog see Dwight Newman, "You Still Know Nothin' bout Me: Toward Cross-Cultural Theorizing of Aboriginal Rights" (2007) 52 *McGill LJ* 725.

[40] *Delgamuukw* v *British Columbia, supra* note 13 at 112.

[41] Markell, *supra* note 5 at 39–43.

[42] Note that while Taylor's work on subjectivity prior to his essay on multiculturalism had a firmly dialogic understanding of the self, he nevertheless holds to the possibility of judging proper recognition against an authentic version of the self. His concession to

on the ontology of identity politics,[43] and the contemporary anthropological approach to culture as a process of creating and defending political boundaries,[44] in highlighting the subject, or culture, as dialogically formed, contingent and contextualized. As Lois McNay argues, one reason that those promoting the politics of recognition might forgo the initial commitment to a dialogic subject or cultural identity in favor of a reified one is that it would require an awareness of the processes and structures of power involved in producing certain identities, the examination of which is too threatening to privileged groups in neo-liberal regimes.[45]

Consequently, power is, broadly, at the heart of a third set of problems that include, in particular, a kind of pathology produced by unequal relations of power in recognition encounters. The cognitive gaze calls up a sense of mastery (recognition as actively grasping something with the mind[46]) that objectifies others by rendering them "known, understood, interpretable.[47] Dialogic recognition does not completely avoid this aspect of recognition either: Taylor, for instance, contemplates recognition as a primarily cognitive affair, and this is bound to be lopsided considering the uneven distribution of the need for recognition and the consequent non-reversible hierarchy of recognizer and recognized. Moreover, given the mutually constituted nature of identity, the selves that seek recognition are likely to have been thoroughly shaped by the oppressive relationship. In this way, the act of recognition repeats the colonial hierarchy that gave rise to oppression in the first place: in Oliver's take on Frantz Fanon, "recognition itself is part of the pathology of oppression and domination."[48]

Three particular suggestions for ways out of this pathology – the hall of mirrors that leads to a never-ending cycle of failures of, and thus further need for, recognition – have been made: a focus on the structures of

this incoherence is that the authentic identity is a projection into the future based on what has come in the past: "this sense of my life as having a direction towards what I am not yet": Charles Taylor, *Sources of the Self: The Making of the Modern Identity* (Cambridge, Mass: Harvard University Press, 1989) at 48.

43 For example, Judith Butler, *Gender Trouble: Feminism and the Subversion of Identity* (New York: Routledge, 1999).

44 Niezen, *supra* note 28 at 2.

45 Lois McNay, *Against Recognition* (Cambridge: Polity, 2008) at 10.

46 Paul Ricoeur, *The Course of Recognition*, translated by David Pellauer (Harvard: Harvard University Press, 2005) at 7.

47 Majid Yar, "Recognition and the Politics of Human(e) Desire" (2001) 18:2–3 *Theory Cult Soc* 57 at 62.

48 Oliver, *supra* note 35 at 23.

domination that would transform rather than affirm oppressed identities;[49] turning inward toward other members of the group to develop a progressive mirror reflecting a positive self-image back to them, and a struggle for freedom on their own terms or according to their own traditions;[50] and a recovery of the material aspects of intersubjective relations – the body and its location in place and time – that cannot be captured by categories of recognition.[51] An example of this final approach commensurate with many Indigenous philosophies would be grounding action in the land – and in particular, in its specific and material characteristics, capacities and limitations – rather than in identity or culture.

Nevertheless, there is a fourth, deeper, ontological problem with the politics of recognition in Markell's critique that none of these solutions adequately addresses, although they may avoid it in some ways: in attempting to guarantee that we are effectively represented in social and political life through proper recognition so that we may "act in accordance with who we are,"[52] we forget that the very reason why we need recognition from others is our basic human condition of constitutive vulnerability to them. In a careful re-reading of Hegel, Markell argues that the source of oppressive practices is not misrecognition, but "the desire for sovereign agency" which drives both the master and the slave to risk life in the struggle for recognition.[53] However, what produces the unequal outcome is not the asymmetry of recognition, but the slave's realization, first, that "life is as essential to it as pure self-consciousness,"[54] and, second, that the original desire for freedom is impossible to fulfill because of our finitude and dependence on others. The master, on the other hand, has used the slave's labor to insulate him from his own dependence in a simulation of sovereignty that leaves the other "to bear a disproportionate share of the costs and burdens involved in social life."[55]

[49] Catharine A MacKinnon, *Feminism Unmodified: Discourses on Life and Law* (Cambridge: Harvard University Press, 1987) at 38–9; Nancy Fraser, *Justice Interruptus: Critical Reflections on the "postsocialist" Condition* (New York: Routledge, 1997) at 30.

[50] Franz Fanon, *Black Skin, White Masks*, translated by Charles Markmann (New York: Grove Press, 1967) at 222; bell hooks, "Postmodern Blackness" (1990) 1:1 *Postmod Cult*, online: www.press.jhu.edu/journals/postmodern_culture at 11; Coulthard, *supra* note 21 at 454.

[51] Brenna Bhandar, "Plasticity and Post-Colonial Recognition: Owning, Knowing and Being" (2011) 22:3 *Law Crit* 227 at 230.

[52] Markell, *supra* note 5 at 12. [53] *Ibid* at 22.

[54] G W F Hegel, *Phenomenology of Spirit (1807)*, translated by A. V. Miller (Oxford: Oxford University Press, 1977) at 115.

[55] Markell, *supra* note 5 at 22.

This reading allows us to see that the pursuit of sovereignty in Aboriginal rights jurisprudence is not just the obvious one in which the Canadian state asserts jurisdiction over Indigenous territories to the exclusion of Indigenous sovereignty, or where Indigenous groups push for the converse. It is also the one in which Aboriginal rights are shaped so as to reduce Aboriginal claims to a set of finite, legible practices, thereby ensuring that the majority's sense of itself will not be perpetually threatened by an unlimited range of claims for recognition.[56] This is a sense of sovereignty as masterful agency – having a firm grasp of the fact of oneself as a solid basis on which to act and to control one's destiny. The conditions of interdependence behind the ontological problem allow us to see, first, that the inadequate cultural test for Aboriginal rights cannot be overcome by a better mapping of Indigenous realities as culture, since those cultural realities are not just dynamic but are productively contingent on relationships to other cultures. Second, we see that legal institutions in which struggles for recognition take place are among the elicitory mechanisms for culture.[57] State legal forms, practices and language cause people to articulate their culture – genuinely – in particular ways. Further, interdependence suggests that while the Canadian state gives no appearance of seeking or participating in an *exchange* of recognition, nonetheless its pursuit of sovereignty (in both territorial and agentic senses) is a simulation maintained by displacing the burdens of justification onto Indigenous peoples.[58] The following section attempts to think through whether transforming Aboriginal rights from a question of culture to one of law, and thus of legal pluralism, offers an alternative to these problems of recognition.

[56] Indeed, ethnographic legibility has a disciplinary effect, in Foucault's terms, such that Indigenous peoples internalize the positivist language of rights claims. Julie Cruickshank, for instance, has noted that Indigenous groups, having discovered the strategic importance of claims of cultural distinctiveness and authenticity, can find post-modern anthropological approaches threatening: *The Social Life of Stories: Narrative and Knowledge in the Yukon Territory* (Vancouver: UBC Press, 1998) at 162.

[57] James Weiner, "Culture in a Sealed Envelope: The Concealment of Australian Aboriginal Heritage and Tradition in the Hindmarsh Island Bridge Affair" (1999) 5:2 *J R Anthropol Inst* 193 at 202.

[58] Revealing this simulation seems to be behind the insistence of John Borrows that Aboriginal rights jurisprudence should focus on an examination of the basis of the Crown's claim to lands and sovereignty. See for example Borrows, *supra* note 31 at 112–13.

5.4 Legal Pluralism and the Recognition of Indigenous Law

As mentioned, critics of the place of culture or "aboriginality" in Aboriginal rights commonly argue for a more robust recognition of Indigenous law and of Indigenous political autonomy, one that takes Indigenous law to be not merely a fact of life in Indigenous communities, but a potential source of norms, standards and criteria for decision-making concerning Aboriginal rights.[59] A turn toward theories of legal pluralism as a way of understanding the relative place of, and interaction between, Indigenous law and state law, would thus seem apt. Posed as a problem of the recognition of non-state law, however, legal pluralist approaches potentially throw up a progression of problems similar to the ones we have just looked at in the context of culture and identity.

Let us first work from the perspective of judges who, taking note of the principle that Aboriginal perspectives should contribute to shaping the *sui generis* nature of Aboriginal rights, want to recognize Aboriginal law *as law* in their decisions. In this task, they might take their cue from the definitional debates in pluralist legal theory,[60] namely, about how to identify the legal in a way that is not centered on the state. Following some of the most influential trends in socio-legal theory, they might look to functional equivalents to state law (or to its legal concepts such as property) or to similar structures such as obligatory norms. Hoebel and Llewellyn for example, in their pioneering work of legal anthropology *The Cheyenne Way*, developed a common-law inspired "trouble case method," in which legal principles were constructed from the way the community had resolved disputes in the past, when they were unsuccessful in getting their informants to articulate explicit rules directly[61] Courts in Canada have in the past used a functional equivalent approach, for example, in the cases that take Aboriginal customary marriages and adoptions to have the same status as *de jure* marriages and adoptions for some purposes.[62]

[59] *Ibid* at 20–7.

[60] As William Twining notes, legal pluralist theory has often devolved into conceptual concerns belonging more to the general theory of law or of norms: William Twining, "Normative and Legal Pluralism: A Global Perspective" (2009) 20 *Duke J Comp Intl L* 473 at 479.

[61] K N Llewellyn & E Adamson Hoebel, *The Cheyenne Way: Conflict and Case Law in Primitive Jurisprudence* (Oklahoma: The University of Oklahoma Press, 1941).

[62] See examples cited in Borrows, *supra* note 31 at 6–7.

But the functional approach was problematic for legal pluralists. Although the ethnocentric assumption that the state was the central marker of a legal order might have been rejected, theorists struggled to supply a different criterion for recognising the existence of law[63] – not only did functional categories pose analytical problems (being both under- and over-inclusive with respect to phenomena habitually considered as law), they were also themselves ethnocentric.[64] Taking the West-Coast Gitxsan *yukw* (traditional feast hall) on its face as a dispute resolution institution, for example, reduces the specificity of a Gitxsan form of life to a universal derived from non-Indigenous categories and reifies this one aspect of law. In the more specific example of property, we have already seen the difficulties entailed in looking to Indigenous practices through the lens of exclusive possession as the qualifier of Aboriginal title, and even in the more radical attempt to characterize property in terms of, for instance, trusteeship. However, the issue for our judges is not to parse these (perhaps futile) definitional debates so as to be able to apply criteria for the identification of law – since the jurisprudence calling for regard to "Aboriginal perspectives" is not framed in such limited terms – but rather what it would mean to take Indigenous normativity *as* law, and the need to characterize or translate in doing so, to recognize something *as* something.

To those who suggest that any such translations would necessarily be a form of colonial assimilation, John Borrows points out that all law is a kind of translation process, and that his efforts, for instance, to present Anishnabek stories in the form of case law, are undertaken both to participate in legal conversations and "to remind Canadian law-makers of their reluctance to engage in [those] conversations with First Nations."[65] Further, he claims, the transformations are consistent with the trickster genre of Indigenous story-telling, in which the narrator adapts stories to suit the current context.[66] In stressing law as a "culture

[63] Merry, *supra* note 2; Franz von Benda-Beckmann, *supra* note 3.

[64] See Brian Tamanaha, "The Folly of the 'Social Scientific' Concept of Legal Pluralism" (1993) 20 *J Law Soc* 192 at 194–9.

[65] Borrows, *supra* note 31 at 21. See my argument elsewhere that there are better and worse translations, and that better ones must struggle somehow with the particularities of the Indigenous version, with what is untranslatable: Kirsten Anker, "Translating Sui Generis Aboriginal Rights in the Civilian Imagination" in Alexandra Popovici, Lionel Smith & Régine Tremblay, eds., *Intraduisible en droit civil* (Montreal: Editions Thémis, 2014) at 5–8; Kirsten Anker, *Declarations of Interdependence: A Legal Pluralist Approach to Indigenous Rights* (Farham, Surrey: Ashgate, 2014) at chapter 4.

[66] Borrows, *supra* note 31 at 21.

of argument," Borrows echoes certain solutions to both the analytical problems and ethnocentricity found in the legal theory debates that focus on linguistic practice and convention, and that, I would suggest, run parallel to the constitutive rather than cognitive approaches to recognition we looked at earlier.

As an example of legal pluralism's turn to a discursive approach, Gunther Teubner defines legal pluralism not as a situation of overlapping sets of norms, but a "multiplicity of diverse communicative action that observe social action under the binary code legal/illegal."[67] Legal discourses misread the norms of other discourses to render them sensible in internal terms and this is, in Teubner's autopoietic theory, productive of the distinction between law and "the rest". In Brian Tamanaha's formulation, "[l]aw is whatever people identify and treat through their social practices as 'law'."[68]

Conventional criteria avoid the essentialism problem, but on their own are inadequate to account for certain of law's discursive features. For instance, as Emmanuel Melissaris points out, simple convention combined with indifferent relativism negates the possibility of claiming recognition for, or even communication about, these diverse phenomena as "law," which depends on a commitment to a thin sense of something universally true of "law" at the same time as acknowledging that any specific properties of law spring from a contextual understanding that is true relative to the experience of individuals or communities.[69] Conventional criteria also, on the face of it, do not seem sufficiently nuanced to distinguish between the different ways in which legal language may be used: as a joke, a metaphor or a bald-faced lie. In order to do justice to the many ways in which language both communicates and performs, it seems necessary to subscribe to the fuller sense of legal language as a "culture of argument" or a form of rhetoric in which there is a community of speakers with a background (and often implicit) sensibility toward how to read specific statements or practices via which we could identify the legal.[70]

[67] Gunther Teubner, "The Two Faces of Janus: Rethinking Legal Pluralism" (1992) 13 *Cardozo Rev* 1443 at 1451.

[68] Brian Tamanaha, "A Non-Essentialist Version of Legal Pluralism" (2000) 27:2 *J Law Soc* 296 at 313.

[69] Emmanuel Melissaris, *Ubiquitous Law: Legal Theory and the Space for Legal Pluralism* (Farham, Surrey: Ashgate, 2009) at 50.

[70] See for example, the approach of James Boyd White, "Law as Rhetoric, Rhetoric as Law: The Arts of Cultural and Communal Life" (1985) 52:3 *Univ Chic Law Rev* 684; Marianne Constable, "Law as Language" (2014) 1:1 *Crit Anal Law* 63 at 67–8.

In the Indigenous context, linguistic translation per se is an issue in the conventional approach. Where communities themselves start to articulate their lifeworlds using the English language of law (mostly in response to the need to make cognizable claims), we might see an "emergence" of the legal in the conventional sense. Where they do not, Tamanaha also suggests that the conventional principle applies to whatever word is used by actors to designate state law in their context.[71] But an approach more consistent with the richer idea of law as a culture of argument would be that of interpretive anthropology, which would have us engage in a cross-cultural hermeneutical exercise. As advocated by anthropologist Clifford Geertz, the comparativist would start with an Indigenous term, not to identify an equivalent of "law," but as a way of unraveling what is distinctive about the legal sensibility of the Indigenous speakers. In the back-and-forth process of interpretation, we come to a new understanding of our own law in contrast.[72] Similarly, Melissaris's view of the possibility of recognition or communication about law is that our context-bound "thick" commitments should be open to being falsified or altered through dialog with other normatively committed agents, leading to a process reminiscent of Taylor's fusion of horizons.[73] Taking communicative actions, convention and dialog as the site for identifying the legal highlights law as process rather than thing, and legal processes as responsive to context and to interactions with others, making legal pluralist interactions constitutive ones in these theories.

However, in asking whether judges can engage in a fusion of horizons or a constitutive dialogue, we confront something particular about their role within the apparatus of the state, the orthodox understanding of law that endows their legal speech with legitimacy within that apparatus, and the set of recognition problems related to power.[74] This question of the role of judges in legal pluralism speaks to the distinction in legal pluralist literature between juristic and sociological or discursive legal pluralism. The typical strategies for state recognition – such as translation,

[71] Brian Tamanaha, *A General Jurisprudence of Law and Society* (New York: Oxford University Press, 2001) at 203.

[72] Clifford Geertz, *Local Knowledge: Further Essays in Interpretive Anthropology* (New York: Basic Books, 1983) at 181–3.

[73] Melissaris, *supra* note 69 at 33.

[74] Although the possibility for, and particular shape of, cross-cultural theorizing of Aboriginal rights is considered in detail by Newman, *supra* note 39, he does not consider the particularity of the role of judges as opposed to academics such as political theorists.

accommodation, deference, incorporation or delegation[75] – are labeled juristic or "weak" legal pluralism by anthropologist John Griffiths, because ultimately these arrangements do not challenge the supposition – driven by the ideological interests of the state in maintaining supremacy – that all law is the law of the state, unified into a single system.[76] From the state's perspective, non-state law in these strategies is either taken as "fact," or becomes law only once attached and subordinated to state law.[77]

If that is the case, then is it *ever* possible for "strong" pluralist situations – in which there is a radically "other" law, a distinct jurisdiction – to be recognized by the state? One answer could be yes, given that states apparently do this all the time in applying the law of foreign states under choice of law or private international law rules. In these cases, judges are external observers of foreign law akin to social scientists, and yet, in applying the foreign law, they attempt to take on the perspective of a participant in that legal system.[78] Sébastien Grammond makes this analogy in arguing for the reception of Indigenous law by the Canadian state, arguing that the difference between reception and, say, delegation (the powers accorded to band councils under s.81 of the Indian Act being a prime example), lies in whether Indigenous law is subordinated to state law or not in the process.[79] Similarly, Ralf Michaels probes the possibilities of using choice of law principles to recognize non-state law, but

[75] These refer to the following strategies: taking customary arrangements as functional equivalents of legal relationships (such as in marriage or adoption, or taking physical occupation as the basis for title) [translation], taking customary law as part of the factual context relevant to determining, for instance, appropriate sentencing or "reasonableness" [accommodation], granting a measure of autonomy or non-interference (such as with freedom of religion) within the basic structure of state law [deference], embodying particular norms as part of the general law applicable by courts either by codification or open reference [incorporation], or permitting the self-regulating activities of groups, such as via contractual agreements, to be enforced via the mandate of the state [delegation]. See Australian Law Reform Commission, *The Recognition of Aboriginal Customary Laws*, ALRC Report no.31 (1986) at 199–208; Ralf Michaels, "The Re-State-Ment of Non-State Law: The State, Choice of Law, and the Challenge from Global Legal Pluralism" (2005) 51 *Wayne Rev* 1209 at 1231–5.

[76] John Griffiths, "What is Legal Pluralism?" (1986) 24 *J Leg Plur Unoff Law* 1 at 5.

[77] Michaels, *supra* note 75 at 1235.

[78] Recalling the ethnographic aspiration to the "native's point of view" in Bronislaw Malinowski, *Argonauts of the Western Pacific: An Account of Native Enterprise and Adventure in the Archipelagoes of Melanesian New Guinea* (New York: EP Dutton, 1961) at 25.

[79] Sébastien Grammond, "L'appartenance aux communautés inuit du Nunavik: Un cas de réception de l'ordre juridique inuit?" (2008) 23:1–2 *Can J Law Soc* 93 at 98.

concludes that states are only persuaded of the comity of applying the law of other *states* because of the "collective interest [of states] in maintaining their cartel of law-making,"[80] mutually recognizing each other's monopoly in certain cases, and thus the role that states assume as the transcendent deciders of conflicts between societal factions. Presuming that the persuasive hurdle has been, or could be, cleared in the special case of Indigenous law, one factor in the distinction then is whether the state claims a transcendent role with respect to Indigenous norms, or whether, as in private international law, recognition is a mutual and reciprocal process.

Let us look at some examples that could be taken as instances of the reception of Indigenous law, in that they consider normative or discursive materials (aspects of a culture of argument) as part of the standards for making decisions. In *Mitchell* v *MNR* – one of the few Canadian decisions to consider what might be thought of as a substantive principle of Indigenous law – the Mohawks of Akwesasne claimed a right to take goods across the border free of customs tariffs derived from a fundamental historic relationship of non-interference between Aboriginal and non-Aboriginal peoples.[81] In his minority judgment, Justice Binnie refers to the fact that, "in the Mohawk tradition this relationship is memorialized by the 'two row wampum'" [para. 127] and proceeds to work with the imagery of the two parallel paths of the European ship and the Aboriginal canoe in the Wampum[82] in order to articulate a contemporary principle guiding the relationship between Haudenosaunee and the Canadian Crown. Binnie J nevertheless goes on to state that the "modern embodiment of the 'two-row' wampum concept, modified to reflect some of the realities of a modern state, is the idea of a 'merged' or 'shared' sovereignty" in which the metaphor is a single ship made up of different elements of wood, iron and canvas.[83] Consequently, according to Binnie J, Mitchell's claim could not then be based solely in his Haudenosaunee citizenship, as he is also part of a collective Canadian sovereignty, one which has a paramount interest in areas such as border control and military defense.[84]

[80] Michaels, *supra* note 75 at 1243. [81] *Mitchell* v *MNR*, *supra* note 9.

[82] For an explanation, see Wilbur Jacobs, "Wampum: The Protocol of Indian Diplomacy" (1949) 6:4 *William Mary Q* 596; John Borrows, "Wampum at Niagara: The Royal Proclamation, Canadian Legal History, and Self-Government" in Michael Asch, ed., *Aboriginal and Treaty Rights in Canada: Essays on Law, Equality and Respect for Difference* (Vancouver: UBC Press, 1997) 155.

[83] *Mitchell* v *MNR*, *supra* note 9, at 129–30. [84] *Ibid* at 136, 160 & 164.

As Gordon Christie comments, Binnie J here effectively rewrites the Two-row Wampum, legitimating his unilateral act with reference to "reality" and perhaps the implicit consent of Mohawks.[85] Binnie J's reading seeks, in both form and substance, to achieve a transcendent, neutral position for the state in contravention of the original agreement represented by the Wampum, and in the face of a long history of resistance by Haudenosaunee to colonial attempts to override the agreement, and of explicit expressions of their non-consent to merged sovereignty. In this rare example of the use of an Indigenous legal source in a discursive way to contribute to the development of Canadian jurisprudence, the Court flagrantly ignores Indigenous interpretations in favor of exercising unilateral power to rewrite the significance of that source.

A stronger form of recognition, one that includes the power to decide on the interpretation and application of Indigenous law, lies in the eligibility requirements under the James Bay and Northern Quebec Agreement, discussed by Grammond as an example of reception, one criteria of which is to be Inuk "as determined in accordance with Inuit customs and traditions."[86] Grammond notes that, on paper at least, this appears to be a strongly-pluralist recognition (what he terms "extra-state" legal pluralism) in which the Canadian legal order removes itself entirely from the question of the status of beneficiaries.[87] Nevertheless, as part of the political process of negotiating the inclusion of this provision, the Inuit had to convince the government that they would not "abusively" extend the list of beneficiaries so as to increase the financial burden on the government or discriminate on the basis of gender, and developed tentative criteria for that purpose that effectively codified Inuit tradition on identity.[88] Other provisions in the Agreement establish Western-style mechanisms of due process and democratic accountability in decision-making, even as it was agreed that decisions would be made by committees of local Inuit people.[89] Further, the Agreement leaves open the possibility for recourse to the courts and thereby for a final decision on whether the criteria are compatible with the Canadian Charter of Rights and Freedoms.[90] Grammond concludes by questioning

[85] Gordon Christie, "The Court's Exercise of Plenary Power: Rewriting the Two-Row Wampum" (2002) 16 *Supreme Court Law Rev* 285.

[86] *James Bay and Northern Quebec Agreement, Complementary Agreement No.18* at 3A.3.

[87] Grammond, *supra* note 79 at 114. [88] *Ibid* at 114–15. [89] *Ibid* at 116.

[90] *Ibid* at 117.

whether, in these terms, there is such a difference between the constraints surrounding delegations of authority and the "renvoi" to an autonomous legal order that appears in the James Bay Agreement: to win recognition, the Inuit had to express the content of their law as positive (and Charter conforming) rules and adopt an administrative-style decision-making process, with the political negotiators of the Federal Government acting as *a priori* judges of their suitability.[91]

Justin Richland's chapter in this volume shows even more clearly how it is that the form of recognition, even in some of the "strongest" versions of state-sponsored legal pluralism, guts non-state orders of their normativity. The Hopi courts he describes were set up under the Hopi Constitution – a product of recognition by the United States of Aboriginal tribes as "domestic dependent nations" with inherent self-governing authority remaining in certain areas of jurisdiction – and are staffed by a mix of Hopi and Anglo-American personnel. The Court is mandated to "give more weight as precedent to the . . . customs, traditions and culture of the Hopi tribe" in matters of both procedure and substance. However, the procedural structure laid out – basically that of an adversarial court – is Anglo-American in style.[92] As described in his chapter, the formal structure, in which the (Hopi) judge questions Hopi witnesses so as to establish the local tradition that the judge will apply to the facts of the case, finds "law" (that of the Court) hedging out other authoritative discourses that might be attempting the parallel task of connecting facts to norms. In the chapter's detailed example, a judge succeeds in drawing out a statement of a generalized principle of succession (accomplished via linguistic forms that combine the infinitive (what one does) and the habitual verb form (what has always been done)).[93] However, the process is immediately resisted by witnesses who wish to speak in the specifics of the here and now (by offering their opinion as to the results of the case), and thus to perform their tradition instead of offering up knowledge of it.[94] This is a contest between law as a set of inert facts and law as the exercise of jurisdiction, the authority to speak the law; it is the contrast between law as a product and law as a process.

[91] *Ibid* at 118.

[92] Justin B Richland, *Arguing With Tradition: The Language of Law in Hopi Tribal Court* (Chicago: University of Chicago Press, 2008) at 47–50.

[93] Justin Richland, "On Perpetuity: Tradition, Law, and the Pluralism of Hopi Jurisprudence" in this volume (Chapter 6).

[94] Ibid.

Is it thus inevitable, as one intervener in the Centaur Jurisprudence conference discussion suggested, that any given legal order tries to turn other law into fact, because all law is a claim to exclusive normative authority in its domain? While the "choice of law" example seems to show that where there is a political incentive to do so, it is theoretically possible to hold at once a perspective from inside our own order and to apply another law as if we were a participant in a different order, and thus to treat it as law, it may well only be practically possible where there is structural parity as well as political parity. That is, the foreign law, being the law of another state, issues from of a similar system of legislation, adjudication and enforcement, as well as being characterized as the positive, objectified rules produced by that system – something that can be applied by another person in another time and place. For all the contrasts between internal and external perspectives, and between juristic and sociological legal pluralism, the positive lawyer shares a similar "factual" or cognitive gaze with the empirical social scientist. The above three examples suggest that it is as much this gaze as it is the ideology of state legal monopoly that is responsible for the problems of recognition of Indigenous law.

5.5 Conclusion

In discussing the way that the labels "weak" and "strong" legal pluralism express a clear preference for the sociological approach to law in which it is freed from the dominant ideology of the state, Sherman Jackson observes that the objective of much sociological and anthropological writing on non-state law nevertheless seems to be to gain some form of state recognition "as the sine qua non of any truly meaningful legal pluralism."[95] This is certainly true of those critics of Aboriginal rights jurisprudence who would have courts and the Canadian state take Indigenous law, and law-making, seriously. And yet it often seems that the very act of recognition turns Indigenous law, in that context, into a fact. This may be merely a clash of participant perspectives because the sense in which Indigenous law is normative for its practitioners cannot be experienced by agents of state law other than as an empirical fact: if not the degree of cultural difference alone, then the state's own self-definition as the centralized source of legal authority may preclude it

[95] Sherman Jackson, "Legal Pluralism between Islam and the Nation-State: Romantic Medievalism or Pragmatic Modernity" (2006) 30 *Fordham LJ* 158 at 161.

being otherwise. However, if translation across cultures is possible and the main risks – the problems of ethnocentricity and assimilation discussed in Part II – can be assuaged by a dialogic approach to recognition, it remains to be seen whether the state's claim to monopolize legitimate legal authority makes it impossible to realize a centaur discipline as an approach to formal legal decision making. The problem of power and pathological recognition seems endemic to the concept of state law.

What our excursion into the critical politics of recognition helps us see is that both sets of problems are symptoms of an aspiration to exercise a certain form of sovereignty. Following Markell, I have argued that the pursuit of sovereignty in the sense of mastery, authoritative agency or self-determination is misguided – or maintained as an illusion at someone else's expense – given the human condition of finitude or the "constitutive vulnerability to the unpredictable reactions and responses of others."[96] First, the urge to identify, map or render Indigenous cultures and laws legible and knowable, and to make Indigenous parties bear the burden of proof, is a product of this aspiration. Second, although the state purports either to pre-exist or transcend the struggles between its constituent subjects, it too emerges from exchanges of recognition, from a constant process of differentiation between it and civil society; conversely, 'the people' whom it represents are defined and reproduced through citizenship and other laws. As Markell argues, although it typically commands more social and political resources than other entities, the state is "both a participant in and an artifact of the politics of recognition."[97] The state's claim to monopoly, and the law's claim to determinacy, are just that – a claim.

One possible response to the critical politics of recognition for Aboriginal rights is to insist that the state cannot assume its own stable identity or the juridical bases of its claim to sovereignty, to land and to its resources. Indeed, this is the thrust of the work of Indigenous scholars like John Borrows and Sákéj Henderson who seek continually to turn the questions asked by courts of Aboriginal petitioners back on the state or on the non-Aboriginal majority. What is the core of your cultural distinctiveness? Where do you get your right to harvest timber? This shift goes hand in hand with one that changes the justice issue from one of getting better or more recognition – a better map of Indigenous law or culture – to one of asking where the burdens of the state's simulation of

[96] Markell, *supra* note 5 at 36. [97] *Ibid* at 28.

6

On Perpetuity

Tradition, Law and the Pluralism of Hopi Jurisprudence

JUSTIN B. RICHLAND*

6.1 Introduction

In November 1999, the Hopi Appellate Court, the highest court with jurisdiction to resolve civil disputes on the Hopi Indian Reservation, heard arguments in a case involving a conflict between a woman and her sister's daughters over a plot of farming land in one of its nine mesa-top villages.[1] At trial, the woman had argued that, following village customs and traditions, her father had given her the land through an oral bequest prior to passing away in the 1950s. Her nieces argued that even if this were true, given that the woman had married outside the tribe and resided off the reservation for the last forty years, custom and tradition mandate that she lose whatever rights to the land she may have

* This chapter has been read and commented on by a number of colleagues, most of whom I would also call close friends. I especially wish to thank Hussin Agrama Iza Hussin, Susan Gal Bill Maurer, Elizabeth Mertz, Jothie Raja, ,Michael Silverstein, Kaushik Sunder Rajan , Susan Coutin. The research and write-up of this chapter was supported by a grant from the National Science Foundation's Law and Social Science and Cultural Anthropology Programs, Award Number # 1061063, Co-PI, with Susan Coutin). In addition, smaller grants from the University of Chicago Department of Anthropology's Lichtstern Fund for supporting the research assistance and write-up time associated with this chapter. Early iterations of this chapter have been presented at several conferences and workshops over the past two years, including the 2012 Annual Meeting of the Law and Society Association, in Honolulu, HI June 2012, the American Bar Foundation Seminar Series, Chicago, IL November 2012, and the Centaur Jurisprudence Conference, McGill Centre for Human Rights and Legal Pluralism, Montréal, CA February 2014. To those who planned and organized these events, I am also deeply indebted.

Finally, let me note that this chapter builds on and elaborates the arguments I make in a previously published work of mine, Justin B. Richland "Perpetuities Against Rules: Law, Ethnography, and the Measuring of Lives" (2012) 8 *Law Culture, and the Humanities* 3, 433–47, and "Jurisdiction: Grounding Law in Language" (2013) 42 *Annual Review of Anthropology* 209–29. The three should be read in conjunction with each other.

[1] *Smith* v *James*, 1999.

inherited from her father. The Hopi trial judge ultimately found in favor of the nieces, and their aunt, through her non-Hopi attorney, appealed.[2]

Among the issues the Appellate court was to address was whether or not the Hopi trial judge who originally heard the case at the trial level had acted properly in allowing the parties to call elder witnesses to testify at a special hearing about their village's traditions concerning property and inheritance.[3] In coming to its decision, the court first congratulated the trial judge – a Hopi man from another village – for taking testimony from village elders on questions of tradition, stating that he had acted "wonderfully in the absence of guidelines for conducting such a hearing."[4] At the same time, the Appellate Court expressed concern that because the hearing on the facts of the dispute was held *before* the Court took testimony from the elders, the parties could not know at the time they presented evidence what kinds of factual proof would be relevant and sufficient to meet the legal standards required by village tradition. In the end, the Court found this procedural error fatal to the lower court's decision and remanded the case for a rehearing.[5]

The Appellate Court would later go on in its decision to announce guidelines for future hearings on custom and tradition. These guidelines drew largely on the testimonial format used by the Hopi judge in the original trial. In so doing, they filled in procedural gaps that had made it difficult for trial judges to follow Hopi Tribal legislation that, since 1976, mandated the court to give greater precedential weight to Hopi custom and tradition than to Anglo-American principles of inheritance and property law.[6]

But the parties appearing in court that day in 1999 were clearly frustrated when they heard that their case was going to have to be retried. Several gasps were audible to those of us sitting in the back of the

[2] *Joyce James, et al* v *Ruth Smith*, 1998. [3] *Smith* v *James*, *supra* note 2 at 2. [4] *Ibid.*

[5] *Ibid* at 7.

[6] Resolution, Hopi Tribe H-12–76, § 2. In relevant part, it reads:

(a) "The courts in deciding matters of both substance and procedure, shall look to and give weight to: (1) The Hopi Constitution and Bylaws; (2) the ordinances of the Tribe; (3) the resolutions of the Tribe; (4) the customs, traditions and culture of the Tribe; (5) the laws, rules and regulations of the federal government and the cases interpreting them; (6) the laws and rules of the state of Arizona and the cases interpreting them; and (7) the common law."

(b) "The Courts of the Hopi Tribe shall not recognize nor apply any federal, state, or common law rule or procedure which is inconsistent with either the spirit or the letter of the Hopi Constitution, ordinances, resolutions, or the customs, traditions, or culture of the Hopi Tribe."

court. One of the three nieces screamed, "No!" after the Hopi Justices announced their decision while another turned to the audience as she loudly exclaimed to no-one and everyone, "That's not right!" All were noticeably shaken as they left the courtroom. To this day, the parties have not returned to re-hear the case, the property remains unused, and perhaps most significantly, the nieces still do not talk to their aunt, their "clan mother" who would otherwise carry much influence with them.

While the nieces' sudden outburst might be explained as frustration at having to return, yet again, to the lower court, I am not inclined to understand their objections in quite this way. Long and bitter disputes over property inheritance, sometimes spanning generations, are nothing new to Hopi people – indeed, as I shall argue later, nothing new to Anglo-American law either. And while the dispute in question here had already been in the Hopi legal system for nearly two years when it was remanded, the parties both testified that they had been fighting over the property for nearly three decades before ever coming to court.[7]

This case is actually one the first of a series of six inheritance disputes that came before the Hopi Appellate Court between 1994 and 2003.[8] The decisions rendered by the Appellate Court in these cases would together result in the most significant refinements of Hopi legal procedure and expansion of tribal court authority since the court was first created in 1972. In each one of these cases, both sides argue that their village customs and traditions support their claims to the disputed property. The legal procedures announced in the case described above were thus all designed to take better measure of custom and tradition as raised by the parties. And yet, despite these efforts, none of the underlying disputes in any of these six cases reached final resolution through the Hopi legal system.[9]

[7] *Ibid.*

[8] *In The Matter of the Estate of Neomi Komaquaptewa*, 2002 Hopi Appellate Court; *Nutongla-Sanchez* v *Garcia et al*, 1999 Hopi Appellate Court; *Smith* v. *James*, *supra* note 2; *Honie* v *Hopi Tribal Housing Authority*, 1998 Hopi Appellate Court; *Coin* v *Mowa*, 1996 Hopie Appellate Court; *Ross* v *Sulu*, 1991 Hopi Appellate Court. All cases can be found at: www.hopicourts.com/index.php?option=com_docman&Itemid=50&group=13 (accessed October 16, 2010).

[9] One of these *cases* did reach a final determination in Hopi Tribal Court, *Honie* v *Hopi Tribal Housing Authority*, *supra* note 8. But it is not at all clear that the underlying dispute has ever been resolved. Indeed, the *Honie* case achieved a final determination only because it was deemed to have already been adjudicated by a traditional leader before the matter was filed in Hopi court. Thus, when the case finally came to hearing at the Appellate Level, the lower court's decision was overturned for reasons of *res judicata*.

What I suggest so vexed these nieces, and so vexes all the Hopi court's efforts to adjudicate inheritance disputes more generally, is its introduction of additional layers of Anglo-style legal procedure to determining matters of custom and tradition. This case is thus representative of a larger trend evident in Hopi tribal cases since the mid 1990s, one that results from a turn to increased procedural formalism in Hopi jurisprudence since that time. This turn, as I have argued elsewhere, grows directly from the ways in which the legitimacy of tribal legal practice and power is constituted by actors navigating between the long reach of U.S. colonial oversight and the demands of a tribal cultural sovereignty that calls for a "return" to indigenous "traditions" as a source of tribal law.[10]

In this chapter, I will suggest that the litigants' response here is an example of the regular and recurrent interactional effects of these competing legitimacy demands as they alight in the discourses of tradition in Hopi court. More specifically I argue that these demands shape how tradition gets formulated by Hopi tribal court actors – namely judges and Anglo-law trained attorneys – as either *statements of law* or *evidence of fact* in a way that is legible to and in service of the Anglo-style legal authority of the Hopi court, but which is illegible, and illegitimate, to the Hopi parties' and witnesses' understanding of tradition.

The English word "tradition" or the concept of "traditional knowledge" is translated by Hopi as *navoti* (a nominalization of the verb *navota* "to hear").[11] As a genre of speech, *navoti* is a form of discourse characterized by the recurrent, clause by clause occurrence of reported speech markers, either the Hopi quotative particle *yaw* ("it is said"), Hopi verbs of speaking such as *kita, pangkawu, pang akw* (which roughly translate as "says," "tells," "tells to [one]") or their English equivalents. These forms, particularly when they co-occur with indefinite subject forms and verbs inflected with the habitual tense affix – *ngwu*, constitute the speech event in which they occur as both pointing to and constituting an act of Hopi ceremonial authority. And in the theocratic style of esoteric political authority that defines all traditional pueblo governance

[10] Justin B Richland, "'What Are You Going to Do with the Village's Knowledge?' Talking Tradition, Talking Law in Hopi Tribal Court" (2005) 39*Law and Society Review* 235–271; Justin B Richland, "The Multiple Calculi of Meaning" (2006) 17:1 *Discourse & Society* 65–97; Justin B Richland, "Pragmatic Paradoxes and Ironies of Indigeneity" (2007) 34:3 *American Ethnologist* 540–558.

[11] Peter Whiteley, *Rethinking Hopi Ethnography* (Washington, DC: Smithsonian Institution Press Washington DC, 1998).

But, just as much as it forges certain kinds of connections between facts and norms by linking them to other facts and norms across time–space, the pragmatics of law also does the work of rupturing or foreclosing other such connections.[20] It is this rupturing that I am concerned within this chapter. I argue that it is precisely when law is confronted with other interpretive genres whose power is also generated by working the time–space immanent in and transcending facts and norms, is-ness and ought-ness, that the smooth veneer of legal authority comes under threat. One such threat is posed by the discourses of Hopi tradition, especially when raised in property and inheritance disputes in the Anglo-style court of the Hopi tribal nation in Arizona.

It is when the perpetuity of Anglo-law and the perpetuity of Hopi tradition confront each other, I argue, that the trial proceedings in these inheritance disputes begin to falter. For when Hopi judges and lawyers attempt to formulate tradition as either akin to the citations to precedent that characterize Anglo-style law or as the reports of prior statements of speech equivalent to the suspect evidence called "hearsay," they in effect foreclose the mediative ground that tradition can claim between facts and norms, sundering the claims to tradition's normative transcendence from their immanence in the facts at hand. As such, their acts are understood by litigants and witnesses as attempts not just to appropriate Hopi traditional authority, but to undermine it as well. Indeed, as I will show, at every turn these efforts are challenged by Hopi litigants and witnesses called to testify. The result, I suggest, is a kind of legitimation crisis in the fullest sense – that is, a crisis of law-making – that emerges in Hopi court precisely because the perpetuities of Hopi tradition and Anglo-style law are understood as mutually excluding each other – each defying the ways in which norm and fact are brought together in the pragmatics of the other's perpetuity.

As such, my arguments very much align with the insights of comparative legal scholar, H. Patrick Glenn in revealing that for both law and tradition, there emerges a "necessity . . . [in] having been continuously transmitted, in a particular social context."[21] Indeed, the concept of perpetuity that I put forward here owes much to Glenn's arguments that legal traditions are recognizable precisely in the ways they are each committed to their own continuity – a continuity best described as

[20] *See, e.g.*, Robert M Cover, "Foreword: Nomos and Narrative" (1983) 97 *Harv Rev* 4–66.

[21] H. Patrick Glenn, *Legal Traditions of the World : Sustainable Diversity in Law*, 4th edn. (London: Oxford University Press, 2014) at 13.

capturing the utility of tradition as a rhetoric that sutures the changing circumstances of the present and an uncertain future to the timeless rhetoric of the past that gives it coherence. Where the claims of this chapter differ, however, is in suggesting that it is precisely these parallels that, at least in the context of the pluralistic demands of Hopi jurisprudence, form the site for conflict and contestation, rather than reconciliation between the normative commitments of Anglo-American style legal discourse, and those of Hopi custom and tradition. Use of the term "perpetuity" to describe this contestation as a constitutive element of law and legal discourse itself. It is meant to foreground this site of contestation, operative in the ways that law, from within its own logics, can be seen to generate authority precisely by holding the middle ground between facts and law to the exclusion of other discourses that would also claim such ground. In the Hopi court context, we could thus say that Hopi tradition and Anglo-style law, are to themselves the exclusive engines of legitimacy, and to the other, the most proximate threat of illegitimacy. It is the tension between the two, as it is worked out in the adjudication of disputes before the Hopi tribal court, that can be said to be the productive problem of contemporary Hopi jurisprudence.

Before turning to the data, I would like to make two points about this concept of perpetuity and its relation to two more common notions of Anglo-American jurisprudence, citation and jurisdiction.

First, in introducing the concept of law's perpetuity, I am speaking of something that is certainly related to, but nonetheless distinct from, the role that citationality plays in law. Of course, citing to precedent is key to the ways in which law is textually and discursively perpetuated across space and time. But in introducing the concept of perpetuity, I am precisely interested in the ways in which discourses of law, and in the Hopi case, tradition, not only cite to prior instances of their expression, but collapse the spatio-temporal distance between the past, present, and future, figuring law as a kind of time–space envelope that transcends all three, even as it binds norms to facts by finding them immanent in the materials of the case at hand. Citationality, as a theory that foregrounds the transmission of discourse through chains of quotation can point either to law's transcendence or its immanence,[22] but it cannot

[22] For theories of citationality, *see* Jacques Derrida, *Limited Inc*, Gerald Graff, ed. (Evanston, IL: Northwestern University Press, 1988); Judith Butler, *Gender Trouble* (London and New York: Routledge, 1990).

foreground both simultaneously in the way I hope to imply through the concept of perpetuity.

Secondly, to the extent that I will argue that the "perpetuities" of law and tradition work discursively to exclude each other in Hopi law, I want to also argue that the concept of "perpetuity" more generally fleshes out how I have come to understand recent re-thinkings of jurisdiction as *juris-diction* (derived from combining the latin forms *iuris* and *dicta*, to form a double genitive meaning simultaneously "law's speech/speaking of the law"[23]) as the ways in which the scope of law's power and authority are announced and delimited in the everyday details of legal discourse.[24] In so doing, I build upon the work of law and humanities scholars like Costas Douzinas, Shaun McVeigh, Bradin Cormack and others who suggest that it is precisely in jurisdictional questions that one can observe governmental institutions in their law-making, -applying, and -executing capacities, posing the question of their own authority to themselves.[25] More importantly, it is in those moments of jurisdiction – such as preambles of constitutions or when litigants ask after a court's authority to hear their case – that the law at once assumes its power to decide generally (that is, that the law is that legitimate adjudicatory power of the state over something) but at the same time asks after the particular limits of that power as it may apply to the case at hand, and then elides the fact that in asking it is announcing that power anew. The net effect of this juris-diction is to convert difficult questions regarding the ultimate sources of legal power and authority into much easier questions of its practical scope and distribution. As Bradin Cormack writes, "[j]urisdiction obliquely encounters the impossibility of grounding the juridical norm by remolding the problem and projecting it onto the manageable … axis of competence or scope."[26] And in this sense, it

[23] Emile Benveniste, "Indo-European Language and Society" in L R Palmer & G C Lepschy, eds., *Studies in General Linguistics* (London: Faber Faber, 1969).

[24] Justin B Richland, "Jurisdiction: Grounding Law in Language" (2013) 42 *Annu Rev Anthropol* 209; Justin B Richland, "Hopi Tradition as Jurisdiction: On the Potentializing Limits of Hopi Sovereignty" (2011) 36:1 *Law Soc Inq* 201.

[25] Bradin *A Power to Do Justice. Jurisdiction, English Literature, and the Rise of Common Law, 1509–1625* (Chicago: University of Chicago Press, 2008); Shaun McVeigh, ed., *Jurisprudence of Jurisdiction* (New York: Routledge Cavendish Press, 2007); Costas Douzinas, "The Metaphysics of Jurisdiction" in McVeigh, Ibid at 21–32; Richard T Ford, "Law's Territory (A History of Jurisdiction)" (1999) 97:4 *Mich Law Rev* 843.

[26] Cormack, Ibid at 8.

takes those more troubling questions out of discursive circulation. It is through jurisdiction that "the law functions by keeping the source of its authority in fixed view as, insistently, the merely technical (and for that reason discursively unassailable) . . . ."[27]

What I argue for in this chapter is that juris-diction is accomplished in and through the quality of legal discourse as perpetuity. It is in the linking up of facts and norms of a present dispute to those of prior and as-yet-to come cases, and the binding of facticity and normativity that is thereby accomplished, that legal power is at once created in, but figured as already preexisting and thus authorizing (that is as at once immanent in and transcendent of) the pragmatics of everyday legal speech. It is a collapsing of what Walter Benjamin described as law's two modes – the constitutive (or law-making) and the perpetutive (law-preserving) – and in so doing, foregrounding the latter while presupposing the former.[28] As Costas Douzinas writes, "[e]very trial explicitly or implicitly addresses the power of the court to judge . . . every judgment is the violence at law's inception, the original performative *dictio*."[29]

What is so suggestive in the Hopi courtroom discourses I analyze here is the conflict that emerges when the perpetuity of Anglo-style legal jurisdiction is confronted by the perpetuity of Hopi tradition as jurisdiction – especially in Hopi property disputes where both are being invoked by differently situated Hopi actors – judges, lawyers, litigants and elders, to authoritatively claim the exclusive right to hold the mediative ground between facts and norms. In this sense the perpetuity of law, and the perpetuity of tradition struggle both in and as jurisdiction over the unstable ground of Hopi property disputes. And as we shall see, neither can fully carry the day. Hopi law is revealed as a jurisdiction caught between jurisdictions, and thereby held in suspense. Contemporary Hopi law might thus be said to be caught up in a crisis of perpetuities against rules.

To show how this unfolds, I will turn to an analysis of the courtroom discourses in which such matters unfold in the realtime interaction between Hopi judges, witnesses, litigants and lay and professional advocates.

[27] *Ibid* at 7.

[28] Walter Benjamin, "Critique of Violence" in Peter Demetz, ed., *Walter Benjamin Reflect Essays Aphorisms Autobiographical Writ* (New York: Schocken Books, 1978) at 277–300.

[29] Costas Douzinas, *supra* note 25 at 28.

6.2 Hopi Tribal Court: Arguing with Tradition

Approximately 6,600 Hopi tribal members reside on the Hopi reservation,[30] which occupies 1.5 million acres of aboriginal Hopi lands in northeastern Arizona. These residents occupy twelve villages located on or around three mesas which before the 1930s operated under autonomous village leadership.[31] In 1936, and pursuant to the Indian Reorganization Act,[32] these autonomous villages federated into a Hopi Tribe to be governed by a representative Tribal Council. The Hopi Constitution also includes an explicit reservation of power to village leadership, giving them regulatory and adjudicatory power over intravillage matters, including addressing family and property disputes.

Tribal governance was elaborated again in 1972 with the creation of the Hopi Judiciary, one that is largely Anglo-Adversarial in its processes and procedures. At the same time, tribal legislation and case law require the Hopi court to give a preferential place to Hopi customs, traditions, and culture. In Resolution H-12–76, the Hopi Tribal Council mandated that "in deciding matters of both substance and procedure," the Tribal Court give more "weight as precedent to the . . . customs, traditions and culture of the Hopi Tribe" than to U.S. state and federal law.[33]

These customs, traditions, and cultures are largely understood by Hopi as pointing to and enacting the norms, practices, and institutions related, either directly or indirectly, to the clan traditions and ceremonies that animate ritual life in the several Hopi villages. Both before and after 1936, the idealized image that Hopis have of village organization sees them as constituted of several matrilineal, matrifocal, exogamous groups they call *ngyam* or clans.[34] Each clan has its own origin story which describes the migration of ancestors to their current residence and their original

[30] United States Census, *American Indian and Alaska Native Summary File (AIANSF)* (2000).

[31] Frederick R Eggan, *Social Organization of the Western Pueblos.* (Chicago: University of Chicago Press, 1950); Richard O Clemmer, *Roads in the Sky: The Hopi Indians in a Century of Change* (Boulder, CO: Westview Press Boulder, 1995).

[32] *Indian Reorganization Act of 1934 (Wheeler-Howard Act)* [*Indian Reorganization Act of 1934 (Wheeler-Howard Act)*] at ss. 461–79.

[33] *Resolution H-12-76*, 1976 Hopi Tribe (copy on file with the Hopi Tribal Court)

[34] Peter M Whiteley, *The Orayvi Split: A Hopi Transformation* (New York: American Museum of Natural History, 2008). *See also*, Eggan, *supra* note 28; Mischa Titiev, *Old Oraibi: A Study of the Hopi Indians of Third Mesa*, Harvard University Peabody Museum of American Archaeology and Ethnology Papers (Cambridge, MA: Harvard University Press, 1944).

admission to the village community, admission which was premised on their performance of rituals efficacious for bringing rain. It was in exchange for performing those rituals, pursuant to each clans' esoteric traditional knowledge, that clans were first given land to farm. It is also those ceremonies that constitute the ritual cycle performed every year, a performance that is generally understood as (re)instantiating this originary moment and the social charter it created among the village clans every year.

It is in part the significance of this ritual cycle as at once an icon and enactment of Hopi village sociality that helps explain the Hopi commitment to the now well-described pattern of Pueblo ceremonial and cultural "conservatism," in which the felicitous execution of ritual activity "comes only from letter-perfect attention to detail and correct performance, . . . [with] emphasis on formulas, ritual, and repetition. . . ."[35] Letter perfect performance of its ritual obligations is how the component clan and ritual sodalities perpetually (re)make their community. This also helps explain why it is access to, and possession of, the traditional knowledge that informs these performances that serve as a key source of social power among Hopi. As Peter Whiteley explains, "one of the most distinguished terms for a man is *navoti'ytaqa,* 'a man of knowledge.'"[36] It is because of this, he argues, that for Hopi "ritual knowledge is a 'strategic resource'"[37] serving as "the 'currency,' perhaps, of power."[38] At Hopi then, tradition is at once the stuff of social power and an index of its perpetuity.

Hopi people generally agree that clans are the corporate holders of land, ceremonial homes, ceremonial power and its corresponding offices of ritual authority, and that these symbolic and material resources were bestowed upon them because of their proper performance and commitment to a "traditional" Hopi way of life. It is therefore not surprising that discourses of tradition, who legitimately knows it, and what it provides for, are a regular and recurrent feature of the legal texts and courtroom interactions that constitute Hopi property disputes.

6.3 The Perpetuities of Tradition in Hopi Tribal Court

In the over ninety hours of courtroom interaction I observed, discourses invoking notions of traditional knowledge, who can express it and how, are a recurrent feature of both the written texts and oral arguments proffered by litigants, witnesses, lawyers and judges in Hopi property

[35] Ortiz, *supra* note 12 at 143. [36] Whiteley, *supra* note 11 at 94. [37] *Ibid* at 71.
[38] *Ibid* at 74.

disputes. Qualitatively, the instances of tradition talk that emerge in Hopi courtroom interactions reveal a wide diversity of form, content, and distribution of speaking rights. And as shown in Figure 1.) below, many of these instances appear to us as articulating normative principles of behavior, either explicitly or as refracted through clan relations and ceremonial and other social obligations – expressing what Kroskrity has called an ideology of "regulation by convention"[39] that is a key element to the idealization of ritual formulae as a model for Hopi behavior generally.

a.) An "Anglo" advocate during direct examination pursuing an argument that her client rightfully inherited a plot of land from her father (March 1995):

Now it's true, isn't it, that in Hopi tradition, orchards are generally considered to be the man's property?

b.) A Hopi witness describing to a Hopi judge principles of clan relation between a party and the grandfather she claims bequeathed her clan land (December 1997):

Wit. You won't be the same clan as your grandpa.
You'd have to be the- some other clan
As you are aware at Hopi clanship.

Figure 1.) Tradition as Normative Principle.

But in other moments within and across Hopi courtroom interactions, an orientation to specific instances of speech, made by particular persons, do seem to enter into arguments being formulated in and around notions of Hopi tradition and ritual responsibility. Thus consider the exchange in Figure 2.

ATTORNEY: Ahm Louise, in your knowledge ah **as a community member of Hotevilla**, and **as a member of Hopi ah your entire life**, is that in line with - the understanding of how things work –

LOUISE: I believe that was true because, like I said, our grandmother left Old Oraibi, solely for the reason of remaining Hopi. **She didn't want the White Man's Way. She didn't want any other way but the Hopi way**. And I believe that, **I believe that she would say that** because that was **also her instructions to all of us.**

Figure 2.) Tradition as Prior Speech Event. (March 1995)

[39] Kroskrity, *supra* note 12 at 36.

Note here how the attorney questions the witness in an effort to get her to respond in a way that indexes her claims to Hopi tradition as significant because of the social conventions of practice and belief that are known to all Hopi members of her village – that is generalized normative principles. But the witness's response ignores these constraints, instead formulating the truth-value of her claims as derived from the particular motivations, desires, and "instructions" of her grandmother.

In other instances, however, whether tradition is formulated as the report of particular individuals' prior expression of their motivations or as a general principle of tradition is not so easy to tease apart. This is particularly true when the testimony of tradition is given in Hopi. Consider first the stretch of talk in Figure 3. It comes from a hearing held August, 2000, offered by a woman, Jean, who was in a dispute with her brother, Dan, over a ceremonial home left vacant by their now-deceased mother. Such homes are generally recognized by Hopis as carrying certain gender specific ceremonial responsibilities that require they pass from clan mothers to their daughters. The dispute arose when Dan claimed that their mother left a will in which she bequeathed the home to him. In this stretch of talk, Jean, representing herself, was allowed to make her closing argument as to why she believed the disputed home should go to her and not her brother:

001 **Jean:**	Ingu	**yan**	wuuyoqtiqe
	My mother	**there/then**	become old
	When my mother became old		
002	Kur	hakiy	aw nìiqe
	Apparently	who	to so
	She did not know who to turn to so		
003	**Pu'**	inumi	maatavi.
	here/now	to me	relinquish.
	She gives me that.		
004	**Pu'**	i'	[DAN],
	Here/Now	this	[DAN]
	Now DAN,		
005	Pam	pay	taaqa.
	He	merely	man
	He is just a man.		

006 Pam son put ang hinman**i**.
He NEG that. along there/then be carrying along.
FUT
He won't be able to carry that out.

007 Pi qa tiimaytongwu!
Truly not witness dance **HAB**
He doesn't even come to the dances!

008 Pam **YAW** yep sinmuy oo'oy'**ni**?
He **QUOT** at this point people be serving.**FUT**
Will he (as they say) be receiving the people?

009 Pam **YAW** yep sinmuy amungem
noovalaw.**ni**?
He **QUOT** at this point people for them prepare
food. **FUT**
Will he (as they say) come and prepare food for the people to eat?

010 Pangsosa sinom ökiwis. **ngwu**
To then/there people be approaching. **HAB**
The people all come to that house.

011 I' **YAW** panti.**ni**?
This **QUOT**do it that way. **FUT**
Can he (as they say) do all that?

012 Qa'e!
NEG.
No!

Figure 3.) Arguing with Tradition in Hopi Court (August 2000):

Note the shifting array of temporalities, in which past and anticipated interactions are fused in a succession of events that link the present courtroom discourse to a temporally transcendent narrative of "tradition". Starting with lines 001–7, the speaker generates a time–space envelope "within" which remain constant the ceremonial responsibilities communicatively passed from her mother to her in the "then/there" (***yan,*** line 1) of the past, with those that would be passed on to Dan if he were to get the home in the "here/now" (***pu'*** , line 4, the "habitual" suffix ***ngwu,*** line 7) of this court proceeding, and with those which he is imagined as failing to fulfill in the "then/there" that would follow ("future" suffix -***ni***, line 6).

Indeed, in the second half of the narrative, the woman combines use of the Hopi quotative particle ***yaw*** ("they say") with verbs inflected with the future ***–ni*** suffix. In this way, she conveys within single clauses at lines 8, 9, and 11 the sense of a three-fold temporality that frames her present claim as reporting "timeless" talk of traditions that have occurred and are occurring from some point in the past to now and which reach forward to anticipated social moments of Dan's potential violation of those traditions. A time–space envelope is thus crafted in which the bequest of the home and the present courtroom arguments are transcended by norms of tradition that were announced and in-force before, during, and after the factual events relevant to this hearing. In so doing, the woman's utterance serves as a performance of the perpetuity of Hopi tradition, and her authority in and through it. Tradition here serves both to reference the Hopi norms that legitimate her claims in much the same way that lawyers cite legal precedent to legitimize their claims in U.S. courts, and to point up her own authority as emerging from the line of transmission of that tradition, from prior speech events to the now – a perpetuity that speaks the past and carries it hither.

Compare this to the two stretches of talk at Figure 4a and b. The interaction in Figure 4a comes from the trial court hearing in the case described in my introduction, in which a Hopi judge queries an elder about how often a woman must return to her village to continue to claim the customs of her village.

a). Hopi Judge questioning elder witness about principles of tradition (August 1995):

001 **Judge:** Pam hapi pay **yephaqam** **hak** ayo'
In that way truly now **somewhere here**
someone to there
In that manner someone may go over there

002 **Hìisakis** sen **pam** pas pew pìpte'
How often perhaps she much to here return
How often must s/he return

003 Put pay naat
It now still
And still –

To understand the full contribution these complexities of tradition and its perpetuity play in the on-going legitimation crises posed by Hopi inheritance disputes before the Hopi tribal court, it is necessary to explore how Hopi legal actors – namely judges and law trained attorneys attempt to constrain the significance of tradition discourses as either statements of law or evidence of fact, but not both, and how the witnesses and litigants producing those discourses respond to those efforts.[40]

Let us return, then, once again to the dispute between the three nieces and their aunt in dispute over a piece of property. And let us pick up where we left off in Figure 4a, with the Hopi Judge questioning elders and attempting to get them to speak about general "principles of tradition." Though the first elder to respond seems to follow suit, she shortly thereafter begins to talk not about general principles at all, but about her knowledge of the facts of the case – namely that the woman, the nieces' aunt "this one [the woman], never came back frequently."

a). Witnesses challenging the formulation of tradition as generalizable legal principles (August 1995):

011 **Witness:**	Pu' **pam** angqw	**suushaqam** pìtu**ngwu**	
	Then **s/he** from there	**for once** return+**HAB**	
	S/he should return once in a while.		

012	**I'**	pay	qa	hìsat,	sutsep	papki
	This	now	not	sometime	always	return
	This one [the woman disputant] never came back frequently.					

The judge then quickly jumps in, requesting that they not speak about the specifics of the case, reminding them that:

016 **Judge**	Pay nu' ayanwat as	umuy tuuvìngta
	I asked you in a different way instead.	

[40] For a similar view of the ways in which law and fact find presentation in various contexts in ways that defy the easy fact-law distinction we make in certain Euro-American legal traditions, *see* Clifford Geertz, "Local Knowledge: Fact and Law in Comparative Perspective" in Clifford Geertz, ed., *Local Knowledge: Further Essays in Interpretive Anthropology. 3rd Edition* (New York: Basic Books, 2000). Thanks to René Provost for pointing out this parallel insight.

017 Pay qa hakìy pas itam aw suuk aw taykyahkyàngw
We are not to look at some one person

018 turta put yu'a'totani
As we talk about this.

This time, however, the elder balks:

023 **Witness:** *Noqw my understanding is*
But my understanding is

. . .

024 *Su`upan as itam pumuy- pay pumuy as engemyaqw*
I thought we were [doing this] only for them?

025 *Kur hapi pay pas itam so`osokmuy engemya.*
But appears [to me] now we are doing this for all.

026 **Judge:** *Pay puy umuhnavot`ıy itamumumitungla'yyungwa*
We are asking you for your traditions

[Some lines omitted]

Another elder speaks up from the floor of the court,

032 **Witness 2:** *Um it kitsokit– navot`ıyat uma hintsatsnaniqe oovi*
What are you going to do with the village's
tradition?

[Some lines omitted]

036 *Nu' aw wuuwaqw,*
When I think of it,

037 *it yep [Village name] navotiyat kitsokit navotiyat*
this village's traditional way,

038 *tut pay kya so'on hak pas hin*
that is something that probably no one

039 *pas navoti'ytani*
will know very much about.

Figure 6.) Challenging the legitimacy of tribal court appropriations of tradition.

The elders object here because, as they see it, when the judge attempts to get them to speak about generalized principles of tradition, it violates their understanding of tradition as a body of potent but esoteric knowledge-power (*navoti*) that is not distributed equally across all villages or even within each village. It is indeed a common refrain among Hopi people I know that no two villages, or even two clans within the same village, can have the same understanding of tradition.[41]

As these two elders rightly recognize, when the judge asks them to speak about general norms of tradition, he is asking them to subsume their capacity to perform tradition to the norms of an Anglo-American style legal system that requires general norms to be applied by triers of fact (here the judge) to the facts of the case.

To the elders, however, this appears as little more than a power grab, one that would illegitimately separate the iconic qualities of tradition as an expression of general rules from its indexical force as an instantiation of their authority to perform it, and would do so for the purposes of authorizing his power as a Hopi tribal judge applying tradition in the resolution of the property dispute. When the second elder (witness 2) finally informs the judge at lines 36–9 that the village's traditional way is "something that no one will know very much about," he is in fact shutting down the interaction, refusing to testify in the way the judge wants. Ironically, his denial of knowledge about tradition could, in a sense, be read as a kind of performance in the negative – an assertion of his traditional authority by non-assertion.

At least from the elders' perspective, what the judge here sees as merely enacting Anglo-style tribal law of inheritance, albeit grounded in Hopi tradition, is to them the illegitimate appropriation and dismantling of their social authority, as they generate it, through their legitimate perpetuation of tradition. By responding with a non-response, the elder witnesses attempt to turn the tables back around, risking the appearance of offering testimony that is illegitimate to the aims of the court's Anglo-style legal procedures, but so as to preserve the legitimacy of their traditional authority. The breakdown in the hearing – and the rupture it causes to the perpetuation of law – is then, in a sense, in the service of the preservation of the perpetuity of tradition.

[41] For a more complete discussion of the way traditional knowledge is understood as distributed among the various villages and clans, *see* Justin B Richland, *Arguing with Tradition: The Language of Law in Hopi Tribal Court* (Chicago: University of Chicago Press, 2008); Justin B Richland, "The State of Hopi Exception: When Inheritance Is What You Have" (2008) 20:2 *Law Lit* 261.

Finally, consider the spate of interaction in Figure 6b. Here again, contests over the interpretation of tradition arise again, but this time it is because the non-Hopi attorney cross-examining them attempts to frame the niece's testimony as exclusively evidence of the facts of a prior speech event. The attorney here is following up on what the niece had already testified as her "understanding of tradition," She asks:

b). Challenging the formulation of tradition discourse as hearsay evidence (March 1995):

001	**ATY:**	And **if** a- **a man** gives his daughters rights,
002		in his lands,
003		before he passes on.
004		**If the daughter** leaves the reservation,
005		would she have to relinquish her rights in those
006		lands?
007	**Neice:**	In Hopi,
008		**they- our mothers** say they do.
009	**ATY:**	You think then,
010		that **your mother would** say,
011		that even if the daughters got land from their
012		fathers,
013		if they leave,
014		they have to give up that land.
015	**Neice:**	Yes. That's what **my mother** tells me.
[Some lines omitted]		
019	**ATY:**	And you don't ahm- know
020		about whether or not
021		this is **how everybody feels** at Hotevilla?
022	**Neice:**	I don't know how they feel.
023	**ATY:**	Okay, so this would just be your own feelings
024	**Neice:**	Yes.
025	**ATY:**	Based on what **your mother told you.**
026	**Neice:**	Yes.

Figure 6.) *(cont.)*

Note how the attorney initiates her question, posing it as a hypothetical situation ("if a-a man. . . If the daughter. . ."), one that makes relevant an answer that will speak of normative responses that Hopis have to such circumstances. And the witness starts her answer in this way at lines 007 and 008: first explaining that "In Hopi they say," before restarting to

the time the provision was created. The idea is that a testator should not be able to create a perpetuity, dictating in the present the distribution of their property infinitely into the future. The Rule thus attempts to impose a limit, invalidating any distribution that would occur beyond the time when the grandchildren of the youngest generation alive at the end of the testator's life (approximately the fourth subsequent generation) would reach maturity and thus take ownership.

So what is the problem? It turns out that it is quite difficult to determine in the present when a property interest will vest in the future, if at all. This is particularly true when what matters to the Rule is not even what *actually* happens in the future, but what is imagined in the present as a *possible* future.

The problems this has posed for lawyers has been in evidence for over one hundred years. Writing in the nineteen century, John Chipman Gray notes the "few lawyers of any practice drawing wills and settlements who" in failing to anticipate the possible futures that their testamentary documents create in violation of the RAP, "have not at some time either fallen into the net which the Rule spreads for the unwary, or at least shuddered to think how narrowly they have escaped it."[42] Yet despite this long-standing awareness of the problem, the traps posed by the Rule remain. Indeed, as recently as 1998, Britain's Law Commission proposed substantial reforms to the Rule Against Perpetuities.[43] Before that, in 1990, at the National Conference of Commissioners of Uniform State Laws enacted the Uniform Statutory Rule Against Perpetuities, a revision to the 1987 Uniform Rule that, in only three years, was already found faulty in its application.[44] And perhaps, most famously, in 1963, the California Supreme Court in *Lucas* v *Hamm*[45] held that a lawyer is not liable for malpractice when the will he prepared was void for violating the Rule Against Perpetuities. This is true, the court explained, because the Rule has always proved difficult to follow.

Interestingly, the decision quotes Chipman Gray for the fact that, since its earliest formulation, "there is something in the subject which seems to

[42] John Chipman Gray, *supra* note 14 at xi.

[43] The Law Commission, *Item 7 of the Sixth Programme of Law Reform: The Law of Trusts. The Rule Against Perpetuities and Excessive Accumulations. To the Right Honorable the Lord Irving of Lairg, Lord High Chancellor of Great Britian* (1998).

[44] Uniform Law Commission, *The Uniform Statutory Rule Against Perpetuities, with 1990 Amendments, Prefatory Note*, The National Conference of Commissioners on Uniform State Laws (1990).

[45] *Lucas* v *Hamm*, 1963 California Supreme Court.

facilitate error."[46] I am inclined to think that it is the subject *of* the Rule that poses the problem. That is, I wonder if the challenges posed by the Rule speak to a larger challenge that inheritance, and tradition, and any other discursive modality that has perpetuity at its heart, poses to law, and its perpetuity, more generally.

The question the rule seeks to address – if understood in retrospect as a court would when trying to apply it – would ask after the extent to which the possible future imagined in the past (in a testator's will, say) should constrain how inheritance is distributed in the actual future that has arrived now in the present. Understood in this way, the founding question of the Rule poses precisely the questions of perpetuity that animate the authority of law more generally. If, as I have tried to show, law generates its authority "between facts and norms" through discursive moves that figure law as at once immanent in and transcending any single instance of bringing facts and norms together, it appears to do so by the same kind of "speaking the past" and "carrying it hither" that is imagined at the execution of any act of testation.

If we can say that the abiding question of inheritance (literally, the act by which one "makes heirs") – is the question of a testator perpetuating her will into the future – her perpetuity – then the dilemmas of the Rule Against Perpetuities just described can perhaps be understood as yet another instance of law's crisis in the face of any perpetuity other than its own. Law is itself constituted as a kind of continuity – a perpetual transmission that endeavors to speak its past and carry it hither every time it is enacted anew in courtroom hearings or legal opinions. It is, also, however, a perpetuity whose legitimacy and authority is premised on representational practices that work by excluding other discourses whose authority is claimed in mediating between and transcending norms and facts via perpetuity.

When viewed in this light, it is not surprising then that Hopi customs and traditions seem to be done a violence by the formulating practices of Anglo-style tribal legal actors. As with the Rule Against Perpetuities, the temporal displacements operating in the ideologies of the Anglo-style legal processes of the court, and by which its legal actors formulate tradition as either a statement of law or evidence of fact, both do a kind of violence to the perpetuity of tradition – preventing its capacity to bind norm and fact, transcendence and immanence, such that those who wish

[46] *Ibid* at 58. *Quoting* John Chipman Gray, *supra* note 14 at xi.

to argue in and through tradition are denied the opportunity to either legitimately "speak the past" or forcefully "carry it hither." But these problems arise not because these perpetuities are so radically different, but rather so very similar. Thus Hopi litigants, like the three nieces or their witnesses, expect that their traditions, and the inheritance matters they inform, *should* find adequate resolution and re-presentation in law and its perpetuities. And yet, time and again, they discover that the fit of Hopi tribal law to the legitimate expression of their traditions is just not right. It is this, in the end, that explains the crises of *juris-diction* – of the speaking of law/law's speech that, in the Hopi courtroom, seems to be held in suspense – that the perpetuities of its Anglo-style legal discourses and the perpetuities of Hopi tradition, produce when they confront each other in inheritance disputes. And, perhaps even more importantly, it suggests the extent to which it is perpetuity, or perpetuities, that sits at the very heart of that which stands as, and against, law.

7

"Existing in the Hyphen"

On Relational Legal Culture

JENNIFER HENDRY

"Law is in society, or laced through, between and in society's culture."

Seron & Silbey[1]

"Only if one is willing to ignore the cultural dimension of the law can one say that [. . .] the law can be considered irrespective of geography, of place."

Legrand & Munday[2]

7.1 Introduction

In her book *For Space*, Doreen Massey suggests that we imagine space as "a simultaneity of stories-so-far," with the aim of explaining the perpetual being-made-ness of space.[3] For Massey, space is "a product of interrelations, constituted through interactions" and thus must necessarily be a process.[4] This insight is important in elucidating the shift from conceptualizing place, as it were, to conceptualizing *space* – an area of potentiality and radical openness that not only precludes closure and completion but clearly rejects it, and as such is always already under construction. By detaching the notion of space from the geography of place it thus becomes possible to use space in a non-embedded and non-located sense as well as to conceptualize it as unbounded or, rather,

[1] Carroll Seron & Susan Silbey, "Profession, Science and Culture: an Emergent Canon of Law and Society Research" in Austin Sarat, ed., *Blackwell Companion to Law and Society* (Oxford: Blackwell Publishing, 2004) 30–60 at 13.

[2] Pierre Legrand & Roderick Munday, eds., *Comparative Legal Studies: Traditions and Transitions* (Cambridge: Cambridge University Press, 2003) at 276.

[3] Doreen Massey, *For Space* (London: Sage, 2005) at 9. [4] *Ibid.*

concept of legal culture with a view to highlighting from where the main points of contention arise.

What, then, is meant by "culture"? It could be stated that culture is "that which is socially as opposed to genetically transmitted,"[11] although this albeit accurate characterization is, unfortunately, broadly stated to the point of having limited critical utility. One beneficial aspect of this definition, however, is the attention it draws to culture's *social* dimension: indeed, it is pertinent at this stage to distinguish between culture understood in this social sense and culture in the more popular sense of the term, encompassing for example art, literature, and music. This is not to downplay the importance of these cultural influences and representations[12] but rather to separate out those things commonly referred to as "cultural" from the more communal, connection-based, social form that is the focus of this chapter. *This* kind of culture, Terry Eagleton has argued, is only formed when, regardless of locus, status or age, people "begin to share speech-habits, folklore, ways of proceeding, frames of value [and] a collective self-image." What this interpretation endorses is the idea that culture can be said to encompass those qualities that "embody a distinctive way of seeing the world but not necessarily a unique way of seeing."[13] Understood in this sense, therefore, culture is attributable to agreed-upon perspectives held in common or, as Pierre Legrand puts it:

> Culture refers to a horizon of intelligibility within which a constellation of (often inexplicable) world-defining dispositions allowing for responses to situations and for the effectuation of discriminations manifest themselves.

It is notable here that both Eagleton (briefly) and Legrand (implicitly) appear to include an active "practice" component alongside the more overly stated "belief" elements, which suggests that these common perspectives also require some form of actualization, arguably so that they can be both socially observed and engaged with. A more noticeable consensus between the two standpoints, however, is the idea that a culture requires a degree of having things in common, a recognition of sameness that generates an impetus to coalesce around that similarity. A corollary of recognizing sameness, of course, is that in order to do so

[11] Anthony O'Hear, "Culture" in Edward Craig, ed., *Routledge Encyclopedia of Philosophy* (London: Routledge, 1998).

[12] See Douglas-Scott, *supra* note 8 at 4–7.

[13] Terry Eagleton, *The Idea of Culture* (Oxford: Blackwell, 2000) at 37.

there must be a simultaneous recognition of difference – this is the basis upon which differentiation occurs, and which in turn allows (to use Legrand's language) for the manifestation of discrimination.

This introduction of alterity is not intended to reduce the issue of culture to a Them/Us debate, but rather to draw attention to the conundrum at the heart of the issue of *belonging*, which is defined (and this in a depoliticized sense) in contradistinction to the idea of someone or something *not belonging*. Of speaking differently, of understanding differently, of behaving differently, and of asserting their own difference on those bases with the view to demonstrating their *own* membership of their own culture... Put simply, the establishment of sameness necessitates the recognition of difference. There are four important points to take from this insight. First, there is no overt spatial determination or place-embeddedness in either of these definitions of culture; second, the snapshot of In/Out is merely that, a moment in time where the situation "viewed" apparently lacks all openness and malleability; third, the acknowledgement of difference highlights the inherent heterogeneity and plurality of space; and fourth, the belief and practice of belonging to a culture is *constitutive* of that culture.

While Eagleton would make the coming-into-being of a culture dependent upon the numbers involved – "It would be odd to see three people as forming a culture but not three hundred or three million"[14] – strictly speaking the premises of alterity and belonging should in fact be sufficient with just two individuals to identify commonality and one to be omitted. This is of limited importance *in situ* but increases in import when culture and indeed legal culture are detached from their geographic places. Neither should we fixate upon the numeric in terms of the quantity of such cultural affiliations experienced and maintained by an individual. While an individual's identity can be conceptualized as an a aggregation of many components and cultural affiliations, even partial ones, community identities are dependent upon linkages among individuals who have identified some feature in common with other individuals, and it is the combination of this belief and active practice on its basis that serves to create the common culture. Although certain social features have a quality of permanence, these alone are insufficient in the generation of a culture *ex nihilo*; the associated belonging-belief and belonging-practice is required for the coming-into-being of a culture.

[14] *Ibid.*

7.3 "Legal Culture" (definitions)

What, then, is the benefit of yoking the "legal" to the "cultural"? What are the specific aims of such an endeavor? Employment of the concept of *legal* culture, it could be argued, involves acknowledgment of and engagement with the compound nature of law, which is to say, with the social norms, socio-political constellations, historical underpinnings, institutional arrangements, societal practices and population dynamics that inform the law's social context, within a jurisdiction or legal "space." In this regard, there is a clear connection between this concept and the definitions of culture provided earlier: as Emmanuel Melissaris puts it, "the conception of the law in terms of shared normative experiences reflects the fragmentation of our identities and memberships."[15] This observation pulls together the aggregate quality of individual affiliations and those all-important linkages and connections between and among individuals that are constitutive of culture, while at the same time blending these with an associated normative dimension. It is important to note, however, that this composite character of legal culture is subject to variation on a temporal basis – as those aspects constitutive of its context alter over time, so does the legal culture itself.

The *legal* aspect of legal culture comes through more overtly in David Nelken's conception. His work concerns itself with how "aspects of law are themselves embedded in larger frameworks of social structure and culture which constitute and reveal the place of law in society."[16] Nelken's main approach to the concept of legal culture has been the utilization of sociological insights to scrutinize and highlight law-related behavior within society. However, while he seems to be open-minded to legal culture's application beyond the confines of the nation state, seeing equivalent constellations at regional, sub-, and transnational level, as well as in discipline- or function-related vertical constructions, his discussions appear to concern the demarcation of the *unit* of legal culture and questions regarding its own internal coherence.[17] Whether it is viewed as a discrete unit or through a lens of structural functionalism, however, the true complexity of legal culture so understood is restricted. Only by

[15] Emmanuel Melissaris, *Ubiquitous Law* (Surrey: Ashgate, 2009) at 125.

[16] David Nelken, "Comparative Sociology of Law" in Reza Banakar and Max Travers, eds., *Introduction to Law and Social Theory* (Oxford: Hart, 2002) chapter 19 at 333.

[17] See, for example, David Nelken, "Defining and Using the Concept of Legal Culture" in David Nelken and Esin Örücü, eds., *Comparative Law: A Handbook* (Oxford: Hart, 2007) 109 at 117–22.

conceptualizing legal culture as a process can this limitation be overcome. To be fair to Nelken, there does appear to be a gradual move within his work toward a multi-level, post-State understanding of legal culture, an example of which could be professional bodies operating transnationally, although this does seem to relate to a hierarchical or sectoral unit. Taken further, this understanding of legal culture as being premised upon behavior could arguably facilitate the attenuation of legal culture from any specific locus, while at the same time staying true to its conceptualization as a unit.

By comparison, Pierre Legrand's conceptualization of legal culture takes a more epistemological approach. Often referring to legal culture as legal *episteme*, Legrand introduced the complementary idea of "legal *mentalité*," making the argument that the distinct cognitive structure prevailing within a legal culture generates meanings that cannot be disentangled from its rules;[18] in this way, place plays an intrinsic role in the creation of legal meaning. Place, he argues, "is not a mere static backdrop to legal meaning: it is a dynamic constituent of it."[19] The result of this perspective, however, is that such "discrete epistemological formations"[20] assume a character that, if not entirely closed, is certainly far from open. Moreover, its emphasis on considering both place and *mentalité* has the effect of introducing issues of comprehension across legal cultures.[21] Although the well-known billiard ball metaphor is certainly too strong here, the difficulties of communication and interaction – at the epistemic as opposed to behavioral level – serve to *hypercontextualize* the legal culture, thus contributing both to its essentialization and its conceptual constraint. This is not to say, of course, that context is not vital both to an understanding of legal culture specifically and law more broadly: a discussion of legal culture in an a-contextual sense would be both pointless and horrendous, and certainly not the purpose of this chapter, which takes the overt position that law is "as much a matter of culture as it is a system of rules".[22] Nevertheless, care must be taken not

[18] Pierre Legrand, "European Legal Systems Are Not Converging" (1996) 45 *Int Comp Law Q* 52; Pierre Legrand, "How to Compare Now" (1996) 16:2 *Legal Studies* 232.

[19] Pierre Legrand, "Econocentrism" (2009) 59:2 *Univ Tor Law J* 215 at 215.

[20] Pierre Legrand, "The Impossibility of 'Legal Transplants'" (1997) 4 *Maastricht J Eur Comp L* 111 at 48.

[21] For a discussion of cross-cultural understanding and translation, see Jennifer Hendry, "Legal Comparison and the (Im) Possibility of Legal Translation" in Simone Glanert, ed., *Comparative Law – Engaging Translation* (Abingdon: Routledge, 2014) at 87.

[22] Douglas-Scott, *supra* note 8 at 25.

meet in order to achieve the status of law within a particular legal space.[31] Justifications and explanations of what constitutes (or fails to constitute) legal character is not, however, the focus of this chapter. What rather concerns this investigation is the potential afforded by legal *plurality* when understood in the sense of fragmentation. Legal pluralism is inherently connected to the concept of legal culture as a result of the potential for multiplicity included in the very designation of "legal" as something both conceptually and characteristically variable.

This fragmentation of law within and across jurisdictions and legal spaces is facilitated by the existence of boundaries that operate along normative, cultural, functional, geographical, and alternatively spatial lines. Such boundaries operate both as delimiters of legal space and obstacles for legal movement: indeed, in terms of the latter, it is arguable that this hurdle could be conceptualized as something of a filter – a semi-permeable membrane in the osmosis of the law from locus to locus. Importantly here, the delimitation is not merely confining but also enabling. Even more than that, the boundary embodies and represents the liminal by itself existing in-between; it is a constitutive connection between what is inside and what is outside. To put this in another way, such a border line is a selecting delimitation that signifies structures and patterns of normativity within those borders, and which "others" equivalent processes out with them. What is of interest here is the extent to which such boundaries affect interaction among and across different legal cultures, specifically those recognized as subaltern normative spaces. Plural legal circumstances generate contradictory views of both borders and spaces, but they also serve to hold them in tension, keeping them in a state of perpetual juxtaposition, or hyphenation.

7.5 Legal Hyphen Culture (as process)

Massey's tripartite definition of space is as "the sphere of possibility of the existence of multiplicity," "the product of interrelations constituted through interactions," and "always under construction... always in the process of being made... never finished; never closed."[32] The aim of this section is to apply this reasoning to the contested compound concept of legal culture, with the objective of opening up its radical potential, its

[31] See William Twining, "Normative and Legal Pluralism" (2010) 20 *Duke Journal of Comparative and International Law* 473–517.

[32] Massey, *supra* note 3 at 9.

ability to accommodate complexity and fragmentation, and its comfort with the multiple tensions at its heart.

Until now, the focus has been upon the spatial aspect of legal culture, which is perhaps more accurately stated as being an approach, as opposed to a perspective. Intrinsic to this understanding, however, and as revealed by Massey's trifecta, is the temporal dimension. This chapter opened with a discussion of space as "stories-so-far" with a view to introducing these ideas of temporality and interactivity within legal-cultural space. Legal culture's conceptual flexibility has already been discussed – it can be readily applied to an overarching inclusive legal space such as the European Union (EU) or the Council of Europe, for example, or to situations of state-internal or classical (weak) legal plurality – but this chapter argues that the concept of legal culture comes into its own when blended with an approach that takes into account the spatiality of law. The reasons are twofold. First, a spatially-detached or non-embedded understanding of legal culture frees it from the confines of both jurisdiction and hierarchical (albeit oftentimes interpenetrating) levels of legal institutions and operations. Second, the inclusion of a temporal dimension provides for the radical openness necessary to a relational procedural conception of legal culture. Conceptualizing legal culture as a process not only allows for its interaction-based constitution (unit) but also facilitates its evolution and development over time and in relation both to its internal dynamics and external influences.

This relational element is particularly important as this is the means by which learning occurs, and this process is necessarily one that has two-way causality. The interactions between the legal and the cultural (or, more accurately, between and among multiple legal-cultural spaces) are characterized by reciprocity in that they *cannot but* influence each other. These unavoidable social interactions give rise to tension-laden and unsteered[33] adaptations in both and all spaces, results that drive the process onward and, importantly, maintain the vital gap between these spaces. This process can be viewed as a juridified process of social learning, one that is embodied (at the meta-level) by the tensions stemming from unavoidable interactions in society between the legal and the

[33] My systems theory leanings cause me to consider any adaptation to be *de facto* unsteered, although this is an issue that requires more consideration. That adaptation occurs is, however, undisputed, because norms, legal features and processes that cross boundaries have thereafter "different conditions for their continuance": Niklas Luhmann, *Social Systems* (Stanford University Press, 1995).

cultural. The importance of this cannot be overstated, for if a legal culture can be understood as a process of adaptation (social learning), then nothing can be considered to be *essential* (in the sense of fundamental/original), and if nothing is essential, then everything within that legal culture has come about through interaction, the result being that nothing is "unknowable": epistemic restrictions are ultimately things that can be overcome. Such a conception of legal culture undermines the "deep structures" position while still allowing for a strong sense of the contextual to be maintained.

Moreover, the strength of detaching the two variables from their socio-geographic context is that the sphere of interaction is thus widened, with all the radical potential that holds. The detachment from *locus* gives rise to (the potential for) new interactions and linkages with individuals and groups, linkages that could certainly, if they do not already, comprise a fledgling common culture.[34]

The ongoing process of legal culture, for which I have argued in favor, is continually reaffirmed and re-negotiated on the basis of external information being included within the operations of that process. While it is premised upon alterity, that is to say, the means by which it establishes its inside and outside, the boundary is subject to contestation and revision. The dynamic connection of the law and culture is recognized and privileged, as is the separation of the two vitally distinct variables – in this regard, and the extent to which it prevents the two from collapsing into each other, we cannot underestimate the importance of the hyphen.

[34] There is scope here to explore the issue, ancillary to legal culture, of an epistemic community in existence at the transnational level of the UN Indigenous space, arguably in terms of both a deliberative space and the potential for a functional perspective; these are considerations for another project.

8

The Unexpected Effects of the Recognition of Indigenous Rights in New Caledonia

The Story of an Assimilation Measure Becoming the Trigger for the Acculturation of the French Legal System

THOMAS BURELLI
RÉGIS LAFARGUE

"Legal pluralism is as much an issue of norms and obstinacy of the litigant, as of institutional mechanisms. This is also a 'reality check,' and a lesson in humility because legal pluralism is not an ethnographic dream: reality is there, although far away from our courtrooms, but very much alive."[1]

8.1 Introduction

For a French lawyer, the terms *Republic* and *legal pluralism* often feel incompatible. In principle, the French State does not allow for much pluralism in its legal system. France is a unitary state, and there is one legal order: the State legal order.[2]

Régis Lafargue left us on August 30, 2016, prior to the publication of this article. He was an extraordinary mentor, colleague and friend to the many people whose lives he touched. We shared a common passion and commitment for research and advocacy on the protection of the rights of Indigenous Peoples. This contribution encompasses our reflections on research we conducted about the rights of the Kanak Peoples of New Caledonia. To keep his memory alive, it is up to us to embrace his lessons, especially on intercultural relationships, and to continue our engagement with Indigenous Peoples.

[1] Régis Lafargue, "Dire le droit de l'autre" : contribution à une approche réaliste du pluralisme juridique" in Jean-Yves Faberon, ed., *Collectivités Français d'Amérique Au Carrefour des Institutions* (Paris: la Documentation française, 2006) at 98. ("Le pluralisme juridique est bien, tout autant, affaire de volonté que de norme, d'entêtement du plaideur que de mécanique institutionnelle. C'est aussi une leçon de réalisme, et d'humilité, car le pluralisme juridique n'a rien d'un rêve ethnographique: la réalité est là, certes éloignée de nos prétoires, mais bien vivante").

[2] In the French Constitution of October 4, 1958, the first article states that: "France is an indivisible, secular, democratic and social Republic. It shall ensure the equality of all citizens before the law, without distinction of origin, race or religion."

However, far away from Paris, some territories are resisting this model and offer a different reality. This is the case in particular of certain French territories marked by France's colonial legacy. In these territories, the model of the unitary State has been challenged, causing the French State to adapt its system and institutions in order to maintain its legitimacy and the unity of its territory in light of local responses.

The French State has been confronted in some of these territories by indigenous populations refusing to be assimilated. In most cases, these populations have maintained distinctive ways of living and conventions for organizing their societies. Such cases can be seen with the indigenous peoples of French Guyana, French Polynesia, Mayotte, in Wallis and Futuna Islands, as well as New Caledonia, the historical land of the Kanak people.

However, the legal and political adaptations adopted by the French State are not uniform across its global territories. Instead, the French State has defined and developed a specific status and relationship with almost each of its twelve territories. For instance, in the case of the "Départments et Régions d'outre mer" (namely: Guadeloupe, French Guyana, Martinique, Mayotte and La Réunion), France does not recognize any legislative autonomy for these territories.[3] Thus, only the laws fashioned in Paris apply there (with the possibility of minor variations).[4] In other cases, such as the "Collectivités d'outre-mer" (la Polynésie française, Saint-Barthélemy, Saint-Martin, Saint-Pierre-et-Miquelon et Wallis-et-Futuna), the State does recognize legislative autonomy for these territories in some domains of law.[5] Finally, the territory of New Caledonia maintains a *sui generis* status as defined in Title XIII of the French Constitution, as a result of the history of its indigenous people's resistance and resilience towards France's institutions. This status, analyzed later more at length, constitutes an official recognition of legal pluralism by the French State, while, curiously, the same cannot be said of France's other territories, despite the conservation of distinct legal cultures among the territories' indigenous peoples.[6]

New Caledonia represents a unique case among France's territorial holdings. In order to recognize the specificities and the rights of the

[3] Article 73 of the *French Constitution of 4 October 1958*, JORF, 5 October 1958 [*French Constitution of October 4th 1958*] at 9151.

[4] Jean-Yves Faberon and Jacques Ziller, *Droit des collectivités d'Outre-mer* (LGDJ, 2007) at 48; Lucile Stahl, *Le droit de la protection de la nature et de la diversité biologique dans les collectivités françaises d'Outre-mer* (Thèse en droit de l'environnement, Lyon 3, 2009) [unpublished] at 47.

[5] Article 74 of the *French Constitution of 4 October 1958*, *supra* note 5. Stahl, *supra* note 6 at 82, 86–9.

[6] François Garde, Les autochtones et la République (1999) AJDA at 2.

Kanak people, the French State is actively working to adapt its institutions and establish an official form of legal pluralism. This territory is now a fascinating laboratory where multiple forms of legal pluralism and legal interfaces between the State legal order and other legal orders (particularly, the Kanak legal order) have been implemented.

Legal pluralism[7] is a theory that surveys social realities in heterogeneous societies.[8] It rejects the idea of a State monopoly on the creation of law,[9] purporting that several legal orders coexist and interact with each other in every heterogeneous society. In New Caledonia, the Kanak people have maintained distinctive principles and rules to govern their society and their relationship to the land and environment at large.

Legal pluralism provides conceptual tools to analyze the interactions between legal orders,[10] enabling a thorough examination of the interactions between the legal orders of the Kanak and French State. According to Ghislain Otis, three different types of interactions resulting from this coexistence can be observed:[11] (1) A *monism* or a refusal of interaction: that is, a clear separation between legal orders;[12] (2) The subordination of one or more legal orders by another legal order;[13]

[7] Legal pluralism does not constitute a uniform theory, some authors have said that there might be as many theories of legal pluralism as there are researchers working on it. Christoph Eberhard, "Penser le pluralisme juridique de manière pluraliste–Défi pour une théorie interculturelle du droit" (2003) 2 *Cahiers d'anthropologie droit* at 51. In this article we rely mainly on legal pluralism as described by Professor Roderick Macdonald and Professor Jacques Vanderlinden.

[8] Roderick A Macdonald, "L'Hypothèse Du Pluralisme Juridique Dans Les Sociétés Démocratiques Avancées" (2002) 33:1–2 *RDUS* 133 at 138–9.

[9] Ghislain Otis, "Les figures de la théorie pluraliste dans la recherche juridique," in *Méthodologie Plur Jurid* (Karthala, 2012) 9 at 15; Macdonald, *supra* note 8 at 135; John Griffiths, "What is Legal Pluralism?" (1986) 24:1 *J Leg Plur* at 1.

[10] "Outre le constat du fait de la pluralité, le chercheur tentera d'affiner la description et la compréhension du phénomène. Il se penchera parfois sur les valeurs, les représentations, les acteurs, les espaces, les dynamiques, les institutions et les techniques des divers systèmes normatifs. Il s'attachera en d'autres mots à cerner les 'traditions juridiques' ou les 'cultures juridiques' qui se font jour." Otis, *supra* note 9 at 11.

[11] *Ibid* at 16–17. See also Bradford W Morse & Gordon R Woodman, "Introductory Essay: The State's Options," in Bradford W Morse & Gordon Woodman, eds., *Indigenous Law and the State* (Foris Publications, 1988) at 5–24, which is used by Professor Otis to build his analytical framework. Professors Morse and Woodman describe well the separation and subordination type of interactions.

[12] Morse & Woodman, *supra* note 11 at 17. The refusal of interactions does not mean the absence of a diversity of legal. This situation results in what Sermet describes as "Pluralisme hors l'État," a pluralism outside the State legal order. Laurent Sermet, "Le pluralisme juridique : une approche française ?" (2013) 22 *Rev Jurid Polit Économique Nouv-Caléd* at 6.

[13] Otis, *supra* note 9 at 20; Lafargue, *supra* note 1 at 91.

(3) The coordination between several legal orders.[14] The latter two interactions represent what Laurent Sermet calls a "Pluralisme d'État": a situation of legal pluralism recognized and organized by the State. Sermet adds the possibility of pluralism occurring outside the State, where there is the coexistence of legal orders in a society with the State adoption of a monist position refusing to consider and to interact with other legal orders[15].

Here is a table summarizing and combining the two models proposed by Otis and Sermet:

Monism[16]		State Organized Legal Pluralism	
Strict monism	Flexible monism	Subordinated pluralism[17]	Habilitated pluralism[18]
The State is the only authority sanctioned to create norms. There is a clear and strict refusal to interact with other legal orders.[19] Type of interaction (s) between legal orders: Negation, marginalization[20]	The State is the only authority sanctioned to create norms, however it can consult other authorities.[21] Type of interaction (s) between legal orders: Negation, marginalization[22]	The State authorizes other authorities to create norms, however it controls them by checking the conformity of the norms adopted with the State's legal culture.[23] Type of interaction between legal orders: Subordination[24]	The State authorizes other authorities to create norms without controlling them. There is no hierarchy between the coexisting legal cultures.[25] Type of interaction between legal orders: Coordination[26]

[14] Otis, *supra* note 9 at 22; Lafargue, *supra* note 3 at 96–7. [15] Sermet, *supra* note 14 at 6.

[16] Otis, *supra* note 9 at 17–19. [17] Sermet, *supra* note 14 at 6. [18] *Ibid.*

[19] *Ibid* at 6, 17.

[20] Otis , *supra* note 9 at 17–19; Morse & Woodman, *supra* note 11 at 5–24.

[21] Sermet, *supra* note 15 at 6.

[22] Otis , *supra* note 9 at 17–19; Morse & Woodman, *supra* note 11 at 5–24.

[23] Morse & Woodman, *supra* note 11; Otis, *supra* note 9 at 20.

[24] Otis, *supra* note 9 at 20–1; Morse & Woodman, *supra* note 11 at 5–24.

[25] Sermet, *supra* note 15 at 6 ; Otis, *supra* note 9 at 23 [26] Otis, *supra* note 9 at 22–6.

The focus of this chapter is on the legal interfaces[27] (or intercultural forums) that emerge between State legal order and the legal order of the Kanak in New Caledonia, resulting from the recognition and valorization of legal diversity by the French State. These legal interfaces (i.e., where customary assessors assist judges in State court) constitute contact zones, which are defined by Boaventura de Sousa Santos, as zones "in which rival normative ideas, knowledges, power forms, symbolic universes and agencies meet in unequal conditions and resist, reject, assimilate, imitate, subvert each other, giving rise to hybrid legal and political constellations in which the inequality of exchanges are traceable[28]." For Santos one key issue in the analysis of the contacts zone is: "who defines who or what belongs to the contact zone and what does not? To whom belongs the line that delimits the contact zone both externally and internally? Indeed, the struggle for the appropriation of such line is the meta-struggle for cosmopolitan legality in the contact zone[29]."

More importantly, is the analysis of the type of sociability resulting from a contact zone or a legal interface? Santos outlined four types of sociabilities, each characterized by the type of relationship established between the present legal orders:

> I distinguish four types of sociability: violence, coexistence, reconciliation, and conviviality. Violence is the type of encounter in which the dominant culture or normative life world vindicates full control over the contact zone and as such feels legitimated to suppress, marginalize or even destroy the subaltern culture or normative life world. Coexistence is the sociability typical of cultural apartheid in which different cultures are allowed to unfold separately and in which contacts, intermingling or hybridizations are strongly discouraged if not outright forbidden. Reconciliation is the type of sociability based on restorative justice, on healing past grievances. It is a past-oriented rather than a future-oriented sociability. For this reason the power imbalances of the past are often allowed to go on reproducing themselves under new guises. Finally, conviviality is, in a sense a future-oriented reconciliation. Past grievances are settled in such a way as to make possible sociability grounded in tendentially equal exchanges and shared authority[30].

These four sociabilities are not mutually exclusive within a specific contact zone. Instead, they constitute an evolving spectrum of

[27] *Oxford Dictionary* defines an interface as "a point where two systems, subjects, organizations, etc. meet and interact"; in our case two legal cultures.

[28] Boaventura De Sousa Santos, *Toward a New Legal Common Sense*, (Butterworths Lexis Nexis, 2002) at 472.

[29] *Ibid*, at 473. [30] *Ibid*, at 473–4.

sociabilities between the actors in a given legal interface (or intercultural forum). A sociability of conviviality results in increased equal exchanges between legal orders and in a better recognition of differences, and thus leads to the social inclusion of marginalized groups and to social justice. According to Santos, the types of exchanges occurring in a sociability of conviviality also have the potential to benefit the dominant culture as intercultural dialogue is established and leads to the emergence of alternatives, for instance in the field of justice. These alternatives can consist for example in innovative ways of dealing with social conflicts.[31]

This chapter examines the situation in New Caledonia, through the descriptive and analytical lens of legal pluralism, recognition, and valorization. This model of analysis will highlight the means and lengths to which courts and other legal institutions have become culturally sensitive to the Kanak people and their legal culture. This chapter will then analyze the institutional implications of the current situation in New Caledonia for both the State and for the Kanak people. In the process, it will illustrate how these experiences have led to recognizing the cultural specificities and expectations of the Kanak people. We will then attempt to characterize the types of sociabilities resulting from the emergence and evolution of these experiences in order to determine if they are leading to relationships based on equality and shared authority between the State and the Kanak legal orders. In conclusion, we will determine whether these experiences have led to renewed relationships between the State and the Kanak legal orders.

The chapter also shows how a measure – Section 75 in the Constitution – initially designed as a tool of assimilation became the trigger for the progressive recognition of Kanak rights and the acculturation of State judges, as soon as were set up "customary" courts from 1990. This mechanism, ineffective and inefficient over years, was the first step towards recognizing Kanak norms, acting as a catalyst for the resilience of the Kanak legal order.[32]

[31] Some researchers have applied the analytical framework proposed by Professor Santos. They have shown the potential of this framework to describe and to analyze the relationships between the State legal order and indigenous legal orders. See for example, Charlotte Chicoine-Wilson, *La reconnaissance de l'autonomie judiciaire autochtone: regard sur l'expérience colombienne* (LL.M Thesis, University of Ottawa, 2015).

[32] Régis Lafargue, *La coutume face à son destin: réflexions sur la coutume judiciaire en Nouvelle-Calédonie et la résilience des ordres juridiques infra-étatiques* (LGDJ, 2010) at 88–119.

8.2 The Initial Project of France: The Progressive Assimilation of the Kanak People

In 1853, France took possession of the territory of New Caledonia according to the principles of international law at that time and held onto it as a French colony officially until 1945 (in fact until 1956 and the Deferre Status[33]).[34] From the other perspective, the Melanesian population (today referred to as the Kanak people) of New Caledonia witnessed James Cook's arrival in 1774 only to be followed by successive waves of immigration.[35] Accordingly, the indigenous population has been displaced and has suffered greatly from contacts with newcomers and the colonial process. As a result, studies have estimated that by 1921 only 20 percent of the initial Kanak population still survived, the lowest recorded level. Today, however, the Kanak population has grown to represent about 40 percent of New Caledonia's population.[36]

New Caledonia has known many legal status, some in favor of more autonomy for the territory and recognizing the diversity of the population, and others more in favor of centralization.[37] The first turning point in the modern history of the territory can be marked in 1946 after the Second World War. At this time, New Caledonia ceased to be a colony and the code of Indigenous Status was abolished, but lasted until new means up to 1957 (freedom of movement being restricted for the Kanak till that date).

As a result of the abolition, all subjects of the French Empire became French citizens and indigenous people in the French territories abroad

[33] Loi n°56–619 du 23 juin 1956, *Mesures propres à assurer l'évolution des territoires relevant du Ministère de la France d'Outre-mer*, JORF du 24 juin 1956 page 5782. Available online at: www.legifrance.gouv.fr/affichTexte.do?cidTexte=JORFTEXT000000692222

[34] Joseph Du Bouzet, *Déclaration du chef de division, Gouverneur des établissements français de l'Océanie, relative à la propriété et l'aliénation des terres, en Nouvelle-Calédonie et dépendances* (1855).

[35] Garde, *supra note* 6 at 2.

[36] *Population census in New Caledonia* (2009).

[37] The Deferre status was adopted in 1957. This law transfers powers in several fields, such as education, urbanism, and public health, to the territory. Several more centralist status followed the Deferre status. Finally, the Matignon and the Nouméa (JORF n°121 du 27 mai1998 page 8039) agreements in 1988 and 1998 represented a new stage for the autonomy of New Caledonia and for the recognition of Indigenous people in New Caledonia. www.transfertsdecompetences.gouv.nc/portal/page/portal/transfert/transfert/processus/datescles. Jean-Yves Faberon, *Des institutions pour un pays: la Nouvelle-Calédonie en devenir* (Presses universitaires d'Aix-Marseille, 2012) at 24–50; Mathias Chauchat, *Les Institutions en Nouvelle-Calédonie* (Centre de Documentation Pédagogique de Nouvelle-Calédonie, 2011) at 1–8.

8.3.1 *The Slow Implementation of the Customary Civil Status*

As discussed in the previous section, the French constitution left the door open for Kanak people to keep their personal civil status based on customary law. In fact, the Courts have recognized the existence of their personal civil status since the 1920s and 1930s,[45] and later, by a regulation in 1934 which created an indigenous civil registry.[46]

The mechanism incorporated in article 75 of the 1958 French Constitution can, thus, be conceived as constitutional recognition of the personal status of indigenous people, and, more importantly, as a transitional measure. However, as discussed, the Kanak people did not accept the invitation, and the vast majority of them have retained their customary civil status.

Despite state and constitutional recognition, the French courts have marginalized the customary civil status of the Kanak for years. Between 1946 and the 1980s, the Kanak people could only rely on this provision of the French Constitution to claim the application of their customary rules, but the events at Ouvéa (from April 22, 1988 to May 5, 1988) have forced the French government to move forward in recognizing Kanak identity.[47] It is in this context that the Matignon (1988) and the Nouméa (1998) agreements were adopted. The former was adopted and targeted to achieve a lasting peace by formally recognizing all the indigenous communities represented in New Caledonia. The Nouméa agreement constitutes a detailed road-map toward the self-determination of New Caledonia. It is also a sort of constitutionalized *devolution of powers* for the territory recognizing Kanak identity and certain Kanak rights.[48]

No mechanism in the French legal system was established before 1982 (and applied in 1989) to make room for Kanak customs.[49] As a

[45] The Courts recognized, as soon as the 1920s, the existence of the personal status of Kanak people by refusing them to be enrolled in the civil registry. Lafargue, *supra* note 34 at 63.

[46] Arrêté n. 631 du 21 juin 1934 portant création d'un état civil des indigènes, JONC, 15 juillet 1934, 299.

[47] On the 22nd of April 1988, a group of Kanak *independentists* attacked the Fayaoué gendarmerie on the Ouvéa Island. Four police officers were killed during the attack and three *independentists* were injured. Twenty-seven police officers were kept as hostages for several days in a cave. On the 5th of May 1988, an assault was conducted by French soldiers. Nineteen Kanak *independentists* and two soldiers were killed during the assault. "Grotte d'Ouvéa : La République a été dévoyée pour des raisons de basse politique," *J Monde* (November 2, 2011), online: www.lemonde.fr/idees/article/2011/11/02/grotte-d-ouvea-la-republique-a-ete-devoyee-pour-des-raisons-de-basse-politique_1597407_3232.html.

[48] The article 77 of the French Constitution refers to the Nouméa Agreement.

[49] This does not mean that the Courts did not have to apply customary law before 1982. Lafargue, *supra* note 32 at 71.

consequence, for more than forty years the Kanak people had to experience the paradox of having their customs recognized by the French Constitution with the refusal of judges to apply it.

Until 1989, when the Kanak people began bringing cases to French judges asking for the implementation of their customary civil status, judges had declared that they had no jurisdiction to hear their claims and to apply customary rules, and sent the Kanak people back to their own judges.[50] In addition, French judges systematically imposed an implicit renunciation of the customary civil status through the fact that Kanak people were coming to them and then judges were applying the civil law status to them.[51] Judges could argue that they had no basis (in written law) to say the law of the Kanak applied.[52] However, judges could have been helped by experts through the *amicus curiae* mechanism which allows judges to ask someone who is not a party to the case to offer assistance to the court. The attitude of judges during that period of time demonstrates the goal to assimilate, or marginalize, Kanak people and their legal culture.

During the 1930s, while the French courts were refusing to hear Kanak litigants, judge Éric Rau proposed the creation of customary courts as already existed in the France's empire to enforce respect for local populations and their legal cultures.[53] This only occurred in 1982 with the local government headed by independence leader Jean-Marie Tjibaou who proposed the creation of bicultural courts to apply the previously ignored customary law. This change took the form of a new regulation adopted in 1982 that stated that judges were to be assisted by customary assessors in cases involving two people with a customary civil status.[54] However, this mechanism was only implemented in 1989 with the adoption of a new statute creating two Courts in Koné and Lifou; at which time, the Courts became accessible to the population, promoting better access to justice.[55]

In 1991, an unprecedented decision of the Cour de Cassation[56] stated that the Courts had to apply the Kanak custom when two disputing

[50] Lafargue, ibid. at 65. [51] *Ibid* at 64. [52] *Ibid.*

[53] Eric Rau, *Institutions et coutumes canaques* (Paris: L'Harmattan rééditions, 2006).

[54] *Ordonnance n° 82-877*, October 15, 1982 [*Ordonnance n° 82-877*] instituant des assesseurs coutumiers dans le territoire de la Nouvelle-Calédonie et Dépendances au tribunal civil de première instance et à la cour d'appel (J.O.R.F, 17 octobre 1982, 3106).

[55] *Loi, n° 89-378* [*Loi, n° 89-378*] at 1402, publiée au Journal officiel de la Nouvelle-Calédonie du 27 juin 1989; Lafargue, *supra* note 43 at 122, 126.

[56] The *Cour de Cassation* is the French Supreme Court in civil and criminal matters.

parties each maintained customary civil status.[57] The Court added that judges have to apply customary rules even in cases where the two parties would have refused the participation of customary assessors.

Finally, article 19 of the Loi organique n° 99–209 du 19 mars 1999 recalled the rule that "Civil courts are the sole authorities competent to hear disputes and queries relating to customary civil status or customary land. It is then supplemented by customary assessors as provided by law." The customary assessors are designated according to the customary areas of the parties (there are eight customary areas in New Caledonia). Customary assessors must be over twenty-five years old and they are selected through customary rules. Customary assessors are always the majority in the court, always in pairs, and are present to explain the case and the customary rules to the State judge. In these circumstances, in our opinion, the role of judges is mainly to transcribe the solution in a decision, and thus more oral rules become written law principles.[58]

One limit to this framework is where a person of "ordinary civil status" disputes with another of "customary law civil status." In this case, the judge will apply the civil status regime. In practice, there is no superior status, only a rule to deal with conflicts between norms inspired by the heritage of assimilation.

8.3.2 *The Acculturation of State Legal Institutions*

Since 1989, it has been observed that the Kanak are less reluctant to go to court to assert their rights. As a result, the case law in the field of customary civil status and customary land continues to grow significantly.[59] An increasing number of lawyers are interested in commenting on the case law and in studying this unique legal dynamic. The success of this experience rests on several elements: the legitimacy of the customary assessors, the creation of the Courts in Koné and Lifou, and finally the personality of the State judges.[60]

[57] Cass. civ. 2e, 6 février 1991, Bull. civ. 1991, II, n° 44; D. 1992, jur., 93, note G. Orfila.

[58] Régis Lafargue, "La 'voie' néo-calédonienne pour sortir de 'l'enchevêtrement normatif': Jeu D'ombres et de Lumières Sur La Coutume," in Jean-Yves Faberon & Armand Hage, eds., *Mondes océaniens : études en l'honneur de Paul de Deccker* (L'Harmattan, 2010) at 65.

[59] With all jurisdictions taken together, the number of cases represents approximately 300 cases every year, which is few compared to ordinary cases. The Nouméa Court of Appeal issued 9 decisions in 2012, and 23 in 2013. The Cour de Cassation issued 3 decisions in 2013.

[60] Some of these State judges can be seen in action the documentary of Éric Beauducel, *Une justice entre deux mondes* (ELKA Production, 2013).

The procedure for selecting customary assessors guarantees their legitimacy, especially because they come from the customary areas of the parties.[61] The creation of the Courts in Koné in the North Province and in Lifou in the Province of Loyalty Islands has clearly brought justice closer to the Kanak people. A comparison of the New Caledonian experience with that of the Amerindian people of French Guyana is illustrative here. The Amerindian people have never renounced their personal status, and many of them still live according to customary rules. Therefore, they should be able to claim the application of their customary rules in civil matters. However, the judicial phenomenon as observed in New Caledonia did not occur in French Guyana. From a legal point of view, this can be explained by the absence of a customary Civil Registry. This was present in New Caledonia before the adoption of a new regulation in 1934.[62] Even with such a registry, French Guyana would still need a rule or a mechanism to deal with the conflict between norms and would require modified Courts capable of interpreting their oral custom. In fact, French Guyana's current situation is similar to that of New Caledonia approximately a century ago. From a practical point of view, it can also be explained, at least in part, by the large distance between the Court in Cayenne (the capital of French Guyana) and the predominant residencies of some tribes (e.g., a distance of several days by boat), resulting in the hesitance of many to bring their claims before the State courts.[63] This reluctance of the indigenous population is illustrative of one of the four types of sociabilities outlined by Boaventura De Sousa Santos, namely a sociability of coexistence[64].

The situation of French Guyana has been denounced in the years 1995–98, by a former President of the Cayenne Court of justice:

> . . .it seems that once paid a tribute of principle to the picturesqueness, the potential legal value of Customs should remain hidden precisely in the

[61] Lafargue, *supra* note 32 at 79.

[62] Arrêté n. 631 du 21 juin 1934 portant création d'un état civil des indigènes, JONC, 15 juillet 1934, 299

[63] A lack of trust or simply a lack of interest could also explain this situation. However, it is surprising to note that among all the strategies used by the Amerindian people, this one is not represented. See in particular the work of Alexis Tiouka in French Guyana who is using mostly international instruments in order to promote the rights of the Amerindian people. Alexis Tiouka "Les Amérindiens et l'avenir institutionnel de la Guyane," in Jean-Yves Faberon, ed., *Les collectivités françaises d'Amérique au carrefour des institutions* (La Documentation française, CEREC, 2006) at 65–71.

[64] De Sousa Santos, supra note 28 at 473–4.

> place where it is of great interest to a significant part of the population [...] Hence this paradox: those who tolerate without hesitation (but sometimes with a touch of condescension towards the 'primitive') the coexistence of conflicting legal systems, fear that the obvious conflict between some laws and some customs would be brought to courts able to judge the case. Custom does not enter the courtroom in Cayenne, for a simple reason: indigenous people don't sue anybody. This would never occur to them. Would you knock on the door of a House of which all doors seem to be closed? If they would do so, how would their applications be received?[65]

State judges are usually unprepared to face the Caledonian reality, but have proven able to adapt their practices. Their main difficulty is in understanding the explanations of the assessors who usually describe how things should have been done, rather than to give general rules. Some people criticize the lack of theory in the explanation of the customary assessors.[66] As a result, State judges need to take time to listen and to translate the explanations of the Kanak people into legal principles. Since the late 1990s and the 2000s, legal writings and case law have been published that can aid judges to prepare.

As a result of the interactions between judges and the Kanak, exchanges between their respective legal orders and a mutual acculturation can be observed. This is the particular case of State judges who have adapted some of their practices by working with the customary assessors.

65 "...On a l'impression qu'une fois rendu un hommage de principe au pittoresque, la valeur juridique potentielle des coutumes devrait demeurer cachée précisément à l'endroit où elles concernent une masse significative de personnes [...] D'où ce paradoxe: les mêmes qui tolèrent sans barguigner (parfois avec un brin de condescendance à l'égard des 'primitifs') la coexistence de systèmes juridiques contradictoires redoutent que le conflit patent entre certaines lois et certaines coutumes soit élevé devant les tribunaux aptes à les trancher. La coutume n'entre pas dans le prétoire à Cayenne, pour cette raison bien simple: les autochtones ne font jamais de procès civil à quiconque. C'est que cela ne leur vient jamais à l'esprit. Frappe-t-on à la porte d'une maison dont toutes les ouvertures paraissent obstruées ? S'ils le faisaient, comment accueillerait-on leurs demandes?" Didier Peyrat, *Le Juge et le Lieu. Essai sur le besoin de droit en Guyane* (Ibis Rouge Edition, 1999) at 63.

66 "Le rôle joué par l'assesseur coutumier est parfois nié ou minimisé, au motif qu'il n'exprimerait jamais d'emblée un point de vue 'théorique'. Il explique quelles procédures, quelles attitudes, auraient été idoines en la circonstance, ou conformes aux devoirs coutumiers, en donnant des exemples, par analogie, conciliables avec la solution proposée. L'assesseur n'explique pas, du moins spontanément, les ressorts intimes d'une règle, car il ne porte pas de jugement extérieur sur sa société: pour lui, la solution proposée relève de l'évidence (...). L'assesseur évoque donc des 'faits normatifs' plus aisément qu'il n'évoque des principes: il dit ce qui fait ordre et ce qui fait désordre sans sa société." Lafargue, *supra* note 58 at 70.

The duplication of the proceedings reveals the customary norm: because customary rules are not codified, State judges have been forced to adapt Court procedures. They had instituted a pre-litigation phase[67] where a collection and explanation of Kanak customary law was assessed to judge its relevance.[68] This phase was essential for the emergence of customary rules, especially if indigenous rights in New Caledonia were to be recognized. This practice affected the material content of the Court's decisions. State judges recalled the legal and cultural context of the Kanak society which led to very detailed and "culturally colored" decisions.[69] However, this practice was only used on rare occasions and has been fully abandoned today. Lawyers now have enough information in the form of "precedents" to avoid the need for this procedural phase.

The customary interlude: The practices of several successive State judges have led to the emergence of a new process. In some cases, State judges have decided to defer the court's decision in preference to allowing the parties to hold a customary palaver ("*palabre*").[70] The customary assessors are then sent to follow the discussion and to act as mediators. When discussions end, assessors return to the State judge and inform him/her of whether an agreement has been reached.[71] Even without an agreement, this phase at least helps to explain the issue and relevant customary rules.[72]

The customary interlude is normally an option for judges. However, in the case of the customary dissolution of a marriage, it is a legal obligation according to the Deliberation[73] n. 424 of April 3, 1967. Article 44 of this text provides that before bringing the case to the court, Kanak people must have engaged in a "*préalable coutumier.*" This involves bringing their case to the clans before appearing before a judge.[74] Without a "*préalable coutumier,*" a judge will refuse to hear the case, reaffirming the authority of the clans.

By adopting such a procedure, State judges recognize that they are not the only relevant normative order addressing legal issues. In fact, they recognize the responsibility of customary authorities to resolve disputes. In this case, there is clear coordination between the roles played by State

67 Lafargue, *supra* note 32 at 316. This is explored in the context of ADR by Morgan Brigg in his contribution to this volume: Chapter 10 – "Rebalancing Power and Culture: The Case of Alternative Dispute Resolution."

68 *Ibid.* 69 *Ibid*, at 317. 70 Ibid at 318. 71 *Ibid.* 72 *Ibid.*

73 A Deliberation is a binding text adopted by the Congress of New Caledonia.

74 *Waute* vs *Pujapujane*, 2013 Nouméa Court of Appeals.

judges and customary authorities. Moreover, this procedure also upholds the legitimacy of the Court and the decision of judges.[75]

As a result, the role and the practice of State judges are deeply evolving as they engage with the Kanak legal order. Judges are working more like their common law counterparts though their reliance on precedents.[76] However, this adaptation and shift in their vision of justice requires more attempts at mediating the legal orders present in New Caledonia and more efforts from State judges in this regard.[77] They must be willing to question their traditional role and the place of customary authorities. Moreover, much like an ethnologist, judges must be accepted by customary authorities for legal pluralism to hold meaning.[78]

By recognizing the customary personal status of the Kanak people, we can talk of a "clarified and balanced legal pluralism" leading to peaceful coexistence between the State legal order and the Kanak legal order.[79] Hence, the personal status mechanism also constitutes an effective way to organize the coexistence of the various communities, each with their own values, on the Caledonian territory.[80]

The institutional and legal mechanisms and the practices of actors are capable of reaching the sociability of conviviality model defined by Boaventura de Sousa Santos. In this legal interface, the authority of the State court is shared between the Kanak legal orders (represented by the assessors) and the State legal order (represented by State judges). The Kanak assessors actively control customary rules as custom is oral in New Caledonia. Under this framework, we can observe a gradual evolution towards a heightened degree of mutual recognition and hybridization, which characterizes a sociability of conviviality. The Kanak and the State legal orders share the role of authority, while working toward a hybrid form of law: *la coutume judiciaire*[81] (judicial custom). These practices are proactive and future-oriented (characterizing a sociability of conviviality), rather than reactive and past-oriented (characterizing a sociability of reconciliation).

Despite many explicit and implicit attempts to subordinate the Kanak legal order through different strategies,[82] the State and the Kanak people

[75] Lafargue, *supra* note 32 at 319. [76] Lafargue, *supra* note 58 at 65.
[77] Lafrague, *supra* note 32, at 321. [78] Ibid at 320; Lafargue, *supra* note 43 at 134.
[79] Lafargue, *supra* note 1 at 96. [80] Lafargue, *supra* note 43 at 63.
[81] Some authors talk about the "judicial custom" to refer to this hybrid form of law. Lafargue, *supra* note 32.
[82] Otis, *supra* note 9 at 21.

have managed to build an effective forum for customary laws to be implemented. In this framework, State judges act as mediators between the customary legal order and the State legal order. The acculturation of both the Kanak people and the judges, as well as the growing trust between them, has led to increasingly effective coordination between the State and the Kanak legal systems. However, this is a fragile process as it is based mainly upon mutual trust. Moreover, this coordinated process suffers from its limitation to only civil matters as opposed to criminal matters.

8.4 The Frontiers of Recognizing the Kanak Legal Order

8.4.1 The Non-Recognition of Customary Law in the Field of Criminal Law

Customary law in New Caledonia only applies to civil matters. As a result, the State does not accept legal pluralism in the field of criminal law. In its decision from the April 28, 2009, the Nouméa Court of Appeal stated that the expulsion by using violence of occupants from customary land even based on customary doctrine and the ruling of a customary authority may be a criminal offence. This is the case when such customary rulings result in the destruction of the occupied buildings and the personal belongings of former occupants forced to reluctantly obey the legal decision of the customary authority.[83]

However, the Courts in criminal matters in New Caledonia differ from the Courts in metropolitan France. Since 1989, civil assessors in charge of representing Caledonian society assist judges.[84] They are not in charge of expressing the custom which is not recognized by judges in criminal matters. However, the inclusion of the assessors in the composition of the courts constitutes a step towards the recognition of the social and cultural specificities of New Caledonia. This is particularly the case in the North province and the Loyalty Island province where the majority of Kanak people reside and from which a pool of civil assessors may be selected.[85]

Almost ten years after the implementation of customary assessors, the Nouméa agreement from 1998 stated that "[t]he role of the customary authorities for the social prevention and the criminal mediation will be

[83] *Ministère Public* vs *Fisdiepas*, 2009 Cour d'appel de Nouméa; Lafargue, *supra* note 32 at 181–2.

[84] Lafargue, ibid at 78. [85] *Ibid*, at 175.

recognized." This role in the field of "customary criminal mediation" still needs to be defined in law. Until now, only experimental procedures have been implemented.[86] For numerous reasons, the implementation of this mechanism is exceedingly problematic. Firstly, who holds ultimate authority over its governance has yet to be determined. Secondly, understanding the meaning of Kanak custom contemporaneously with the concepts and rules of the criminal law system can be very difficult, as some of them cannot be translated into the Kanak legal order. By maintaining strict authority over criminal law issues pertaining to the Kanak, without attempting to ameliorate the combination of the two legal traditions, the French State may potentially render a narrow and artificial recognition of the Kanak legal order in criminal matters.[87]

It is important to note that the distinction between civil and criminal law is strictly irrelevant for Kanak society.[88] Furthermore, recognizing custom only in regard to civil matters is hard to understand and to justify in the Caledonian context. It removes from customary authorities the power to punish people who violate customary rules. It thus weakens the enforcement of the customary legal framework.

In the context of criminal law, the application of Santos's model inherently recognizes that by refusing to appreciate and acknowledge the legitimacy of the Kanak legal orders, the State is creating a sociability of violence which is characterized by their dominant culture, otherwise exercising control over the contact zone. This refusal of recognition, is a source of cognitive injustices and thus of social injustices according to Santos[89].

Some alternatives can be imagined on the basis of the "social prevention" role of the Kanak authorities (the tribal elders) recognized in the Nouméa Agreement.[90] They could be achieved through the creation of an alternative criminal status and by the adoption of a customary

[86] Pierre Frezet, "Chronique d'un jugement qui ne sera jamais rendu" (2006) 51 *Droit Cult Rev Int Interdiscip* 233 at 234.

[87] Lafargue, *supra* note 32 at 176–8. See Brigg, Chapter 10.

[88] Régis Lafargue, "'Prévention sociale', droits des victimes et statut personnel," in Jean-Yves Faberon et al, eds., *Destins des collectivités politiques d'Océanie : peuples, populations, nations, États, territoires, pays, patries, communautés, frontières : actes du colloque international organisé du 7 au 10 mars 2011 à Nouméa* (Singularités, Presses universitaires d'Aix-Marseille, 2011) at 641.

[89] Boaventura De Sousa Santos, *Epistemologies of the South: Justice against Epistemicide* (Paradigm Publishers, 2014).

[90] *1.2.4. Accord de Nouméa*, mai 1998 [*1.2.4. Accord de Nouméa*].

deontology.[91] New Caledonia should now consider this. It is in a phase where the territory should look at foreign cases and analyze how other states such as Canada, Australia, and South Africa have managed to integrate indigenous customary laws within the criminal legal system as well as recognizing customary structures for the treatment of criminal issues.[92]

8.4.2 *The Subordination of the Kanak Legal Order to the State Legal Order in the Legislative Field*

In New Caledonia the legislative powers are shared between the French State, New Caledonia, and the Provinces. Article 22 of the Loi Organique 99–209 gives New Caledonia and its institutions the authority to adopt statutes in the field of customary civil status, customary lands, customary palaver, and the limits of customary areas, and since July 1, 2013 all issues in the field of civil legislation.

However, the government and the Congress (the local parliament) do not specifically represent the Kanak people even if some Kanak are elected in these institutions. Instead, the Nouméa Agreement has created a new institution devoted to representing the Kanak people: the Customary Senate, an assembly composed of sixteen representatives from the eight customary areas of New Caledonia and designated according to customary rules.

The Customary Senate must be consulted on projects relating to Kanak identity. It thus allows the Kanak people to be heard with respect to legislative projects. The Senate can give an opinion on projects that call upon symbols of New Caledonian identity, the customary civil status, the customary land regime, the customary assemblies, and the limits of customary areas. However, the Senate cannot block a project. It has no veto power in the legislature and can only slow the adoption of a project.[93] Thus, although the State allows for the expression of Kanak voices, it can still impose its own views. As a result, the Customary Senate cannot actually safeguard Kanak custom in the legislative arena. However, customary law is protected by the French Constitution as far as the

[91] Lafargue, *supra* note 88 at 642–3. [92] *Ibid*, at 645–6.

[93] Articles 137 to 148, *Loi n° 99-209 du 19 mars 1999 organique relative à la Nouvelle-Calédonie*, March 21, 1999 [*Loi n° 99-209 du 19 mars 1999 organique relative à la Nouvelle-Calédonie*] at 4197.

rights of the sea clan of this area. This was the result of a negotiation between the South province and the sea clan accepting the creation of a reserve.

In both cases, it seems that the type of sociability emerging is coexistence because the process of hybridization is not initiated. In our opinion it is merely a mutual recognition of the existence of different legal orders. However, with time and with increased exchange between them, this sociability could evolve towards a sociability of conviviality. For example in the context of the research project, while contact is currently confined to an authorization to conduct research, we can imagine that Kanak people could collaborate with scientists during the collection and the analysis of material and data in the future. These practices would only emerge as a result of contact and will result in increased opportunities for hybridization.

8.5.1.2 The Participation of the Kanak People in a Major Industrial Project

The Kanak successfully compelled a private company – whose purpose was to exploit nickel resources in southern New Caledonia – to enter into a contract that adapted the company's initial project design to fit their needs. As a result, the Goro Nickel Company, the customary council from the Djubea Kapone area, the Customary Senate and the Rheebu Nuu committee[100] have entered into an agreement.[101] No public authority such as the South Province or the government of New Caledonia is part of the agreement.

This contract is based on the 1998 Nouméa Agreement recognizing that New Caledonia was inhabited when European people arrived,[102] the principles developed during the 1992 Rio Summit, the Declaration of the United Nations on the Rights of Indigenous people,[103] and finally the perceptions and the history of the Kanak people living in southern New Caledonia.[104]

[100] Rhéébù Nùù is an environmental organization from New Caledonia. Rhéébù Nùù means "eye of the land" in the local Djubea language. The group was created in order to watch the activities of the Goro Nickel mining company operating on the customary land of Kanak people in the extreme south of Grande Terre in New Caledonia. www.oeil.nc/cdrn/index.php/acteur/view/45

[101] *Protocole d'accord portant pacte pour un développement durable du grand sud* (2008) at 1.

[102] *Ibid*, at 2. [103] *Ibid*, at 3–4. [104] *Ibid*, at 4.

In this agreement, the company committed itself to define a plan for the participation of local populations as part of its efforts towards sustainable development.[105] The contract provided for the creation of a foundation,[106] one of its objectives being the social and cultural development of the local population. Finally, the parties also agreed to create an environmental consultative customary committee responsible for giving recommendations and acting as an interface between the company and the local population.[107] This committee is in charge of ensuring that Kanak knowledge is integrated into the project.[108] To do so, the committee is responsible for establishing a strategy for the integration of Kanak knowledge in the operations of the company.[109]

To achieve these ends, the committee gives its opinion on the company's environmental management program and its monitoring protocol.[110] It can decide to conduct environmental studies with use of the budget allotted by the company (approximately 200,000 euros per year).[111] At least in theory, this enables opportunities to mobilize and integrate indigenous knowledge. Even if the company has no obligation to follow committee opinions and recommendations, its existence nonetheless compels the company to engage in some reflection over the Kanak's expressed expectations.[112]

That the committee is well represented is ensured through its composition of fifteen Kanak representatives. Two representatives from the company attend meetings, but only as observers.

The creation of this committee is then, at least at first blush, a significant step toward the recognition and the consideration of Kanak expectations regarding industrial projects and their environmental impacts. However, while the committee officially began meeting in 2009, it is difficult to assess its real impact. It is nonetheless still interesting to see that the Kanak have managed to force the creation of a customary deliberative and consultative organ in a major industrial project, and, moreover, that this was achieved without the participation of State or public authorities.

It is difficult to assess the type of sociability stemming from the agreement between the Kanak people and the company due to the lack

[105] *Ibid*, at 5–6. [106] *Ibid*, at 7–9. [107] *Ibid*, at 9–11. [108] *Ibid*, at article 11.
[109] *Ibid*. [110] *Ibid*, at article 12. [111] *Ibid*.
[112] "La Société Goro Nickel s'engage à contribuer de façon significative et durable au développement social et économique des populations voisines du projet, sans affecter les composants vitaux de l'écosystème ni la faculté des membres de ces populations d'utiliser les ressources terrestres et maritimes de façon traditionnelle." *Ibid*, at article 10.

of information about the process and outcome of the Environmental Consultative Customary Committee. In theory, the recognition of the Kanak voice and the project to take into account indigenous knowledge into environmental assessments would tend to a sociability of conviviality. However, the role of the committee is only consultative, and foreign experiences have demonstrated the difficulties of integrating indigenous knowledge where projects are co-managed[113]. As a result, the type of sociability resulting from this legal interface could either be weighted towards reconciliation (and in some aspects even violence in case where indigenous knowledge is not seen as serious enough to be taken into account) or conviviality. It is however too early to draw a conclusion as to its outcome.

8.5.2 The Work of the "Agence pour le Développement de la Culture Kanak" (ADCK)[114]

The Kanak have developed their own practices in other areas where the State does not recognize Kanak law. This is demonstrated through the management of the Kanak traditional knowledge by the ADCK.

8.5.2.1 A Spontaneous Project

Since 2002, the ADCK has reactivated a process of traditional knowledge collection in the eight customary areas of New Caledonia. The ADCK collaborates with the customary councils and trains Kanak traditional knowledge collectors. They are in charge of collecting the Kanak oral heritage. The ADCK also spontaneously receives knowledge from holders who do not wish or who cannot pass it on to young people through traditional canals. In some cases, elders are unwilling to transfer their knowledge because no young people will receive it or because they are scared of what the young generation could do with it.[115]

113 See for instance: Graham White, "Cultures in Collision: Traditional Knowledge and Euro-Canadian Governance Processes in Northern Land-Claim Board" (2006) 59:4 *Arctic* at 401–14; Paul Nadasdy, *Hunters and Bureaucrats. Power, Knowledge, and Aboriginal-State Relations in the Southwest Yukon* (UBC Press, 2003); Thierry Rodon, *En partenariat avec l'État: les expériences de co-gestion des Autochtones du Canada* (Presses Universitaires de Laval, 2003).

114 The Agency for the Development of the Kanak Culture.

115 MWA VEE, "À la recherche des savoirs kanak" (2003) 40 *Rev Cult Kanak* at 68.

The ADCK also plays a role in the conservation of indigenous knowledge by digitally storing it. In addition, the Agency promotes the transmission of customary knowledge by means of producing cultural events.

Measures for the management of the knowledge have also been implemented. The Agency has established various degrees of access to knowledge holders depending on their wish to be contacted and the type of customary knowledge they hold.[116]

Neither the French State nor New Caledonia have adopted specific rules for recognizing, protecting, and conserving Kanak traditional knowledge. Thus, the ADCK is an entity firmly born from the need of the local Kanak populations to have an alternative framework to traditional intellectual property rights.

8.5.2.2 An Inspiration for a New Legal Framework

In 2010, the New Caledonian government drafted a new bill that recognizes and protects intangible aspects of Kanak cultural heritage[117]. This effort found its roots in the different international treaties that France had signed, its dealings with traditional knowledge,[118] and the willingness of the Kanak people to protect and conserve their cultural heritage[119].

The statute provides for a unique framework in France.[120] It was inspired by the Indian and the Peruvian state experiences and by the work of the ADCK.[121] In fact, the statute promotes the creation of an independent

[116] *Ibid.*

[117] The bill was drafted by Régis Lafargue assisted by a committee composed of Kanak people.

[118] *The Convention on Biological Diversity*, 1992 [*The Convention on Biological Diversity*]; *The Nagoya Protocol*, 2010 [*The Nagoya Protocol*]; *The Convention for the Safeguarding of Intangible Cultural Heritage*, 2003 [*The Convention for the Safeguarding of Intangible Cultural Heritage*]; *The United Nations Declaration on the Rights of Indigenous People*, 2007 [*The United Nations Declaration on the Rights of Indigenous People*].

[119] Thomas Burelli, dans Jean-Yves Faberon, Thierry Mennesson (eds.), *Peuple premier et cohésion sociale en Nouvelle-Calédonie: identités et rééquilibrages: actes du colloque organisé à Nouméa les 30 et 31 août 2012 par la Maison de la Mélanésie-Paul de Deckker* (Presses universitaires d'Aix-Marseille, 2012) at 116–18.

[120] *Ibid*, at 123–8; Sarah Vanuxem, "Le devenir des régimes d'Accès aux ressources génétiques et de Partage des Avantages (APA)" (2013) 214 *Droit Environ* at 256–64.

[121] Geoffroy Filoche, "Les connaissances, innovations et pratiques traditionnelles en matière de biodiversité: un kaléidoscope juridique" (2009) 2 *Droit Société* 433 at 433–58; Thomas Burelli, "La reconnaissance et de la protection des savoirs traditionnels associés à la biodiversité dans l'outre-mer français: une nécessité jusqu'à présent négligée," in Stéphane Pessina Dassonville, dir., *Le statut des peuples autochtones. À la croisée des savoirs* (Les Cahiers d'anthropologie du droit, 2012) at 137–62.

especially true for those territories where the recognition of indigenous rights is not as developed as in New Caledonia.

The process of recognizing the legal order of the Kanak people and their culture is not over. The case law is currently growing and ambitious projects respecting this area of inquiry are taking root, including the effort to formally recognize and protect Kanak indigenous cultural heritage.

The bicultural courts have proven to be an effective catalyst for recognizing Kanak identity and revitalizing the Kanak legal order. However, this system is still under threat, because it is still viewed suspiciously. Some voices question the need for such jurisdictions, especially since the purpose of the 1998 Nouméa agreement was to forge a common legal destiny. Some authors interpret the notion of a common destiny as a unitary one and plead for the abolishment of the Kanak customary status. This is the same reasoning that prevailed when article 75 of the French Constitution was adopted: that Kanak people should give up their personal status and accept the civil status and related French values. This is an assimilationist interpretation of the common destiny agenda. This chapter purports that the common destiny, in light of the Nouméa Agreement and of the evolution of the situation, calls for a more pluralist approach in which Kanak values and rules have their place alongside the civil rules. The Kanak customary status is not a cage, but rather the dynamic expression of Kanak identity. They can decide to give it up for the civil status or they can do the opposite by proving that they are living in accordance with custom as accepted by the clans.[126] A recent case has widened this possibility.[127]

For more than two millennia, the Kanak legal culture has proven capable to evolve and adapt to all kind of interactions – even the most brutal. It has also proven to be a great source of inspiration for the Civil Law in terms of providing new concepts and offering innovative legal solutions.[128] This is why we believe that rather than try to marginalize

[126] Lafargue, *supra* note 58 at 62.

[127] Cass. Civ. 1ère, June 26, 2013, no. 12-30.154, Bulletin civil 2013, I, n°139, *Procureur Général* v. *Poadey*. Sandrine Sana, Journal de droit international, juillet-septembre 2014.

[128] Such as the recognition of "cultural damages" or "spiritual damages" related to pollutions and environmental damages. Régis Lafargue, "Le préjudice civilisationnel pour atteinte à l'environnement. Droit au cadre naturel et réalités socioculturelles: interdépendances et interdisciplinarité" (2010) 1 *Droit Société* 151 at 151–69; Régis Lafargue, "Le préjudice culturel né du dommage environnemental: par-delà nature et culture, un préjudice écologique spécifique," in Laurent Neyret & Gilles J. Martin, eds., *Nomenclature des préjudices environnementaux* (LGDJ, coll. Droit des affaires, 2012) at 219–50.

or destroy the Kanak legal culture in the name of so-called superior principles, the French legal system should develop and deepen its interactions with it. This may eventually lead not only to a better understanding and respect between cultures, but also encourage the phenomena of interlegality and mutual development for both legal cultures.

PART III

Alternative Dispute Resolution

resolution. It uses the history of ADR advocacy as a site for considering the rhetoric used to describe and "sell" ADR to sometimes enthusiastic and sometimes skeptical (or even hostile) Western audiences as either not so culturally different, or as salutary despite (or indeed because of) cultural difference.[2] The cultural claims made in the ADR literature play with notions of time, space, and alterity to present alternatives to Western legal institutions. These cultural models or transplants are presented as different, yet not so different; as potentially transformative, yet not revolutionary; as exotic, yet at the same time tame.

This chapter begins with an overview of the different paths of "non-Western" influence on ADR – both real and supposed[3] – from the 1960s or so forward. My focus is on three ways that culture has entered and moved through the ADR discourse, evident in processes of *criticizing* the existing system, of *yearning* for alternatives, and of *shopping* for models of change. The rhetoric is my focus: how were proposals for new processes characterized so as to negotiate the intertwining demands of cultural sameness and difference? To illustrate these issues, I turn to examine in detail the use made within the ADR literature of a particularly frequently cited African conflict-resolution model, the Kpelle "moot." In the conclusion, I return to the question of culture and law to consider questions surrounding cultural influence and cultural transplants in the elaboration of Western ADR.

9.2 Criticizing

The cultural claim in ADR has from the beginning to the present day rested on critique: on dissatisfaction with the existing Western legal world of judges, courts, lawyers, and adversarial litigation. These critiques have taken different forms, of course, but all begin with a sense that the Western

[2] For intellectual histories of ADR, see Carrie Menkel-Meadow, "Introduction: What Will We Do When Adjudication Ends? A Brief Intellectual History of ADR" (1997) 44 *UCLA L Rev* 1613; Carrie Menkel-Meadow, "Mothers and Fathers of Invention: The Intellectual Founders of ADR" (2000) 16 *Ohio St J Disp Resol* 1; Michal Alberstein, "Forms of Mediation and Law: Cultures of Dispute Resolution" (2007) 22 *Ohio St J Disp Resol* 321. An early and more political look at aspects of ADR history is Richard L Abel, ed., *The Politics of Informal Justice* (New York: Academic Press, 1982). For a disappointing general history, see Jerome T Barrett & Joseph Barrett, *A History of Alternative Dispute Resolution: The Story of a Political, Social, and Cultural Movement* (San Francisco: Jossey-Bass, 2004). Other accounts will be referred to later.

[3] This qualifier reflects the often vigorous debate about whether influence moved from or to the West, or both. See below, text accompanying notes 35–6.

justice system is in crisis or – to cite frequently heard medical metaphors – unhealthy for individual litigants or sick systemically.[4] The crisis is in turn cast in identity terms: things do not work as well as they could, or do not work at all, because of what the West has become and how Westerners relate to one another – Westerners are competitive, adversarial, self-interested liberal individuals, and their disputing culture reflects this self-identity. Turning to its effects, this crisis or sickness has led to various dire consequences. For some, it means inefficiency and inaccessibility, as the court system subjects litigants to long delays, high costs, and their associated material and psychological pressures. For others, it means undermined justice, as the system encourages self-interest and zero-sum adversarialism, which lead to poor outcomes and failure to address the larger problems behind social conflict. The rhetoric of crisis and sickness has led many to conclude – beginning in the 1960s and continuing to the present – that radical solutions are needed, and this in turn has led ADR advocates to direct wistful looks to other times or places, where the malaise characterizing Western litigation was not so evident.[5]

The critique of the Western – and more particularly the North American – court system, with its adversarial procedure and its inefficiencies, has deep roots. In 1906, Roscoe Pound canvassed "the causes of popular dissatisfaction with the administration of justice," and in the late 1940s U.S. Appeals Court judge and legal realist Jerome Frank suggested various creative solutions to what he saw as the problematically exclusive focus on rationalism and objectivity in the formal justice system.[6] The critique received renewed and wide attention in the United States (and beyond) following the 1976 National Conference on the Causes of Popular Dissatisfaction with the Administration of Justice. Popularly known as the Pound Conference, because it was convened to take stock of Pound's criticisms

[4] On the different forms of critique within the ADR literature, see Christine B Harrington & Sally Engle Merry, "Ideological Production: The Making of Community Mediation" (1988) 22 *Law Soc Rev* 709; Kevin Avruch & Peter W Black, "ADR, Palau and the Contribution of Anthropology" in Alvin W Wolfe & Honggang Yang, eds., *Anthropological Contributions to Conflict Resolution* (Athens, GA: University of Georgia Press, 1996) 47 at 50; Joseph Folger, "Harmony and Transformative Mediation Practice: Sustaining Ideological Differences in Purpose and Practice" (2008) 84 *ND L Rev* 823.

[5] Alongside this advocacy were defenders of the existing system, who argued that the inefficiencies should not become an excuse to sacrifice the procedural and other guarantees of adversarial justice. See e.g., Owen M Fiss, "Against Settlement" (1984) 93 *Yale LJ* 1073.

[6] Roscoe Pound, "The Causes of Popular Dissatisfaction with the Administration of Justice" (1906) 14 *Am Law* 445; Jerome Frank, *Courts on Trial: Myth and Reality in American Justice* (Princeton: Princeton University Press, 1949).

from seventy years earlier, it featured a keynote address by U.S. Chief Justice Warren Burger, who raised concerns about the unhealthy state of the U.S. legal system, calling for lawyers to become "healers of society's conflicts" and to explore alternatives to adversarial litigation. Frank Sander followed with an early version of what he later termed the "multi-door courthouse," which would present potential litigants with alternatives to trial more efficiently tailored to their particular needs.[7]

In Canada, the legal professional and academic establishment underwent similar soul-searching a few years later. At the 1979 Conference on the Cost of Justice, Harry Arthurs argued for pluralism in the justice system, with options for litigants outside the courts, particularly conciliation. Benefits would include efficiency, but also putting the entire system on a more "humane and intelligent" footing.[8] In the years following, others in Canada echoed the call for alternatives to litigation,[9] as the ADR movement gathered momentum across North America.

The ADR critique contained (and still contains) various streams, and distinguishing these nuances is important for understanding the cultural aspects of the development of ADR. The efficiency critique has received the most press: the idea that the formal system is too costly and too slow to deal with the number and kinds of matters coming before it, leading to exacerbation of delays and frequently denial of justice. Alongside the efficiency critique is another that focuses not on the numbers, but on the purpose of a dispute resolution system and the quality of the outcomes it produces. Here the argument is that the formal justice system is ill-suited to achieve whatever wider goals one might wish for in dispute resolution, whether these be keeping social peace, promoting personal growth, or fostering a transformation of society away from conflict.[10] Both the

[7] The proceedings of the Pound Conference can be found in "Addresses Delivered at the National Conference on the Causes of Popular Dissatisfaction with the Administration of Justice" (1976) 70 *FRD* 79. See especially Warren E Burger, "Agenda for 2000 A.D.: Need for Systematic Anticipation," *ibid.* 83 at 96; Frank EA Sander, "Varieties of Dispute Processing," *ibid.* 111 at 131. (advocating "a Dispute Resolution Center.")

[8] H W Arthurs, "Alternatives to the Formal Justice System: Reminiscing About the Future" in *The Cost of Justice: Papers Prepared for Presentation at the Canadian Institute for the Administration of Justice Conference on the Cost of Justice* (Toronto: Carswell, 1980) at 14.

[9] Willard Estey, "Who Needs Courts" (1981) 1 *Windsor YB Access Just* 263; Russell L Horrocks, "Alternatives to the Courts in Canada" (1982) 20 *Alta L Rev* 326.

[10] See, e.g., Ted Becker, "Conflict and Paradox in the New American Mediation Movement: Status Quo and Social Transformation" (1986) *Mo J Disp Resol* 109 at 114–15; Robert A Baruch Bush & Joseph P Folger, *The Promise of Mediation: Responding to Conflict Through Empowerment and Recognition* (San Francisco: Jossey-Bass, 1994); Mark

efficiency critique and the justice critique lead to a search for alternatives. But where the efficiency critique evaluates alternatives in mainly operational terms (how will alternative *x* reduce costs or delays?), the justice critique defines alternatives in explicitly cultural terms (how will re-orienting conflict resolution along Buddhist or Indigenous or Afrocentric lines help us to reach better results?).[11]

The efficiency and justice critiques have fixed in the minds of justice system insiders and outsiders alike the conclusion that the system is in "crisis" – an argument that has been challenged as smacking of "golden age" nostalgia, but whose rhetorical power is undeniable.[12] Though most often voiced in the language of economics, the critiques also took on cultural terms, with the image that the North American justice system had become "uncivilized" or "inhumane" in its treatment of litigants.[13] In particular, adversarial litigation was seen as treating humans not as multi-faceted beings situated within a web of life relationships, but as one-dimensional disputants, a characterization that ignored affective motivations (emotions, caring, relationships) in its focus on the pecuniary interests of the parties.[14] The sense of urgent crisis has spurred the

S Umbreit, "Humanistic Mediation: A Transformative Journey of Peacemaking" (1997) 14 *Mediat Q* 201. Though many make the critique in general terms, it also appears in specific terms, such as that the existing system does not serve the needs of particular communities, and so must be reformed along different cultural lines. See e.g., Morris Jenkins, "Gullah Island Dispute Resolution: An Example of Afrocentric Restorative Justice" (2006) 37:2 *J Black Stud* 299. Similarly, the gendered nature of modes of dispute resolution fits here as well – mediation and other negotiated forms of justice are often seen as "feminine," in contrast to "male" adversarial modes. See e.g., Frank, *supra* note 7 at 384–8; Sally Engle Merry, "Sorting Out Popular Justice" in Neal Milner & Sally Engle Merry, eds., *The Possibility of Popular Justice: A Case Study of Community Mediation in the United States* (Ann Arbor: University of Michigan Press, 1995) 31 at 36.

11 E.g., Ran Kuttner, "From Adversity to Relationality: A Buddhist-Oriented View of Integrative Negotiation and Mediation" (2010) 25 *Ohio St J Disp Resol* 931. This point will be developed further later.

12 See Marc Galanter, "Lawyers in the Mist: The Golden Age of Legal Nostalgia" (1996) 100 *Dick L Rev* 549. For an overview of the crisis rhetoric of the 1970s, see Oscar G Chase, *Law, Culture, and Ritual: Disputing Systems in Cross-Cultural Context* (New York: New York University Press, 2005) at 100–9.

13 E.g., Maurice Rosenberg, "Devising Procedures That Are Civil to Promote Justice That Is Civilized" (1971) 69 *Mich L Rev* 797 at 820. ("We can improve the quality of justice for individuals by establishing a system that will be more humane, compassionate, and civilized than today's because it will be fitted with the men and means to function as it should—and not be abused by profligate overuse.")

14 See, among a growing literature, Daniel L Shapiro, "Emotions in Negotiation: Peril or Promise" (2004) 87 *Marq L Rev* 737; Erin Ryan, "The Discourse Beneath: Emotional Epistemology in Legal Deliberation and Negotiation" (2005) 10 *Harv Negot L Rev* 231.

search for informal alternatives to court-based litigation, making use of negotiated settlements, neighborhood justice centers, and the like.

Metaphors – and particularly medical ones – add urgency to the general rhetoric of crisis. The problems of litigation – whichever problems are the focus of the critique being made – are compared to a society-wide sickness of suboptimal dispute resolution mechanisms that threatens individual and collective well-being.[15] Alternatives to the courts thus become forms of therapy, a metaphor that in the early days of ADR resonated with the more general psychoanalytic turn within society.[16] Though some saw the "therapy" of ADR as akin to mind control, training the vulnerable to abandon their legal rights in favor of vague promises of a healthy conflict-free life,[17] for many ADR came to offer the promise of therapy for individuals and society alike, leading them out of deeply seated but harmful ways of relating.[18] Even hard-nosed efficiency critics likened "fitting the forum to the fuss" to emergency-room "triage," with cases being directed to the optimal dispute-resolution process within the multi-door courthouse.[19] The rhetoric of crisis and sickness, along with the promise of alternatives as therapy for the Western legal system, led naturally to longing looks to other times or places, where the malaise was not evident.

9.3 Yearning

Alongside and reinforcing the criticism of the Western legal system, ADR has always elicited and made use of a rhetoric of yearning. The "A" in ADR itself suggests a certain longing: whether construed as "alternative" or as the more recent "appropriate," it bespeaks a desire to have something we currently do not. As Jerold Auerbach notes, perhaps with a

[15] E.g., Warren E. Burger, *supra* note 8 at 96. (lawyers should be "healers of society's conflicts"); Jane A Waldron et al, "A Therapeutic Mediation Model for Child Custody Dispute Resolution" (1984) 3 *Mediat Q* 5.

[16] Discussed in Harrington & Merry, *supra* note 5 at 715–6.

[17] This argument is especially associated with Laura Nader, for example, in Laura Nader, "Controlling Processes in the Practice of Law: Hierarchy and Pacification in the Movement to Re-Form Dispute Ideology" (1993) 9 *Ohio St J Disp Resol* 1 at 12–13.

[18] E.g., Robert Benham & Ansley Boyd Barton, "Alternative Dispute Resolution: Ancient Models Provide Modern Inspiration" (1996) 12 *Ga St U L Rev* 623.

[19] E.g., Menkel-Meadow, "Introduction" *supra* note 3 at 1616 (describing Sander's multi-door courthouse); Peter Salem, Debra Kulak & Robin M Deutsch, "Triaging Family Court Services: The Connecticut Judicial Branch's Family Civil Intake Screen" (2007) 27 *Pace L Rev* 741.

certain degree of irony, by the mid-twentieth century the ideal of ADR had "shimmered elusively like a desert mirage" until it was revived by "the euphoric hope that burst forth during the sixties, when community empowerment became a salient theme of political reform."[20] The yearning takes a range of intensities, and its objects vary as well. Rhetorically, it serves equally well as support for conservatism or for change. I would like here to focus on two modes of this yearning evident in the literature, which I roughly characterize as historical nostalgia and exotic longing. The former looks to a purer or simpler time the West had but has lost, while the latter looks to exogenous values the West never had, but wishes it did. What both share is a sense of absence (usually of missing community values of harmony, connectedness, altruism), a temporal or geographical (that is, cultural) Other, and a hope that society might be transformed so as to recapture at least some of what is missing.[21]

In some cases this yearning is a kind of historical (or more often quasi-historical) nostalgia, asserting a supposed shared Western past that has been lost in the wake of modern adversarial litigation. ADR would mean a return to communitarian values native to the West but since lost; in this formulation, ADR becomes a largely conservative remembrance of things past, a return to essential truths within the Western tradition. ADR advocacy is often supported by casual references to the "roots of justice," a vague historical claim that evokes a world without courts, without lawyers, without restrictive procedure, when a pure and direct and accessible justice had not yet become hyper-legalized and out of the reach of the general public.[22] Often an attempt is made to clothe this in the gravitas of "historians' history," such as in the "history of ADR"

[20] Jerold S Auerbach, *Justice without Law? Resolving Disputes without Lawyers* (New York: Oxford University Press, 1983) at 116.

[21] Discussion of these values (and in some cases critique of their role) runs through most of the ADR literature. See especially Laura Nader, *Harmony Ideology: Justice and Control in a Zapotec Mountain Village* (Stanford: Stanford University Press, 1990); Laura Nader, "Harmony Models and the Construction of Law" in Kevin Avruch, Peter W Black & Joseph A Scimecca, eds., *Conflict Resolution: Cross-Cultural Perspectives* (New York: Greenwood Press, 1991) 41 at 41–59; Graham Kemp & Douglas P Fry, eds., *Keeping the Peace: Conflict Resolution and Peaceful Societies around the World* (London: Routledge, 2004).

[22] Jennifer Llewellyn & Robert L Howse, *Restorative Justice: A Conceptual Framework* (Ottawa: Law Commission of Canada, 1998) at 5 (restorative justice is "a return to the roots of justice, and not as some new-age 'cure-all' for an ailing system."); David N Smith, "A Warmer Way of Disputing: Mediation and Conciliation" (1977) 26 *Am J Comp L Sup* 205 at 205 (ADR "represents a return, in part, to the more modest modes of dispute resolution of an earlier epoch"); Barrett & Barrett, *supra* note 3 at 2 (ADR's "roots run deep in human history").

section included at the beginning of many works advocating ADR,[23] or in more formally historical studies of Western disputing, such as Auerbach's widely cited 1983 book.[24] In the North American context, the argument is usually that early Americans tended to avoid the courts in favor of community-based negotiation or conciliation, and only in the increasingly urban and industrialized late nineteenth and twentieth century did the litigious society come to predominate.

It is worth pausing a moment to distinguish historical nostalgia within North American majority culture, my focus here, from the similar phenomenon of historical constructions by minority cultural groups (such as Aboriginal peoples or Blacks) to reclaim their own traditions.[25] The evocation of historical traditions by minority groups makes political claims of authenticity and identity in more specific and immediate ways than in the majority culture. As well, the tradition being claimed is one that distinguishes from the majority tradition ("our" as opposed to "their" tradition), whereas within majority culture historical models tend to be assumed to be common to all (such as the "Western tradition").[26] In both, historical specificity is deployed for political purposes, but the power differential between majority and minority culture changes the nature of the claim in the two cases, making it an identity-based claim in the latter context, a more general values-based claim in the former. Finally, as we will discuss later, the power differential affects how in each case institutions and methods derived from the claimed historical past are adopted.[27]

Historical nostalgia draws on a largely imagined past, reminiscent of Eric Hobsbawm's "invented tradition," and shaped to mesh with the rhetorical and political purposes of promoting reform.[28] Whether what

[23] E.g., the following early examples: Arthurs, *supra* note 9 at 5–6; Christine B Harrington, "Delegalization Reform Movements: A Historical Analysis" in Richard L Abel, ed., *The Politics of Informal Justice* (New York: Academic Press, 1982) 35.

[24] Auerbach, *supra* note 21.

[25] See e.g., John George Hansen, *Cree Restorative Justice: From the Ancient to the Present* (Kanata, Ont.: J. Charlton, 2009) (on Aboriginal traditions) and Jenkins, *supra* note 11 (on survivals of distinct forms of dispute resolution among Black communities in the Gullah Islands of South Carolina).

[26] Jeremy Webber's remarks on legal traditions in the context of legal pluralism are relevant here: see Jeremy Webber, "Legal Pluralism and Human Agency" (2006) 4 *Osgoode Hall LJ* 167 at 186–8.

[27] See below, text accompanying note 79.

[28] Eric Hobsbawm, "Introduction: Inventing Traditions" in Eric Hobsbawm & Terrence Ranger, eds., *The Invention of Tradition* (Cambridge: Cambridge University Press, 1983) 1 at 1–14.

is being invoked is colonial North America or the mists of the human past, history provides an evidentiary basis upon which to promote ADR's "fit" within contemporary Western legal systems. It helps soften the novelty of ADR by making a cultural claim of sameness whose implications we will explore at the end of the chapter. The purpose is transformational, but a conservative transformation that will take place firmly within the limits of a shared Western culture. The goal is not revolution, but reformation: to resurrect, within Western disputing culture, values from a more congenial time in the Western past.

A different form of yearning – which we might term "exotic longing" – looks beyond the West to other cultures as living exemplars of ancient wisdom and ways of doing things largely foreign to the West. Here too the past is the focus, but it is a past-in-the-present that evokes the primitive Other in order to confirm Western ideas of pure and uncorrupted pre-modernity. The purpose is again transformational, but unlike the conservative return to Western roots associated with historical nostalgia, exotic longing looks to a more radical cultural transformation of society's values and institutions through the importing of "foreign" or "exotic" ideas. To effect this transformation, the West must look to societies characterized by so-called non-Western values of peacefulness, mindfulness, community, and harmony, distinct from the supposedly cut-throat, zero-sum world of Western litigation. (As we will see, these exotics still need to be "sold," and so their exoticism must be tempered in various ways.) Robert Benham and Ansley Boyd Barton make this point in particularly stark terms:

> American society today is plagued by division along racial, gender, and class lines. The wisdom of the ancient societies in cherishing a sense of community provides a powerful lesson for us at a time of deep suspicion and isolation. We need to look beyond retribution and vindication to a restorative justice that not only rights the wrongs, but heals the wounds. It is certain that the first step must be an end to posturing and a commitment to honest communication as well as the recognition of both the differences and the kinship that we share as a society.[29]

As these remarks indicate, this exotic longing is central to restorative justice,[30] but it appears in relation to mediation, community justice, and

[29] Benham & Barton, *supra* note 19 at 648.

[30] See e.g., Gerry Johnstone, *Restorative Justice: Ideas, Values, Debates*, 2nd edn (New York: Routledge, 2011); Jenkins, *supra* note 11.

other aspects of ADR as well.[31] It draws on what Anne McClintock has called "anachronistic space," cultures that "do not inhabit history proper but exist in a permanently anterior time within the geographic space of the modern empire as anachronistic humans, atavistic, irrational, bereft of human agency – the living embodiment of the archaic 'primitive'."[32] The ADR literature depicts the inhabitants of this space in a more positive than dismissive light, however (though it is arguably no less colonialist for that). The primitive Other is presented not as recipient of the White Man's Burden but as teacher, as holder of primordial wisdom and ancient values that the West ignores at its peril.

This exotic longing is of course open to criticism. Longing for a historical or cultural Other tends to mythologize or idealize the object of that longing, and scholars have pointed out the dangers of the "casual beatification of activities and attitudes deemed as traditional or indigenous."[33] Some have argued as well that these supposed non-Western values like peacefulness and harmony are in fact Western colonial exports. They see Christian values of turning the other cheek and antipathy toward conflict as having been actively promoted in colonized societies so as to ensure the compliance and passivity of potentially unruly imperial subjects.[34] Others, however, resolutely defend the ancient, traditional roots of "Indigenous" dispute resolution.[35] Regardless, the idea that

[31] See e.g., David W Augsburger, *Conflict Mediation across Cultures: Pathways and Patterns* (Louisville, KY: Westminster/John Knox, 1992); E Victoria Shook & Leonard Ke'ala Kwan, "Straightening Relationships and Settling Disputes in Hawai'i: Ho'oponopono and Mediation" in Matsunada Institute for Peace, University of Hawai'i at Manoa, *Program on Conflict Resolution*, PCR Working Paper Series 1987–10 (Manoa, Hawaii: n.p., 1987) 1 at 1–56.

[32] Anne McClintock, *Imperial Leather: Race, Gender, and Sexuality in the Colonial Contest* (New York: Routledge, 1995) at 30.

[33] Roger Mac Ginty, "Indigenous Peace-Making versus the Liberal Peace" (2008) 43 *Coop Confl J Nord Int'l Stud Assn* 139 at 149–50 (in the context of international peacemaking). See also Merry, *supra* note 11 at 38–9 n. 9; Carole E Goldberg, "Overextended Borrowing: Tribal Peacemaking Applied in Non-Indian Disputes" (1997) 72 *Wash L Rev* 1003 at 1005; Kathleen Daly, "Revisiting the Relationship Between Retributive and Restorative Justice" in Heather Strang & John Braithwaite, eds, *Restorative Justice: Philosophy to Practice* (Aldershot: Ashgate, 2000) 33 at 33–54; Annalise Acorn, *Compulsory Compassion: A Critique of Restorative Justice* (Vancouver: UBC Press, 2004).

[34] See especially Boaventura de Sousa Santos, *Toward a New Common Sense: Law, Science and Politics in the Paradigmatic Transition* (New York: Routledge, 1995); Nader, "Harmony Models" *supra* note 22; Laura Nader, "The Globalization of Law: ADR as Soft Technology" (1999) 93 *Am Soc Intl L Proc* 304.

[35] E.g., Carlo Osi, "Understanding Indigenous Dispute Resolution Processes and Western Alternative Dispute Resolution: Cultivating Culturally Appropriate Methods in Lieu of Litigation" (2008) 10 *Cardozo J Confl Resol* 163 at 165–6, 194.

non-Western Others are keepers of unadulterated ancient ideals of peacefulness and harmony has exerted a powerful pull in ADR scholarship, and the colonialist nuances are frequently lost.

We will look at some of the objects of exotic longing in the next section, but at the level of attitudes, what we are seeing is a different form of the illness or malaise viewpoint that gave rise to the efficiency critique. The West yearns for its own uncorrupted past or for links to a foreign but analogous and also uncorrupted past. The former is presented as culturally similar but not too similar, the latter as culturally different but not too different: each depends as a model on an implicit claim that they are not really so culturally foreign at all. Before looking at how this works rhetorically, we need to turn to the next step in the process: shopping for models.

9.4 Shopping

Criticizing and yearning lead naturally enough to conflict-resolution shopping, as scholars and practitioners alike scour the globe in search of potential models from the Western past or (more frequently) from other cultures where people do things differently and (it is argued) better.[36] The models come from a long ethnographic literature on conflict resolution,[37] which continues in more recent studies of resurrected

36 For a brief overview of this impetus toward ADR shopping, especially in relation to the American ADR movement, see Merry, *supra* note 11 at 38–9. It should be noted that some resisted foreign imports, for a variety of reasons. See, for example, the arguments against ombudsmen and conciliation-based institutions in John Willis, "Foreign Borrowings" (1970) 20 *UTLJ* 274.

37 See generally the bibliography in Laura Nader, Klaus F Koch & Bruce Cox, "The Ethnography of Law: A Bibliographical Survey" (1966) 7 *Curr Anthropol* 267. Among the frequently cited case studies are Bronislaw Malinowski, *Crime and Custom in Savage Society* (New York: Harcourt Brace, 1926); E E Evans-Pritchard, *The Nuer: A Description of the Modes of Livelihood and Political Institutions of a Nilotic People* (Oxford: Oxford University Press, 1940); Karl N Llewellyn & E Adamson Hoebel, *The Cheyenne Way: Conflict and Case Law in Primitive Jurisprudence* (Norman, Okla: University of Oklahoma Press, 1941); Roy Franklin Barton, *The Kalingas: Their Institutions and Custom Law* (Chicago: University of Chicago Press, 1949); J H M Beattie, "Informal Judicial Activity in Bunyoro" (1957) 4 *J Afr Adm* 188; Elizabeth Colson, *Social Organization of the Gwembe Tonga* (Manchester: Manchester University Press, 1960); James L Gibbs, "The Kpelle Moot: A Therapeutic Model for the Informal Settlement of Disputes" (1963) 33 *Africa* 1; Laura Nader & Duane Metzger, "Conflict Resolution in Two Mexican Communities" (1963) 65 *Am Anthropol* 584; Isabel Emmett, *A North Wales Village: A Social Anthropological Study* (London: Routledge & Kegan Paul, 1964); Laura Nader, "An

"traditional" dispute resolution mechanisms like the post-genocide Rwandan *gacaca*, the Indian *panchayats*, Ethiopian wise-counsel mediation, and others.[38]

Shopping builds on the cultural claims we have been canvassing while at the same time exposing their limits. It is based on the claim that the West has much to learn from other cultures: values to use in approaching disputes and institutional models to adopt or adapt to resolve conflicts. In this it makes the yearning we examined above more tangible, by turning the desire for change into concrete proposals for reform. Already in the 1940s, Jerome Frank pointed to the Chinese preference for negotiation over adjudication as a salutary model for the American justice system, arguing it could help individualize justice. Frank was somewhat skeptical about the importability of the Chinese model, but in the end suggested that it might "be wise in part to emulate their approach."[39]

In the 1960s and 1970s, this phenomenon took a more interesting turn, as reformers advocating popular justice initiatives and community mobilization looked to the growing legal anthropological literature for models of the kind of relational and communitarian thinking they felt was missing from Western courts. The point of entry was James Gibbs's 1963 article on the Kpelle of Liberia, which explicitly lauded the therapeutic advantages of the Kpelle community "moot" and which we will consider in more detail in the next section below.[40] Though Gibbs stopped short of explicitly proposing the Kpelle "moot" as a model for Western law reform the implication was clear,[41] and within a few years

Analysis of Zapotec Law Cases" (1964) 3 *Ethnology* 404; Max Gluckman, *Politics, Law and Ritual in Tribal Society* (New York: Basil Blackwell, 1965).

[38] Among a large literature, see Phil Clark, *The Gacaca Courts, Post-Genocide Justice and Reconciliation in Rwanda: Justice Without Lawyers* (Cambridge: Cambridge University Press, 2010); Catherine S Meschievitz & Marc Galanter, "In Search of Nyaya Panchayats: The Politics of a Moribund Institution" in Richard L Abel, ed., *The Polititics of Informal Justice* (New York: Academic Press, 1982) 47; Daniel Atkilt et al, *Shimgelina (Under the Shade): Merging Ethiopian Wise-Counsel Mediation and Facilitative Mediation: A Training Manual* (Addis Ababa: House of Federation, 2013); G Sidney Silliman, "A Political Analysis of the Philippines' Katarungang Pambarangay System of Informal Justice through Mediation" (1985) 19 *Law Soc Rev* 279.

[39] Frank, *Courts on Trial, supra* note 7 at 381–4, quotation at 383.

[40] Gibbs, *supra* note 37 at 6 (emphasis in original) ("... the moot is not only conciliatory, but *therapeutic*. Moot procedures are therapeutic in that, like psychotherapy, they re-educate the parties through a type of social learning brought about in a specially structured interpersonal setting.")

[41] Gibbs later stated that his intent was descriptive and not prescriptive: personal communication reported in Alexandra Crampton, "Addressing Questions of Culture and Power in

legal scholars like Michael Lowy and Richard Danzig were proposing that the African tribal "moot" be imported to American cities as a community-based alternative to adversarial justice.[42] Though Gibbs's African model was by far the most influential, other authors in this early period of ADR writing looked elsewhere as well, for example to conciliation in China and Korea and to the Cuban People's Courts.[43]

More recently, other traditions have been brought into the discussion, widening the cultural range of alternatives. Restorative justice, for example, was initially inspired by Aboriginal traditions (such as sentencing circles in Canada or Navajo peacemaking in the United States),[44] and has since broadened to include Afrocentric ideas and Hawaiian ho'oponopono, among other approaches.[45] These approaches were initially proposed as alternatives within the dominant culture for minority communities whose traditions the proposals were reviving, forms of dispute resolution that would be more culturally compatible than Western adversarialism. In origin, then, many of these cultural imports reflected a political drive for recognition, for a culturally pluralist refashioning of law and its institutions. Such approaches rapidly moved outside the minority communities for which they were initially proposed, as proponents offered

the Globalization of ADR: Lessons from African Influence on American Mediation" (2006) 27 *Hamline J Pub L Pol'* 229 at 235 n. 16.

42 The initial proposals focused on the criminal justice system: Michael J Lowy, "Modernizing the American Legal System: An Example of the Peaceful Use of Anthropology" (1973) 32 *Hum Org* 205; Richard Danzig, "Toward the Creation of a Complementary, Decentralized System of Criminal Justice" (1973) 26 *Stanford L Rev* 1. Later they joined forces to argue for the applicability of African negotiation models to civil matters: Richard Danzig & Michael J Lowy, "Everyday Disputes and Mediation in the United States: A Reply to Professor Felstiner" (1975) 9 *Law Soc Rev* 675.

43 E.g., Jerome Alan Cohen, "Chinese Mediation on the Eve of Modernization" (1966) 54 *Calif L Rev* 1201; Stanley Lubman, "Mao and Mediation: Politics and Dispute Resolution in Communist China" (1967) 55 *Calif L Rev* 1284; Pyong-Choon Hahm, "The Decision Process in Korea" in Glendon A Schubert & David Joseph Danelski, eds., *Comparative Judicial Behavior: Cross-Cultural Studies of Political Decision-Making in the East and West* (New York: Oxford University Press, 1969) at 19–47; Jesse Berman, "The Cuban Popular Tribunals" (1969) 69 *Columbia L Rev* 1317.

44 See e.g., Mark S Umbreit & Robert B Coates, "Multicultural Implications of Restorative Justice" (1999) 63:2 *Fed Probat* 44; Llewellyn & Howse, *supra* note 23; Jon'a F Meyer, "'It Is a Gift from the Creator to Keep Us in Harmony': Original (vs. Alternative) Dispute Resolution on the Navajo Nation" (2002) 25 *Int J Public Adm* 1379. See also the general overview in Johnstone, *supra* note 31.

45 Jenkins, *supra* note 11; Andrew J Hosmanek, "Cutting the Cord: Ho'oponopono and Hawaiian Restorative Justice in the Criminal Law Context" (2005) 5 *Pepp Disp Resol LJ* 359.

them up as examples to reform the crisis in the broader justice system, a project whose implications we will consider later.[46]

The case of ho'oponopono is a good example of shopping and its implications. A form of spiritual dispute resolution said to have been traditionally practiced within extended families in Polynesian cultures, it involved a relative or community member of high social status convening a gathering of disputants in which prayer, discussion, questioning, confession, and forgiveness were employed to "put things right" (the meaning of the term ho'oponopono) and to reconcile offender and community.[47] The practice had virtually disappeared by the mid-twentieth century, pushed aside (both passively and actively) by Christian beliefs brought in during colonization,[48] but was revived in the 1970s as a culturally resonant dispute-resolution mechanism for dealing with youth criminality within the native Hawaiian community.[49] From there, the general conflict resolution literature picked it up and advocated it as a new "non-Western" approach to various kinds of conflicts in society at large. This literature – first among conflict-resolution practitioners in Hawaii and then broadening outward from there – presented ho'oponopono in explicitly cultural terms, touching many of the points we have been making. Though evidence for its origins and pre-colonial (or even pre-revival) usage is virtually absent,[50] authors making a case for importing it into Western legal systems have stressed its antiquity and links with tradition,[51] its therapeutic potential,[52] its fostering of values of

[46] E.g., James A Wall & Ronda Roberts Callister, "Ho'oponopono: Some Lessons from Hawaiian Mediation" (1995) 11 *Negot J* 45; Gretchen Ulrich, "Widening the Circle: Adapting Traditional Indian Dispute Resolution Methods to Implement Alternative Dispute Resolution and Restorative Justice in Modern Communities" (1999) 20 *Hamline J Pub L Pol* 419.

[47] This summary is based on Wall & Callister, *supra* note 46 at 47–8.

[48] On the history of ho'oponopono, see E Victoria Shook, *Ho'oponopono: Contemporary Uses of a Hawaiian Problem-Solving Process* (Honolulu: University of Hawaii Press for East-West Center, 1985) at chapter 1.

[49] Central to the revival was the work of Mary Kawena Pukui: see the overview with citations in Hosmanek, *supra* note 45 at 362.

[50] Karen L Ito, "*Ho'oponopono*, 'To Make Right': Hawaiian Conflict Resolution and Metaphor in the Construction of a Family Therapy" (1985) 9 *Cult Med Psychiatry* 201 at 201.

[51] E.g., Shook, *supra* note 48 at 1 ("A rich body of knowledge about the physical, emotional, and spiritual well-being of an individual in relationship to family, community, and environment has existed in the Hawaiian culture for centuries"); Wall & Callister, *supra* note 46 at 46 ("Ho'oponopono is an integral and ancient part of Polynesian culture.")

[52] Ito, *supra* note 50; Hosmanek, *supra* note 45 at 359 (bringing victims and offenders together through ho'oponopono means "true healing can occur.")

community and cultural sensitivity,[53] and its potential "payoffs" (in terms of better results) for Western conflict resolution practitioners.[54] In general studies on ADR, ho'oponopono has come to be canonized alongside the Kpelle "moot" as one of the paradigmatic "exotic" approaches to conflict practiced in "traditional societies".[55] Doubts about its antiquity have been left behind in favor of its rhetorical power as a radical though useful alternative to adjudication that can help Western society transform its disputing culture.

To use a different metaphor, shopping might be seen as a kind of mining,[56] in which nuggets of cultural knowledge are extracted from sites around the world to be shipped back to the West, refined, and fashioned into products for Western consumption.[57] This refashioning is itself a cultural process, however, and to illustrate it I would like to return to Gibbs's Kpelle "moot".

9.5 "Moots": Kpelle and Otherwise

To draw together some of these threads and to move the discussion toward the broader point of what this rhetorical mobilization of culture to promote ADR might mean in terms of the points of contact between law and culture in the West, I would like to pause to consider in more detail a key source of the cultural claim: anthropologist James Gibbs's 1963 article on dispute resolution among the Kpelle of Liberia.[58] As we saw, Gibbs's article has been the go-to citation in discussions of the cultural foundations of ADR.[59] Its title, "The Kpelle Moot: A Therapeutic Model for the Informal Settlement of Disputes," is rich

[53] Hosmanek, *supra* note 45 at 367 (ho'oponopono can provide "an alternative culturally sensitive means of resolving legal disputes.")

[54] Wall & Callister, *supra* note 46 at 51–2 (in a section entitled "Lessons for the Western Mediator.")

[55] E.g., in Benham & Barton, *supra* note 19 at 629–31; Umbreit, *supra* note 11 at 203; Barrett & Barrett, *supra* note 3 at 3.

[56] I thank Tim Bryan for suggesting this metaphor in response to an earlier version of this chapter.

[57] A further step – export of the Westernized "traditional" practices back to their places of origin – is beyond the scope of this chapter. See e.g., Ann Black, "Alternative Dispute Resolution in Brunei Darussalam: The Blending of Imported and Traditional Processes" (2001) 13:2 *Bond L Rev* article 4 (unpaginated); Carrie Menkel-Meadow, "Exporting and Importing ADR: 'I've Looked at Life from Both Sides Now,'" (2006) 12 *Disp Resol Mag* 5.

[58] Gibbs, *supra* note 37.

[59] In Hein Online's Law Journal Library, the article is cited in seventy-five other articles from 1965 to 2011, most dealing with dispute resolution.

in possibilities for detailed glossing and deconstruction. Here I want to focus first on the word "moot," before taking up the idea that the "moot" is a "therapeutic model."

Gibbs's subject is a dispute resolution institution among the Kpelle in which certain kinds of cases – generally disputes involving continuing relationships between the parties like domestic or matrimonial matters – were aired within the home before assembled kin and neighbors, with an elder or local notable acting as mediator. Gibbs first gave the Kpelle name for the institution – *bɛrɛi mu neni saa*, which he translated roughly as "house palaver" in an echo of Mary Kingsley's pioneering work[60] – before translating it as "moot," the word he used throughout the article and in the title. The name "moot" should give us pause, as should any attempt at cross-cultural labelling. My concern however is not to revive long-dormant nomenclature debates among ethnographers,[61] but rather to examine the normative implications in a law reform context of the deployment of a Western term to ease the importation of a non-Western institution into Western legal systems. A "moot" (sometimes spelled "mote" or "mot") was the Anglo-Saxon equivalent of the Norse "thing" – a generic term for a meeting or assembly. It was usually used in compounds, as in the "folk-moot" (the assembly of the tribe), the "shire-moot" (the regional assembly), and so on up to the "*witenagemót*" (the assembly of elders or wise men, most recently the inspiration for J.K. Rowling's *wizengamot*, the assembly of the principal wizards in Harry Potter's world). Thus even before its adoption by U.S. law schools at the beginning of the last century to describe their mock courtroom exercises,[62] the word had venerable roots in Western culture.

But it had more than just antiquity attached to it. The ancient Anglo-Saxon moots served a variety of functions – deliberative, judicial, legislative – whose historical specificity could easily be finessed for symbolic or

60 The Kpelle term and "house palaver" appear only once, on the first page of the article. On "palaver," see e.g., Mary H Kingsley, *West African Studies*, 2nd edn (London: Macmillan, 1901) at 401–2.

61 Paul Bohannan's dispute with Max Gluckman over the universality or specificity of the concept of law and its terminology raised this issue in the 1960s; see Max Gluckman, "Concepts in the Comparative Study of Tribal Law" in Laura Nader, ed., *Law in Culture and Society* (Chicago: Aldine, 1969) 349 at 349–73; Paul Bohannan, "Ethnography and Comparison in Legal Anthropology" in Nader, *ibid.* 401 at 401–8; Laura Nader, "Introduction" in Nader, *ibid.* at 4–5; Sally Falk Moore, "Certainties Undone: Fifty Turbulent Years of Legal Anthropology, 1949–1999" (2001) 7 *J R Anthropol Inst* 95 at 98–9.

62 J Benjamin Van Veen, "Moot Courts and the Law School" (1924) 1 *NYU L Rev* 37.

ideological ends. Nineteenth-century whiggish English historians, for example, saw in the moots the ancestors of British justice and representative government; the moot provided the crucial native English lineage for these ideals, one whose Teutonic roots pre-dated the Norman Conquest and its imported Latinate influence. Bishop Stubbs made this clear in 1880 in his *Constitutional History of England.* After spending much of his first volume going through the various Anglo-Saxon moots in considerable detail, he came to his larger point:

> The great characteristic of the English constitutional system, in that view of it which is offered in these pages,–the principle of its growth, the secret of its construction,–is the continuous development of representative institutions from the first elementary stage, in which they are employed for local purposes and in the simplest form, to that in which the national parliament appears as the concentration of all local and provincial machinery, the depository of the collective powers of the three estates of the realm.[63]

Stubbs's point got condensed and sharpened (and stripped of all nuance, not that there was much room to mistake his ideological purpose) in the entry "Parliament" in the *Encyclopædia Britannica* from the same era: "... in the Anglo-Saxon moots may be discerned the first germs of popular government in England."[64]

American historians, who could out-whig even their English counterparts, brought forward the symbolic and ideological import of the ancient moot even more clearly. As George Elliot Howard vividly put it in 1889:

> In our national history the town-meeting fills a glorious page. In fostering the growth of a sentiment of union among the colonists, it played a part so important politically as almost to justify the claim of those who regard it as an American product. It was a genuine folcgemot [folk-moot], but a folcgemot far more developed and independent politically than that of the old English tun [town]. It was here that the idea of nationality, of colonial unity, germinated and was fostered into a sublime reality.[65]

Alongside its use in "moot court," then, the moot was part of a longer tradition that saw it as a central symbol of, on the one hand, the origins

[63] William Stubbs, *The Constitutional History of England in Its Origin and Development* (Oxford: Clarendon Press, 1880) at 611.

[64] Thomas Erskine May, "Parliament," in *The Encyclopædia Britannica: A Dictionary of Arts, Sciences, and General Literature*, 9th edn (American reprint), vol. 18 (Philadelphia: J.M. Stoddart, 1885) at 308.

[65] George E Howard, *An Introduction to the Local Constitutional History of the United States* (Baltimore: Publication Agency of the John Hopkins University, 1889) at 74.

we looked at above. It took an exotic institution (the *bɛrɛi mu neni saa*) with transformative potential and domesticated it through the application of a Western name redolent with some of the most fundamental values of Western liberal democracy. Who could resist bringing Western dispute-resolution processes into line with the pure, uncontaminated wellsprings of participatory democracy and direct community justice?

9.6 Conclusion: Cultural Models and Western Law

The story of ADR's engagement with exotics – the Kpelle moot, Hawaiian ho'oponopono, colonial American conciliation – suggests some points about the meaning and possibilities of legalizing culture and enculturating law. The rhetoric we have been considering, evoking as it does ancient institutions or Indigenous practices or primordial values like the "roots of justice," brings to the ADR discussion particular kinds of models, presented as ancient yet present, foreign yet familiar, indigenous yet universal. What does it mean to extract aspects of other cultures or other times and import them to the West? To what extent are these cultural artifacts changed by Westerners trying to comprehend them and, more important, to put them to use?

The antiquity and exoticism of these models pull at once in two different directions, evident in the lively debate over the possibilities of inter-cultural borrowing in the ADR literature.[73] On the one hand, their very exoticism explains their excitement and their appeal. They appear in the literature precisely because they are foreign, and so promise to pull Western dispute resolution out of its cabined, instrumentalist, individualist rut. Exotics serve to emphasize the "alternative" in ADR by harnessing the transformative potential of radical Others – African cultures, Confucianism, Buddhism, Navajo peacemaking – to provide ways of curing the ills of Western litigation.[74] And it is important to remember that ADR is a technique as well as a law reform program, and for

[73] E.g., Leonard Pospisil, "Comment" (1973) 32 *Hum Org* 211 (comment on Michael J. Lowy, *supra* note 43); William LF Felstiner, "Influences of Social Organization on Dispute Processing" (1974) 9 *Law Soc Rev* 63; June Starr, "Mediation: Anthropological Perspectives" (1982) 6 *ALSA Forum* 221 at 254–5; Avruch & Black, *supra* note 5; Goldberg, *supra* note 34.

[74] See e.g., Oscar Chase's discussion of the Azande (drawn from Evans-Pritchard) at the beginning of Chase, *supra* note 13 at 15–29 and passim (the Azande of Central Africa); Leonard L Riskin, "Mediation and Lawyers" (1982) 43 *Ohio St LJ* 29 at 29 (Confucianism); Kuttner, *supra* note 12; Meyer, *supra* note 44.

practitioners such techniques may achieve better results, or reinvigorate practice, or open up new ways of understanding conflict and conflict resolution.[75]

On another level, however, the exoticism of the models represents a threat that needs to be neutralized or at least tempered. An early commentator noted this fear of the Other when he wrote that for many, "The African approach [based on mediation and compromise] – except in a familiar family court or constitutional setting – gives us ethnocentric nightmares."[76] Similar discomfort is evident in John Willis's Orientalist rejection of the ombudsman as "in his purest, though unimportable, form a cadi under a palm tree setting all things right."[77] Here is fear of pluralism and accommodation: the line between "us" and the Other exposes the boundary between law and culture. And for some, crossing that boundary to bring "culture" into "law" means coming into contact with the messy, problematic, threatening things that cannot fit without undermining the integrity of the system.

These cultural encounters between Western law and exotic viewpoints or techniques raise the question of which exotics will "fit" within the strictures of Western legal systems, and how.[78] It is a question of "legal transplants," in other words, though not transplantation of norms, but transplantation of institutions, values, and ways of thinking.[79] To what extent, for example, can African household-based conciliation be

[75] Though the initial wave of literature we have been considering was explicitly aimed at institutional and systemic reform, more recently much of the focus has shifted to suggesting techniques for practitioners.

[76] John E Coons, "Approaches to Court Imposed Compromise–The Uses of Doubt and Reason" (1964) 58 *Nw U L Rev* 750 at 787–8. Coons reports this viewpoint, but rejects it in favor of embracing the possibility of importation of alternatives.

[77] Willis, *supra* note 37 at 275, cited in Roderick A. Macdonald, "Call–Centre Government: For the Rule of Law, Press #" (2005) 55 *University of Toronto Law Journal* 449–495.

[78] Among a large literature on conflict-resolution imports and exports, see especially Catherine Bell, "Indigenous Dispute Resolution Systems within Non-Indigenous Frameworks: Intercultural Dispute Resolution Initiatives in Canada" in Catherine Bell & David Kahane, eds., *Intercultural Dispute Resolution in Aboriginal Contexts: Land Claims, Treaties, and Self-Government Agreements* (Vancouver: UBC Press, 2004) 241; Menkel-Meadow, *supra* note 57; Pratiksha Baxi, "Access to Justice and Rule-of-[Good] Law: The Cunning of Judicial Reform in India" (2008) 2 *Indian J Hum Dev* 279; Osi, *supra* note 36.

[79] The idea of "legal transplants" gained currency through the work of Alan Watson, especially Alan Watson, "Legal Transplants and Law Reform" (1976) 92 *Law Q Rev* 79; Alan Watson, *Legal Transplants: An Approach to Comparative Law*, 2nd edn (Athens, GA: University of Georgia Press, 1993). Among critics, I draw especially on Pierre Legrand, "The Impossibility of 'Legal Transplants'" (1997) 4 *Maastricht J Eur Comp L* 111.

transported to North American cities to serve as a model for community mediation programs? To what extent can restorative justice ideas drawn from Aboriginal communities be used to reform sentencing practices or offender reintegration programs outside those communities? As mentioned above, these sorts of imports have taken varied routes into Western legal systems, some more direct, others more indirect, and with varying degrees of cultural resonance between origin and target groups. Some, like Ho'oponopono and sentencing circles, were initially proposed for (and sometimes by) particular minority communities culturally connected to the proposed techniques, and afterward spread outward from there. Others, like Buddhist mindfulness teachings or indeed Gibbs's Kpelle moot, were presented as direct imports, to work as models for reform of the majority legal system.

If we take seriously the criticisms of the idea of legal transplants, and I think we must, then Western audiences cannot even understand these exogenous institutions and ways of approaching conflict without in some measure translating them into Western categories and ways of thinking. As Pierre Legrand put it (speaking of norm transplantation):

> Meaning simply does not lend itself to transplantation. There always remains an irreducible element of autochthony constraining the epistemological receptivity to the incorporation of a rule from another jurisdiction, therefore limiting the *possibility* of effective legal transplantation itself. The borrowed form of words thus rapidly finds itself indigenized on account of the host culture's inherent integrative capacity.[80]

Like Bohannan's and Gibbs's "moots," then, exotic or Indigenous institutions must be appropriated by being put into Western terms in order for them to be made comprehensible to Western culture. This is of course a political and ideological process; it is no accident that words like "moot" or "mediation" or "conciliation" or, more fundamentally, "justice" – Western concepts all – are applied to the models. A Tiv *jir sa ya* or a Kpelle *bɛrɛi mu neni saa* will always be foreign; translated into a "moot" they become familiar and so importable. Moreover, given the global reach and institutional power of Western ideas like the rule of law, human rights, and sovereignty, the "inherent integrative capacity" of the West is powerful indeed.

Exotics get framed so as to ease entry into the receiving culture, and this most often means framing them within the dispute resolution

[80] See Legrand, *supra* note 79 at 118.

enterprise as contributing in an instrumental way to classically Western goals like efficiency or justice. One author describes Ho'oponopono as "traditional" but as leading "to better outcomes for victims, offenders, and society as a whole"[81]; another sees it as an "integral and ancient part of Polynesian culture" but as having "potential payoffs" for Western mediators.[82] Traditional Gullah Island dispute resolution is described as an "ancient" approach to justice, but one that "could reduce not only crime and delinquency but also the apprehension many Blacks have about the political and legal systems."[83] We see in these examples – to which we could add the Kpelle "moot," Ethiopian wise-counsel mediation, forms of Indigenous-inspired restorative justice, and so on – a seemingly paradoxical balancing of exoticism (the stress on antiquity and indigeneity) and Western instrumentalism (the promise of efficiency or utility or other empirically verifiable benefits).

The cultural claims of ADR – that non-Western values can refocus Western disputing on restoring balance, promoting harmony, and emphasizing community well-being rather than individual self-interest – are predicated on a reaffirmed liberal worldview of the fundamental similarity of humans and their institutions,[84] the idea that African or Aboriginal or other non-Western cultures are different, but not incommensurably different from Western institutions and values. Our "common humanity" – a phrase that turns up often in the ADR literature – ensures that whatever the superficial differences between cultures, ADR can be presented as tapping into primordial values that transcend culture.[85] Techniques too, for example negotiation or third-party mediation, have often been presented as fundamental human processes and so as readily adaptable to different cultures.[86] But these processes and values and institutions are similar not in themselves, but because we project that

[81] Hosmanek, *supra* note 45 at 359 and 375.

[82] Wall & Callister, *supra* note 46 at 46 and 52.

[83] Jenkins, *supra* note 11 at 301 and 304.

[84] Morgan J Brigg, *The New Politics of Conflict Resolution: Responding to Difference* (New York: Palgrave Macmillan, 2008) at 6–12 and passim.

[85] E.g., Umbreit, *supra* note 11 at 202 ("This article presents a model of mediation that intentionally taps into the full potential of mediation to offer a genuine transformative journey of peacemaking that is grounded in compassion, strength, and our common humanity.")

[86] See especially PH Gulliver, "Dispute Settlement Without Courts: The Ndendeuli of Southern Tanzania" in Laura Nader, ed., *Law in Culture and Society* (Chicago: Aldine, 1969) 24 at 67–8; PH Gulliver, "Negotiations as a Mode of Dispute Settlement: Towards a General Model" (1973) 7 *Law Soc Rev* 667.

similarity onto them, what Pierre Legrand has called the difference between "them" and "us speaking of them."[87] Differences get pushed aside and the focus becomes the perceived or asserted similarities to what we in the West already know and understand. What are these exotic institutions for? Since they instantiate our own wishes, we see them as being for resolving conflicts (and not for preserving lineages, or for reaffirming household status, or for re-inscribing family boundaries against outsiders). What values animate these exotic models? Since they reflect our own understanding of other cultures and our hopes for our own culture, we see them as being animated by restoring harmony and fostering community (and not by re-establishing status relationships, or by maintaining the dynamics of social conflict by channelling violence into other forms). Where do these models come from? Since they project our own understandings of indigeneity and antiquity, we see them as ancient and unadulterated links to an uncorrupted past (and not as themselves evolving organically or even as shaped by the colonial encounter). These exotic imports or resurrections of ancient Western values may well help us achieve better results, or permit wider access to justice, or perhaps even transform Western cultures of disputing. But what we are importing or resurrecting are Westernized images of exotic institutions, domesticated in name and, more importantly, in substance to achieve decidedly Western purposes like efficiency or therapy or justice.

[87] Pierre Legrand, "Comparative Legal Studies and the Matter of Authenticity" (2006) 1 *J Comp L* 365 at 371.

10

Rebalancing Power and Culture?

The Case of Alternative Dispute Resolution

MORGAN BRIGG

10.1 Introduction

Modern political systems and institutions have in recent centuries gained increased governmental purchase over both individual subjects and collective lived experience. The growth and spread of formal institutions, most notably the state, sovereignty and rule of law, have been central to this development. By subjugating, bypassing, standing above, or aggregating and consolidating both the regulatory forces and ways of being that operate through guilds, communes, clans, tribes, religious communities and so on, the institutions of state, sovereignty and rule of law have facilitated the subordination and regulation of what can, for the sake of convenience, be termed (local) 'cultures'. In place of the everyday indigenous and local regulation of social life, the emergence of sovereignty and rule of law in European history, as well as the export of these political and legal forms through colonialism, development and globalisation, facilitate the individual's subjection to often-distant and abstract entities and processes alongside the transfer of authority to the quasi-transcendental authority of sovereignty and state. These processes are imbricated with wider political developments. The nineteenth-century emergence of legal positivism, for instance, was bound up with both the consolidation of sovereignty within European states and the differential allocation of sovereignty on a global scale through processes that facilitated legal imperialism.[1]

The University of Queensland, with acknowledgement to the Käte Hamburger Kolleg / Centre for Global Cooperation Research, University of Duisburg-Essen, Germany, where the author was a visiting fellow in 2013.

[1] Turan Kayaoglu, *Legal Imperialism: Sovereignty and Extraterritoriality in Japan, the Ottoman Empire, and China* (Cambridge University Press, 2010).

Although political and legal formalism have enjoyed considerable success in recent centuries, the rise of formal systems in politics and law from the local to the global has, as is perhaps to be expected, encountered resistance and limits. The increasing pressure for conventional approaches to law to respond to the cultural claims of those to whom it is applied – along with the rise of legal pluralism – are indicative of this phenomenon. Indeed, in the early twenty-first century there appears to be less confidence in the capacity and reach of rational and secular means for governing social life and a dawning recognition that the universal ideals, categories and injunctions of modern formal politics have less purchase than may have been anticipated by modernisers. This may be because such formal and rational forces tend to belong to the realm of imagination rather than lived experience. As Partha Chatterjee points out, people can only imagine themselves in the empty, homogenous and civic space of the nation; they do not live there.[2]

The recent burgeoning of the alternative dispute resolution (ADR) movement in modern capitalist democracies has emerged as part of the response to demands for law and the formal administration of justice to be more responsive to lived experience. Indeed, an early article advocating ADR cast conflicts as the property of conflicting parties; property that had been stolen from them by officials and the state, and which should be returned to its rightful owners.[3] Culture, too, has been an important part of ADR advocacy and the ADR story in two complementary ways. Moots and other informal processes (especially of non-European peoples) have been used to argue that modern industrialised justice systems have lost touch with everyday life, to make arguments for reform, and to inspire and invent revised and new processes such as mediation in capitalist democracies.[4] ADR has also been promoted as being more consistent with the decision-making processes of diverse cultures and therefore more appropriate than formal court processes for dispute management involving a wide range of cultural groups. ADR thus functions as a site of exchange between abstract legal and political governance and quotidian

[2] Partha Chatterjee, *The Politics of the Governed: Reflections on Popular Politics in Most of the World* (Columbia University Press, 2004) at 5–6, passim.

[3] Nils Christie, 'Conflicts as Property' (1977) 17:1 *Br J Criminol* 1.

[4] E.g. see Richard Danzig, 'Toward the Creation of a Complementary, Decentralized System of Criminal Justice' (1973) *Stanford Law Rev* 1; Jerold S Auerbach, *Justice without Law?* (New York: Oxford University Press, 1983).

social means of regulating social life – between formal power and informal culture.

This chapter analyses the relationship between formal power and informal culture through ADR to ask if ADR is, or can be, a site of meaningful legal pluralism. That is, can it facilitate elements of mutual recognition, accommodation and exchange between diverse legal orders? The analysis is illustrated with reference to the case of ADR policy and processes in relation to Australian Aboriginal peoples. Australia shares a broadly similar liberal political culture with the heartland of modern ADR, the United States of America (USA), and yet, as an adopter more than an originator of modern ADR processes, it also offers a slightly different vantage point.[5] At the same time, the Australian settler-colonial setting sees an exchange between European-liberal political culture and very different Aboriginal culture. While the social setting involves a mutual entanglement that militates against a simplistic binary rending of these differences, the entanglement does involve an antagonism arising in part out of ways of relating to the world and other people that are at times all but incommensurable.[6]

The first part of this chapter considers the cultural politics of the early ADR movement to argue that, during the period from the 1970s to 1990s, the possibilities for legal pluralism within ADR were highly attenuated. Despites links with – and apparent openness to – cultural difference, ADR policy and practice was substantially informed and governed by modes of reasoning about conflict and social life that reflect and reproduce dominant western law and political systems. Furthermore, and somewhat subtly and paradoxically, the very informalism of ADR facilitates a mode of liberal governance that has ADR participants govern their selves in ways that are consistent with formal law and governance. At the same time, the prospects for legal pluralism through ADR are not entirely closed.

The second part of this chapter considers a shift in the Australian ADR policy debate of the 1990s, focusing particularly on a move to open mediation processes to Aboriginal participation and values. A more genuine exchange may become possible by turning more fully to the

[5] The Australian case is also one with which I have direct knowledge, both as a mediator (including in relation to conflicts involving Aboriginal people) and as a contributor to policy debates and discussions.

[6] Nicholas Thomas, *Possessions: Indigenous Art, Colonial Culture* (Thames and Hudson London, 1999) at 10, 14.

lived experience of people and their social forms in order to mitigate the influence of western-liberal modes of reasoning about conflict and social life, but for this to lead to meaningful legal pluralism it must attend to ontological frameworks and reference points – the categories and associated conceptual scaffolding that specify what is to be taken as 'real', and which structure political and social order – rather than rest at the level of behaviours and practices. This chapter concludes by reflecting upon the possibilities and perceived risks of legal pluralism in ADR.

10.2 The Cultural Politics of ADR

In recent decades, the informal yet structured processing of disputes has grown markedly in western democratic contexts and has spread rapidly to so-called transitional and emerging countries. These developments have longstanding roots, with significant intellectual forerunners to modern ADR[7] and processes such as arbitration and conciliation playing a role in collective dispute management in labour and industrial disputes for over a century. However, it was increasing dissatisfaction with legal processes from the 1960s, including calls for greater access to justice and for the justice system to be more responsive to the lived experience of consumers, that saw the expansion and wider application of these and other informal processes from the 1970s. The process of mediation, in particular, became very influential in the United States.[8] The resulting 'ADR movement' takes in arbitration, conciliation, facilitation, mediation, and allied processes. In some respects, the ADR movement can be located in an ongoing history of legal reform and recurrent shifts and contests within western legal culture, but its impact should also not be underestimated.[9] As ADR has met both the ideological and practical needs of legal reform it has altered the landscape of dispute management. Mediation and other ADR processes are now mainstream ways of processing disputes. The application of mediation, in particular, is now sufficiently widespread and institutionalised to warrant, for many, removing the qualifier 'alternative'.[10]

[7] Carrie Menkel-Meadow, 'Mothers and Fathers of Invention: The Intellectual Founders of ADR' (2000) 16 *Ohio St J Disp Resol* 1.

[8] Auerbach, *supra* note 5.

[9] Laura Nader, 'Harmony Models and the Construction of Law' (1991) *Reformul Dispute Resolut* 41 at 50–3.

[10] ADR and dispute resolution appear to be succumbing to the wider term 'conflict resolution', but ADR remains important in some contexts and dispute resolution may

The informalism of ADR invariably involves an engagement with non-legal, societal, or 'cultural' ways of managing conflict, but culture has also been directly important to the emergence and promulgation of ADR.[11] In the development of the ADR movement in the 1970s, moots and other informal processes were used to illustrate how modern industrialised justice systems had lost touch with everyday people, to make arguments for reform, and to inspire and invent revised and new processes such as mediation in the modern capitalist democracies.[12] The key source material was legal anthropology, which had burgeoned in the 1950s and 1960s.[13] Several commentators mention the relevance of this influence for ADR reform,[14] and debates about if and how to introduce non-western processes into the United States occur in the literature.[15] There are also accounts of anthropological work directly inspiring mediation programs[16] and one prominent ADR advocate, Chief Justice Warren E. Burger.[17]

The linking of ADR with non-western dispute management processes through legal anthropology did not, however, lead to a substantive exchange with non-western dispute processing mechanisms. Although the idea that mediation practiced in western countries might align with

be preferred in any dealing with the legal system for the way it evokes a more discrete and contained matter rather than a set of ramifying concerns that travels through the social fabric.

11 Kevin Avruch & Peter Black, 'ADR, Palau and the Contribution of Anthropology' (1996) 29 *Anthropol Contrib Confl Resolut* 47.

12 Christie, *supra* note 4; Auerbach, *supra* note 5.

13 E.g. see Max Gluckman, *The Judicial Process among the Barotse of Northern Rhodesia* (Manchester University Press, 1967); James L Gibbs, 'The Kpelle Moot: A Therapeutic Model for the Informal Settlement of Disputes' (1963) 33:01 *Africa* 1; Paul Bohannan, 'The Differing Realms of the Law' (1965) 67:6 *Am Anthropol* 33; Max Gluckman, *The Ideas in Barotse Jurisprudence* (Manchester University Press, 1965); Laura Nader, 'The Anthropological Study of Law' (1965) 67:6 *Am Anthropol* 3; Paul Bohannan, 'Law and Legal Institutions' (1968) 9 *Int Encycl Soc Sci* 73; *ibid.*

14 Sally Engle Merry, 'The Social Organization of Mediation in Nonindustrial Societies: Implications for Informal Community Justice in America' (1982) 2 *Polit Informal Justice* 17.

15 See Danzig, *supra* note 5; William LF Felstiner, 'Influences of Social Organization on Dispute Processing' (1974) *Law Soc Rev* 63; Richard Danzig & Michael J Lowy, 'Everyday Disputes and Mediation in the United States: A Reply to Professor Felstiner' (1975) *Law Soc Rev* 675.

16 Paul Wahrhaftig, 'An Overview of Community-Oriented Citizen Dispute Resolution Programs in the United States' (1982) 1 *Polit Informal Justice* 75.

17 Laura Nader, 'Civilization and its Negotiations' in P. Caplan, ed., *Understanding Disputes: The Politics of Argument* (Berg, 1995) 39–63.

Peter Fitzpatrick[29] and George Pavlich[30] demonstrate, against ADR folk logic, that the informalism of ADR is bound to the formalism of law rather than constituting a challenge to it. While ADR invokes 'a realm where people are or could be truly, or even normally, themselves, a realm apart from the artifices of form, a realm of a natural and undifferentiated reality',[31] informal justice and formal regulation are, paradoxically, united. This is because, on one hand the state and law rely upon the informal operation of power to 'constitute a massive, non-rebellious normality'[32] necessary for the operation of law while, conversely, the law serves to demarcate – both through notions of individual rights and by limiting the extent of its sanctions – a zone of 'freedom' in which individuals are apparently free from the injunctions of the sovereign or state.

Within this governmental constellation, ADR processes govern by assisting individuals to perform and regulate their selves as non-disputing and rational beings. By combining governmentality analysis with Foucault's rendering of the Christian confessional as a regulatory practice transferred into the secular realm,[33] Pavlich shows, for instance, that confessing one's conflict to the external figure of the mediator opens and prepares participants for reconfiguring their selves.[34] Over the course of the mediation process, careful selection of certain aspects of clients' behaviour and the use of both praise and castigation 'pressures individuals to adopt subjective aspirations and conceptions of self that rid them of conflict with others'.[35] Furthermore, because the modes of reasoning about conflict and social life in mediation as well as the forms of selfhood demarcated and enabled by formal law (e.g. the self-maximising and self-sufficient subject) are those of western political liberalism and the law itself rather than of the informal or cultural sphere, participants in ADR processes (re-) configure themselves – with the help of mediators – in ways that reproduce rather than challenge formal legal power.

[29] Fitzpatrick, *supra* note 23; Peter Fitzpatrick, 'The Impossibility of Popular Justice' (1992), online:

[30] George Pavlich, *Justice Fragmented: Mediating Community Disputes under Postmodern Conditions* (Routledge, 1996); George Pavlich, 'The Power of Community Mediation: Government and Formation of Self-Identity' (1996) *Law Soc Rev* 707.

[31] Fitzpatrick, *supra* note 22; *Ibid* at 191.

[32] Fitzpatrick, *supra* note 22 at 190.

[33] Michel Foucault, *The History of Sexuality: An Introduction/Transl. from the French by Robert Hurley* (Penguin Books, 1984) at 60–3.

[34] Pavlich, *supra* note 31.

[35] *Ibid* at 125–6.

While cultural difference does potentially intrude upon and challenge formal legal power, this possibility was vitiated in the early decades of the ADR movement by a focus upon apparently apolitical questions of the processes and techniques of conflict management and a lack of substantial engagement with cultural difference. In these circumstances, ADR is constituted as a sphere of practice that substantially reflects – and therefore reproduces rather than challenges – dominant western law and political systems. In the Australian context, for instance, ADR practices operate in relation to particular values and modes of self-formation that can re-inscribe western liberal forms of selfhood at the expense of indigenous ways of being and processing conflict.[36] The informalism of ADR may indeed make ADR processes more appropriate than formal legal processes for assisting with conflict management in culturally diverse populations, including with Aboriginal people, but at least in its early forms ADR does not promise to reconfigure the relationship between formal power and informal culture. Despites its links with and apparent openness to cultural difference, ADR policy and practice typically subordinates culturally different ways of being-together and dealing with difficulties among people to those frameworks and approaches that find their grounding in the rule of law and the state. The very informalism of ADR paradoxically facilitates a mode of liberal governance that has ADR participants govern their selves in ways that are consistent with formal liberal law and governance. The early decades of ADR do not suggest, then, that ADR is a promising site for the emergence of thoroughgoing or serious legal pluralism.

10.3 Opening the Mediation Process: Legal Pluralism in ADR?

Although the ADR movement has links with cultural difference, the cultural politics of ADR are somewhat counterintuitive. Despite gaining inspiration and moral support from cultural difference, the ADR movement engaged minimally with culture in its early decades and paid limited attention to its own political and ideological entailments. Furthermore, because ADR processes are more flexible than most of the processes of formal law – and therefore are often seen as more appropriate for culturally diverse groups – ADR facilitates operations of informal governance which, counter-intuitively, vitiate the possibility of legal

[36] Morgan Brigg, 'Mediation, Power, and Cultural Difference' (2003) 20:3 *Confl Resolut Q* 287.

pluralism by governing selves in relation to liberal forms of selfhood and social order while bypassing non-western alternatives. Nonetheless, ADR is bound with a wider impulse and set of forces encouraging engagement with informal societal processes for managing conflict, including by recognising cultural difference. For this reason the governance landscape in relation to ADR, and the accompanying possibilities for legal pluralism, are neither static nor closed. Moreover, an important paradox of contemporary liberal governmentality is that an accommodating stance towards cultural difference forms part of liberal rule. By following a key self-critical principle of liberal political rationality that '"One always governs too much" – or, at any rate, one always must suspect that one governs too much',[37] liberal rule creates spaces of (ultimately constrained) freedom in which difference may realise and express itself. To understand the prospects for the relationship between formal law and informal culture through ADR requires asking after these spaces. Are such spaces sufficiently limited such that meaningful legal pluralism is impossible, or does ADR offer a site for realising a more expansive and culturally diverse repertoire of frameworks and techniques – including political categories and normative reference points – for managing disputes?

The initial enthusiasm for the application of ADR processes with Australian Aboriginal people from the 1970s to the 1990s met with mixed success. Efforts to recruit and retain Aboriginal mediators within agencies – the preferred model for many advocates and practitioners in the sector – was less successful than had been hoped for and the take-up of mediation by Aboriginal people and communities was less than what was deemed satisfactory when Aboriginal people were not heavily involved in service provision. These issues coincided with a range of critical analyses about the relevance and political implications of western ADR models for Aboriginal peoples[38], including some calls for recognition of indigenous dispute processing mechanisms.[39] Once again local

[37] Michel Foucault, *The Essential Works of Foucault, 1954–1984* (New York: New Press, 1997) at 74.

[38] Michael Dodson, 'Power and Cultural Difference in Native Title Mediation' (1996) 3:84 *Aborig Law Bull* 8; Kevin Dolman, 'Native Title Mediation: Is It Fair? [Condensed version of a paper submitted for assessment at the University of NSW]' (1999) 4:21 *Indig Law Bull* 8; Brigg, *supra* note 36; Madeleine Sauvé, 'Mediation: Towards an Aboriginal Conceptualisation' (1996) 3:81 *Aborig Law Bull* 10.

[39] Peter R Grose, 'An Indigenous Imperative: The Rationale for the Recognition of Aboriginal Dispute Resolution Mechanisms' (1995) 12:4 *Mediat Q* 327; Larissa Behrendt,

developments aligned with the wider international conflict resolution field, this time with a growing recognition that culture, rather than simply being a factor to be taken into account in universal mediation processes, needed to be more seriously engaged as a phenomenon with serious implications for how disputes are waged and resolution pursued.[40]

In the context of frustrated aspirations about the application of ADR with Aboriginal people and international recognition of the importance of culture in dispute processing, the 2000s saw three policy-focused national projects – all involving NADRAC, the (now defunct) National Alternative Dispute Resolution Advisory Council – begin to grapple more seriously with Aboriginal participation in ADR. A NADRAC consultative process found, in contrast to earlier enthusiasm for ADR, that '[i]n Indigenous communities, issues often do not fit the structures which have been developed to address western needs'.[41] For example, the understanding of conflicts as arising from clashes or incompatibilities between individual interests or needs, and the design of processes to address such clashes, do not align with Aboriginal understandings of selfhood as frequently extending beyond an individual skin-bound being through other people, and into landscape. As a result it can be difficult to address a whole range of conflict issues – from interpersonal grievances to community governance and land management – through western mediation approaches.

During the same period and in close collaboration with NADRAC, the national Indigenous Facilitation and Mediation Project (IFaMP)[42] sought, as one of its broad aims, to '[f]ind ways of building on indigenous ways of making decisions and managing conflict in the design and implementation of flexible, responsive, reliable and sustainable decision-making and dispute management systems'.[43] Later in the decade, a project under the auspices of the Federal Court of Australia and conducted in collaboration with the institutions that ran the earlier

Aboriginal Dispute Resolution (Sydney: Federation Press, 1995); S Gray, 'Monsters Round the Stomping-Ground: An Alternative Dispute Resolution Proposal for Indigenous Communities in the Northern Territory' (1999) 5:24 *Altern Law J* 216.

40 Kevin Avruch, *Introduction: Culture and Conflict Resolution* (1991).

41 NADRAC, *Indigenous Dispute Resolution and Conflict Management* (Canberra, Australia: National Alternative Dispute Resolution Advisory Council., 2006) at 5.

42 Within the Australian Institute of Aboriginal and Torres Strait Islander Studies (AIATSIS).

43 AIATSIS, *Mediation, Negotiation & Facilitation* (2013).

population influenced by mainstream western values. The result is a model that conforms to the requirements of the criminal justice system[50] and that is broadly consistent with western mediation, including through an emphasis on non-violent speech (rather than admonishment by elders or ritualised physical combat) as the key means for restoring relationships and social order.[51] Nonetheless, the conduct of MIRJ mediations also differs sufficiently from those undertaken in the mainstream community to warrant documentation by project staff.[52]

There seems little doubt that the opening of mediation process design to Aboriginal participation and values, or the participation and values of other peoples, involves – and indeed perhaps even encourages and supports – some degree of cultural pluralism in conflict management, and yet this opening is also constrained by formal liberal rule of law. The question becomes, then, whether this is a serious cross-cultural negotiation that deserves the label of legal pluralism or a mere accommodation that extends liberal governmentality through the contemporary recognition of cultural and identity differences. This is, in turn, part of a larger puzzle about 'how liberal is liberalism': Can certain key principles of liberalism (liberty and equality, in particular) help it to overcome its extant ontological and political commitments (including certain understandings of the individual, rights, representation, and property) such that its openness to difference brings about its own substantial transformation and, thereby, (partial) surpassing? While such questions are not susceptible to a definitive answer in the short run, it is possible to clarify what is at stake and to identify what would be required for the emergence of serious legal pluralism through ADR.

To interrogate the possibilities of substantive legal pluralism through ADR is not, to be clear, to ask a question about whether governing occurs or not through ADR and related conflict resolution processes. Conflict management invariably governs.[53] It involves individuals reconfiguring their orientations to their selves, to others and the institutions and world that bind them. What *is* of primary importance are the frameworks and ontological reference points in relation to and through which governance and the practice of conflict management occurs. This chapter, in opening, contrasted the formal abstract ideals, categories and injunctions of liberalism with the informal lived experience of (local) culture as a key fault line of contemporary governance.

[50] Philip Venables, *supra* note 48 at 5. [51] *Ibid* at appendix 5. [52] *Ibid* at appendix 6.
[53] Brigg, *supra* note 45.

Part of what is at stake here for ADR are the possibilities, as I have previously argued, for mitigating and transforming the operations of power and governance in ADR through a shift in the practice of mediation practitioners from an emphasis on technique, cognition, and reason, to affect, susceptibility and relationality.[54] A combination of technicality and susceptibility allows ADR practitioners to manage parties' reconfiguration of their selves and their relationship to conflict in ADR processes. Technicality is necessary to deal with the complexity of conflict; susceptibility to achieve rapport and fellow-feeling understanding. Just as these capacities allow mediators to direct a party towards their underlying interests and towards a rational response to their concerns (for instance) within a liberal ontological frame, the flow may be reversed. A mediator may become susceptible to, for instance, Aboriginal spirit ancestors and kinship networks in ways that disrupt ADR expectations about professional distance and neutrality. She or he may also come to think of parties as bound with ancestors and families rather than a bundle of interests. Susceptibility can open a fissure in the programmatic technology of mediation as governance. Because governing occurs in mediation through affective relations among parties and mediators, mediators can cultivate affective susceptibility in order to more fully and responsively engage others and difference, including different ontological reference points and lived experience. This opens the possibility that 'forces other than those of western liberalism (with its accompanying assumptions about selves, order and dispute) might come to operate through informal conflict resolution practice'.[55]

However, for mediators to be open and susceptible to cultural difference does not guarantee legal pluralism because difference can be readily enfolded within the ontological framework of formal liberalism. It can be, then, that difference is merely accommodated – and even appropriated – as an aesthetic orientation, or to underscore an aspect of mediation practice. We see, for instance, the use of Native American wisdom – in the form of traditional Native American quotes – to help present a series of values that can assist mediators to facilitate the mediation process.[56] The risk of operating only or primarily at the level of practices is that

[54] Morgan Brigg, 'Governance and Susceptibility in Conflict Resolution: Possibilities Beyond Control' (2007) 16:1 *Soc Leg Stud* 27.

[55] *Ibid* at 44.

[56] Joe Epstein & Darby Sais, 'Native American Wisdom: Lessons Learned for Mediation' (2003) 22 *Prev Rep* 27.

mediators may engage in a cursory detour via cultural difference that folds back upon dominant liberal forms of selfhood and social ordering which are (in turn) brought to bear in the governing relations facilitated in mediation processes. The sensibilities and practices that are generated in the process may be valuable for connecting across cultural difference and improving mediation practice, but without engagement with the ontological frames and reference points that structure the regulation and ordering of social life in different cultures, meaningful legal pluralism cannot be said to be at play.

Similarly, to identify and respond to cultural differences in the behaviours of disputing parties – a common approach in efforts to develop cultural awareness and appropriateness within culturally-sensitive ADR practice – does not constitute legal pluralism. Indeed, while a progressive move at face value, the adjustment of mediation practices to reflect a more culturally-sensitive approach may well facilitate more subtle modes of liberal governmentality rather than advance legal pluralism. For this reason it is hard to accept Menkel-Meadow's sanguine contention that her earlier concerns about the export of ADR from the United States as potentially ethnocentric and colonising are adequately ameliorated by the two-way exchange of practices, including by the import of revised or new practices by exporters following their overseas consultancy assignments.[57] ADR is part of a globalised liberal peacebuilding apparatus[58], and thinking at the level of practices does not adequately engage with its governing effects.

For ADR to be a serious site of cultural negotiation and legal pluralism, it must not only attend more fully to the lived experience of people at the level of behaviour and mediation practices; it must reach beyond behaviour and practice to engage with ontological questions about ways of being and forms of social and political order. To accept that Aboriginal parties to an ADR process might sometimes want to meet outdoors in the landscape of their ancestors is very different from understanding that parties may become subject to forces embedded in the landscape and the contemporary incarnation of an ancestor, with the implications this has for the dynamics of negation and agreement-making during an ADR

[57] Carrie Menkel-Meadow, 'Exporting and Importing ADR' (2005) 12 *Disp Resol Mag* 5.

[58] Oliver P Richmond, 'Becoming Liberal, Unbecoming Liberalism: Liberal-Local Hybridity via the Everyday as a Response to the Paradoxes of Liberal Peacebuilding' (2009) 3:3 *J Interv Statebuilding* 324; Oliver Richmond, 'Resistance and the Post-liberal Peace' (2010) 38 *Millenn-J Int Stud*, 665.

process. It is such ontological reference points that generate the ideals, categories, injunctions and norms that constitute the frameworks that are used within ADR and other conflict management processes to reveal, order and govern behaviour in dispute management.

Culturally variable understandings of personhood and social order (and, flowing from these, the interplay and relative importance of various human faculties including imagination, reason, and emotion) have significant implications for how conflicts are managed and social order achieved,[59] but these matters are relatively underexplored in ADR. Opening ADR processes to wider cultural participation, as has happened in the recent shift in ADR policy debate in Australia, provides opportunities to mitigate the influence of western-liberal modes of reasoning about conflict and social life by taking into account other worldviews. However for so long as ADR focuses on behaviours and practices rather than deeper ontological concerns ADR is more likely to remain a site for the accommodation – and governing – of cultural difference rather than for meaningful legal pluralism.

10.4 Conclusion

The relationship between formal law and informal culture in ADR is nuanced and somewhat counter-intuitive. By considering the relationship between cultural difference and ADR in the early decades of the movement as well as the case of ADR policy and practice in relation to Aboriginal peoples in Australia, this chapter first argued that ADR processes tend to govern and subordinate cultural difference despite their apparently natural fit with the informal conflict management processes of diverse cultural groups. Although the early ADR movement drew inspiration from cultural others to advocate for and otherwise support the development of ADR processes, this was a superficial engagement serving more to differentiate mediation from formal law than to create exchange between culturally different ways of managing disputes. Some exchange took place at the level of technique and practice, and this has been expanded with the export of ADR processes from the United States, but this serves to mask the way that informal ADR processes govern participants in relation to the ontological frameworks and reference points of formal liberalism. ADR may well be more culturally appropriate

[59] Wanda D McCaslin, *Justice as Healing: Indigenous Ways* (Living Justice Press, 2005).

than the processes of formal law, and yet governmentality analysis shows that the governance effects of ADR may well be all the more complete and accomplished for such cultural sensitivity. The implication is that for so long as ADR operates at the level of behaviours and practices without reference to culturally diverse foundations for social order and dispute management it has limited prospects as a site of serious legal pluralism.

Nonetheless, the relationships between formal law and informal culture that generate the foregoing governing effects and limit the prospects for legal pluralism are not stable or static, not least because they themselves arise out of a call for law to be more responsive to the lived experience of local cultures. The case of recent ADR policy discussions in relation to the participation of Australian Aboriginal peoples illustrates the possibility for change. In response to a less than satisfactory uptake to ADR processes by Aboriginal peoples, policy discussion – and some practice in the area of mediation program development – has recently taken the incremental yet significant step of opening the design of some mediation processes to Aboriginal participation and values. Such opening remains, as might be expected, constrained by formal liberal rule of law, but it takes policy discussion from the limited consideration of behaviours and practices to a more expansive purview that begins to bring into play more substantive questions of cultural values and ontological reference points. This raises the question: can ADR open to difference or is it destined to only accommodate and govern cultural difference as it upholds extant liberal ontological and political commitments? Can key principles of liberty and equality (alongside an apparent contemporary openness to cultural difference) enable liberalism to surpass itself in exchange and negotiation with cultural traditions that operate with different understandings of personhood and place differing emphases on the role of violent force, speech, and the interplay and relative importance of various human faculties?

The prospects for progress towards substantive legal pluralism through ADR are subject to the agonistic and unpredictable dynamics of politico-cultural engagement. On one hand, the liberal formal politico-legal imaginary exerts a powerful and deeply embedded influence both within the developed west and in wider global politics, and this militates against negotiation and serious exchange with the worldviews and ontological reference points of Aboriginal and other peoples. Equally, neither cultural difference nor associated politico-cultural claims show any signs of abating, and some governments appear to be willing to make practical accommodations of cultural difference. If these accommodations extend to putting the ontological frameworks and reference points of liberalism into exchange with those of diverse peoples through the development of ADR policies and processes for dispute management, then ADR will contribute to the pursuit of liberty and justice as an ongoing endeavour.

No doubt some would be concerned about support for the development of such a centaur justice within ADR. But against such objections, the forcefulness of formal liberalism more than ensures that the normative foundation of the law as we know it is not threatened. Rapid change is unlikely and, moreover, the normative foundation that some would seek to protect is itself always already hybridised and changing. A pragmatist muddling through – a mode of operating which has itself generated our current relatively regularised legal world – would thus see the gradual evolution of entirely workable and politico-culturally acceptable ADR arrangements arising out of legal pluralism. Against potential objections, the benefits of a centaur justice, should it come about, would include a rebalancing of culture and power beyond liberalism to more accurately reflect the global diversity of peoples and worldviews as well as everyday lived experience and understandings of justice.

11

Grassroots Law in Context

Moving beyond the Cultural Justification

KRISTIN DOUGHTY

11.1 Introduction

After the 1994 genocide, consistent with global fetishization of law and transitional justice, the Rwandan government resolved to build a state "governed by the rule of law, based on respect for fundamental human rights."[1] This led to building new courts and legal jurisdictions, and training new lawyers and judges. Yet, most ordinary Rwandans were still directed to take to the Western-style courts only as a last resort. Instead, whether facing criminal genocide charges, a land dispute with a neighbor, divorce from a spouse, or a contract disagreement with an employer, I suggest that Rwandans were most likely to experience the social force of law through efforts at mediation, whether in forums based on customary law or those rooted in universal human rights principles. This emphasis on mediation was perhaps most notoriously a part of the restorative justice aims of Rwanda's highly publicized genocide courts (*gacaca*), but was also a part of enduring legal institutions and practices including mediation committees for low-level civil and criminal disputes (*comite y'abunzi*), and a university-led legal aid clinic.

In this chapter, I examine Rwanda's *gacaca, comite y'abunzi,* and the legal aid clinic as united by a common undergirding philosophy that, whenever possible, disputes should be solved through compromise and reconciliation with the help of a third party. They were designed to bring participants together as joint problem-solvers to find mutually agreed solutions, rather than one side winning and the other side losing. I thus

[1] Preamble para. 6, *Constitution of the Republic of Rwanda and its Amendments of 2 December 2003 and of 8 December 2005* [], June 4, 2003, available at: www.refworld.org/docid/46c5b1f52.html [accessed October 12, 2014]

situate these forums as "harmony legal models"[2] within a broader context of alternative dispute resolution.[3] Nader identifies harmony legal models as legal forums that combine the principles of harmony ideology – "a view of harmonious behavior as more civilized than disputing behavior, the belief that consensus is of greater survival value than controversy" – with state-backed punishment.[4]

Rwandan government authorities justified the emphasis on mediation and harmony as a cultural model of dispute resolution, consistent with "cultural claims made in the ADR literature" more widely.[5] By highlighting a cultural basis for legal practice rather than universal legal principles or human rights, the official Rwandan discourse dovetailed with how legal anthropologists have over the past decade shown the limitations of the growing hegemony of international human rights and criminal law, and have renewed calls to recognize the cultural dimensions of law.[6] For example, Clarke discusses how the International Criminal Court's aims are disconnected from local desires and practices in Kenya. Anthropologists of transitional justice have shown how truth commissions' Judeo-Christian valorization of talk risks overwriting people's cultural practices of silence or deliberate forgetting, including in Sierra Leone,[7] Angola and Mozambique,[8]

[2] Laura Nader, *The Life of the Law: Anthropological Projects* (Berkeley: University of California Press, 2002).

[3] See Briggs, Chapter 10, this volume and Reiter, Chapter 9, this volume.

[4] Laura Nader, *Harmony Ideology: Justice and Control in a Zapotec Mountain Village* (Stanford: Stanford University Press, 1990) at 2.

[5] See Reiter, Chapter 9, this volume.

[6] See Kamari Maxine Clarke, *Fictions of Justice: The International Criminal Court and the Challenge of Legal Pluralism in Sub-Saharan Africa* (Cambridge: Cambridge University Press, 2009); Tim Kelsall, *Culture under Cross-Examination: International Justice and the Special Court for Sierra Leone* (Cambridge: Cambridge University Press, 2013); Sally Engle Merry, *Human Rights and Gender Violence: Translating International Law into Local Justice* (Chicago: University of Chicago Press, 2006); Alison Dundes Renteln, *The Cultural Defense* (Oxford: Oxford University Press, 2005); Lawrence Rosen, *Law As Culture: An Invitation* (Princeton: Princeton University Press, 2006). See also Provost, Chapter 1, this volume.

[7] Rosalind Shaw, "Rethinking Truth and Reconciliation Commissions: Lessons from Sierra Leone," *USIP Spec Rep* (2005) 130, 1; Rosalind Shaw, "Memory Frictions: Localizing the Truth and Reconciliation Commission in Sierra Leone," *Int J Transitional Justice* (2007) 1, 183.

[8] Alcinda Honwana, "Healing and Social Reintegration in Mozambique and Angola" in E Skaar, S Gloppen & A Suhrke, eds., *Roads to Reconciliation* (New York: Lexington Books, 2005) 83; Victor Igreja and Beatrice Dias-Lambranca, "Restorative Justice and the Role of Magamba Spirits in Post-Civil War Gorongosa, Central Mozambique" in L Huyse & M Salter, eds., *Traditional Justice and Reconciliation After Violent Conflict: Learning from African Experiences* (Stockholm: International IDEA, 2008).

Burundi,[9] Liberia,[10] and Peru.[11] The rightful critiques of legal universals have come alongside a recognition of the importance of "the local" in transitional justice.[12] Practitioners and scholars have responded with a search for "authentic" cultural practices, such as in Northern Uganda where backlash against the International Criminal Court's perceived weaknesses has led to increased attention on reconciliation rituals such as *mato oput* or *gomo tong*.[13]

This volume similarly responds to this trend to reintegrate culture and law, considering the challenges of the legalization of culture and the enculturation of law. But, as I discuss in this chapter, culture is often used as a blunt analytic tool and risks obscuring as much as it reveals. I show here the dangers of relying on cultural legitimization, as culture can be used as a seemingly benign justification for non-benign forms of governance. Laying bare the fallacy of the cultural justification for harmony in African examples is perhaps particularly important, because they are routinely romanticized as "pure tradition" in ways that can blind us to how power actually operates within them.[14] This chapter shows that while there are in fact deep historical socio-cultural roots to mediation in Rwanda, at the same time, these forums, and the mediation principles at their heart, are related to broader, historically situated neoliberal logics of governance. The relationship between culture and law is too often stripped of power and politics, rather than culture being analyzed alongside the broader, and highly unequal, moral economy of justice.[15]

[9] Ann Nee and Peter Uvin, "Silence and Dialogue: Burundians' Alternatives to Transitional Justice" in R Shaw, L Waldorf & P Hazan, eds., *Localizing Transitional Justice* (Stanford: Stanford University Press, 2010) 157.

[10] Sharon Alane Abramowitz, *Searching for Normal in the Wake of the Liberian War* (University of Pennsylvania Press, 2014).

[11] Kimberly Theidon, *Intimate Enemies: Violence and Reconciliation in Peru* (Philadelphia: University of Pennsylvania Press, 2012) at 42–4.

[12] Alexander Laban Hinton, ed., *Transitional Justice: Global Mechanisms and Local Realities after Genocide and Mass Violence* (New Brunswick, NJ: Rutgers University Press, 2010); Rosalind Shaw, Lars Waldorf & Pierre Hazan, eds., *Localizing Transitional Justice: Interventions and Priorities after Mass Violence* (Stanford: Stanford University Press, 2010).

[13] Tim Allen, "Ritual (Ab) Use? Problems with Traditional Justice in Northern Uganda" in Nicolas Wadell & Phil Clark, eds., *Court Confl Justice Peace ICC Afr* (London: Royal African Society, 2008) 47; Sverker Finnström, "Reconciliation Grown Bitter? War, Retribution, and Ritual Action in Northern Uganda" in R Shaw, L Waldorf & P Hazan, eds., *Localizing Transitional Justice* (Stanford: Stanford University Press, 2010) 135.

[14] See Reiter's discourse analysis of the cultural justification for ADR in this volume.

[15] Clarke, *supra* note 6.

In recent decades, scholars have shown how identity and culture are increasingly commodified and politicized,[16] and these effects can be just as problematic (if not more so) in the hands of the state.

Looking at harmony principles as cross-cutting Rwanda's genocide courts, mediation committees, and legal aid clinics shifts the debate from whether or not mediation is in fact the culturally appropriate model for Rwanda, as the government claims it is, to help us better understand what is at stake in the cultural justification, and how this mode of power constitutes people as particular kinds of subjects, within a carefully constructed "community." I argue that combining the cultural justification with state-backed authority insidiously amounted to making the beliefs and values of collective unity mandatory in and of themselves. Thus, I suggest that if we are to consider the enculturation of law and advocate for culturally sensitive legal processes, we could benefit by identifying even more nuanced analytic instruments. Contextualization is perhaps a useful metric for explaining how legal forums can become relevant to people's efforts to rebuild their social worlds. Thus, my goal is to contribute to this volume's question of whether legal pluralism can bring culture within the domain of law by helping us to more specifically name what we mean by "culture" and how it is relevant to people's everyday practices of resolving disputes.

11.2 Post-Genocide Rwanda's Harmony Legal Models

I begin by providing three typical examples – one each from *gacaca* (genocide courts), *comite y'abunzi* (mediation committees), and a legal aid clinic – compiled from eighteen months of ethnographic fieldwork I conducted in Rwanda between 2007–8. I present these examples in order to show the mediation focus within each of the three legal forums, and thus to situate them within one analytic frame as harmony legal models. These empirical examples illustrate the deeply contextualized conversations that were occurring within law-backed mediation. These forums were physically proximate, public, routine, participatory, and based on oral testimony. Residents who sat together in grassroots legal proceedings one day a week typically saw one another the rest of the week, as they lived in mutual interdependence in a densely populated area. Sessions were episodes in a set of debates and knowledge claims that

[16] John Comaroff and Jean Comaroff, *Ethnicity, Inc.* (Chicago: University of Chicago Press, 2009).

this, saying that his intentions were good, reiterating that his powers were limited at the time. Elise then spoke directly to Celestin, telling him that he had been very rude to her, and "the way you replied hurt me so much." Celestin said he understood, but he had not intended to hurt her. A judge intervened in support of Elise, asking Celestin how he could have hurt Elise by challenging her rights to inherit, when the bigger issue was that her brother had just died. Celestin explained that he really did not intend to hurt her, "she knows me, I was a friend of her father's, please forgive me, I never intended to keep the bike just because it was fancy." Another judge pushed him again, saying that if his powers were limited, why did he not ask someone for help in making that decision? Celestin explained that there were so many problems at the time, maybe he did forward it on to others for help, but there were too many for him to remember precisely.

This discussion continued, with the judges asking the general assembly for their assessment of the situation, and several additional people rising to provide questions or suggestions. Celestin's daughter then stood from where she had been seated in the general assembly. She spoke in defense of her father. She explained that if he had wanted, he could have kept both bikes, but giving one was a gesture which showed that he had no negative intentions. She explained that even after her father left his leadership post, she and Elise had lived together, but Elise never said that she had tried to recover the bike. She wondered why it took Elise thirteen years to bring up the bike, suggesting that it was an opportunistic claim, not an honest one.

This example illustrates how the judges took seriously the mediating dimension of their task, focusing on a process to try to build consensus and ensure buy-in to their logical process, and attending to the relationships amongst the participants – Elise and Celestin's daughter were close friends who had lived together, and Celestin and Elise's father had been friends. I suggest here that part of what made this process powerful, despite its flaws (concerns of bias, lack of procedural regularity, lack of standardization), was how deeply embedded this legal process was in people's everyday lives and social networks. Whether or not the participants felt a naturalized cultural connection to the practice of dispute resolution in which they were engaged, they did feel invested and that they had a stake in its outcome, in large part because it was proximate to them, it prioritized oral testimony with wide latitude for what could be included as evidence, and it involved people with whom they were in ongoing relationships.

11.2.2 Comite y'abunzi: *Mediation Committees*

The Rwandan government created mediation committees (*comite y'abunzi*) shortly after the nationwide launch of *gacaca* courts. *Comite y'abunzi* had jurisdiction over low-level civil and criminal disputes. *Comite y'abunzi* were established by national law around the same time as *gacaca* courts based on the same general procedure, in order to "provid [e] a framework of obligatory mediation" for ordinary civil and criminal disputes, where locally elected *abunzi,* Kinyarwanda for mediators or reconcilers, would "seek first to conciliate the two parties."[19] Even while the *abunzi* aimed to find compromise solutions with which parties would voluntarily comply, state-backed authorities could seize land, livestock, crops, and other personal property based on case judgments.[20]

Consider the following example from late 2007 of a dispute between a woman and her aunt, both subsistence farmers living in Southern Rwanda, over a piece of land. This example shows how mediators sought to reason with the participants to get them to voluntarily comply, even as the sessions themselves were highly contentious. It further illustrates the deeply localized, specialized knowledge of family and ownership practices needed to make a decision on the case.

Beatrice claimed Annonciata, an aunt on her father's side, was living on a parcel of land to which she herself also had rights because it was family land from her father's side of the family. Beatrice had already taken the case to the local authorities, but they had not been able to resolve the issue. She wanted the *abunzi* to order Annonciata to split the land with her. The discussion before *comite y'abunzi* quickly became quite complicated, with the more than forty people in the crowd and the panel of mediators all trying to follow along. The case sessions involved a long oral history of land use and acquisition in the area, as elderly people provided detailed narratives about things they remembered from their childhood. My research assistant and I drew a family tree, which we kept correcting as witnesses added people and clarified relationships.

Specifically, Beatrice claimed that the land had originally belonged to her great-great-grandfather, named Ndayisenga. Ndayisenga had two sons, Moise (from whom Beatrice was descended) and Frederic (from

[19] *Organic Law N.31/2006 On Organisation, Jurisdiction, Competence and Functioning of the Mediation Committee*, August 14, 2006 [*Organic Law N.31/2006 On Organisation, Jurisdiction, Competence and Functioning of the Mediation Committee*].

[20] *Ibid* at Article 24.

whom Annonciata was descended). Beatrice claimed that Ndayisenga had died before formally portioning the land among his inheritors, so that it remained family land and should be shared by surviving descendants, herself included. Annonciata, who was living on the land, claimed that the land had been partitioned by Moise and given to her father, Gatanazi, and therefore was no longer part of the family land to which Beatrice would be entitled. Further, Annonciata argued, if Beatrice wanted some of her land, then she should share the land on which she was currently living. By contrast, Beatrice claimed that land to which Annonciata referred had been acquired separately by Moise, and therefore was not part of the family land that she would need to share.

The complexity in the case was that the family relations and blood lines were unclear, and therefore inheritance was ambiguous. Precision on the relationship between Annonciata and Beatrice only emerged after hours of discussion. Technically, Annonciata was Beatrice's grandfather's cousin's child. Annonciata's father, Gatanazi, was Moise's brother's son (nephew). But Gatanazi had been raised by Moise, because his own father, Frederic, had died while he was still young. So, if Moise had formally adopted Gatanazi, then Annonciata could be considered Beatrice's father's cousin. The difference in these degrees of relatedness was central to the ownership of the disputed property.

So the first question was whether Ndayisenga had partitioned his original land between his sons. If he had, and if the disputed land was Frederic's portion, then it would belong to Annonciata, as she claimed. If, by contrast, Ndayisenga had given all his land to his surviving son Moise upon Frederic's death, then the question became whether Moise had explicitly given the disputed land to Gatanazi as his adopted son (as Annonciata claimed), or if Moise had partitioned the land among his own family, and descendants from Gatanazi were improperly occupying the land (as Beatrice claimed). If Moise had partitioned the land between his son (Beatrice's grandfather) and Gatanazi (the adopted nephew, Annonciata's father), then Annonciata could maintain sole rights to it. If he had not, and if the adoption was in question, then Beatrice should have access.

A series of witnesses presented testimony, describing what they recalled hearing people say decades before, during the contested time period, about who owned the land, who lived on it, and how it came to be owned. They relied on memories passed down over time, and on informal practices such as whether saying that Gatanazi thought of Moise as a father (as proof, one witness described that he would "swear on his father's name" using the name Moise). The mediators recounted testimony they had heard from visiting elderly people living on the adjacent land. The conversations remained heated, with frequent disagreements and interruptions from people seated listening to the case. The mediators adjourned the discussion after several hours, claiming that they would wait to hear from two other witnesses that Annonciata wanted to bring.

Three months later, the case still had not been resolved, and the disputants came back for another session. Beatrice sat on her haunches by the door, while Annonciata stood on the other side of the door, leaning against the window. They rarely looked at each other. Beatrice insisted that the mediators should make a decision. The mediators said they wanted to hear from more witnesses for Annonciata, including an aunt and another man in the family. Beatrice said that those people had already spoken before the local authorities and said that they knew nothing about the case (as the papers that she had already presented to the mediators attested), and therefore she insisted the mediators should make a judgment. Beatrice had brought another witness, Annonciata's younger sister, who testified that the land in question was in fact family land that had never been partitioned. Annonciata objected to having her sister as a witness, saying that their relationship was not good and therefore she would be biased. Annonciata claimed that her sister was not happy with how the land was currently being shared and so she was conniving with Beatrice to gain access to the land to sell it. One of the mediators then lectured Annonciata, noting that she needed to share the land among anyone who had rightful access to it. Ultimately, Annonciata agreed aloud that she would have to share the land with Beatrice. The mediators wrote their decision, and set a date on which the local authorities would accompany the women to the land to officially partition it.

This case example, while quite distinct from the *gacaca* case – a land dispute among family as compared to a property dispute during a genocide case among neighbors – nonetheless reveals commonalities in law-backed mediation. It demonstrates the emphasis on process, collective conversations, and negotiation amongst participants, with an emphasis on a solution that involved compromise for the collective good. It also shows how discussions were heavily contested, rather than harmonious. It further shows the importance of contextualization here. Cases rested on complex details that could not be easily proven with independent, objective evidence, but rather required deeply nuanced understandings of local practices of family belonging, ownership, and local landscape. Without arguing that the decisions were more or less

out. The legal aid clinic was less deeply contextualized than *gacaca* and *comite y'abunzi,* but was much closer to their localized social and knowledge networks than were the ordinary courts in Rwanda.

This case example shows that while there was variation in mediation across these three legal forums in post-genocide Rwanda, if we attend only to the emphasis on harmony and unity within the so-called customary-style law of *gacaca* and *comite y'abunzi,* then we risk misunderstanding how law-based mediation operated as a mode of power. Mediation at the legal aid clinic perhaps most closely resembled alternate dispute resolution as it is found in other contexts. I turn now to the cultural justification for harmony and mediation in Rwanda, and how by examining it in historical and comparative context, we can better understand power, politics, and even coercion in harmony.

11.3 Denaturalizing the Cultural Justification

In May 2008, I sat with a middle-aged Rwandan man who described to me the cultural justification for unity and reconciliation at the heart of Rwanda's harmony models. He said:

> *Gacaca en fait c'est la verdure, c'est la verdure, on cohabitait ensemble, s'il y avait un conflit entre un tel et tel, on prenait les sages, les vielles se mettaient là, on prenait les gens en conflit, on s'assoyait. Gacaca ça signifie le gazon, on s'assoyait, on disait « tu es coupable, toi tu n'es pas coupable, toi tu dois celui-là indemnisation d'une vache ou un pot de bière. » Ça on disait procès gacaca. Au même temps qu'abunzi, c'est que dire « unir ». On a différencié ces juridictions populaires parce que les gacaca pour le génocide, abunzi pour unir, déjà abunzi c'est unir, unir les gens. Gacaca, abunzi, c'est ensemble des personnes pour la réconciliation.*
>
> (Gacaca, basically, means the grass, it's the grass. People lived together, if there was a conflict between two of them, they gathered the wise men, the elderly, and they sat together, brought together the people who were quarelling, and all sat together. Gacaca means the lawn, they sat together, they said "you are guilty, you, you need to repay that one a cow or a bottle of beer." That, we say, was the gacaca process. At the same time, abunzi, that means "unite." They differentiated these popular jurisdictions because gacaca was for genocide, abunzi to unite. So already, abunzi is uniting. Gacaca, abunzi, it's gathering people together for reconciliation.)

This characterization was consistent with how the Rwandan government authorities legitimized the harmony legal models as, according to printed brochures, "traditional community courts" based on "the inspiration of the traditional context of conflict resolution." They claimed that Rwandans historically had dispute resolution systems that eschewed the winner-take-all basis of Western courts, instead using respected elders to solve specific disputes between individuals and families to strengthen communal ties.

Indeed, scholars writing on Rwanda note a long-term presence of conciliation-based, decentralized mechanisms for resolving disputes in the region now known as Rwanda,[21] consistent with broader-reaching customary law practices across much of sub-Saharan Africa. Sources agree on a general view of *gacaca* in the pre-colonial period without specifying precisely when it came into being or differences across centuries pre-colonially.[22] During the pre-colonial period in Rwanda, as late as the eighteenth century, there existed no codified law, no formal tribunals, and no structure for appealing judicial decisions.[23] *Gacaca* hearings were convened when conflicts arose within or between families over issues such as land rights, property damage, marital disputes or inheritance. They were presided over by elders or male heads of household, and based on shared social norms. The primary goal was to restore social order and create reconciliation by reintegrating the offender into the community after sanctioning the offender's violation of shared values and rules. Offenders appeared voluntarily, insofar as they were not compelled by the king (*mwami*). The elders could determine the sanction. Decisions were intended to represent a compromise between the individual interests of the participants and collective norms. Sanctions were enforced through social pressure.

[21] Jennie E Burnet, *Genocide Lives in Us: Women, Memory, and Silence in Rwanda* (Madison, WI: University of Wisconsin Press, 2012) at 196; Catharine Newbury, "Ethnicity in Rwanda: The Case of Kinyaga", *Africa* (1978) 48(1), 17 at 20; Filip Reyntjens, *Pouvoir et Droit au Rwanda: Droit public et Evolution Politique, 1916–1973* (Tervuren, Belgique: Musée royal de l'Afrique centrale, 1985) at 150–2; Filip Reyntjens, "Le Gacaca Ou La Justice Du Gazon Au Rwanda," *Polit Afr* (1990) 31, 31; Laurel Rose, "Are Alternative Dispute Resolution (ADR) Programs Suitable for Africa," *September Afr Notes* (1996) 5 at 6–7.

[22] See, for example, Amnesty International, *Rwanda Gacaca: A Question of Justice* (London, Amnesty International, 2002) 20–1; Phil Clark, *The Gacaca Courts, Post-Genocide Justice and Reconciliation in Rwanda: Justice without Lawyers* (Cambridge: Cambridge University Press, 2010) at 52; Filip Reyntjens & Stef Vandeginste, "Rwanda: An Atypical Transition" in E Skaar, S Gloppen & A Suhrke, eds., *Roads Reconcil* (New York: Lexington Books, 2005) 101 at 118; Simon Gasibirege, "Resultats Definitifs de l'Enquete Quantitative sur Les Attitudes des Rwandais vis-a-vis des Juridictions Gacaca," *Cahiers de Centre de Gestion des Conflits* (2002) 6, 39–92; Nicholas Jones, *The Courts of Genocide: Politics and the Rule of Law in Rwanda and Arusha* (New York: Routledge, 2010) 56.

[23] Jan Vansina, *Antecedents to Modern Rwanda: the Nyiginya Kingdom* (Madison: University of Wisconsin Press, 2004) at 89–90.

This philosophy was consistent with classic analyses of African adjudication, which stressed that local courts in Africa, whether formal or moots, aimed to restore breaches in relationships among members in an ongoing community in order to restore equilibrium.[24] Similar to the classic ethnographic examples, post-genocide Rwanda's harmony legal models had no lawyers, incorporated broad participation and had minimal hierarchy among disputants, judges, witnesses, and other attendees, all consistent with a spirit of compromise rather than adversity. They used wide rules of evidence, given that the issue at hand was understood as a breach of deeply embedded relationships and practices, rather than narrowly focused on a specific point of law. Finally, the processes explicitly and clearly articulated social norms in an effort to socialize litigants as well as other participants.

Yet, debating whether Rwanda's post-genocide legal institutions are "customary" can disguise the degree of state involvement in so-called informal or popular mediation in the past and present, and it can hide historical and contemporary power imbalances and coercion. For decades we have known that we cannot take the ethnographic record of African customary law at face-value, given how the focus on compromise within it reflects primarily a "Durkheimian emphasis on harmony of interests and shared goals"[25] as the primary analytic lens, rather than theoretical attention to conflict and discord. Even seemingly consensus-based customary practices contained hierarchy and coercion.[26] In precolonial Rwanda, the king's justice was swift but not impartial, and

[24] Paul Bohannan, *Justice and Judgment among the Tiv* (London: Oxford University Press for International African Institute, 1957); E E Evans-Pritchard, *The Nuer: A Description of the Modes of Livelihood and Political Institutions of a Nilotic People* (Oxford: Oxford University Press, 1940); Max Gluckman, *The Judicial Process among the Barotse of Northern Rhodesia* (Manchester: Manchester University Press for Rhodes-Livingstone Institute, 1955); Elizabeth Colson, "Social Control and Vengeance in Plateau Tonga Society," *Africa: The Journal of the International African Institute* (1953) 23(3), 199–212; James L. Gibbs, "The Kpelle Moot" in Paul Bohannan, ed., *Law and Warfare: Studies in the Anthropology of Conflict* (American Museum Sourcebooks in Anthropology Series, Garden City: Natural History, 1967) 277–90; Laurel Rose, *The Politics of Harmony: Land Dispute Strategies in Swaziland* (Cambridge: Cambridge University Press, 1992); Isaac Schapera, *A Handbook of Tswana Custom and Law* (London: Published for the International African Institute by the Oxford University Press, 1955).

[25] June Starr & Barbara Yngvesson, "Scarcity and Disputing: Zero-Ing in on Compromise Decisions," *Am Ethnol* (1975) 2, 553 at 559.

[26] Elizabeth Colson, *Tradition and Contract: The Problem of Order* (Chicago: Aldine Publishing Company, 1974); Sally Falk Moore, *Social Facts and Fabrications "Customary" Law on Kilimanjaro, 1880–1980* (Cambridge: Cambridge University Press, 1986).

dispute resolution could be part of politics of violence.[27] Scholars have shown in Rwanda how customary-style tribunals during the colonial period served primarily as instruments through which the ruling elites, appointed as judges and key personnel, retained privileges.[28]

Further, customary practices and institutions in Rwanda and elsewhere in sub-Saharan Africa changed significantly during the colonial period and since independence, specifically through increasing state control. While in pre-colonial Rwanda, local lineages enjoyed relative autonomy and resolved many conflicts, such as those over land,[29] by the late nineteenth century, prior to colonial contact in Rwanda, the king (Rwabugiri) introduced new chiefs who took over many of the functions, such as resolution of land disputes, which had previously been performed by lineage heads.[30] During the colonial period, a hierarchy of customary law rigidified gradually over several decades, in interplay between Rwandan chiefs and Belgians.[31] Both German and Belgian colonial leaders created two categories of rules: they formalized the colonial legal system where written law applied to Europeans, while indigenous jurisdictions maintained the right to judge Rwandans for civil and penal affairs based on custom. In reality, custom was only allowed where it did not contradict public order as defined by the colonizers and Rwandan people were subject to both indigenous law and Belgian written law.

Under the First and Second Republics after Rwandan Independence, systems based on the principles of customary law continued to exist and were intertwined with state law, though not formalized. Specifically, after independence, the new government extended Belgian written law to apply to all Rwandans, so citizens were formally subject to "modern" law.[32] Customary law was no longer part of the state system, though local systems of dispute resolution continued to exist and in some areas to flourish. *Gacaca* was in place as late as the 1980s, distinct from the formal system of law and not regulated by any codified legal texts as it would be in the post-genocide period, but not purely popular or traditional, as it

[27] Vansina, *supra* note 23 at 185.

[28] René Lemarchand, *Rwanda and Burundi* (New York: Praegar Publishers, 1970) at 75; Reyntjens, *supra* note 21 at 155.

[29] Newbury, *supra* note 21 at 20. [30] *Ibid.*

[31] Most information about law under colonial rule comes from Reyntjens, *supra* note 21.

[32] Bibane Mbaye Gahamanyi, "Rwanda: Building Constitutional Order in the Aftermath of Genocide" in AA An-Na'im, ed., *Hum Rights Afr Const Realiz Promise Ourselves* (Philadelphia: University of Pennsylvania Press, 2003) 252 at 266.

victim narratives consistent with a psychotherapeutic model, and eschews punishment in an effort to "heal individuals and society after the trauma of mass atrocity."[44] In this vein, billboards across Rwanda in 2004 and 2005 publicized the launch of the *gacaca* process by announcing *Ukuri kurakiza,* "the truth is healing." Further, the imbrications of Christianity with mediation in Rwanda are pronounced. Rwanda has been predominantly Christian for over a century, due to the missionary influence under colonial rule.[45] Post-genocide Rwanda saw a resurgence in transnational forms of Christianity, particularly evangelical churches brought in from East and Central Africa by returning diaspora, as well as by church congregants on missions from churches in Europe and the United States. Though churches were not formally involved in the legal process, Christianity served as a broader part of the socio-political context that reinforced mediation principles. Both local pastors (some of whom served as *abunzi* or *inyangamugayo*) and international pastors advocated harmony principles within and outside courts in Rwanda. Other scholars have noted this trend elsewhere. Wilson has argued that Christian notions of confession and redemptive healing were crucial to many people's understandings of reconciliation in the South African TRC.[46] Shaw and Kelsall have described how Christian elements were crucial to the Sierra Leonean TRC hearings, and Theidon has detailed the interrelationships between evangelical Christianity and the TRC in Peru.[47]

None of this is to suggest that there is no basis for claiming cultural roots of harmony in Rwanda, or that *gacaca, comite y'abunzi,* or the legal aid clinic are identical to ADR. Rather, in the face of such clear interconnections between Rwanda's post-genocide grassroots mediation-based legal forums and global trends, I want to ask, what is at stake in the insistence that these forums are naturally Rwandan? Challenging the benign cultural framing of harmony legal models in Rwanda is vital,

[44] Martha Minow, *Between Vengeance and Forgiveness: Facing History after Genocide and Mass Violence* (Boston: Beacon Press, 1998) at 57. See also Nader, *supra* note 37 at 44. Nader & Grande, *supra* note 37.

[45] Timothy Longman, *Christianity and Genocide in Rwanda* (Cambridge: Cambridge University Press, 2010).

[46] Richard Wilson, *The Politics of Truth and Reconciliation in South Africa: Legitimizing the Post-Apartheid State* (Cambridge: Cambridge University Press, 2001) at 109–20.

[47] Theidon, *supra* note 11; Shaw, *supra* note 7; Tim Kelsall, "Truth, Lies, Ritual: Preliminary Reflections on the Truth and Reconciliation Commmission in Sierra Leone," *Hum Rights Q* (2005) 27(2), 361.

especially given the growing acknowledgement that the increasingly authoritarian Rwandan government uses law and "lawfare"[48] selectively as another strategy to consolidate the ruling elites' power and suppress dissent.[49] National unity was promoted alongside the implementation of increasingly repressive laws that proscribed ethnic labels and criminalized "divisionism," "revisionism," or "genocide ideology," anything seen as "marginalizing… degrading… [or] stirring up ill feelings."[50] These laws served to reduce political dissent, especially when coupled with ongoing detentions and state-backed violence at home and in neighboring Democratic Republic of Congo.[51] While in theory *gacaca* had the possibility to promote peace-building through a historically contextualized process,[52] much critical research agrees that *gacaca* was an "imposition of the central government on local communities,"[53] wherein the "near-total state control"[54] and pursuit of victor's justice[55] often

[48] John Comaroff, "Colonialism, Culture, and the Law: A Foreword", *Law Soc Inq* (2001) 26, 305 at 306.

[49] E.g., Anuradha Chakravarty, *Investing in Authoritarian Rule: Punishment and Patronage in Rwanda's Gacaca Courts for Genocide Crimes* (Cambridge: Cambridge University Press, 2015); Constance Morrill, "Show Business and 'Lawfare' in Rwanda: Twelve Years After the Genocide," *Dissent* (2006) 53(3), 14; Scott Straus & Lars Waldorf, eds., *Remaking Rwanda: State Building and Human Rights after Mass Violence* (Madison: University of Wisconsin Press, 2011).

[50] *Law N.18/2008 Relating to the Punishment of the Crime of Genocide Ideology*, July 23, 2008 [*Law N.18/2008 Relating to the Punishment of the Crime of Genocide Ideology*] at Article 3.

[51] Susan Thomson, "Whispering Truth to Power: The Everyday Resistance of Rwandan Peasants to Post-Genocide Reconciliation," *Afr Aff* (2011) 110(440), 439 at 442; Lars Waldorf, "Instrumentalizing Genocide: The RPF's Campaign against 'genocide ideology'" in S Strauss & L Waldorf, eds., *Remaking Genocide* (Madison: University of Wisconsin Press, 2011) 48 at 49.

[52] Clark, *supra* note 22; Philip Clark & Zachary D Kaufman, eds., "After Genocide: Transitional Justice, Post-Conflict Reconstruction and Reconciliation in Rwanda and Beyond" in *Rwanda Beyond* (New York: New York University Press, 2009); Timothy Longman, "Justice at the Grassroots? Gacaca Trials in Rwanda" in N Roht-Arriaza & J Mariezcurrena, eds., *Transitional Justice Twenty-First Century* (Cambridge: Cambridge University Press, 2006) 206; Elise Venter, "Eliminating Fear through Recreating Community in Rwanda: The Role of the Gacaca Courts," *Tex Wesley Law Rev* (2006) 13, 577.

[53] Burnet, *supra* note 21 at 212.

[54] Susan Thomson, "The Darker Side of Transitional Justice: The Power Dynamics behind Rwanda's Gacaca Courts," *Africa* (2011) 81(3), 373 at 373. See also Susan Thomson & Rosemary Nagy, "Law, Power and Justice: What Legalism Fails to Address in the Functioning of Rwanda's Gacaca Courts", *Int J Transitional Justice* (2011) 5(1), 11 at 13.

[55] Reyntjens & Vandeginste, *supra* note 22 at 111; Lars Waldorf, "Mass Justice for Mass Atrocity: Rethinking Local Justice as Transitional Justice," *Temple Law Rev* (2006) 79(1) at 9, 29, 65, 81–5.

reinforced ethnic divides[56] and people often felt coerced, fearful, and insecure as a result, both during case sessions and in everyday life.[57]

I suggest that the cultural justification for harmony was an effort to insulate against international critique of, and interference in, Rwandan governance. For Rwandan leaders to claim they could rebuild Rwanda based on their own rather than foreign cultural principles served to protect against persistent allegations that domestic legal forums did not meet international legal and human rights standards.[58] This echoes how cultural justification for customary law was used in many contexts in Africa both to insulate from colonial interference and to support nationalism at independence.[59] It parallels Nader's argument that harmony can be a counter-hegemonic strategy,[60] though in Rwanda, the move appears directed not at colonial leaders or state law, but at the hegemony of international regimes of law and human rights.

I suggest that what was particularly problematic was the cultural justification for unity itself. Given that mediation was presented as a practice natural to all Rwandans, then to reject overtures to "be mediated" or "reconciled" was to reject the unity of all Rwandans, and even to reject shared citizenship and the legitimacy of the state. By a decade after

[56] Jennie Burnet, "The Injustice of Local Justice: Truth, Reconciliation, and Revenge in Rwanda" in A Hinton, ed., *Transitional Justice Glob Mech Local Realities Genocide Mass Violence* (New Brunswick, NJ: Rutgers University Press, 2011) 95 at 114; Thomson & Nagy, *supra* note 54 at 29.

[57] Burnet, *supra* note 56; Chakravarty, *supra* note 49; Bert Ingelaere, "The Gacaca Courts in Rwanda" in L Huyse & M Salter, eds., *Traditional Justice and Reconciliation After Violent Conflict: Learning from African Experiences* (IDEA, 2008) 25; Bert Ingelaere, "'Does the Truth Pass across the Fire without Burning?' Locating the Short Circuit in Rwanda's Gacaca Courts," *J Mod Afr Stud* (2009) 47(04), 507; Bert Ingelaere, "Peasants, Power and Ethnicity: A Bottom-up Perspective on Rwanda's Political Transition," *Afr Aff* (2010) 109 (435), 273; Max Rettig, "Gacaca: Truth, Justice, and Reconciliation in Postconflict Rwanda?," *Afr Stud Rev* (2008) 51(3), 25 ;Susan Thomson, "After Genocide: Transitional Justice, Post-Conflict Reconstruction," *Int J Afr Hist Stud* (2010) 43(1), 192; Thomson, *supra* note 54; Thomson & Nagy, *supra* note 54; Waldorf, *supra* note 55; Lars Waldorf, "'Like Jews waiting for Jesus': Posthumous Justice in Post-genocide Rwanda" in R Shaw, L Waldorf & P Hazan, eds., *Localizing Transitional Justice* (Stanford: Stanford University Press, 2010) 183.

[58] E.g., Amnesty International, *Rwanda Gacaca: A Question of Justice* (London: Amnesty International, 2002); Penal Reform International, *Research Report on the Gacaca Report VI: From Camp to Hill, the Reintegration of Released Prisoners* (Kigali: Penal Reform International, 2004).

[59] Colson, *supra* note 26 at 77–8. Chanock, *Law, Custom and Social Order: The Colonial Experience in Malawi and Zambi.* (Cambridge: Cambridge University Press, 1985) 24.

[60] Nader, *supra* note 4.

the genocide, many scholars argued that Rwandans "rehearsed consensus,"[61] or "pretended peace,"[62] which papered over much deeper divisions.[63] This is consistent with Nader's caution that harmony ideology "may be used to suppress people's resistance, by socializing them toward conformity by means of consensus-building mechanisms, by valorizing consensus, cooperation, passivity, and docility, and by silencing people who speak out angrily."[64] Recent research underscores how most Hutu who had been in Rwanda during the genocide felt that strident resistance to *gacaca* risked conveying criminally divisive intentions.[65] Many Hutu men and women described to me confessing and requesting forgiveness under duress, fearing that not to do so would invite arbitrary accusations, false convictions, and heavy sentences, as well as other social sanctions. Similarly, victims often described feeling pressured – by defendants, by *inyangamugayo,* by pastors, by neighbors – to forgive perpetrators or to accept less than they were due in property cases for the benefit of community and country. The coercive potential of harmony in *gacaca* was particularly strong, perhaps inescapable, because of how tightly it linked unity principles to state punishment. People were essentially told to forgive and reconcile with a thinly veiled "or else": risk state-backed punishment as someone who did not value unity, and therefore who probably embraced divisionism as a propagator of genocide ideology and an enemy of other Rwandans and the state.

Overall, Rwanda's harmony legal models located the solution to the genocide in interpersonal relations, not in structural and political or economic changes.[66] In the aggregate, *gacaca* courts, *comite y'abunzi,*

61 Bert Ingelaere, "Do We Understand Life after Genocide? Center and Periphery in the Construction of Knowledge in Postgenocide Rwanda," *Afr Stud Rev* (2010) 53(1), 41 at 53.

62 Susanne Buckley-Zistel, "We are Pretending Peace: Local Memory and the Absence of Social Transformation and Reconciliation in Rwanda" in P Clark & ZD Kaufman, eds., *After Genocide: Transitional Justice, Post-Conflict Reconstruction, and Reconciliation in Rwanda and Beyond* (New York: Columbia University Press, 2009) 125.

63 Susan Thomson, *Whispering Truth to Power: Everyday Resistance to Reconciliation in Postgenocide Rwanda* (Madison: University of Wisconsin Press, 2013).

64 Mattei & Nader, *supra* note 37 at 77. See also Greenhouse, et al. *Law and Community in Three American Towns* (Ithaca: Cornell Press, 1994) 130, 141; Lazarus-Black, *Everyday Harm* (Chicago: University of Illinois Press, 2007) 139–57; Merry, *supra* note 36 at 177–80; Wilson, "Justice and Retribution in Post-Conflict Settings," *Public Culture* (2003) 15(1), 187–90, 189.

65 Burnet, *supra* note 56; Ingelaere, *supra* note 57; Thomson & Nagy, *supra* note 54; Waldorf, *supra* note 57.

66 Research has shown this same effect in psycho-social interventions to address trauma: Abramowitz, *supra* note 10.

PART IV

Law in Conflicts

12

Cannibal Laws

RENÉ PROVOST[1]

Chacun appelle barbarie
ce qui n'est pas de son usage

Michel de Montaigne, 'Des cannibales' in *Essais* (1580)

12.1 Introduction

In the Civil Defence Forces trial before the Sierra Leone Special Court, witness TF2-144 reported that she had seen the victim, Mr. Ojuku, beheaded, disembowelled, and his organs placed in a plastic basket by the Kamajors, who then demanded money from Mr. Ojuku's wife 'so, as they said, to buy ingredients to cook Mr. Ojuku's organs. They told her they were going to eat Mr. Ojuku's soup today'.[2] In the Charles Taylor trial, witness Akiatu Tholley testified that she was made to eat the flesh of dead Kamajor fighters on three or more occasions.[3] In both situations the Kamajors appear, once as consumer and the other as consumed.

[1] The writing of this paper owes much to the superb research carried out by Caylee Hong, BCL LLB 2013 (McGill). I also want to thank Maggie Kilgour, Judge Pierre Boutet, and participants in the Centaur Conference at McGill for comments on the draft. Financial support was provided by way of a research grant from the Social Sciences and Humanities Research Council of Canada, which is gratefully acknowledged.

[2] Caroline Pappas, *Law and Politics: Australia's War Crimes Trials in the Pacific, 1943–1961* (University of New South Wales, Australian Defence Force Academy, 1998) [unpublished]. CDF trial transcript, 25 February 2005 at 14.

[3] Charles Taylor trial transcripts, 27 October 2008, at 19229–30. The Kamajors were members of a secret society which formed the core of the Civil Defence Forces, a non-state armed group that was one of the main protagonists of the civil war in Sierra Leone. On the Kamajors, see: Mariane Ferme & Danny Hoffman, 'Hunter Militias and the International Human Rights Discourse in Sierra Leone and Beyond' (2004) 50 *Afr. Today* 73; Danny Hoffman, *The War Machines: Young Men and Violence in Sierra Leone and Liberia* (Duke University Press, 2011).

nature of international criminal law sets one of the limits of formal law in this context. That limit reflects a combination of post-colonial malaise before the law's civilizing aspiration as well as the law's inability to construct a rationalised version of cannibalism that permits its reduction to legal fact.

12.2.1 *The Criminalisation of Cannibalism under International Law*

Despite the lack of an express prohibition of cannibalism in either international treaties or customary law, a persuasive case can be made that this practice is an international crime justifying the imposition of individual penal responsibility. Under international humanitarian law and international criminal law, cannibalism is not identified as a separate war crime. Nevertheless, accepted international standards on the protection of the body of the deceased, on the one hand, and of human dignity, on the other, could provide a sufficient basis for the criminal sanction of acts of cannibalism such as those that were reported to have happened in the conflict in Sierra Leone.

Turning first to the protection of the body of the dead in war, there is a longstanding prohibition against mistreating the remains of enemies killed in battle, a crime historically considered alongside the illegality of declaring that no quarter would be given and the illegality of the ill-treatment of prisoners of war or inhabitants of occupied territories.[4] Following the usual pattern in the legal regulation of armed conflicts, the international legal rules regulating such prohibitions are more numerous and explicit in relation to international armed conflicts than for internal conflicts like the war in Sierra Leone.

For international armed conflict, the obligation to prevent the dead from being despoiled or pillaged was already codified in the 1906 and 1929 Geneva Conventions for the Amelioration of the Condition of the Wounded and Sick in Armies in the Field.[5] In the 1949 First Geneva Convention for the Amelioration of the Condition of the Wounded and

[4] See Hersch Lauterpacht, ' The Law of Nations and the Punishment of War Crimes,' (1944) 21 *Brit YB Intl L* 58 at 78. For a European historical background see: Luc Capdevila & Danièle Voldman, trans. by Richard Veasy, *War Dead: Western Societies and Casualties of War* (Edinburgh: Edinburgh University Press, 2006) 76–113; United Nations War Crimes Commission, 'Law Reports of Trials of War Criminals' (1949) vol. XIII at xi (in the Foreword authored by the Rt. Hon. The Lord of Wright of Durley).

[5] Convention for the Amelioration of the Condition of the Wounded and Sick in Armies in the Field, Geneva, 6 July 1906, Article 3; Convention for the Amelioration of the Condition of the Wounded and Sick in Armies in the Field, Geneva, 27 July 1929, Articles 3 & 4.

Sick in Armed Forces in the Field, Article 15 provides that 'Parties to the conflict shall, without delay, take all possible measures to ... search for the dead and prevent their being despoiled', and Article 17 provides that Parties 'shall further ensure that the dead are honourably interred'. According to the UK *Manual of the Law of Armed Conflict*, these provisions preclude 'burial in quick-lime, exposure as a curiosity or to instil terror, dissection and experiment, and grave-molestation'.[6] The 1949 First Geneva Convention also requires that Parties not only ensure burial or cremation but also demands, 'as far as circumstances permit', that they examine bodies to verify death and establish identity (Article 17). More generally, Article 34(1) of the 1977 Additional Protocol I also provides that human remains be 'respected', which implies a duty to prevent them from being despoiled. These treaty standards are replicated in customary international law, as confirmed in the wide-ranging study of customary humanitarian law carried out by the ICRC in 2005[7]: Rule 113 provides that '[e]ach party to the conflict must take all possible measures to prevent the dead from being despoiled. Mutilation of dead bodies is prohibited'. The ICRC identifies the prohibition against despoiling or mutilating dead bodies as an offence under many states' legislation and military manuals, and as prosecuted in different tribunals.[8] The ICRC also points to one state, Australia, which specifically prohibits cannibalism.[9] The ICRC's study also identifies Rule 115 which provides that '[t]he dead must be disposed of in a respectful manner' and Rule 112, stating that Parties must 'take all possible measures to search for, collect and evacuate the dead'. Under Rule 114, Parties also 'must endeavor to facilitate the return of the remains of the deceased upon request'. These rules are applicable to both combatants and civilian dead.

[6] *Manual of the Law of Armed Conflict* (Oxford: Oxford University Press, 2004) at 7.35 at fn 85.

[7] Jean-Marie Henckaerts, Louise Doswald-Beck & Carolin Alvermann, *Customary International Humanitarian Law: Volume 1, Rules* (Cambridge University Press, 2005).

[8] The US Military Commission Instruction No. 2 of 30 April 2003 makes degrading treatment of a dead body a war crime. Sierra Leone's Instructor Manual (2007), for example, states: '[i]t is therefore the responsibility that at the end of every engagement soldiers should ... [t]ake necessary action to prevent the dead from being despoiled. [...] The above mentioned actions shall be applied to all dead persons, whether civilian or military, own or enemy forces'. See also Article 51 of the Gacaca Organic Law, No. 16/2004, which classifies 'the person who committed dehumanizing acts on the dead body' as category 1 criminals. See *Ibid.*

[9] Australia's *War Crimes Act* states that '"war crime" includes ...cannibalism ...[and] the mutilation of the dead'.

In internal armed conflicts, the humanitarian law provisions on the dead are less specific.[10] The only explicit treaty reference to the dead is in Article 8 of the 1977 Additional Protocol II which states that: '[w]henever circumstances permit, and particularly after an engagement, all possible measures shall be taken, without delay . . . to search for the dead, prevent their being despoiled, and decently dispose of them'. However, according to the ICRC's study on customary law, Rules 112 (obligation to collect and evacuate the dead), 113 (prohibition on mutilation of the dead and obligation to prevent despoiling) and 115 (obligation to respectfully dispose the dead) are applicable in both international and non-international armed conflicts.[11] On the other hand, there is no treaty or customary rule explicitly covering the return of mortal remains in non-international armed conflicts. Rule 114 of the ICRC study – requiring Parties to facilitate the return of remains – is only applicable in international armed conflicts. While the ICRC recognises a trend towards the return of remains, Petrig notes that this can only be found in the general norms of IHL.[12]

While the treaty and customary norms of international humanitarian law applicable in international and internal conflicts do not refer specifically to cannibalism, there is no doubt that the practice of cannibalism inherently implies a violation of these accepted standards. Disembowelling bodies and removing limbs – whether to consume body parts or not – desecrate the body, contrary to the Geneva Conventions and customary law. This echoes other prohibitions on the treatment of the dead such as unlawful autopsies or medical experiments, which protect dead bodies from being dissected or otherwise interfered with.[13] Beyond acts of mutilation, the consumption of human body parts also violates the obligation to dispose of a body in a respectful manner and facilitate the return of the remains to its home country. Although cultural and religious traditions differ on the appropriate treatment of the dead, parties would in most circumstances be hard-pressed to demonstrate that by eating parts of dead belligerents they 'decently dispose[d] of them', as under Additional Protocol II, or 'honourably interred' them,

[10] See Anna Petrig, 'The War Dead and their Gravesites' (2009) 91:874 *Int Rev Red Cross* 2005 341 at 343.

[11] Henckaerts, Doswald-Beck & Alvermann, *supra* note 7 at 406–16.

[12] Petrig, *supra* note 10 at 353.

[13] For a more general discussion see Dorothy Nelkin & Lori Andrews, 'Do the Dead Have Interests? Policy Issues for Research after Life' (1998) 24:2–3 *American Journal of Law and Medicine* 261.

as under Article 17 of the First Geneva Convention. The one conceivable exception concerns a form of mortuary cannibalism, such as practiced by the Wari tribes of Western Brazil: anthropological studies have documented that the Wari practiced both exocannibalism (eating the dead enemy) and endocannibalism (eating their own kin), two forms of anthropophagy that their authors considered to have little in common.[14] For the Wari, the consumption of their own dead was a form of respect and affection for the deceased, a way to ensure the dead's incorporation into the body of a relative rather than rotting in the ground, but the eating of the enemy expressed hostility and domination.[15] While the bodies of the dead protected by humanitarian law covers victims from all sides of the conflict, even this rather extreme example would authorise only forms of endocannibalism in a tribe such as the Wari. As a final point, cannibalism can defeat a key purpose of the rules on missing and dead persons: enabling people to know what happened to their loved ones. As stated in Article 32 of Additional Protocol I, the rules were 'prompted mainly by the right of families to know the fate of their relatives'. Consuming a body, however, can inhibit its identification, return, and honourable burial.[16]

The jurisprudence of war crimes prosecutions before international and national courts is still relatively limited, and within that body of case law there are only a few trials that have touched on the violation of international standards protecting the bodies of the dead in times of war. The International Military Tribunal for the Far East, established to try Japanese political and military leaders after the Second World War, classified cannibalism as a 'conventional war crime'.[17] The majority judgment noted that cannibalism was 'not unnoticed nor even disapproved by the Japanese army' when it came to eating enemies:

[14] Beth A Conklin, '"Thus are our bodies, thus was our custom": Mortuary Cannibalism in an Amazonian Society' (1995) 22:1 *Am Ethnol* 75 at 75.

[15] *Ibid* at 81.

[16] The general recognition of family members' rights to receive remains in international law is also found, for example in the UNGA, *Set of Principles for the Protection and Promotion of Human Rights through Action To Combat Impunity* ('Joinet Principles') (1997) which states, in Principle 36, that the deceased person's family has the 'imprescriptible right to be informed thereof and, in the event of decease, the person's body must be returned to the family'.

[17] Bernard Victor Aloysius Röling & C F Rüter, eds., *The Tokyo Judgment: The International Military Tribunal for the Far East Majority Judgment* (IMTFE), 29 April 1946–12 November 1948, Volume I (Amsterdam: APA-University Press Amsterdam, 1977) at 409–10.

> At times this consumption of the flesh of their enemies was made into something of a festive occasion at officers' quarters. Even officers of the rank of General and Rear-Admiral took part. Flesh of murdered prisoners or soup made from such flesh was served at meals of Japanese below the rank of officers. The evidence indicates that this cannibalism occurred when there was other food available. That is to say, on such occasions, this horrible practice was indulged in from choice and not of necessity.[18]

The Tribunal, however, did not list any specific convictions of cannibalism in its verdicts against the twenty-eight accused. While no other international tribunal has specifically prosecuted a person for cannibalism as a crime under international law, a few have confirmed the criminal nature of the mutilation or despoiling of the dead. In the *Tadić* case, the Trial Chamber of the International Criminal Tribunal for former Yugoslavia examined whether discharging contents of the fire extinguisher into a dead body constitute an inhumane act under Article 5 (i) of the Tribunal's statute.[19] Although the Trial Chamber held that the specific provision only contemplates a living person, it recognised that the maltreatment of the dead is considered a war crime.[20] The Trial Chamber stated 'that certain acts against dead bodies have been punished as war crimes though these relate in principle to cannibalism and the mutilation of, and the failure to bury, dead bodies in breach of specific provisions of the laws and usages of war relating to the mistreatment of the war dead'.[21]

Turning to war crimes prosecutions before national tribunals, there have been a number of convictions for maltreating the bodies of war dead, including instances of cannibalism. In the 1947 trial of Max Schmid, the US General Military Government Court at Dachau relied

[18] *Ibid.* The Tribunal noted that the Japanese army treated endocannibalism in a radically different way: 'Although it is not prescribed in the criminal code, those who eat human flesh (except that of the enemy) knowing it to be so, shall be sentenced to death as the worst kind of criminal against mankind.'

[19] *The Prosecutor of the Tribunal* v. *Dusko Tadić*, Trial Judgment, Case No. IT-94-1-I, 7 May 1997. The original indictment, however, did not relate to the dead since it became a matter of fact as to whether the victim was alive.

[20] The court reasoned that Article 5(i) applied only to the living on the basis of *ejusdem generis* – as Terhi Anneli Jyrkkiö notes, since all the crimes against humanity in the ICTY statute can only be committed against living persons, 'other inhumane acts' should also be only seen as being able to be committed against the living. See '"Other Inhumane Acts" as Crimes Against Humanity' [2011]1 *Helsinki Law Review* 183.

[21] *Tadić*, para. 748. The Trial Chamber only cited the trial of Max Schmid, discussed in the following paragraph.

on Articles 3 and 4 of the 1929 Geneva Convention to convict a German medical officer for the maltreatment of the body of a member of the US Air Force who had been killed earlier in battle. The court held that by severing the man's head, boiling and bleaching it and keeping the skull on his desk, Schmid committed the war crimes of mutilating a dead body and refusing an honourable burial. The notes on the case referred to Hersch Lauterpacht, who identified the maltreatment of the dead as a customary norm: '[a]ccording to a customary rule of the law of nations belligerents have the right to demand from one another that dead soldiers shall not be disgracefully treated and, in particular, that they shall not be mutilated but shall be, as far as possible, collected and buried or cremated on the battlefield by the victor'.[22] The case notes further cited Lauterpacht's observation that 'belligerents are bound to make provisions for honourable interment and for respectful treatment and proper marking of graves so that they can always be found'.[23] There were a few cases of war crimes prosecutions by American and Australian military tribunals in the Far East that dealt directly with the practice of cannibalism. In 1946, the US Military Commission at the Mariana Islands convicted General Tachibana Yochio of the Japanese Army for murder and 'preventing an honourable burial due to the consumption of parts of the bodies of prisoners of war by the accused during a special meal in the officers' mess'.[24] Similarly, an Australian Military Courts sitting at Wewak in 1945 sentenced Lieutenant Tazaki Takehiko in the Japanese Army for 'mutilating the dead body of a prisoner of war' and for cannibalism, while the Australian Military Court at Rabaul in 1946 convicted Lieutenant Tomiyasu Tisato of murder and cannibalism.[25] The trials at the end of the Second World War mark the recognition into positive international of the war crimes of cannibalism. In the Tachibana Yochio trial before a US Military Commission, there reportedly was some hesitation on the part of the prosecution to include a specific charge of cannibalism despite conclusive evidence to support it, because of the lack of modern precedents. Ultimately, cannibalism was invoked instead as an

[22] Case no. 81 (1947), available in The United Nations War Commission, 'Law Reports of Trials of War Criminals', *supra* note 4 at 151. The reference is to Hersch Lauterpacht ed., *Oppenheim's International Law*, 6th edn, vol. 2 (Longman, 1944) para. 124.

[23] *Ibid* at 152.

[24] Trial of Tachibana Yochio (1946), cited in Trial of Max Schmid, *ibid*, at 152. A full set of trial proceedings is available at http://research.archives.gov/description/6997357.

[25] Trial of Jutaro Kikuchi (1946) and trial of Tazaki Takehiko (1945), cited in Trial of Max Schmid, *ibid*, at 152.

aggravating factor to the charge of murder.[26] Australia, on the other hand, took a more proactive stance and explicitly listed cannibalism as a war crime. A commission tasked with inquiring into war crimes committed against Australians during the war recommended listing cannibalism because of the number of reports attesting to this practice as well as the fact that it was not a common law crime.[27] On that basis, unlike their American counterparts, Australian courts issued convictions directly for the war crime of cannibalism. In the Philippines, ten Japanese soldiers were sentenced to death for, inter alia, cannibalism, by a Filipino war crimes tribunal relying on evidence that had been initially collected by US prosecutors.[28]

On the basis of the treaties, customary norms, and war crimes cases studied above, the protection given to the body of the dead during armed conflicts now seems to offer a solid basis for the prosecution of cannibalism as an international crime. In that respect, one could note that the Rome Statute of the ICC does not include this particular crime in its extensive and jurisdictionally exhaustive codification of war crimes. Like the SCSL, the ICC does not have an open-ended competence to try 'violations of the laws and customs of war' as found in Article 3 of the ICTY Statute. On the other hand, the SCSL and ICC do have competence for the war crime of 'outrages against personal dignity', applicable to both internal and international armed conflicts. This opens another door for the criminal repression of cannibalism by an international tribunal, one sanctioning not violence directed at the body per se, but rather behaviour denying the fundamental entitlement of any human being to be treated with dignity. Cannibalism, it could be argued, is one of the most extreme forms of outrage against human dignity.

The prohibition of outrages against personal dignity appears to be a well-established norm of international humanitarian law, applicable in both international and internal armed conflicts. It belongs to the core humanitarian standards codified in Common Article 3 of the 1949 Geneva Conventions, binding on all parties to a situation that corresponds to the lowest threshold for the applicability of the laws of

[26] Philip R Piccigallo, *The Japanese on Trial: Allied War Crimes Operations in the East, 1945–1951* (Austin: University of Texas Press, 1979) at 78–79 (the case name is spelled slightly differently).

[27] See Pappas, *supra* note 2 at 276–77; Piccigallo, *supra* note 26 at 128–29.

[28] Piccigallo, *supra* note 26 at 190; '10 Japanese Soldiers Doomed', *N Y Times* (21 September 1949).

war. A key issue as regards the relevance of this norm to the practice of cannibalism is whether it can be said to guarantee the dignity of a person who is no longer alive (leaving aside the rather unlikely scenario of the consumption of parts of the body of a living person). A number of scholars submit that the protection of dignity is not limited to the living. Petrig, for example, argues, that 'the obligation to treat humanely all '[p] ersons taking no active part in the hostilities, including [members of armed forces who have laid down their arms and] those placed hors de combat by ... any other cause' than sickness, wounds, or detention, could arguably apply to deceased persons".[29] She contends that respecting mortal remains 'is a concretization of the general obligation to protect the dignity of persons and the prohibition of outrages upon personal dignity'.[30] Likewise, Gary Solis offers that 'mistreatment of the dead might be considered a violation [of this provision]'.[31] While it does not appear that anyone has argued before an international tribunal that Common Article 3 applies to the dead, Columbia's Prosecutor has argued before the Consejo de Estado that the obligation to respect the dead is inherent in Common Article 3.[32]

While there is limited direct support for this reading of Common Article 3, the concept of dignity in other international legal instruments provides support for such a view. Most notably, Article 8(2)(b)(xxi) of the ICC Statute defines committing outrages upon personal dignity as a war crime, and the elements of crimes in a footnote specify that '"persons" can include dead persons. It is understood that the victim need not personally be aware of the existence of the humiliation or degradation or other violation'.[33] It was reportedly included to cover World War II case law – including the trial of Max Schmid – where the accused were convicted of maltreating dead prisoners of war. In *The Prosecutor* v. *Germain Katanga and Mathieu Ngudjolo Chui*, the Pre-trial Chamber of the ICC relied on ICTY and ICTR jurisprudence to hold that 'burying corpses in latrine pits' was an act constituting an outrage upon personal dignity.[34] The ICC Chamber added that the 'core element' of the crime

[29] Petrig, *supra* note 10 at 350. [30] *Ibid.*

[31] Gary D Solis, *The Law of Armed Conflict: International Humanitarian Law in War* (Cambridge University Press, 2010) at 322.

[32] Henckaerts, Doswald-Beck & Alvermann, *supra* note 7 at 411.

[33] Knut Dörmann, *Elements of War Crimes under the Rome Statute of the International Criminal Court: Sources and Commentary* (Cambridge University Press, 2003) at 314.

[34] Decision on the Confirmation of Charges, 30 September 2008, at para. 371. See *The Prosecutor* v. *Ntagerura, Bagambiki & Imanishimwe*, Case No. ICTR-99-46-T, where

under Article 8(2)(b)(xxi) is 'the humiliation, degradation, or violation of the person's dignity', which 'must be committed with objectively sufficient gravity so as to be "generally recognized as an outrage upon personal dignity"'.[35] The Chamber further stated that 'so long as the serious humiliation or degradation is real and serious, there is no requirement that such suffering be lasting . . . or that it is "necessary for the act to directly harm the physical or mental well-being of the victim"'.[36] This indicates a broader concept of harm that is not necessarily experienced by living persons exclusively. That said, no such charges were laid against Bosco Ntaganda, despite the pre-trial Chamber noting reports of acts of cannibalism that could have been attributed to the accused.[37]

The extension of the prohibition of outrages against personal dignity to the maltreatment of the bodies of the dead begs the question of the identity of the holder of the protected interest. One interpretation might be that the right to the protection of one's dignity extends even beyond life, although the suggestion that deceased individuals might hold these types of rights has generally been resisted because of their lack of agency.[38] The possibility that an act such as cannibalism may amount to the crime of outrages against dignity does not necessarily turn on a conclusion that the dead still have a right to their dignity. Instead, the reference to 'personal dignity' can be taken to refer to the dignity of all persons, of humanity as a whole, which is affronted by an act such as cannibalism. This interest may be localised in individuals with a personal connection to the victim, such as relatives, whose dignity is denied because of the anguish, psychological suffering, or sense of degradation produced by cannibal acts and the impossibility of disposing of the body of the departed in a dignified manner.[39] Moreover, cannibalism can be an outrage upon personal dignity even if it does not harm relatives or

numerous witnesses allege forced cannibalism, missing organs, limbs, genitals from bodies and disposal of bodies in latrines. The judgment, however, does not address these allegations specifically. See also *Prosecutor* v. *Niyitegeka*, Case No. ICTR-96-14-T, Judgment & Sentence (May 16, 2003).

35 Katanga & Ngudjolo Chui, *ibid* at para. 369. 36 *Ibid.*

37 *The Prosecutor* v. *Bosca Ntaganga*, Decision on confirmation of charges, ICC 01/04-02/06, 9 June 2014, para. 28.

38 See Adam Rosenblatt, 'International Forensic Investigations and the Human Rights of the Dead' (2010) 32:4 *Hum Rights Q* 921 at 941; Antoon De Baets, 'A Declaration of the Responsibilities of Present Generations toward Past Generations' (2004) 43:4 *Hist Theory* 130.

39 Petrig, *supra* note 10 at 354; Rosenblatt, *supra* note 38 at 950.

acquaintances of the deceased. In a number of trials before the ICTR, the tribunal has held that gross maltreatment of the dead violates the dignity of the living, constituting an 'other inhumane act' under the crime against humanity. For example, the ICTR in *Niyitegeka* held that the order to a soldier to sharpen a piece of wood and insert it into the genitalia of a woman who had been killed was a 'cruel and insensitive disregard for human life and dignity' that caused 'mental suffering to civilians, in particular, Tutsi civilians, and constitute[d] a serious attack on the human dignity of the Tutsi community as a whole'.[40] Likewise, in *Kajelijeli* as well as *Kayishema and Ruzindana* the ICTR stated that 'perpetuating gross acts of sexual violence upon a dead woman's body' was an attack on the dignity of the community and 'part of a widespread and systematic attack against the civilian Tutsi population on ethnic grounds'.[41] In all these cases, the accused were found guilty for sexual mutilation of dead persons under 'other inhumane acts'.

In Sierra Leone, cannibalism was used to instil terror in people which – following the decisions of the ICTR – constitutes an attack on the dignity of the whole community. For example, as mentioned earlier, one witness before the SCSL testified that people were beheaded, disembowelled and their organs put in a plastic bucket to reportedly make soup.[42] Another witness stated that women's 'guts were made into checkpoints so that anyone coming past could see them. Part of their entrails were eaten and their bodies were buried'.[43] At the Truth and Reconciliation Commission Hearings, a witness spoke about being given a piece of her son's heart to eat.[44] When cannibalism occurs publicly – in order to dehumanise victims and terrorise living persons – it violates people's sense of humanity and causes extreme suffering. As held in the ICTR jurisprudence, especially where third parties observe acts committed against others, the accused may be held accountable for such mental suffering.

40 *Prosecutor* v.*Niyitegeka*, Case No. ICTR-96-14-T, Judgment & Sentence (16 May 2003) at para. 416 and 465.

41 *Prosecutor* v. *Kajelijeli*, Case No. ICTR-98-44A, Judgment & Sentence (1 December 2003) at 933.

42 CDF trial transcript, 25 February 2005 at 14.

43 CDF Trial Judgement at para. 424. The judgment refers to the CDF trial transcripts, 9 September 2004 at 38–39.

44 Reported in Tim Kelsall, 'Truth, Lies, Ritual: Preliminary Reflections on the Truth and Reconciliation Commmission in Sierra Leone' (2005) 27:2 *Hum Rights Q* 361 at footnote 14.

The analysis of the relevant accepted legal norms suggests that the criminal nature of cannibalism under international criminal law is not subject to significant doubt. In other words, in the current conjuncture of international law as administered by a tribunal like the SCSL, it certainly would not have been outlandish for the prosecution to include charges of cannibalism as a specific crime in the indictment against at least some of the accused before that court. More specifically, a charge could have been brought under the SCSL Statute as a crime against humanity ('other inhumane acts', Article 2(i) of the SCSL Statute) or as a war crime proscribed by Common Article 3 of the 1949 Geneva Conventions ('mutilation' or 'outrages upon personal dignity', Articles 3(a) & (e) of the SCSL Statute). Legal uncertainty would thus not explain why no such charges were laid.

12.2.2 *The Ambiguous Presence of Cannibalism in the Sierra Leone Special Court*

Another potential basis for the inaction of the prosecutor of the SCSL in this regard might relate to the availability and solidity of the evidence that the accused had engaged in the practice of cannibalism, either directly (by committing the deed themselves) or indirectly (as a superior, commander, a party to a joint criminal enterprise, or by aiding and abetting in the act). In one of the rare analyses that consider the criminal prosecution of cannibalism under international law, Caroline Pappas notes that there were few charges of this practice in Australian war crimes trials after the end of the Second World War despite the numerous recorded occurrences of cannibalism among Japanese troops on Pacific islands.[45] She notes that prosecutions were hindered by the fact that there were usually no witnesses apart from those having taken part in the crime. In addition, defendants often advanced credible claims that they had to resort to cannibalism because of a state of necessity, being cut off from their line of supplies and fearing their impending death by starvation. In such cases, the accused had not necessarily discriminated between friend and foe as to the source of food to be so consumed. In fact, such a situation was common enough for the Japanese High Command to issue an order on 10 June 1944, prohibiting cannibalism of fallen Japanese soldiers but not that of others, including fallen Allied soldiers.[46]

[45] Pappas, *supra* note 2 at 275; Yuki Tanaka, *Hidden Horrors–Japanese War Crimes in World War 2* (Boulder, CO: Westview Press, 1996) at 127.

[46] Pappas, *supra* note 2 at 276.

The systematic scanning of transcripts of the trials before the SCSL trial and appeals chambers reveals that cannibalism was mentioned by various parties from time to time. Despite the numerous witnesses who made initial statements to the Prosecution about cannibalism and who testified before the court on the topic, there is no enumerated charge of cannibalism in any of the Indictments in the CDF, RUF, AFRC or Taylor trials. The only reference to cannibalism is in the CDF Indictment which notes in a general section on 'charges' that:

> Civilians, including women and children, who were suspected to have supported, sympathized with, or simply failed to actively resist the combined RUF/AFRC forces were termed "Collaborators" and specifically targeted by the CDF. Once so identified, these "Collaborators" and any captured enemy combatants were unlawfully killed. Victims were often shot, hacked to death, or burnt to death. Other practices included human sacrifices and cannibalism.[47]

On at least two occasions in the CDF trial, the Defence objects to the Prosecution's line of questioning on cannibalism. TF2-021, a witness for the Prosecution, is asked by the Prosecution about the Yamorto squad eating collaborators. After the witness graphically describes how people were killed, cooked and eaten, the defence counsel for Kondewa objects:

> This bit of evidence does not go towards substantiating any of the offences charged. My Lord, it is highly prejudicial. We are not – none of the accused persons are facing a charge for cannibalism. I mean, up to the time of the death or killing, one can understand, but what transpires after, you know, I mean, it is completely different. There is no basis for this line of examination-in-chief.[48]

The Prosecution and Judge Boutet respond:

> JUDGE BOUTET: Prosecution?
> MS PARMAR: Your Honours, I was just going to let the witness finish describing this and move on to another area.
> JUDGE BOUTET: So you're not responding to the objection?
> MS PARMAR: I'm simply stating, Your Honour, that the Prosecution is happy to continue with a separate question with this witness.
> JUDGE BOUTET: Fine, thank you.[49]

Although the Prosecution does not contest the objection, the dispute over the evidence continues when the defence again objects to the line of

[47] CDF Indictment at para. 23. [48] CDF trial transcript, 2 November 2004 at 77.
[49] CDF trial transcript, 2 November 2004 at 77.

questioning and requests that some of the evidence related to cannibalism be removed from the record because it is not relevant to any listed charge.[50] Judge Boutet agreed that the 'evidence dealing with the eating of the human being [...] doesn't appear to be relevant'.[51]

However, later on in the CDF trial, when listening to the testimony of a Tongo Field witness, the Presiding Judge and Judge Boutet express interest in hearing about cannibalism and point out to the Prosecution that even though cannibalism is not an enumerated crime, it could support existing indictment counts. Counsel for the Prosecution, Mr. Sauter, expresses reluctance to lead evidence about cannibalism, citing the objections discussed earlier:

Q. Once again, the question again, Mr Witness: Did you see him, Mr xxxxx xxxxxx, being killed?
A. Yes.
Q. In which way he was killed?
A. He himself, his throat was cut.
Q. Did anything else happen to his body?
A. Yes.
Q. Please tell the Court.
A. His stomach was – his stomach was slit open and they took some of his parts.
Q. And after this?
A. These two people were eaten.
Q. Did the Kamajors leave the body of Mr xxxxxx at the place where he was killed?

PRESIDING JUDGE: Let him repeat. What did I hear him say? These two people were eaten?
THE WITNESS: Yes.
PRESIDING JUDGE: Is that what he is saying; that these two people were eaten?
MR SAUTER: This is what he was saying but I intentionally did not follow this point of his testimony.
JUDGE BOUTET: Why not?
PRESIDING JUDGE: Perhaps you could [overlapping speakers]
MR SAUTER: Because I was told earlier that cannibalism is not a count in this indictment.
JUDGE BOUTET: Yes, but without being – this is true, there is no such charges. However, there are charges that deal with threats to the civilian population.

50 CDF trial transcript, 2 November 2004 at 80–81.
51 CDF trial transcript, 2 November 2004 at 81.

MR SAUTER: As My Lord pleases.
JUDGE BOUTET: So obviously you are leading this for charges of cannibalism but it may be for other purposes.
MR SAUTER: As Your Lordship pleases.
JUDGE BOUTET: But that is your case. I mean, as the presiding judge has just raised, the witness has mentioned something and all of a sudden you moved away from it. If it is not part of your case, that's fine.
MR SAUTER: Mr Witness, you said the Kamajors took away inner parts from the body of Mr xxxxx?
JUDGE BOUTET: That was not his evidence. All he says is that his stomach was opened and they took some of his parts.
MR SAUTER: Yes.

Q. Do you know what they did with these parts?
A. They ate them. I said so. They ate them.
Q. Did you see this –
PRESIDING JUDGE: Who ate them, to begin with. When you say "they", who?[52]

The exchange highlights the contested and sensitive appearance of cannibalism in the trials and the seemingly inconsistent approach to the subject by the court. The Prosecution is reluctant to pursue questions about cannibalism especially given the prior reaction of the Judges. Although Judge Boutet initially sustains the Defence's objections on the relevance of evidence of cannibalism, he later reminds the Prosecution that evidence of cannibalism could be relevant for other charges. While the distinction may be due to the Defence's failure to object later on or the context of the discussion, in other instances Judges also express interest and seek clarification in regards to cannibalism. For example:

A. We trained and we killed human beings, we ate the flesh Mustapha Fallon in the Poro Bush –
PRESIDING JUDGE: Halt. They are eating what?
THE WITNESS: Human flesh. We killed Mustapha Fallon. We cooked his liver and ate it in the Poro Bush.[53]

There is clearly a significant degree of ambivalence for both the prosecution and the bench vis-à-vis testimony on the occurrence of cannibalism. On the one hand, the mention of it by witnesses is taken to be highly

[52] CDF trial transcript, 1 March 2005 at 40–43.
[53] CDF trial transcript, 11 March 2005 at 42.

prejudicial without going towards establishing any of the crimes listed in the indictments. On the other hand, mentions of cannibalism never seem to fail to attract the attention of the parties to the trial, despite the admitted limited relevance of this practice for the outcome of the trial.

Likewise, the defence in the Charles Taylor trial uses cannibalism in a surprising and inconsistent manner. First, cannibalism is largely raised by the Defence as a tactic to undermine the credibility of key witnesses like Joseph Marzah and highlight the absurdity of the accusations. Specific descriptions of cannibalism including how people were butchered and the edibility of select body parts ring of incredibility.[54] For example, defence counsel Courteney Griffiths seems to mock Marzah when asking him whether white people, Nigerians, or Krahns taste better.[55] Marzah's response that he has a 'likeness for them' makes him seem not credible and undermines his allegations against Taylor.[56] Griffiths amplifies the sensationalist nature of cannibalism by referring to it as 'dramatic', 'hot', 'dirty', and 'wicked'.[57]

Second, the Defence shows interest in how information about cannibalism emerged, and who asked for it. For example, Griffiths asks Moses Zeh Blah, Liberia's former vice-president:

> Q. My question is this. I know from the documents in front of me that you mentioned cannibalism for the first time in May of this year in [The Netherlands]. What I want to know is this. Who raised the topic with you? Did you volunteer that information, or did someone come to you and say, 'I want to talk to you about cannibalism'? Which of those occurred?[58]

He further asks whether 'when you arrived here in The Hague did someone come to you and say "this hot topic has come up, cannibalism?"'[59] He similarly questions former Sierra Leonean soldier, Samuel

[54] For example, Joseph Marzah testified that 'We would kill you first and take those parts that are not good for us and this your palm, your two palms, we would put them together and clean inside your intestine and wrap it around, because it's not correct. It's a hard bone. Charles Taylor knows that. That's how we eat them'. Charles Taylor trial transcript, 13 March 2008 at 6000.

[55] Charles Taylor trial transcript, 13 March 2008 at 6000. [56] *Ibid.*

[57] Charles Taylor trial transcripts, 13 March 2008 at 6005; 19 May 2008 at 10180; 11 February 2008; 14 March 2008 at 6156.

[58] Charles Taylor trial transcript, 19 May 2008 at 10179.

[59] Charles Taylor trial transcript, 19 May 2008 at 10180.

Kargbo, 'were you in that last proofing session asked the question "do you know anything about cannibalism?"' and 'was it as a result of [the Prosecution] asking you the question, or was it something that just suddenly popped into your mind'?[60] Kargbo states that he did not think that the Prosecution asked him about cannibalism since if they had, he would have mentioned it in his statement. Rather he tells Mr. Munyard, Counsel for Taylor, that 'it was as a result of the questions you asked me'.[61] Munyard presses Kargo for why 'just two weeks ago, between 13 and 15 May, here in Holland, you suddenly remember that people told you that Gios had a habit of engaging in cannibalism?' especially since 'you described it to us as a crucial piece of information, but it's a piece of information that you had forgotten until very recently'.[62]

The Defence also questions another Prosecution witness, Karmoh Kanneh, 'When did you first tell the Prosecution about seeing Zigzag Marzah having a dinner of human flesh?' and 'were you asked in prepping 'Did you ever see Zigzag Marzah eating human flesh?'[63] Kanneh states that he first mentioned cannibalism in his statement and that he was never asked about it by the Prosecution but recalled it when being interviewed.[64] Griffiths attempts to show internal inconsistencies in the witnesses' disclosure of information, insisting that the extraordinary nature of cannibalism should have meant that it would have been mentioned earlier, hinting that the witness heard it from media reports of earlier testimony on cannibalism.[65]

The Prosecution's engagement with cannibalism also seems tactical sometimes. For example, the Prosecution questions Yanks Smyth, a witness for the Defence, and tries to show that he is either lying or completely uninformed by interrogating his complete denial of cannibalism:

Q. So you don't know what happened in any secret society that Charles Taylor belonged to, do you?

A. I don't know the inside, but there is nothing like cannibalism in Liberia. There's nothing like cannibalism being practised in Liberia. That I can tell you that.

60 Charles Taylor trial transcript, 2 June 2008 at 10661.
61 Charles Taylor trial transcript, 19 May 2008 at 10661.
62 Charles Taylor trial transcript, 19 May 2008 at 10660.
63 Charles Taylor trial transcript, 13 May 2008 at 9620, 9633.
64 Charles Taylor trial transcript, 13 May 2008 at 9620 and 9633.
65 Charles Taylor trial transcript, 13 May 2008 at 9621–2, 9632 & 9636.

Q. You've never heard of cannibalism in Liberia?
A. I never heard of cannibalism in Liberia.
Q. If someone in this Court came into this Court and testified that a famous man was killed and his body eaten on the streets of Monrovia, would that person be lying?
A. That would sound very ridiculous to me because he would be really definitely lying.[66]

Charles Taylor, takes the opposite approach while on the stand. Instead of categorically denying the practice of cannibalism in Liberia, he acknowledges that it happens in 'certain parts of Liberia' and also points to cannibals in Europe.[67] However, he argues that 'that's not something that is a part of our trait and surely not mine. I never, ever did that'.[68] This is a completely different approach to cannibalism: whereas it was otherwise presented as fantastical, a neo-colonial projection by the prosecution, it is here associated with a deeply deviant personality by linking it to cannibalism in Europe for which there is no possible cultural background.[69] Taylor himself suggests that this is all a publicity stunt to attract the attention of the world's media: 'Charles Taylor, the former president of Liberia, the cannibal, is on trial'.[70]

This somewhat lengthy exploration of a small fraction of the ways in which cannibalism surfaces in the testimonies before the SCSL reveals that there was indeed evidence of its occurrence. At the same time, it shows that the Prosecution, the Defence and the Bench were either unwilling or unable to approach this particular practice with a view to constructing a coherent narrative of its place in the conflict in Sierra Leone. It could be that, as noted by Donald Sutton, 'cannibalistic accusations tell us much less about those accused than about the accusers'.[71] The tentative and contradictory reaction to evidence of cannibalism in the SCSL suggests that it was difficult to reduce to simply one more gory fact in the representation of the grim realities of war. The heavy historical baggage of cannibalism, said by some to have been a myth created to justify the colonial *mission civilisatrice*, seems to have

[66] Charles Taylor trial transcript, 1 March 2010 at 36419–20.
[67] Charles Taylor trial transcript, 27 July 2009 at 25256.
[68] Charles Taylor trial transcript, 27 July 2009 at 25256.
[69] Marzah is described by Taylor as a 'sick boy' in need of psychological help: Charles Taylor trial transcript, 30 September 2009 at 29942.
[70] Charles Taylor trial transcript, 27 July 2009 at 25255.
[71] Donald S Sutton, 'Consuming Counterrevolution: The Ritual and Culture of Cannibalism in Wuxuan, Guangxi, China, May to July 1968' (1995) 37:01 *Comp Stud Soc Hist* 136 at 139.

induced a very cautious approach within the SCSL.[72] Indeed, as suggested by Frédéric Mégret, international criminal law may evince a tendency to 'orientalise' crimes in Africa, so that certain practices like bush wives or child soldiers are explained as 'typical'.[73] The SCSL, despite its cautious approach to such matters, was challenged for playing on the deep-seated Western fascination of African savagery for instrumental or ideological motives.[74] Charles Taylor himself, in his testimony before the SCSL, suggested that the references to cannibalism had been built into the case to demonise him, part of a racist pattern to justify Western intervention in Africa: 'You come into Africa, the African got a leader in Liberia, a president, who is eating human beings'.[75] Seen in this light, despite the relative clarity of international criminal law and the availability of evidence, cannibalism could not be constructed as a simple crime. Legal positivism leads to a distorted or flattened rendering of cannibalism which seems rather dyspeptic for a legal institution like the SCSL. In cannibalism, the symbolic always overcomes the real.[76]

12.3 Cannibal Law: The Law Cannibals Make, or the Search for the Ethical Cannibal

Só a antropofagia nos une. Socialmente. Economicamente. Filosoficamente. Única lei do mundo.

Oswald de Andrade, *Manifesto antropófago* (1928)

The second cannibal law is the law that the cannibals make. In this relation, law offers a normative framework for understanding the

[72] William Arens , 'Rethinking Anthropophagy' in Francis Barker, Peter Hulme & Margaret Iversen, eds., *Cannibalism in the Colonial World* (Cambridge: Cambridge University Press, 1998) 39 at 43; Maggie Kilgour, 'The Function of Cannibalism at the Present Time' in *id.*, 238 at 239.

[73] Frédéric Mégret, 'Cour pénale internationale et néocolonialisme: au-delà des évidences' (2014) 45:1 *Études Int* 27.

[74] See Gerhard Anders, 'Testifying about "Uncivilized Events": Problematic Representations of Africa in the Trial against Charles Taylor' (2011) 24:04 *Leiden J Int Law* 937 at 941–42; Tim Kelsall, 'Politics, Anti-politics, International Justice: Language and Power in the Special Court for Sierra Leone' (2006) 32:04 *Rev Int Stud* 587 at 592.

[75] Charles Taylor trial transcript, 30 September 2009 at 29968–70. For Taylor, his prosecution fits into a pattern of racist interventions that include the murder of Patrice Lumumba and the jailing of Nelson Mandela (*id.*)

[76] See Marshall Sahlins, 'Raw Women, Cooked Men, and Other "Great Things" of the Fiji Islands' in Paula Brown & Donald Tuzin, eds, *The Ethnography of Cannibalism* (Washington, DC: Society for Psychological Anthropology, 1983) 72 at 88.

practice of cannibalism not merely as an irrational or depraved act, but as a part of a system of norms that fulfils a specific function in the context of an internal armed conflict such as Sierra Leone. Anthropologists have shown that the practice of cannibalism is very often linked to magic, as the provider of the most potent ingredients to make 'medicine' to make a person bullet-proof, able to fly, all-powerful, and many more wondrous things. Those who engage in this practice claim not only the language of science (witch-doctors speaking of 'research and development' to make medicine more effective), but also of law (witch-doctors 'give the law' to fighters to explain prohibitions the breach of which will break the magic spell). Cannibalism can be understood as not necessarily the acts of drug-crazed primitive bush fighters, but as a system of norms that communicates meaning, constitutes communities, and regulates certain relationships. This is a provocative expansion of a legal pluralist understanding of law, which tests the limits of social practices which we are willing to construct as 'law'.

To ask the law question about cannibalism requires a shift in perspective: whereas the international criminality of cannibalism offered in the previous section was anchored in the perspective of the international community, the enquiry into the possible construction of cannibalism as a legal practice must be grounded in a perspective internal to the community putatively supporting such a legal regime. This in turn begs the question of whether such an internal perspective is at all possible, whether cannibals can be said to exist in a meaningful way as a community. The paper first turns to this point, analysing a debate that has taken place in anthropology over the last forty years regarding the existence and extent of cannibalism as an indigenous practice. The conclusion that there are indeed instances of community-based cannibalism then opens the possibility that it may form a normative code. This suggests the potential of cannibalism as the marker of boundaries, but not the one intimately associated with that practice, between civilised people who eat nicely and barbaric people who eat savagely, but rather as marking boundaries among different orders of participants within a group that otherwise stands as undifferentiated. Cannibalism thus emerges not as a universal taboo against anthropophagy but as a regulated practice setting out the norms of who eats whom, what parts, how, when, and why. Cannibals would thus produce their own identity by way of the type of normative commitments that define law.

12.3.1 *The Existence and Construction of Cannibalism*

The eating habits of people are often seized upon as capturing the essence of difference. The French eat frogs, the English eat mushy peas, and the Chinese eat dogs. The prevalence or rarity of frogs on the ordinary menu of the majority of French households does not significantly enter the question of whether this inclination can be held up as summing up what is distinctive about the inhabitants of France. Cannibalism, it has been argued, has played that role in asserting a difference between civilised humanity and savage barbarism.[77] The footprint of cannibalism in the western imaginary about what lies beyond the boundaries of civilised humanity has been so deep that the allegory may have killed the reality of the practice. This poses a challenge for an attempt to study the occurrence of cannibalism as a normative practice, as this can only be meaningful as a reflection of the actual stance of the members of a given community, as opposed to an external construction or even invention for ideological purposes.

William Arens' 1979 volume, *The Man-Eating Myth*, was a frontal assault on the historical significance of cannibalism in what was considered uncivilised parts of the world in an earlier time.[78] Arens didn't deny that anthropophagy did occur in some places visited by European explorers, but he argued that there was a marked disconnect between the reality of anthropophagy and the place it came to occupy in colonial discourse and, later, anthropological analysis. Cannibalism in the relations of many explorers became a trope for the inhumanity of those who engaged in it. Arens set out to demonstrate that survival anthropophagy may have occurred from time to time in situations of famine, but that there is no credible report of cannibalism as a regular custom embraced by a community. He dissected the so-called first-hand eyewitness historical accounts to show that they were concocted long after their author returned to his home country, often with the assistance of others who had no direct knowledge of the facts, including elements that such an eyewitness would not likely have experienced himself because of linguistic or other barriers. The result is a representation of a reality so clouded by externalities that it becomes near-impossible to know what grain of

[77] Kilgour, *supra* note 72 at 239.

[78] William Arens, *The Man-Eating Myth : Anthropology and Anthropophagy* (Oxford University Press, 1979).

truth there may have been to the 'encounter' with cannibals.[79] The fact that some explorers like Columbus recorded the natives' impression that the Europeans were themselves cannibals is an irony that is not lost on Arens, but which failed to suggest to most observers that the cannibalism of the observed might be just as unreal as that of the observers. Conversely, Arens noted that anthropophagic practices were not unknown in the West either, in the form of the use of body parts for the preparation of medicines.[80]

The suggestion was made by Peter Hulme to reserve the label 'anthropophagy' to describe the rare instances of practice, and to use 'cannibalism' to refer to the ideological obsession with this trait in the colonial imaginary.[81] In the more recent past, colonial officers and explorers in the 19th century (such as David Livingstone and Henry Morton Stanley) and anthropologists in the twentieth century (such as Margaret Mead and Edward Evans-Pritchard) either were very cautious in endorsing second-hand accounts of cannibalism (Livingstone, Evans-Pritchard) or overenthusiastic in proclaiming a cannibal custom on the basis of scant and unverified evidence (Stanley, Mead).[82] The common thread in these accounts is a tendency to ascribe cannibalism to others, separated from the informant either by time ('we used to be cannibals, but not anymore') or by place ('the other tribe, over the hill, up the river or on the next island, they are cannibals').[83] The anthropological sin of slipping from the non-existent sign of anthropophagy to the created signified of cannibalism explains for Arens the resilience of cannibalism even in contemporary thinking. Without the cannibal 'other' as an absolute marker of cultural difference, anthropology loses its *raison d'être*.[84]

Turning to the substance of cannibal narratives thus challenged by Arens and others in his footsteps, a link is posited between groups practicing anthropophagy and lawlessness. As a contrast to the narrator's

[79] See *ibid* at 43–80.

[80] Arens et al, *supra* note 72 at 47. See also Karen Gordon-Grube, 'Anthropophagy in Post-Renaissance Europe: The Tradition of Medicinal Cannibalism' (1988) 90:2 *Am Anthropol* 405; Shirley Lindenbaum, 'Thinking about Cannibalism' (2004) *Annu Rev Anthropol* 475 at 479.

[81] Peter Hulme, 'Introduction: The Cannibal Scene' in Francis Barker, Peter Hulme & Margaret Iversen, eds., *Cannibalism and the Colonial World* (Cambridge: Cambridge University Press, 1998) 4.

[82] See Arens, *supra* note 78 at 83–116.

[83] See e.g. Paul Shankman, 'Le Rôti et le Bouilli: Lévi-Strauss Theory of Cannibalism' (1969) 71:1 *Am Anthropol* 54 at 59–60.

[84] See Arens, *supra* note 72 at 55.

civilised nature, reflecting a modernity that could not be reconciled with eating other human beings, cannibals linger in a state of nature that eschews all laws, even that most basic taboo against consuming the flesh of another person. Gananath Obeyesekere, for example, notes how John Wesley viewed Aboriginals as possessing 'no religion, laws, or conceptions of civil society and as murderers of fathers, mothers, and children'.[85] Similarly, Roy Harvey Pearce considers seventeenth century reports by English colonialists in America which asserted that the land 'is inhabited with wild and savage people ... : they have no law but nature'[86] while Bernard Sheehan shows how colonial officials in Canada saw First Nations as living by 'neither divine nor human law'.[87] Montaigne's 'Of Cannibals' also presents people in the colonies as lacking critical features of a civilised society such as 'knowledge of letters', 'science of letters', agriculture, metals and wine, and legal institutions like contracts or magistrates.[88] Arens similarly points to early travelogues which describe alleged cannibals as being completely outside of law, starting with Herodotus: '[t]he Androphai have the most savage customs of all men; they pay no regard to justice, nor make use of any established law'.[89] In Sierra Leone, colonial officers viewed the Human Leopard Society, which allegedly used medicine made up of parts of humans, as '[t]he acme of affrontery, audacity, and defiance of law and order'.[90] These colonial views of the savage as lawless reflect legal theorists like Hobbes or Austin who saw the savage or natural state as existing without law.[91]

The contemporary version of the story locates cannibalism in another lawless zone: warfare, especially 'tribal' or 'ethnic' conflict. The perception that cannibals are outside of law is seen in 'new barbarism', a discourse that Paul Richards characterises as explaining political violence

85 Gananath Obeyesekere, *Cannibal Talk: The Man-Eating Myth and Human Sacrifice in the South Seas* (University of California Press, 2005) at 12.

86 Roy Harvey Pearce, *Savagism and Civilization: A Study of the Indian and the American Mind* (University of California Press, 1988) at 12.

87 Bernard Sheehan, *Savagism and Civility: Indians and Englishmen in Colonial Virginia* (Cambridge University Press Archive, 1980) at 23.

88 Cited in Joshua David Bellin, *The Demon of the Continent: Indians and the Shaping of American Literature* (University of Pennsylvania Press, 2011) at 43.

89 Arens, *supra* note 78 at 10.

90 Milan Kalous, *Cannibals and Tongo Players of Sierra Leone* (M. Kalous, 1974) at 108.

91 Thomas Hobbes, *Leviathan, or the Matter, Forme and Power of a Commonwealth Ecclesiasticall and Civil* (Yale University Press, 1928); John Austin, *The Province of Jurisprudence Determined* (J. Murray, 1861).

through cultural difference.[92] In particular he points to the influential article by journalist Robert Kaplan, 'The Coming of Anarchy', as reifying third world otherness.[93] This 'new barbarism' relies on an idea of lawlessness: Kaplan, for example, states that '[t]yranny is nothing new in Sierra Leone or in the rest of West Africa. But it is now part and parcel of an increasing lawlessness that is far more significant than any coup, rebel incursion, or episodic experiment in democracy'.[94] As Richards notes, cannibalism is directly associated with this modern savagism. He argues that the cannibalism related to a set of beliefs found in Upper Guinea known as *Bɔni hinda*, 'is exactly the kind of material that feeds New Barbarism'.[95] Replicating colonial-era narratives, *Bɔni hinda* is given as especially barbaric because it combines both cannibalism and the occult in the belief that ritual murders are perpetrated by people disguised in skins of wild animals or turn themselves into animals through magic in order to obtain ingredients for a medicine, *bɔfima*.[96] Similarly, sensationalist articles like Daniel Bergner's 'The Most Unconventional Weapon' describing cannibalism in the Democratic Republic of Congo, highlights the assumed links between cannibalism and contemporary states of lawlessness.[97] When combined with magic, cannibalism is seen in this article as being 'fetishism' and a part of a society at the 'pervasive hold of the atavistic, the magical', ending with a *Heart of Darkness*-type summary of Africa: 'a continent suspended, trapped somewhere closer to the ancient than to the modern . . . where so many visas lead to places that feel utterly lost, not only for their wretched poverty and cataclysmic civil wars . . . but also for the primitive understanding their people have of all that happens in their world'.[98] Cannibalism, as elucidated in Bergner's article, becomes the iconic example, and overarching metaphor, of lawlessness, disorder, and when combined with magic, barbaric foolishness.

[92] Paul Richards, *Fighting for the Rain Forest: War, Youth & Resources in Sierra Leone* (International African Institute, 1996) at 162.

[93] Robert D Kaplan, 'The Coming Anarchy', *The Atlantic* (February 1994), online: www.theatlantic.com/magazine/archive/1994/02/the-coming-anarchy/304670/?single_page=true.

[94] *Ibid.* [95] Richards, *supra* note 92 at 81.

[96] Paul Richards, 'Chimpanzees, Diamonds and War: The Discourses of Global Environmental Change and Local Violence on the Liberia-Sierra Leone Border' in Henrietta L. Moore, ed., *The Future of Anthropological Knowledge* (London: Routledge, 1996) 139 at 143. See also Mariane Conchita Ferme, *The Underneath of Things: Violence, History, and The Everyday in Sierra Leone* (University of California Press, 2001) at 181–83.

[97] See Lindenbaum, *supra* note 80 at 481. [98] *The New York Times*, 26 October 2003.

The representation of war zones in Africa as lawless spaces carried over to the judicial proceedings before the SCSL. In his opening statement to the Revolutionary United Front (RUF) trial, the Prosecutor David Crane painted a picture of the civil war in that country as a descent to hell, 'a tale of horror, beyond the gothic into the realm of Dante's inferno', in which 'dogs of war . . . hounds from hell' operated in 'a dark corner of the world, a world without law and accountability' to carry out crimes 'against nature, against logic, against life itself . . . pure evil'.[99] The primal, violent impulse so unleashed 'marks the limits of our language to communicate, it falls outside the realm of expression', it stands as the antithesis of law.[100] If the crimes that were prosecuted before the SCSL mark the outer edge of our sense of humanity, then cannibalism would mark the outer edge of these crimes. How can law be possible in such a context?

'What has the cannibal to say to us now?' asked Frank Lestringant in his book on the subject.[101] One answer came during the Charles Taylor trial before the SCSL, where Taylor's Defence Counsel Courteney Griffith asked Joseph Marzah, a prosecution witness, whether he knew what a cannibal was, prior to questioning him in details about his anthropophagic habits. In answer to the clarifying question 'What do you call someone who eats other human beings?', the witness answered 'The human being that can eat his fellow human being, it's a human being'.[102] In its straightforward simplicity, this is the answer that can be given to the suggestion that cannibalism inherently marks the outer boundaries of humanity, savage and lawless. Indeed, Lestringant asks his rhetorical question at the beginning of his wide-ranging study of some of the same sources that Arens invoked in his challenge to established ideas about cannibalism. It forms part of the response to this challenge, in which the interpretation of the relations of travellers in earlier times is revisited to offer a more nuanced appreciation of the western construction of cannibalism in that epoch. Far from the systematic reduction of the cannibal to a savage animal living in the throes of violent passion, *sans foi ni loi*, Lestringant finds in authors like André Thevet and Montaigne a more

[99] RUF trial transcripts, 5 July 2004 at 19, 21 & 29. See also: Anders, *supra* note 74 at 941; Kelsall, *supra* note 74 at 592.

[100] RUF trial transcripts, 5 July 2004 at 31.

[101] Frank Lestringant, *Cannibals: the Discovery and Representation of the Cannibal from Columbus to Jules Verne* (Berkeley: University of California Press, 1997) at 6.

[102] Charles Taylor trial transcript, 13 March 2008 at 5994.

discriminating understanding of the practice that differentiates between 'bad' and 'good' cannibals: the first feed on human flesh for its taste, driven by appetite, whereas the second do so for revenge, driven by a quest for meaning. In this richer understanding of historical cannibal narratives, the necessary association of cannibalism with unregulated lawlessness is replaced with the possibility that cannibalism can be a form of ethical exploration, however misplaced. As insightfully remarked by Maggie Kilgour in her review of Lestingant, however, 'the figure of the cannibal is oddly never naked: it is shaped by preconceptions, our ideas of human nature, and attitudes towards progress and society'.[103] This appears especially true of the historical texts studied successively by Arens, Lestringant, Obeyesekere and others, because of the fragmented and contested nature of first-hand (so-called) accounts of cannibalism. The systematic allegorisation of cannibalism in these narratives makes them difficult to use in answer to the 'law question' posed at the start of this section beyond rejecting a conceptual or perhaps even ontological claim that cannibalism is irreconcilable with law.

The challenge to anthropology as a discipline and its reliance on the cannibalism trope triggered a different type of reaction among anthropologists, who sought to verify empirically whether there was, in fact, very little anthropophagy as an accepted practice as compared to cannibalism as a dominant rhetorical figure. Instead of pouring over ancient relations of far-away travels, this newer strand of research involved ethnographic studies of anthropophagy that was either still ongoing or recent enough that direct participants could be relied upon as informants. While there is no denying the rarity of anthropophagy as an organised social practice, these more rigorous surveys reveal that when, who, whom, what, how and why one engages in cannibalism are questions that receive specific answers in certain communities. In other words, there is empirical evidence to support a claim that cannibalism can indeed be a regulated activity. Cannibal codes, each with its own social context and cultural logic, have been described in ethnographic studies carried out in various parts of the world, from Africa to Asia, as well as the Americas. They cover an array of situations, some dealing with the consumption of individuals killed in battle (e.g. Fiji Islanders), and others with all deaths in the ordinary unfolding of life in a given

[103] Maggie Kilgour, 'Review of Cannibals: The Discovery and Representation of the Cannibal from Columbus to Jules Verne by Frank Lestringant' (1999) 26:1 *Coll Lit* 209 at 211.

community (e.g. the Wari of Western Brazil).[104] Some codes allow only exocannibalism (e.g. the Bimini-Kuskumin of Papua New Guinea), mostly eating the enemy killed in battle, while others concern endocannibalism and the disposal of the members of one's own tribe members (e.g. again the Wari of Western Brazil).[105] Beyond that, specific norms are often identified with regard to the taxonomy of body parts that are suitable for eating and those that are not, or the ones that are seen as choice morsels (sometimes liver and heart), of the gender of individuals suitable for consumption (in Wuxuan, China, women were not eaten because their flesh was 'too yin' whereas men's flesh was yang).[106] Who participates in the practice is, again, often subject to specific regulation, from the exclusion of some categories of individuals (the Wari eat their in-laws, but not a close relative or a spouse) to an order of preference (the Maka of Cameroun reserve some parts for champions of war and elders).[107] It is not rare for regulated cannibalism to be highly ritualised in its performance (how the flesh is removed, the recipe followed for its preparation), although in some communities that aspect is less developed. The immediate goal of anthropophagy can range from the appropriation of the spirit or power of the consumed (eating the heart of pigmies in Congo is said to provide powers to live in the bush) to seeking to ensure the integration of the dead into the body of loved ones out of a sense of respect and affection.[108] In some of the communities that engage in the practice of cannibalism, it is a permanent tradition that endures from generation to generation, while in others cannibalism may be episodic, emerging at certain conjunctures, while still in others it may have been a one-time occurrence.[109] Even in a case where it flourished

[104] Sahlins, *supra* note 76 at 81; Conklin, *supra* note 14 at 75.

[105] Fitz John Porter Poole, 'Cannibals, Tricksters, and Witches: Anthropophagic Images Among Bimin-Kuskusmin' in Paula Brown & Donald Tuzin, eds., *The Ethnography of Cannibalism* (Washington, DC: Society for Psychological Anthropology, 1983) 6; Conklin, *supra* note 14 at 75.

[106] Sutton, *supra* note 71 at 148.

[107] Peter Geschiere & Janet Roitman, *The Modernity of Witchcraft: Politics and the Occult in Postcolonial Africa* (University of Virginia Press, 1997) at 235 n.11; Conklin, *supra* note 14 at 81.

[108] Daniel Bergner, 'The Most Unconventional Weapon' (2003) 26 *The New York Times Mag* 48; Conklin, *supra* note 14 at 84.

[109] G Guille-Escuret, 'Le corps du délit et l'exoticisme artificiel: à propos de l'anthropophagie guerrière en forêt centrafricaine' in Maurice Godelier & Michel Panoff, eds., *Le Corps Humain Supplicié, Possédé, Cannibalisé* 109–35 (Amsterdam : Editions des archives contemporaines, 1998) at 115–18.

only once for a few months, as in the episode in Wuxuan, China, during the 1968 cultural revolution, Sutton argues convincingly that it was not an aberrant twist of violence but rather a short-lived custom rooted in a bricolage of various elements of local culture including collective family guilt, the diminution of the individual, the mutilation of criminals, and the popular sanction of crimes.[110]

The conclusion to draw from this more recent ethnographic evidence of cannibalism is that anthropophagy can exist as a community-based regulated practice and not merely as an extraordinary or deviant act or as the figment of colonial anxieties regarding the savage other. Indeed, if anything, cannibalism rarely appears as casual, but instead seems ineluctably laden with cultural meaning. However macabre, cannibalism is more than just eating; it is a practice rooted in mythical construction that projects a cultural design and sustains a social order.[111] In other words, cannibalism is not always and necessarily transgressive, but can be in some circumstances constitutive, even normative. It can be constituted by, and productive of, norms, suggesting the possibility of a cannibal code with its own political and cultural logic.

12.3.2 Cannibalism as Legal Ethics

What ought a jurist to think of the suggestion of a 'cannibal code'? We may accept on the basis of what precedes that cannibalism can be a normative practice, but is there something in the concept of law that appears incompatible with the structure of cannibalism? Evidently, the way to approach an answer to these questions will turn on the general concept of law that is adopted. After some preliminary comments on the conception of legal normativity, necessary to meaningfully explore these issues, the analysis turns to the specific articulation of cannibalism as a legal order.

There is no doubt that a narrow conception of law can lead to a quick and decisive answer to the question of the legal nature of a putative 'cannibal code'. If one adopts an understanding of legal normativity as necessarily linked to the state and its institutions, an approach that we could label positivism, then there is no room to argue that cannibalism

110 Sutton, *supra* note 71 at 142–45.

111 Arjun Appadurai, 'Dead Certainty: Ethnic Violence in the Era of Globalization' (1998) 10:2 *Public Cult* 225 at 229; Conklin, *supra* note 14 at 94; Peggy Reeves Sanday, *Divine Hunger: Cannibalism as a Cultural System* (Cambridge University Press, 1986) at 3.

can be anything other than a non-legal practice (as distinct from the question of whether it is legal or illegal under state law). As articulated by Roderick Macdonald, this is a concept of law that rests on four precepts: *monism* (the claim that law is a unified, coherent regime); *centralism* (associating the power to validly create legal standards with state sovereignty); *positivism* (viewing law as ontologically distinguished from fact, thus allowing the systematic delineation of the frontier of legality to reflect pre-existing legal standards); and *prescriptivism* (offering legal norms as external constraints descending upon legal agents to try to modify patterns of behaviour).[112] This is of course an entirely reasonable understanding of the nature of law, one to which most people, and perhaps even most lawyers, would subscribe. Such a concept of law is situated towards one extreme of what constitutes a spectrum of conceptions of legal normativity that allow to a lesser or greater degree the possibility that law properly so called includes norms that are not linked to the state. In its radical exclusion of informal normativity from the ambit of what we are ready to label 'law', this concept of law denies the usefulness of legal discourse for any attempt to explore the normative dimension of cannibalism.

Legal pluralism stands nearer to the opposite end of this spectrum, reflecting a concept of law that challenges each of the four tenets identified as the basis for a positivist understanding of law. Instead, law is given a pluralistic understanding, whereby law is *fragmented* (with no necessary coherence across law as a whole), *decentralised* (where many centres and processes exist to create and interpret law), *contingent* (norms do not exist a priori but emerge from an engagement with the particular circumstances of their invocation, including agents and context), and *deliberative* (law is not so much a series of commands as a discursive space in which meaning is collectively created in relation to social practices). In this light, any community and even any individual constitutes a normative site that produces its own law, both by way of interacting with formal legal standards linked to the state and by outright autonomous production of law.

Michael Reisman's study of microlaw, the legal normativity created informally in the course of ordinary encounters among individuals,

[112] Roderick A Macdonald & David Sandomierski, 'Against Nomopolies' (2006) 57 *N Ir Leg Q* 610 at 610; Roderick A Macdonald, 'Here, There... and Everywhere. Theorizing Legal Pluralism; Theorizing Jacques Vanderlinden' in *Mélanges Jacques Vanderlinden* (Montreal: Yvon Blais, 2006) at 381.

underscores the phenomenon of normative creation attaching to any human interaction.[113] Basing himself on the deconstruction of relations in a number of mundane settings such as queuing to buy theatre tickets, crossing eyes with strangers, or talking to the boss, Reisman argues that every encounter, even fleeting interactions among strangers, is regulated by its own normativity created on the spot. The context in which these relationships take place provides the ground for interlocking expectations as to what type of behaviour is appropriate or not (a child cuts in a line to stand with her parent), and what reaction is warranted by participants in case of violations (verbal protest against a linebreaker). These can be identified as norms despite the fact that they may operate largely at an unconscious level, to the point where participants might be hard pressed to articulate them coherently. The lack of any formal process for the creation, interpretation, application and sanction of norms does not lead to the denial of their very normativity, even legal normativity, as amply demonstrated by the existence of customary regimes in a diversity of contexts. For Reisman, however, a critical feature distinguishing a micro-legal system from mere wishful thinking or polite behaviour is the existence of some type of sanction for noncompliance, whether formal or informal, centralised or diffuse.[114] Thus staring and raising your voice is an accepted response to those trying to cut into a line without an acceptable excuse. Microlegal systems can be described as semi-autonomous, in that they operate in a universe regulated by formal legal norms in which they are grounded and with which they intersect constantly.[115] For instance, someone trying to cut in the line to go through passport control at an airport may trigger informal sanctions from fellow passengers, but also the intervention of state agents. The settings used by Reisman are everyday encounters occurring in a context which are thickly regulated by formal norms, with state institutions always within reach to intervene and police the encounter. Cannibalism, in contrast, tends to occur in remote locations, or during chaotic periods of armed conflict, or both. Far from limiting the significance of non-state

[113] See W Michael Reisman, *Law in Brief Encounters* (Yale University Press, 1999) at 2 ('Real law is generated, reinforced, changed, and terminated continually in the course of almost all of human activity'); Daniel Jutras, 'The Legal Dimensions of Everyday Life,' (2001) 16 *Can JL Soc* 45; Gerald J Postema, 'Implicit Law' (1994) 13:3 *Law Philos* 361; Cass R Sunstein, 'Social Norms and Social Roles' (1996) 96 *Columbia Law Rev* 903.

[114] Reisman, *supra* note 113 at 85, 99 & 140–41.

[115] See S F Moore, 'Law and Social Change: The Semi-Autonomous Social Field as an Appropriate Subject of Study' (1973) 7:4 *Law Soc Rev* 719.

normative sites, the lighter or non-existent presence of formal law leaves a greater space to be occupied by legal norms created by the communities or individuals themselves. A fortiori, then, we should expect that the isolated and autonomous communities that engage in anthropophagy will make their own laws.

Much of the approach to legal pluralism articulated by authors like Macdonald and Reisman is rooted in Lon Fuller's insight that law fundamentally grows from human interaction. In this perspective, law is the crystallisation of interacting expectancies linking members of a community thus created.[116] There is in this fashion a natural and necessary congruence between law and the practices and patterns of interaction in a community.[117] When testing the limits of what even legal pluralists would be willing to call law by way of suggesting that cannibals may create a legal code, I raise the issue of whether there is some substantive incompatibility between cannibalism as a practice and law as a social construct. This intersects with Fuller's central claim of the necessary morality of law, which might be taken to refuse that label for a practice as abhorrent as cannibalism. A close reading of what Fuller meant by his insistence on the necessary morality of law refutes a conclusion that cannibal law is necessarily an oxymoron. For Fuller, the internal morality of law depends on eight identified criteria dealing with the law's generality, accessibility, non-retroactivity, comprehensibility, the absence of internal contradiction, the non-impossibility of compliance, normative stability, and the congruence between legal standards and their application by officials.[118] The central concern that emerges from these eight criteria is the hijacking of the form of law by agents engaged in practices that did not meet the required elements of legal normativity. The prime example that Fuller invoked in this respect was that of Nazi law, which failed to garner several of the criteria listed by Fuller because of 'the general debasement and perversion of all forms of social order'.[119] Without these elements conferring on law its internal

[116] Lon L Fuller, 'Human Interaction and the Law' (1969) 14 *Am J Juris* 1.

[117] Postema, *supra* note 113 at 365.

[118] Lon Fuller, *The Morality of Law. Revised Edition(Second Printing.)* (Yale University Press, 1969) at 34–41; see also Kristen Rundle, *Forms Liberate: Reclaiming the Jurisprudence of Lon L. Fuller* (Hart Publishing, 2012).

[119] Lon L Fuller, 'Positivism and Fidelity to Law: A Reply to Professor Hart' (1958) *Harv Law Rev* 630 at 646; Christiane Wilke, 'Reconsecrating the Temple of Justice: Invocations of Civilization and Humanity in the Nuremberg Justice Case' (2009) 24:2 *Can J Law Soc* 181.

morality, no sense of fidelity to law is generated. Clearly, the issue arises differently when considering the possibility that a community engaged in the regulated practice of anthropophagy might be said to have generated a form of law. As a body of informal, unwritten norms, the question of the form of law is bypassed. That said, this would not lead Fuller to deny that such norms might be law. Quite the contrary, he viewed customary norms as central to the real emergence of any type of legal normativity, whether or not they were consciously adhered to by legal agents.[120] So even for Lon Fuller, who has offered perhaps the most influential modern articulation of the link between legality and morality, there is no easy conclusion that the immoral nature of cannibalism leads to the denial that it could be regulated by law. This aligns with Robert Cover's suggestion that each community not only produces its own interpretation of norms, but also generates its own *Grundnorm* defining the rule of recognition according to which the legal character of a practice is determined.[121] Law and community are thus mutually constitutive, not merely in the delineation of rights and obligations of its members, but also in its narrative of legality.

What would be the content, then, of a cannibal code? A code, in the Civilian tradition of the concept, is a social constitution that succeeds if it captures the underlying values of a society.[122] While there are endless variations in the specifics of the regulation of cannibalism in different communities, as we saw earlier, the norms setting out the conditions of accepted consumption of another human being map the boundaries of belonging for each of these communities. In some significant respect, cannibal laws rely on the consumed body to establish parameters of otherness. Partaking in anthropophagy can thus be a device to adhere to a community that has chosen this practice as a constituent element. Some witnesses before the SCSL declared that eating human bodies was related to membership in the Poro secret society. This has been linked to a wider sense that initiation into the Poro society meant that the initiate was figuratively eaten by the bush spirit.[123] The use of body parts in witchcraft rituals to prepare medicines that give protection or

[120] See Fuller, *supra* note 116. In fact, Fuller suggests that law may be even more authoritative if it is *not* consciously adhered to.

[121] R M Cover, 'Foreword: Nomos and Narrative' (1983) 97 *Harv Law Rev* 4 at 42–43.

[122] John EC Brierley & Roderick A Macdonald, *Quebec Civil Law* (Toronto: Emond Montgomery, 1993) at 32 & 39.

[123] Anders, *supra* note 74 at 955.

provide power are certainly another form of shared beliefs that correspond to a social bond linking participants. For example, in the CDF trial, Albert Moinina Jusu Nallo, a key insider witness for the Prosecution who was a Kamajor and the National Deputy Director of Operation and Director of Operations (Southern Region) for the CDF, testified that 'innocent civilians are killed and transformed into ashes and smeared' and 'then they would use you as initiation materials'.[124] Nallo similarly discusses how the Kamajors used body parts to make objects that empower and protect the user.[125] In the CDF Trial Judgement, the Court found that people were killed as sacrifices and one man 'was repeatedly stabbed and his blood was collected by the rebels'.[126] The same constitutive dimension is apparent in groups where cannibalism is seen as a service to the deceased and his or her family, a way to restore the bond that death has broken or threatened between members of a unified community.[127] Less spiritually and more prosaically, cannibalism is sometimes used as a ritual to maintain unity among combatants in a fighting unit.[128]

If the normative dimension of a rule stands confirmed by its sanction, as suggested by Michael Reisman, then ethnographic evidence strengthens a conclusion that such cannibal codes can indeed be taken as a form of law. For members of a group that engages in cannibalism, there are categories of behaviour that transgress accepted standards, a right way and a wrong way to be a cannibal. Unethical cannibals are often seen as entering the illicit realm of magic and witchcraft. Poole thus observes that:

> the anthropophagic impulses of the insane, the possessed, the morally flawed, and the starving, as well as forest demons, sorcerers, tricksters, witches, and even women and children, are believed to be beyond the pale of moral and jural order and control. Such beings ignore or deliberately violate the ritual rules of appropriate cannibalism and they are contemplated by Bimin-Kuskumin with horror and disgust.[129]

[124] CDF trial transcript, 11 March 2005 at 50 and 34.

[125] CDF trial transcript, 10 March 2005 ('He was hacked to death, and we took off his skin [. . .] They said that they are going to prepare a garment and a walking stick for Chief Hinga Norman and a fan, which is called a "controller", so as to use those things in order to become very powerful' at 59 – 60).

[126] CDF Trial Judgement at para. 1546.

[127] Conklin, *supra* note 14 at 76.

[128] UN Mission in the Democratic of the Congo, 'Report of the Special Investigation Team on the Events in Mambasa, 31 December 2002 – 20 January 2003', UN Doc S/2003/674 at 6 para. 12.

[129] Poole, *supra* note 105 at 9.

Geschiere likewise shows how the Maka identify witches on the basis of violations of cannibalism norms. He observes that the Maka draw careful distinctions between the eating of kin and non-kin. While eating non-kin is considered 'a manifestation of past states of war between villages', the eating of kin – a 'strictly forbidden' practice – is reserved for witches.[130] Geschiere argues that among many African societies, eating one's kin is the 'most compelling urge of the witches' and that '[t]he frightful image of the nocturnal banquet where the sorcerers eat their own family members could be a general element of witchcraft and sorcery in Africa'.[131] Poole similarly shows that 'unrestrained cannibalism' is directly linked to witchcraft. The Bimin-Kuskumin view this unethical cannibalism – for example, eating 'large quantities of both male and females parts' of people killed in battles or hamlet raids – was characterised as a 'desperate attempt to gain some of the fame ritual prowess of the Bimin-Kuskumin through indiscriminate consumption of their bodily substance'.[132] Their deviant cannibalistic practices are taken as breaching norms of the community.

Anthropologists like Pierre Bourdieu, Marcel Mauss and Mary Douglas suggested long ago that the body can be a theatre for social performances. This study of cannibalism adds to this allegory by suggesting that the consumed body can be a theatre for legal performances as well. Douglas, in her landmark study of purity and dirt that intersects to a significant extent with the theme of cannibalism, noted that:

> The body is a model which can stand for any bounded system. Its boundaries can represent any boundaries which are threatened or precarious. The body is a complex structure. The functions of its different parts and their relation afford a source of symbol for other complex structures. We cannot possibly interpret rituals concerning excreta, breast milk, saliva and the rest unless we are prepared to see in the body a symbol of society, and to see the powers and dangers credited to social structure reproduced in small on the human body.[133]

In evoking Douglas' notion that the body may be taken as a symbolic map of the cosmos, working to 'compress and perform wider cosmological understandings about social categories and classifications', we open the possibility that it may in some circumstances allow for the crystallisation

[130] Geschiere & Roitman, *supra* note 107 at 34 & 40.
[131] *Ibid* at 6 and 239–40, footnote 3.
[132] Poole, *supra* note 105 at 10.
[133] Mary Douglas, *Purity and Danger: An Analysis of Concepts of Pollution and Taboo* (Routledge, 2013) at 116.

of these categories into legal norms.[134] Cannibalism, in speaking powerfully to the essence of the body, would offer one such occasion.

I suggested earlier that through cannibalism the body can be used to establish parameters of otherness, leading to the mapping of conditions of belonging to a community. It bears underscoring that this process of constituting a community necessarily implies a process of othering, of signalling to those who are not cannibals that they stand outside of these boundaries. In this fashion, cannibal law is taken as a dialogical practice, reflecting both the communicative function of law as a language of interaction and the role that cannibalism typically plays in constructing difference.[135] This facet of cannibalism emerges from references to the practice in testimonies before the SCSL, more specifically falling into two patterns: first, cannibalism operates as a form of public, performative violence whereby the treatment of the dead is used to terrorise the living. As Donald Sutton argues, cannibalism creates 'a sort of secularized hell', either because of the fear of being killed in this fashion or because of beliefs that this would interfere with a spiritual afterlife.[136] Both the CDF and Taylor's National Patriotic Front of Liberia are alleged to have used cannibalism publicly to instil fear in civilians.[137] The transcripts also show that people were forced to participate in cannibalism by cooking or eating human body parts.[138] Second, and more specifically, most references to cannibalism emerge in the CDF trials over the Kamajors' punishment of collaborators and rebels. For example, Ibrahim Fofana testifies that the 'Kamajors had arrested [people] and said they were juntas sympathisers and RUF sympathisers and collaborators who had not been able to escape from Koidu Town, they were cooked in those pots and eaten'.[139] Witness

[134] Appadurai, *supra* note 111 at 231, referring also to Mary Douglas, *Natural Symbols: Explorations in Cosmology* (Routledge, 2004).

[135] Maggie Kilgour, 'Introduction' in Kristen Guest, *Eating Their Words: Cannibalism and the Boundaries of Cultural Identity* (SUNY Press, 2001) at viii; Fuller, *supra* note 116 at 2.

[136] Sutton, *supra* note 71 at 146.

[137] CDF Trial Judgement at para. 424 ('The Kamajors disembowelled the women and put their entrails in a bucket. The women's stomachs were also removed. Their guts were made into checkpoints so that anyone coming past could see them. Part of their entrails were eaten and their bodies were buried'). The judgment refers to CDF trial transcripts, 9 Sept 2004 at 38–39.

[138] Recall, for example, the testimonies of Akiatu Tholley and witness TF2-144 described in the opening paragraph of this paper. There were also similar testimonies before the Truth and Reconciliation Commission: Kelsall, *supra* note 44 at footnote 14.

[139] CDF trial transcript, 28 October 2008 at 19384. He further testified that 'the Kamajors held the town for about two weeks during which I saw them kill about 15 people they

12.4 Cannibal Law: The Law is Cannibalistic

Toutes les significations
viennent s'abolir dans leur propre signe
et la profusion des signes parodie une
réalité désormais introuvable. C'est ce que
j'appellerais la «carnavalisation», et toute
cette mascarade occidentale repose sur la
cannibalisation de la réalité par les signes.

Jean Baudrillard, *Carnaval/Cannibale* (2005)

The third cannibal law is the way in which legal discourse relates to other forms of social discourse. Viewed as such, cannibalism can be taken as a metaphor for law's consumption of all other ways of understanding, digested and transformed to aliment legal analysis. That which the law cannot digest and transform is simply rejected as irrelevant. There is a degree of circularity to legal reasoning in that law claims an interpretive monopoly over what constitutes legal discourse. We need to step out of law's all-encompassing culture in order to consider it as an artefact of modernity, marked in the field of international criminal law by its nearly exclusively western origins. As a classical trope of savagism, cannibalism stands as international law's anti-modern other. While some have argued that we must distance ourselves from the law to suspend unquestioned belief in its necessity and centrality, it may be that cannibalism's radical anti-modernity stands as altogether too distant for that purpose. As a concept, cannibalism would be radically dyspeptic for law, marking again a limitation of the concept of law as inscribed in an international criminal tribunal like the SCSL. More starkly, the metaphor of the cannibalistic nature of law rests on a misrepresentation of cannibalism as a social practice and a misunderstanding of law as a social structure.

12.4.1 Cannibalism as a Metaphor for Law

Some years ago, Boaventura de Sousa Santos suggested that there was a 'supermetaphor' grounding each legal order and determining its interpretive standpoint.[150] While it would surely be an exaggeration to suggest that cannibalism per se has been so present in the way in which jurists have been conceptualising the place of law in society, it does connect with

[150] Boaventura de Sousa Santos, 'Law: A Map of Misreading. Toward a Postmodern Conception of Law' (1987) 14 *J Law Soc* 279 at 291.

a certain sense that law offers a framework that can capture the totality of human experience in some respect. In his essay, Santos refers to Habermas' bemoaning the 'excessive colonisation of the life-world (*Lebenwelt*) by law'.[151] The point here is not to make an argument regarding the actual scope of law or its normative ability to regulate every facet of human experience, but rather to examine the way in which law is represented by legal discourse itself. In other words, law being a form of representation, the question is whether cannibalism echoes the law's self-representation.

There are at least two distinct ways in which the representation of law has been linked to cannibalism, touching respectively on individuals and institutions and on hermeneutic superiority. As for the first, Maggie Kilgour, in her wide-ranging study of cannibalism as a metaphor of incorporation, notes that 'the representation of the legal system as cannibalistic is an old topos'.[152] She offers a survey from Plato's attack on lawyers as using the law to fill their bellies to Dickens and Rabelais underscoring the ravenous nature of layers, where the desire for money is fused with the desire for blood.[153] The legal system and the digestive system are analogised in this metaphor, paving the way for Levi-Strauss to assert in *Tristes Tropiques* that 'certain of our own customs might appear, to an observer belonging to a different society, to be similar in nature to cannibalism .... For instance ... our legal and prison systems'.[154] In a more contemporary setting closer to the focus of this essay, United States Senator Jesse Helms, for instance, points to the impact of the international criminal law institutions on state sovereignty: '[t]he International Court is a threat to US national interests ... and it is our responsibility to slay it before it grows to devour us'.[155] Cannibalism as a metaphor for law appears consonant with analogies to the body routinely and unconsciously used in describing components of the law: we thus speak of the 'body' of law relating to a given issue or the 'corpus' of jurisprudence, going back to the 'corpus juris civilis' of Roman law

151 Id., referring to Jürgen Habermas, *The Theory of Communicative Action: Lifeworld and System : A Critique of Functionalist Reason* (Beacon Press, 1985).

152 Maggie Kilgour, *From Communion to Cannibalism: An Anatomy of Metaphors of Incorporation* (Princeton University Press, 1990) at 96. See also: Kilgour, *supra* note 72 at 239; Lindenbaum, *supra* note 80 at 476.

153 Kilgour, *supra* note 152 at 97.

154 Claude Lévi-Strauss, *Tristes tropiques* (New York: Atheneum, 1974) at 387–88.

155 'We Must Slay This Monster: Voting against the International Criminal Court is Not Enough. The US Should Try to Bring it Down' (31 July 1998) *Financial Times*.

compiled in the 'Digest'. For Douzinas and Gearey, these representations of the law as a body are literal, so that the law must accordingly 'either digest and transform the non-legal into legality, or it must reject it'.[156]

The last idea links the first and second iterations of the cannibal metaphor for law: in addition to evoking the manner in which individuals (and even countries, for Senator Helms) can be swallowed and digested by the legal system, the metaphor also speaks to the representation of law as a totalizing discourse that absorbs all other perspectives to support its own. Baudrillard, in his *Carnaval/Cannibale* quoted at the start of this section, speaks of the 'cannibalization of reality through signs' and law can certainly be taken as one system of signs that operates on that basis. The same idea is reflected, minus the cannibal metaphor, in Clifford Geertz's arresting formulation that law is 'a distinctive manner of imagining the real'.[157] For Geertz, legal discourse proceeds by way of the normative construction of facts, a process that does imply the production of a reality that will emerge as distinct from, say, that produced by a political, sociological, religious, or popular process. Like all these other, competing discourses, law elevates and celebrates parts of what is real and denigrates and marginalises other parts of 'the real'. One example, close to our concern with international criminal law, is Kamari Maxine Clarke's incisive critique of the interventions of the International Criminal Court in Africa that only allow for a singular notion of justice that is based on an individualisation of criminal responsibility. She points out that this construction of justice marginalises other ways of making sense of violence, such as 'histories of colonial subject formation, contested governance and boundary-making dictates, foreign resource ownership and extraction in the midst of poverty and unresolved conflict'.[158] Tim Kelsall likewise points out how international criminal law rests on a rejection of other ways of understanding and explaining power. He argues that the SCSL's prosecution 'excavate[s] a particular version of the truth from a contested history'.[159] In particular, Kelsall argues that

[156] Costas Douzinas & Adam Gearey, *Critical Jurisprudence: The Political Philosophy of Justice* (Oxford: Hart, 2005) at 47.

[157] Clifford Geertz, 'Local Knowledge: Fact and Law in Comparative Perspective' in Clifford Geertz ed., *Local Knowledge: Further Essays in Interpretive Anthropology* (Basic Books, 1983) 167 at 184.

[158] Kamari Maxine Clarke, *Fictions of Justice: The International Criminal Court and the Challenge of Legal Pluralism in Sub-Saharan Africa* (Cambridge University Press, 2009) at 19.

[159] Kelsall, *supra* note 74 at 587.

the prosecution tries to 'delegitimize leaders of violent movements by constructing their acts as 'criminal' rather than 'political'.[160] By depoliticizing and relocating people to legal categories – most notably the 'criminal' – Kelsall shows how international criminal law constrains the complex ways of understanding and addressing violence. Through the discursive labelling of the political or sociological as legal, 'these strategies, acts and modes of behaviour are extracted [from the political sphere] and rendered susceptible to the intervention of policing, juridical and penal agencies'.[161]

As we see in these examples, the operation of law implies the production of a certain vision of reality. It is important to note that this occurs not merely by the application of substantive legal rules, but by way of the deployment of legal culture as a whole as instantiated in rules of evidence and procedure, in courtroom etiquette, advocacy styles, judicial rhetoric, approaches in legal education, the political economy of legal practice, legal terminology, and so on.[162] That said, the same type of comments could be directed at religion, art, politics, economics, to the effect that they tend to construct a reality that is grounded in the culture of religion, art, politics, or economics. What is it, then, that leads authors to invoke the cannibalism metaphor and argue, for example, that 'law cannibalises history in order to establish its authority'?[163] The key, to return once more to Clifford Geertz, is the manner in which law, as a representation of reality, is itself represented.[164] It is in this respect that the law stands apart from other forms of discourse in society, to claim hermeneutic supremacy. In shifting from a language of imagination, which it shares with others, to a language of decision, it asserts a legitimacy to arbitrate all other forms of discourse. Thus, it is immaterial that the historian might dispute the way in which an eighteenth century agreement between aboriginal people and Europeans is characterised by a court, or that the psychologist might reject the judicial construction of the impact of alcohol consumption on the ability to form a specific intent to commit a crime. The law produces its own answers to such questions, most likely relying on historical and psychological evidence, but doing so on the basis of the law's own canons, rejecting any suggestion that fidelity

[160] *Ibid* at 587–88. [161] *Ibid* at 589. [162] Geertz, *supra* note 157 at 173.

[163] Adam John Waterman et al, *The Price of the Purchase: Black Hawk's War and the Colonization of the Upper Mississippi River Valley* (2007) at 40.

[164] Geertz, *supra* note 157 at 174.

is owed to the canons of these other disciplines cannibalised for that purpose.[165] Even more, the social construction of the place of law in our society implies that the legal construction of reality is not merely one amongst many possible perspectives on any reality, not just one of many manners of imagining the real, but rather the one that will determine the resolution of any possible dispute amongst these perspectives. The cannibal metaphor thus not only suggests that law consumes other ways of thinking about reality to aliment its own operation, but further reflects a more general association of cannibalism with power and dominance.[166]

12.4.2 A Metaphor in Search of Itself

The suggestion that the law might be said to be cannibalistic finds some support in the way in which legal institutions, legal agents, and legal discourse have been described in the literature. While both jurists and non-jurists have invoked the metaphor, they have done so in a manner that reflects a superficial understanding of the practice to which the metaphor refers. A richer understanding of the practice of cannibalism opens the door to a reinterpretation of the metaphor as it is applied to law, challenging the representation of law as dominating other forms of social discourse.

In the examples that I have described above, the metaphor of cannibalism for law is often limited to the mere use of vocabulary like 'cannibalize', 'consume', 'digest', or 'devour'. The concept of cannibalism itself remains largely unexamined outside of literary and anthropological scholarship. In particular, how the act of cannibalism occurs and its implications for the relationship between the 'eaten' and 'eater' lack nuanced examinations or even an informed understanding of what the practice of cannibalism corresponds to. Rather, cannibalism is presented as pure destruction or engulfment. In this representation, cannibalism 'aims at the loss of the Other ... either through the Other's absolute

165 Thus Stanley Diamond holds that '[w]e live in a law-ridden society; law has cannibalized the institutions which it presumably reinforces or with which it interacts. Accordingly, morality continues to be reduced to or confused with legality. In civil society, we are encouraged to assume that legal behavior is the measure of moral behavior': Stanley Diamond, 'The Rule of Law vs. the Order of Custom' (1984) 38 *Soc Res* 42 at 44.

166 See Rosalind Shaw, 'Cannibal Transformations' in Henrietta Moore & Todd Sanders, eds., *Magic Interpretations, Magical Realities: Modernity, Witchcraft and the Occult in Postcolonial Africa* (London: Routledge, 2001) 50 at 65.

destruction or through his absorption into the eater'.[167] When the metaphor is applied to law, the legal system's interaction with other processes is seen as all-powerful, all-consuming, and entirely destructive. There is no room for relationship or resistance. It is a practice grounded in the selfish satisfaction of the cannibal's needs, whether it be hunger or love.[168] I myself must plead guilty of such a reductionist approach in describing how the SCSL used the discourse of international criminal law to absorb witchcraft practices carried out by the accused in the *Civil Defence Forces* case, concluding: 'The customary cosmology of Sierra Leone is kidnapped by the cosmology of international law, which consumes it, saving only the parts that serve its own purposes'.[169] Consumption is thus a one-way exertion of power: to devour is to dominate. In this rendering, cannibalism equals the eater eating the eaten.

To invoke a metaphor is to engage in an interpretive exercise. As brilliantly explored by James Boyd White, translation provides a metaphor that captures the very life of the law.[170] Boyd White observes that the word 'translation' is derived from the Latin *trans* (across) and *latus* (to carry), whereas the word 'metaphor' is derived from the Greek *meta* (across) and *phor* (to carry). In other words, to translate or to interpret is to invoke a metaphor, and vice versa.[171] Part of the challenge of invoking the metaphor of cannibalism in relation to law is that this is a metaphor that refers to a practice that is itself metaphorical at least as much as it is real. Indeed, going back to the anthropological debate examined in the second part of this essay, it seems that the invocation of cannibalism as a metaphor for law reflects cannibalism (the metaphor) much more than anthropophagy (the practice).[172] The aptness of the cannibal metaphor as applied to law can be measured not only in relation to cannibalism as an Orientalizing construct so vigorously attacked by William Arens, but

[167] Ann W Astell, *Eating Beauty: The Eucharist and the Spiritual Arts of the Middle Ages* (Cornell University Press, 2006) at 11.

[168] This is explored by Desmond Manderson in his study of cannibalism in Maurice Sendak's Where the Wild things Are: Desmond Manderson, 'From Hunger to Love: Myths of the Source, Interpretation, and Constitution of Law in Children's Literature' (2003) 15:1 *Law Lit* 87 at 122.

[169] Provost, *supra* note 147 at 200.

[170] James Boyd White, *Justice as Translation: An Essay in Cultural and Legal Criticism* (University of Chicago Press, 1994) at 233.

[171] I discuss this more in depth in René Provost, 'Interpretation in International Law as a Transcultural Project' in Andrea Bianchi, Daniel Peat & Matthew Windsor, eds., *Interpretation in International Law* (Oxford University Press, 2015) 290–308.

[172] This refers to the distinction, discussed earlier, in Hulme, *supra* note 81 at 4.

also in relation to anthropophagy as a community-based regulated practice studied more perceptively in recent ethnographic studies. This thicker construction of cannibalism (or anthropophagy) leads to a richer and more complex metaphor when applied to law.

Contemporary ethnographic studies of cannibalism suggest that it is not the all-destructive practice of pure consumption that corresponds to the metaphorical descriptions of law in the examples cited just above. Rather, it is a process of absorption and incorporation in which the outside enters the inside and the external forms a part of the internal. While the external loses its original characteristics through consumption and incorporation, the internal is not left untouched. Instead, it is also subject to transformation. In short, modern ethnographies show that cannibalism is not merely a process of the eater eating the eaten. Instead, the logic of cannibalism implies the transformation of the eater, not only the consumption of the eaten. As noted by Kilgour, the starting point of cannibalism is the binary distinction between self and other: incorporation 'depends upon and enforces an absolute division between inside and outside'.[173] While the idea of cannibalism necessarily proclaims that division, its practice collapses the binary. In other words, cannibalism 'dissolv[es] the structure it appears to produce'.[174] Through incorporation, the outside comes inside. While this involves the *confusion* between inside and outside, it does not simply result in destruction of either the eaten or the eater.[175] For example Beth Conklin shows how, in mortuary cannibalism, social groups 'defined and reconstituted themselves after a death'.[176] Peggy Reeves Sanday similarly contends that '[e]ndocannibalism recycles and regenerates social forces that are believed to be physically constituted in bodily substances or bones'.[177] I.M. Lewis for his part notes that 'the ritual consumption of parts of the human body enables the consumer to acquire something of the body's vital energy'.[178]

Cannibalism in war is also often presented as the way that the eater obtains the power of the dead. For example, Denis Tull describes conflicts in North Kivu where, 'the eating of flesh, especially organs, serves to absorb the power of their victims and thus to enhance their own strength', echoing the notion mentioned earlier that eating the heart of pigmies is taken to transfer

[173] Kilgour, *supra* note 152 at 4. [174] *Ibid.* [175] *Ibid* at 69.
[176] Conklin, *supra* note 14 at 239. [177] Sanday, *supra* note 111 at 7.
[178] I M Lewis, *Religion in Context: Cults and Charisma* (Cambridge: Cambridge University Press, 1986) at 73.

their power to live in the bush.[179] Sanday also observes that '[b]y consuming enemy flesh one assimilates the animus of another group's hostile power into one's own',[180] These ethnographic explanations for cannibalism show how the eater takes in some element of the person being eaten. Mortuary and conflict cannibalism thus illustrate that cannibalism's very purpose is the *incorporation* of the eaten into the eater.

Bringing this back to law, the metaphor of cannibalism emerges as an insightful way for thinking about law's relationship with other non-legal normative systems. While it captures the terrifying power of law (since what is worse than being eaten?), it also challenges the view that the relationship is defined entirely by domination. Through absorption and incorporation, the eaten is not simply devoured and annihilated but rather becomes integrated in some way with the eater. Unlike the common perception that law 'consumes' or 'devours' other systems *in toto*, eating opens the law to transformation wrought by parallel systems of meaning being relied upon for its operation. Law is transformed through its own process of assessing the other. Boyd White argues that although law works through coercion by 'requiring the argument to proceed in certain terms', it also 'creates something new, a place and mode of discourse'.[181] I made the point earlier that eating habits in general are viewed as markers of difference. Cannibalism explicates the complex dynamic of that difference: all at once, it proclaims the absolute difference between the eater and the eaten, and it dissolves that very difference by making eater and eaten become one through incorporation.[182]

The decision of the SCSL in the CDF trial illustrates how law necessarily opens itself up when it consumes another system through legal analysis. In particular, the Appeal Chamber's reliance on Kondewa's magical power, rooted in his widely-recognised mysticism, shows on the one hand, how law monopolises power – by defining his power through legal responsibility – and, on the other hand, that law is itself transformed by the analysis of magic.[183] For the majority in that case, the magic rituals performed by Kondewa as 'High Priest' of the Kamajor militia – initiation and bullet-proofing ceremonies – gave him a *de facto*

[179] Denis Tull, *The Reconfiguration of Political Order in Africa: A Case Study of North Kivu (DR Congo)*, Hamburg African studies = Etudes africaines hambourgeoises 13 (Hamburg: Institute of African Affairs, 2005) at 239; Bergner, *supra* note 108.

[180] Sanday, *supra* note 33 at 6.

[181] White, *supra* note 170 at 202.

[182] Kilgour, *supra* note 72 at 240.

[183] I study this in much greater detail in Provost, *supra* note 147.

authority that justified imputing onto him criminal responsibility for crimes committed by Kamajor fighters under the doctrine of command responsibility, despite the fact that Kondewa himself never issued orders nor participated in any of the attacks during which the crimes were committed. The law here requires that factual elements be formulated in its own terms, consuming evidence of factual authority but rejecting as immaterial the question of whether Kondewa really did have magical power.[184] The practice is digested to separate what is needed to aliment legal reasoning, the rest is excreted as not legally relevant.

The transformative power of eating means that cannibalism is also potentially dangerous for the eater. It reflects the complex of need-desire-fear associated with food in general: because what we eat intimately interacts with the eater (by forming part of the eater), we need it to survive and yet know it can cause our demise. As Kilgour notes, feasting generally 'is an indication of openness. But this openness in turn is a sign of vulnerability, as the reception of external influences can in different ways endanger the self'.[185] Consumption's potentially negative effects are rooted in fears of food poisoning, ritualised food prohibitions, and discourses on healthy eating. As discussed in the previous Part of the essay, ethnographies highlight how normative rules around cannibalism define whose flesh can be consumed and which parts of the body are edible.[186] These norms are circumscribed by the polluting potential of consumption.

Going back to the treatment of magic in the SCSL Appeal Chamber decision in the CDF Trial, the dissent by judge Gelaga King – who is himself from Sierra Leone – illustrates the limits and dangers of the law's consumption of other systems of meaning. The dissent highlights the incompatibility of the magical power to render someone bullet-proof with the legal reasoning that an international court, based on rationality and a symbol of modernity, is meant to use:

> In my opinion, the roles found to have been performed by Kondewa as "High Priest," are so ridiculous, preposterous and unreal as to be laughable and not worthy of serious consideration by right-thinking persons in civilized society. If the Kamajors believe in the mystical power of Kondewa as an initiator, his imaginary immunisation powers (as if it was scientific), do the Chambers of the Special Court also believe that

[184] See Tim Kelsall, *Culture under Cross-examination: International Justice and the Special Court for Sierra Leone* (Cambridge University Press, 2009) at 128.

[185] Kilgour, *supra* note 152 at 89.

[186] See Poole, *supra* note 105 and accompanying text.

> Kondewa could make Kamajors "bullet-proof" and that Kondewa's "blessings" would make them impervious to machine-gun bullets? And on that basis find him to be a commander? Obviously not.[187]

The explanation of judge Gelaga King's virulent dissent seems to be that magic is so pervasive within Sierra Leone that legal discourse can never fully empty such rituals from their supernatural dimensions. Not only does magic resist total absorption by law, the encounter as depicted in the dissent begs the question of who is consuming whom. For judge King, the judgment stands as a recognition in international criminal law that a 'juju man' wields magical powers that justify the application of the doctrine of command responsibility.[188] In this optic, the skeletonisation of magic to fact by the operation of law simply cannot succeed.

When the cannibal metaphor for law is reimagined on the basis of an understanding of anthropophagy rooted in ethnographic research rather than in colonial projections of savage otherness, it suggests a relation between legal discourse and other systems of meaning that denies facile assumption of its nature and outcomes. Ultimately, the revisited cannibal metaphor for law stands as significantly more apt than its forbearer, rejecting the representation conveyed by legal discourse itself that law stands in a dominant position, unilaterally imposing the terms of its relations to other disciplines and forms of social discourse generally. Instead, it invites jurists to investigate the ways in which such interactions ineluctably transform the fabric of legal discourse. It also suggests that there are things that the law should not attempt to incorporate, for its own good.

12.5 Conclusion

Ultimately, it appears that all three cannibal laws speak to one another, that the explanation of any one calls on the explanatory power of the two others. Perhaps it suggests that the plural form used to describe them in the title of this essay is misguided, that there is a unity in cannibal law that covers cannibalism as a criminal act prohibited by international law, cannibalism as a set of norms regulating the practices of some communities, and cannibalism as a metaphor for the manner in which legal discourse interacts with other forms of social discourse. Cannibal law in

[187] CDF Appeal Judgment, Judge King's dissent, para. 70.

[188] Here again, I borrow from myself some ideas that are developed much more fully in Provost, *supra* note 147.

13

Beyond the Paradox of Exporting the Rule of Law

Resilience and the War on Drugs in the Americas

DAVID CHANDLER

13.1 Introduction

Neoliberal, new institutionalist and social constructivist understandings have increasingly come to dominate the critical debate over rule of law interventions over the last decades.[1] In these approaches, liberal regimes of international intervention seen as relying on top-down frameworks of markets, liberal democracy and the rule of law are viewed as problematic in societies designated as non-liberal. However, these approaches, while useful in articulating an understanding of the limits to liberal universalism, have been unable to provide a programme of policy intervention which goes beyond the paradoxes of liberal approaches to law. Either liberal framings of rights and law are seen as too abstract and distant from the realities of everyday life, often with unintended and problematic consequences, or there is the perceived danger of cultural relativism, undermining democracy and human rights, where law is seen as problematically adapting to local socio-cultural differences.

[1] These frameworks are critical of liberal assumptions of the universal, autonomous, rational subject, drawing attention to ways in which the subjects of rule of law interventions are non- or a-liberal and socio-culturally embedded. See, for example, Roland Paris, *At War's End: Building Peace After Civil Conflict* (Cambridge University Press, 2004); Oliver Richmond, *A Post-Liberal Peace* (Routledge, 2012); Roger Mac Ginty, *International Peacebuilding and Local Resistance: Hybrid Forms of Peace* (Palgrave Macmillan, 2011); Edward Newman, Roland Paris and Oliver Richmond, eds. *New Perspectives on Liberal Peacebuilding* (United Nations University Press, 2009); Susanna Campbell, David Chandler & Meera Sabaratnam, eds. *A Liberal Peace?: The Problems and Practices of Peacebuilding* (Zed Books, 2011); Shahrbanou Tadjbakhsh, *Rethinking the Liberal Peace: External Models and Local Alternatives* (Taylor & Francis, 2011); Oliver P Richmond & Audra Mitchell, *Hybrid Forms of Peace: From Everyday Agency to Post-Liberalism* (Palgrave Macmillan, 2011).

This chapter argues that critiques of the formal, abstract, nature of liberal modernist legal frameworks on the basis of socio-cultural difference have ended in a policy impasse, caught between the Scylla and Charybdis of universalism and cultural relativism.[2] It suggests that we are increasingly seeing a shift away from social constructivist and new institutionalist framings of cultural pluralism to resilience approaches. Resilience approaches do not start from the problematic of socio-cultural difference, but from a different set of problems which no longer involve a focus on a 'hermeneutics of suspicion':[3] problematising the understanding or rationality of those seen to be in need of intervention. These resilience framings suggest that in a complex world, liberal forms of institutional and legal understanding are themselves problematic; that formal frameworks of law can no longer be understood to work to shape or direct social processes in a top-down or hierarchical manner. From this starting point, 'everyday life' is neither conceived of as a problem nor romanticised as 'resisting', but seen as providing a problem-solving resource of practices to be drawn upon. This shift evades the problems of the external imposition of abstract, 'unreal', liberal universalist frameworks, but also evades cultural relativism, because there is no external yardstick or comparison at play in such understandings.

In focusing on how everyday practices can provide the resources to address the problems faced, problems and solutions are no longer debated in the formal framings of the export of liberal institutions, laws and rights; instead, resilience approaches are based on how practices work in a particular context.[4] This approach, which could be understood

[2] It could be argued that this has been implicit within liberal sociological approaches to formal institutional frameworks. See, for example, Max Weber's investigation of the cultural roots of the 'irrationality' of law and administration in Confucian China: Max Weber, Hans Heinrich Gerth & YANG Ch'ing-k'un, *The Religion of China. Confucianism and Taoism... Translated and Edited by Hans H. Gerth. With an Introduction by CK Yang* (Collier Macmillan, 1964).

[3] Paul Ricoeur, *Freud and Philosophy; an Essay on Interpretation. Translated by Denis Savage* (1970) at 27.

[4] The growing attention to concrete practices rather than to explaining the 'gap' between theory and the world through the attention to discursive structures can be clearly seen in the growing attention to practice theory and actor-network approaches. See, for example, Jörg Friedrichs & Friedrich Kratochwil, 'On Acting and Knowing: How Pragmatism Can Advance International Relations Research and Methodology' (2009) 63:04 *Int Organ* 701 at 701–31; Iver B Neumann, 'Returning Practice to the Linguistic Turn: the Case of Diplomacy' (2002) 31:3 *Millenn-J Int Stud* 627 at 627–51; Christian Bueger, 'From Epistemology to Practice: a Sociology of Science for International Relations' (2012) 15:1 *J Int Relat Dev* 97 at 97–109;

along the lines of philosophical pragmatism,[5] starts neither from universalist nor cultural relativist assumptions with regard to formal institutional frameworks, but with the effects of their application in particular circumstances.[6] It is the connection between resilience and philosophical pragmatism which is important to draw out here, and which I argue stakes out an understanding of resilience approaches that is at odds with current critical theorising which tends to understand resilience as explicitly tied to neoliberal frameworks of understanding.[7]

This chapter takes as an example of this shift the recent policy discussion on the limits of international intervention with regard to the war on drugs in the Americas.[8] The war on drugs has been framed in the terminology of international aid for law enforcement in the region and therefore serves as a good example of how international legal interventions have been refocused.[9] International, essentially US-led, approaches

Oliver Kessler & Xavier Guillaume, 'Everyday Practices of International Relations: People in Organizations' (2012) 15:1 *J Int Relat Dev* 110 at 110–210.

5 See, the key text in this regard, John Dewey, *The Public and Its Problems: An Essay in Political Inquiry* (Penn State Press, 2012). Philosophical pragmatism is a broad school of thought from classical US pragmatists such as William James and John Dewey in the early twentieth century to the modern revival of interest in the work of authors such as Richard Rorty and Hilary Putnam. The core aspect is the empiricist attitude of concern with practical consequences rather than abstract concepts and beliefs, reflecting a distinctive epistemological outlook of anti-Cartesian fallibilism. Philosophical pragmatism sought to overcome the divide between Cartesian understandings of objective truth, and sceptical perspectives that truth is always relative or subjective through the emphasis on practical consequences; see, for example, John Dewey, *The Quest for Certainty, The Later Works, 1925–1953, Vol. 4: 1929* (Southern Illinois University Press, 1984). It is this framing which, this article suggests, is at the heart of resilience approaches which go beyond liberal universalist/cultural relativist understandings of rule of law interventions.

6 See further, Amartya Sen's contrapositioning of 'arrangement-focused' and 'realization-focused' views of justice, Amartya Kumar Sen, *The Idea of Justice* (Harvard University Press, 2009).

7 See, for example, Jeremy Walker & Melinda Cooper, 'Genealogies of Resilience From Systems Ecology to the Political Economy of Crisis Adaptation' (2011) 42:2 *Secur Dialogue* 143 at 143–60; Brad Evans & Julian Reid, 'Dangerously Exposed: The Life and Death of the Resilient Subject' (2013) 1:2 *Resilience* 83; Mark Neocleous, 'Commentary: Resisting Resilience' (2013) 178 *Radic Philos* at 2–7.

8 This discussion has been cohered through the publication of a high-profile report from the General Secretariat of the Organisation of American States suggesting that international policy interventions have failed in this area; Organization of American States (OAS), *The Drug Problem in the Americas* (Washington, DC: OAS, 2013).

9 See, for example, Diana Cammack et al, 'Donors and the "fragile states" Agenda: A Survey of Current Thinking and Practice' (2006) *ODI Rep Submitt Jpn Int Coop Agency*, online: www.odi.org.uk/resources/docs/1955.pdf; Paula Miraglia, Rolando Ochoa & Ivan Briscoe, 'OECD Development Co-operation' (2012), online: www.crime-prevention-intl.org/filead min/user_upload/Publications/Transnational_organised_crime_and_fragile_states_2012.pdf; Adam David Morton, 'Failed-State Status and the War on Drugs in Mexico' (2011) 13:1 *Glob*

to the problem have focused primarily on drug production and distribution in Latin American states and the prominence of international criminal organisations and networks operating with relative impunity where many states have fragile frameworks of law and rights enforcement. Heuristically, it is possible to draw out three different approaches to the problem. Firstly, what might be called a 'liberal universalist' approach where resources are put into strengthening state capacity, training police and security forces, improving the operation and independence of the judiciary, increasing state level coordination and information sharing and developing the strength of legal regimes in terms of democracy and human rights.[10] The second approach, launched amid the perceived failures of formal institutional capacity-building, has paid much more attention to plural socio-cultural values and understandings, suggesting that success at the state-level is dependent upon local understandings – that norms and values change is the key to peace and the institutionalisation of a rule of law regime.

The third approach – the 'resilience' approach – does not start from the gap between liberal understandings of law and socio-cultural norms and understandings. Resilience approaches seek to work through understanding the concrete context in which social practices and everyday 'tactics' produce problematic consequences: in this case, the criminal production, trafficking and consumption of drugs. Through a process-based or relational understanding of the construction of a concrete problem (or set of problems), everyday contexts and practices are seen to provide the key to mitigating both the causes and consequences of 'the drug problem' in the Americas.

Resilience is the story of a profound change in perspective about where the solution to the hemispheric drug problem can be found. Rather than focusing primarily on suppressing drug production and trafficking or changing the legal or regulatory regime, national and local leaders recognise that the best approach is to focus on people rather than drugs and to rebuild and strengthen communities from the grassroots level up. Like a

Dialogue; the Pulitzer centre project, *Fragile States: The Drug War in Central America*; Juan Gabriel Tokatlián, *Organised Crime, Illicit Drugs and State Vulnerability* (Norwegian Peacebuilding Centre, 2011); David Sogge, *Repairing the Weakest Links: A New Agenda for Fragile States* (FRIDE, 2009).

10 Richmond describes the liberal peace approach as 'a model through which Western-led agency, epistemology and institutions, have attempted to unite the world order under a hegemonic system that replicates liberal institutions, norms, and political, social and economic systems', Richmond, *supra* note 1 at 1.

healthy body, a healthy community fights off an 'epidemic', whether it is an epidemic of violence or of drug dependence, through its own capacity to respond effectively – its own resilience.[11]

The shift from understanding socio-cultural values as the problem or barrier to be overcome or be adapted to, resilience approaches understand local practices in the context of a societal milieu and view this context as crucial. Here, local responses and practices are seen as the dynamic of positive transformation once there is an enabling context.

The rest of the paper draws out the cultural impasse of rule of law interventionism – where cultural sensitivities lead either to increasingly problematic universalist attempts to remake cultural norms or to the dangers of cultural relativist adaption to the status quo. I will then use the example of the Organisation of American States initiative to rethink the war on drugs to demonstrate how a discussion about how to export liberal institutional frameworks and the rule of law has shifted to one about how to pragmatically deal with a set of varied problems, once they are re-presented as contextually-embedded social practices. From the analysis which follows it will become clear that resilience-approaches can play a role in constructing a positive alternative, evading the dilemma of the export of legal institutional frameworks – the traps of universalism and cultural relativism.

13.2 The Limits of Culture

In a neoliberal or sociological institutionalist understanding, the focus is upon the differential capacity of state institutions and the rule of law, dependent upon their socio-cultural foundations. This neoliberal perspective was probably most famously articulated by Friedrich von Hayek in his view that modern liberal institutions could not be exported or created by edict or plans, but must emerge organically from society.[12] In the organic or culturalist perspective, the constitutional history of Great Britain is often highlighted to argue that even without a written (codified) constitution, the rule of law had more *de facto* purchase than in the former colonies where the rule of law needed to be produced through *de*

[11] OAS, *Scenarios for the Drug Problem in the Americas 2013–2025* (OAS, 2013) at 55.

[12] According to Hayek: 'The conception of man deliberately building his civilization stems from an erroneous intellectualism that regards human reason as something standing outside nature and possessed of knowledge and reasoning capacity independent of experience'. Friedrich A Hayek, *The Constitution of Liberty* (Routledge, 1960) at 22.

jure democratic constitutions.[13] The tautologies of the pluralist, 'organic' or institutionalist position are highlighted in the circular reasoning of studies that attempt to explain the differences and divisions of the present as products of the cultural hold of the past. For example, Brian Tamanaha argues: 'The rule of law existed [in Britain] owing to the widespread unquestioned belief in the rule of law, in the inviolability of certain fundamental legal restraints on government, not to any specific legal mechanism'.[14] Paola Cesarine and Katherine Hite put this well in the context of Latin America:

> The persistence of authoritarian legacies in post-authoritarian democracies may be explained in terms of a combination of socially, culturally, and institutionally induced set of attitudes, perceptions, motivations, and constraints – that is, from traditions or institutions of the past as well as from present struggles within formally democratic arrangements... As a result, democracy in much of Latin America belongs to the realm of constitutions and code books rather than reality.[15]

For constructivist or sociological institutionalist approaches, law could not provide its own legitimacy – its own basis, limits or constraints – anymore than democratic theory could explain the constitution of the demos.[16] The universal, 'natural' or Cartesian assumptions of the liberal rationalist autonomous subject were subject to devastating critique from these sociologically-informed positions.

But while operating to highlight the limits of liberal constructions of the rule of law there appeared to be little that could be done to overcome these limits. Once it was established that merely having legal constitutions (which can, of course, be internationally exported or externally-imposed) was no longer adequate, then the sphere of socio-cultural

[13] This gap, between *de facto* legal standing and a purely *de jure* one, began to enter the sphere of international legal and political understandings of sovereignty with the end of the Cold War. See, for example, Robert H Jackson, *Quasi-States: Sovereignty, International Relations and the Third World* (Cambridge University Press, 1993).

[14] Brian Z Tamanaha, *On the Rule of Law: History, Politics, Theory* (Cambridge University Press, 2004) at 58.

[15] Paola Cesarini & Katherine Hite, 'Introducing the Concept of Authoritarian Legacies' in Katherine Hite and Paola Cesarini, eds., *Authoritarian Legacies Democr Lat Am South Eur* 1 (University of Notre Dame Press, 2004) at 7.

[16] In this context, research projects and, in fact, even entire research institutes (such as the Käte Hamburger Kollege, Centre for Advanced Study, Law as Culture) work on the basis of the need to investigate 'law as culture', see Werner Gephart, *Law as Culture. For a Study of Law in the Process of Globalization from the Perspective of the Humanities* (Frankfurt a. M.: Klostermann, 2011).

understandings appeared to pose a formidable policy challenge. As Augusto Zimmermann notes, with regard to Brazil:

> Indeed, an observation of Brazil's reality reveals a society that is deeply regulated by contra-legem (anti-legal) rules. These are not the rules taught in law schools but rather are socially defined rules that vary remarkably from the state codes and statutes, and the rulings of the courts.[17]

The focus of social constructivist and new institutionalist understandings upon the gap between the formal sphere of law and constitutionalism and the social reality of informal power relations and informal rules established a problematic, but not a way of going beyond it.[18] This attention to cultural differences marked the impasse of the liberal peace framework which shaped international peacebuilding and state-building assumptions in the 1990s. The work of the sociological understanding of constitutionalism and law revealed the shallowness of the state-level or top-down focus of rule of law approaches. In these frameworks, the social reality of countries undergoing democratic or post-conflict legal transition could not be understood merely by an analysis of laws and statutes. In fact, there appeared to be an unbridgeable gap between the surface appearances or artificial constructions of legal and constitutional frameworks and the realities of everyday life, revealed in dealings between individual members of the public and state authorities.

Often this contrast, between the reality of the everyday and the formal framework of law was understood in terms of two opposing spatially-constructed rationalities: that of the 'international' and the 'local'. This clash between the formal and the real has been captured in critical, conceptual approaches which have focused on hybrid outcomes of international interventions which have attempted to transform societies through top-down mechanisms such as legal and constitutional reforms.[19] In the framings of hybridity approaches: 'the "laws" of the

[17] Augusto Zimmermann, 'Rule of Law as a Culture of Legality: Legal and Extra-Legal Elements for the Realization of the Rule of Law in Society, The' (2007) 14 *ELaw J* 10 at 29.

[18] See also, the pessimistic view of Douglass C. North, the policy guru of new institutionalist economics, regarding the difficulties of understanding how exported institutions will interact with 'culturally derived norms of behaviour'; Douglass C North, *Institutions, Institutional Change and Economic Performance* (Cambridge University Press, 1990) at 140.

[19] See, for example, David Roberts, 'Hybrid Polities and Indigenous Pluralities: Advanced Lessons in Statebuilding from Cambodia' (2008) 2:1 *J Interv Statebuilding* 63 at 379–02; Oliver P Richmond, 'A Post-Liberal Peace: Eirenism and the Everyday' (2009) 35:03 *Rev Int Stud* 557 at 557–80; Mac Ginty, *supra* note 1; Richmond & Mitchell, *supra* note 1.

society can easily overrule the laws of the state'.[20] As Zimmermann argues, 'Socially speaking, the former can be far more institutionalised than the latter, which means that the state law can easily be undermined by the lack of connection between its formal precepts and observed behavior'.[21]

These hybrid sociological approaches understood local, national, or community cultures and values as a socially-constructed barrier to the export or development of constitutional frameworks and the rule of law.[22] The discursive framework in which these approaches developed was that of analysing and explaining the limits of external interventions based on liberal understandings. Universalist framings of law were held to fail where societies were understood to be 'non-liberal' and therefore not ready to, or incapable of, organising on the basis of law standing above social and economic conflicts. These barriers to the rule of law were often understood to have deep cultural roots in the colonial era or in the parallel power structures that emerged during internal conflicts and seen to be similarly deep-rooted. It is these deep societal roots that were held to explain the limits of liberal transition and international state-building. As Zimmermann concludes:

> . . .it is impossible to understand the obstacles facing the realization of the rule of law in Brazil if we confine ourselves to a purely legalistic and a less empirical analysis of the legal system. In order to comprehend the reasons for problems blocking the rule of law from taking hold in that society, we must necessarily turn our attention to the many patterns of social behaviour that inhibit normal respect for legal norms and principles.[23]

The framing of socio-cultural norms and understandings as a barrier shifted the emphasis from the formal sphere of rights and law to the informal socio-cultural understandings into which these were deployed.[24] However, while being able to process-trace understandings of these limits to the rule of law backwards into the past, through the

[20] Zimmermann, *supra* note 17 at 29.

[21] *Ibid.* See also, Naomi Mezey who argues that the inter-relationship between law and culture needs concrete ethnographic analysis in each case, 'Law as Culture' (2001) 13 *Yale J L 7* Hum. Available at: http://scholarship.law.georgetown.edu/cgi/viewcontent.cgi?article=1310&context=facpub.

[22] See, David Chandler, 'Promoting Democratic Norms? Social Constructivism and the "subjective" Limits to Liberalism' (2013) 20:2 *Democratization* 215 at 215–39.

[23] Zimmermann, *supra* note 17 at 30.

[24] See further, David Chandler, *International Statebuilding: The Rise of Post-Liberal Governance* (Routledge, 2010).

cultural reproduction of values, societal path dependencies and intersubjective cognitive framings, these approaches offered very little in terms of being able to move forward beyond the impasse of 'culture'.

The exhaustion of these framings can be seen in the 'culture of lawfulness' attempts to transform culture to enable the rule of law. These programmes have been particularly prevalent in frameworks of the war on drugs in Latin America. Heavily funded by the US Government and the World Bank, initiatives led by the US-based NGO the National Strategy Information Centre (NISC) have placed the culture of lawfulness at the centre of the US's global law enforcement strategy. According to US Under-Secretary of State for Global Affairs, Paula Dobriansky: 'Government efforts to enforce the law are insufficient in and of themselves to establish the rule of law in a country. This is a result of the fact that lawlessness and corruption often stem from social norms and historic practices'.[25] For Dobriansky, historic path dependencies and socio-cultural norms meant that the rule of law could not operate universally. She argued therefore that socio-cultural interventions were necessary to educate and win over the 'hearts and minds' of recalcitrant subjects:

The Culture of Lawfulness Project, an international effort fostered by the National Strategy Information Center, has worked aggressively to advance this cause. An NGO that uses public and private funding, the Project has helped a growing number of governments, school systems and civil society leaders to improve public knowledge and attitudes about the rule of law. In culture of lawfulness education, the goal is to reach the next generation of students and through them their parents and communities. Project staff and consultants help teachers develop a lawfulness education program, integrate it into the curriculum, and involve parents and the community in complementary activities. The Project also works with other critical sectors of society, often by offering training. The Project engages representatives from business and labour groups, religious institutions, local non-governmental organisations, and the media.[26]

A typical example is that of the NSIC 'culture of lawfulness' three-year project in the city of Pereira, Columbia, funded from 2008 –10. The project's starting presupposition was that the local culture was a central barrier to the rule of law: 'Prior to this project, rule of law principles had few public advocates and were not well understood by the people of

[25] Paula J Dobriansky, *Promoting a Culture of Lawfulness* (Washington, DC, 2004).
[26] *Ibid.*

Pereira. Apathy and fatalism were the norm for large segments of the population, and many engaged in or tolerated illicit behaviour'.[27] The project started with local knowledge and understandings, developing 'a Pereiran rule of law narrative, locally driven and cognizant of Pereira's unique history, customs and culture' and with the desire of government and civil society leaders to tackle the barriers of the local culture.[28] With the zeal of nineteenth century missionaries, the NSIC attempted to align USAID and local funding, using local knowledge and access to society – at the level of government leaders, civil society organisations, faith groups, local businesses, the media and schools – to initiate awareness of the rule of law, educate and inform and begin to change ingrained patterns of behaviour.

Local culture was to be engaged with on the basis that the locals needed to adapt to and learn about universal liberal understandings of the rule of law:

> ...training judges and prosecutors, rewriting laws, and building investigative facilities for police are not sufficient. To be effective, these efforts need to be accompanied by the development of societal support for rule of law principles. This entails educating citizens about the importance of the rule of law, how it enhances their quality of life, and the role they can play in making it a reality. When education and culture supportive of lawfulness are combined with enhanced law enforcement and institutional reforms, justice and order can be strengthened and crime and corruption reduced – even within one generation. However, reform efforts that do not address the culture at large, neglect a cost efficient, effective, and long-lasting way to deepen democracy.[29]

It was understood that if the barrier of local culture could be successfully overcome, liberal institutions and frameworks could take root 'even within one generation', while reforms that worked at the state and institutional level would be doomed to failure, just remaining at the superficial level of the formal framework and not touching the local reality. To this end, local leaders were encouraged to buy into the programme, and an all-out 'counter-insurgency' campaign was launched to win over the 'hearts and minds' of the community: 'A comprehensive citywide CoL [culture of lawfulness] campaign... touched Pereirans at nearly every point of contact – at school, at work,

[27] National Strategy Information Center, *Fostering a Culture of Lawfulness: Multi-Sector Success in Pereira, Columbia 2008–2010* (2011).

[28] *Ibid.* [29] *Ibid* at 1.

in transit (buses, taxis, billboards), through television/radio/print, at community events and in houses of worship'.[30]

The NISC evaluated their own project very positively, arguing that over the three year period it had a substantial impact on the community 'measured through the degree of the institutionalisation of CoL in long-term community processes, activities and planning as well as significant shifts seen during the program in popular knowledge and attitudes – a foundation of behavioral change'.[31] It is important to note that new institutionalist framings operate at the level of inter-subjective understandings – the empowerment that they offer the local level is that of understanding the importance of the rule of law and their role as active citizens. These cognitive changes then lead to changes in behaviour which enable liberal transformation, facilitating the rule of law:

> A culture of lawfulness guides citizens' relationships with one another and with the state. It can fundamentally alter the dynamics of state institutions, making them more efficient, effective, and just. Lawless behaviour, including corruption, is marginalised as more citizens begin to defend the rule of law and act according to its principles. Law enforcement and justice sector efforts to fight serious crime and corruption are reinforced by ordinary citizens who report crimes, serve as witnesses, and act as a check against corrupt and abusive practices, holding their government accountable for upholding the rule of law and respecting human rights.[32]

Although there is the language of local knowledge and resources, needs and interests and the empowerment of local people, it is clear that the agenda is very much one in which enlightened Western external interveners, equipped with liberal universalist understandings, attempt to transform the barrier of local cultural-social frameworks, through intervening in the inter-subjective understandings of the value and importance of the rule of law regime. Because intervention is consciously aimed at transforming the minds and understanding of local people – and thereby necessarily setting up a hierarchy of understanding – the gap between the external perspective and the 'local' arena becomes clearer the more the international 'empowerment' agenda extends into the society.

This becomes clear in projects such as the comprehensive multi-sectoral campaign considered here. In fact, in reading their report it becomes difficult not to see this work as patronising and demeaning to

[30] *Ibid* at iii. [31] *Ibid.* [32] *Ibid* at 1.

those they are seeking to 'empower'. Examples of good work highlighted in the report include a sixty-hour Culture of Lawfulness course to be taught in schools,[33] encouraging the media to incorporate culture of lawfulness themes into documentaries, soap operas, game and talk shows,[34] therapeutic workshops for citizens to 'give voice to the obstacles and frustrations they face along their 'journey' to a culture of lawfulness',[35] an annual 'Most Legal and Most Safe Neighborhood' competition,[36] culture of lawfulness supported hip hop and rap festivals – including 'The Culture of Lawfulness is an Awesome Challenge' rap contest,[37] public education billboards with personal testimonies concluding with the phrase: 'and YOU, what are YOU going to do for lawfulness?',[38] mime and theatre to discourage speeding and jay walking,[39] pledges for lawfulness by the town mayor in front of primary school children,[40] local Chamber of Commerce prize 'Culture of Lawfulness is my Business',[41] and a Culture of Lawfulness 'paint fest'.[42] Local pastors and lay preachers have even been given manuals on how to introduce rule of law themes into their services.[43] Of course, the paradox is that the more multi-sectoral and comprehensive the culture of lawfulness intervention is, the more artificial and patronising it becomes, while any single activity on its own seems clearly unable to tackle the task at hand, 'to transform an entire culture'.[44]

These approaches were limited by the liberal universalist framings which they explicitly drew upon (and explicitly defended). Here the rule of law was consciously articulated as an external rationality, as somehow the preserve of the West (where, as noted earlier, it was often held that there was no cultural or societal mismatch), meaning that any attempt to artificially construct rule of law regimes, even through 'culture of lawfulness' attempts to transform entire cultures hardly appeared feasible. Even the best and most determined attempts to engage with the 'local', in order to transform cultural values, seemed to fall prey to the problems of 'artificiality' (which had already beset international attempts to export the rule of law through state and institutional level legal and constitutional reforms). Furthermore, no matter how culturally sensitive these interventions were, they still – in fact, inevitably – produced hierarchical understandings, which problematised (even pathologised) local understandings and values, and came across as patronising and neo-colonial.

[33] *Ibid* at 2. [34] *Ibid* at 9. [35] *Ibid* at 11. [36] *Ibid.* [37] *Ibid* at 12; *ibid* at 27.
[38] National Strategy Information Center, *supra* note 27 at 13. [39] *Ibid* at 14.
[40] *Ibid* at 16. [41] *Ibid* at 18. [42] *Ibid* at 24. [43] *Ibid* at 26. [44] *Ibid* at 20.

There are clear limits to attempts to overcome the limits to liberal universalist approaches on the basis of attempts to universalise 'local' socio-cultural understandings. However, the alternative approach to these limits of adapting liberal understandings of legal and constitutional practices to local socio-cultural contexts would appear to be equally problematic. The paradox of liberal legal advocacy is fully highlighted in attempts to defend international intervention, but which deny that local culture will be necessarily seen in these liberal, 'problematic' ways by external interveners. For more critical or radical liberal theorists, intervention needs to be done in more self-reflexive ways, which similarly seek to problematise Western understandings of liberal universality. These critical approaches are often drawn towards pluralist anthropological frameworks in order to develop an ethical methodology of intervention which can break free of the hierarchical understandings explicit in liberal internationalism. Here, the plural and hybrid outcomes of international intervention are seen as positive and to be encouraged. In fact, the experience of intervention, it is alleged, can be a mutual learning exchange between intervener and those intervened upon, as fixed cultural understandings on both sides can be challenged through 'unscripted conversations' and 'the spontaneity of unpredictable encounters'.[45]

The epistemological privileging of 'local' knowledge then becomes the basis of value pluralism, but always from the standpoint of the problems of liberal democracy and universalist approaches to public institutions and the rule of law.[46] The new institutionalist or critical constructivist approach can thereby be understood to operate merely through inverting hierarchical liberal understandings of universal reason.[47] As long as the discourse stays on the level of shared rationalities of spatially differentiated inter-subjective collectivities, both academic and policy discussion remains on the terrain of liberal universalism and value relativism. It is

[45] See, for example, Mark Duffield, *Development, Security and Unending War: Governing the World of Peoples* (Polity, 2007) at 233–4; Richmond, *supra* note 1; Vivienne Jabri, *War and the Transformation of Global Politics [Electronic book]* (Palgrave Macmillan, 2007) at 177.

[46] See, for example, Morgan Brigg, 'Culture: Challenges and Possibilities' in Oliver Richmond, ed., *Palgrave Advances in Peacebuilding. Critical Developments and Approaches* (Palgrave, 2010) at 329–46; Roger Mac Ginty, 'Indigenous Peace-making versus the Liberal Peace' (2008) 43:2 *Coop Confl* 139.

[47] A useful critique of the neoliberal, constructivist and post-structuralist understandings of culture as constructed meaning is David Scott, 'Culture in Political Theory' (2003) 31:1 *Polit Theory* at 92–115.

only in the sphere of practices and strategies in relation to concrete problems that there can be a shift away from spatial constructions to social practices. The 'local' or the 'everyday' then become the focal point, not on the basis of the epistemological differences of liberal reason but on the ontological basis of the practical production of the world.

13.3 The Rise of Resilience

Resilience approaches to the problem do not start from liberal, universalist assumptions of the rational, autonomous subject and are no longer concerned with explaining the limits of liberal universalism or attempting to work on culture to overcome this gap between liberal assumptions and reality. In fact, resilience discourses challenge the liberal discursive construction of 'culture' itself as a fixed or settled spatial community of inter-subjective, constructed meanings.[48] In the world of resilience, few would argue that there is some 'organic' connection between society and law in the liberal West; in fact, the rule of law seems just as alien and 'artificial' in a Western domestic context as it does in the debates on democratic transition and international peacebuilding in the international context.

Legal theorist, Professor Reza Banakar, is typical in drawing upon the radical sociological framings of globalisation theorists, Zygmunt Bauman, Anthony Giddens and Ulrich Beck, to argue that in 'late-,' 'liquid', and 'reflexive' modernity, liberal framings of law no longer have an 'organic' connection to Western societies.[49] In our more fluid, reflexive, transient and networked world, the social institutions and structures - through which the modernist state operated, cohered and legitimated itself – no longer bind communities together through shared frameworks of meaning. Western everyday realities, it appears, also trump any attempts to use the law for purposes of societal regulation: 'Under late modern conditions, where law's normativity can no longer find a durable

[48] As Ann Swindler has noted 'a culture is not a unified system that pushes action in a consistent direction… it is more like a 'tool kit' or repertoire', see Ann Swindler, 'Culture in Action: Symbols and Strategies' (1986) 51:2 *Am Sociol Rev* 273 at 277. See also Victoria E Bonneil & Lynn Hunt, 'Beyond the Cultural Turn: New Directions in the Study of Society and Culture' (1999) *Berkeley U Calif P*, online: http://hrcak.srce.hr/file/52821?origin=publication_detail at 35–61.

[49] Reza Banakar, 'Law and Regulation in Late Modernity' in R. Banakar and M. Travers, eds., *Law and Social Theory* (Hart Publishing). Draft available at: http://papers.ssrn.com/sol3/papers.cfm?abstract_id=2229247.

foothold in fleeting social structures, legal measures aimed at generating new patterns of behaviour or social change grow evermore ineffective'.[50]

It is important to note that, in these approaches, the complexity and fluidity of social practices is highlighted and the spatial dispersal of 'communities' with networked connections which lack a strong sense of shared inter-subjective values. Law fails to connect with society, but not on the basis of the structured or cohered gap between culture(s) and law. In fact, it is possible to argue that the attempts to renegotiate liberal frameworks of representation, in terms of the operation of democratic institutions and legal regimes, on the basis of cultural differences and multiculturalism are precursors to the discussion of governing complexity in terms of resilience.[51] Resilience approaches start from the assumption that there is no 'organic', 'cultural', or inter-subjective construction of community which gives legal frameworks a purchase on social complexity, but do not problematise this. Their concern is with how societal regulation can operate on the basis of fluidity and complexity. As the Stockholm Resilience Centre argues:

> Law is traditionally characterised by 'thou shalts' rather than opening doors for new approaches. As a reaction to this, the concept of reflexive law has emerged. Reflexive law is less rule-bound and recognises that as long as certain basic procedures and organisational norms are respected, participants can arrive at positive outcomes and correct their projects along the way, basically learning by doing. In response to growing complexity, detailed rules are replaced by procedures for regulated entities to follow. Reflexive law is a social innovation which seeks to promote multi-level governance and preserve diversity and experimentation at local level.[52]

Law follows society, but not because there is a clash between liberal universalism and cultural relativism, but because liberal frameworks of law are understood to be the barrier to governing complexity rather than

[50] *Ibid* at 21.

[51] See further, Michael Walzer, *Spheres of Justice: A Defense of Pluralism and Equality* (Basic Books, 1983); Will Kymlicka, *Multicultural Citizenship: A Liberal Theory of Minority Rights* (Cambridge University Press, 1995); James Tully, 'Strange Multiplicity: Constitutionalism in an Age of Diversity' (1995), online: http://philpapers.org/rec/TULSMC; Charles Taylor & others, *Multiculturalism: Examining the Politics of Recognition,* ed. Amy Gutmann (Princeton: Princeton University Press, 1994).

[52] Stockholm Resilience Centre, *What is Resilience: An Introduction to Social-Ecological Research at 14.* Available at:www.stockholmresilience.org/download/18.10119fc11455d3c557d6d21/1398172490555/SU_SRC_whatisresilience_sidaApril2014.pdf

a solution. These approaches share the focus on the local societal milieu of institutionalist or neoliberal debates, but in these framings the milieu is seen as providing the sphere in which transformative agency is generated through practice. In effect, resilience approaches to law repose the problem not in terms of a gap between law and society (or the abstract and the concrete), but in pragmatic terms of specific problems or consequences which can no longer be meaningfully addressed through the mechanisms of law as a guide to practice. It is the internal processes of practical relations and outcomes that need to be understood and worked upon, not the external mechanisms and frameworks which need to be refined.

As Elena Stavrevska notes, in a European Union funded policy brief, instead of problematising the socio-cultural norms and values of people in Bosnia, or a top-down focus on institutional constitutional frameworks and legal settlements, it would be better to focus on the contexts structuring the practical choices of citizens: 'The solution is not to eliminate such individual choices, but to create political, legal and institutional conditions that empower individuals to act on their interests and rights in a socially and politically responsible manner'.[53] The institutional frameworks or the context of choice-making needs to be altered to enable everyday practices and creativity to produce stable and sustainable policy outcomes – here there is neither liberal universalism based on hierarchical judgements of laws and constitutions, nor a cultural relativism suggesting that ordinary people need to be freed from irrational socio-cultural norms and values. This pragmatic approach evades the problems of liberal legal binaries, neither imposing a universal framework over socio-cultural difference, nor recognising or privileging 'local' choices as emancipatory. The problem is the contextual assemblage within which practices take place.

The 'local', or the 'everyday' is understood neither as a product of social and economic structures or fixed ideological and cultural values nor as a barrier or limit, but rather as a set of fluid micro-processes of practices in a constant interaction driven by the agency of ordinary people in concrete circumstances. In this way, 'everyday' life operates across or outside of the structural spatial orderings of critical sociological theory and the homogenising assumptions of top-down understandings of science, law and politics. For the advocates of resilience approaches, it is the 'tactics' of the everyday which constitute the world and its

[53] Elena B Stavrevska, 'Ensuring Political Represen-Tation in a Restructured Bosnia and Herzegovina', online: www.francescoragazzi.com/files/CORE_Policy_Brief_1-2013.pdf.

with can also be argued to undermine such universalist understandings of 'good government'. For many of the states concerned, the focus on law enforcement and drug prohibition 'produces more damage that the drugs themselves'.[61] It is understood that enforcement efforts not only fail to sufficiently reduce the supply and the demand for drugs, but that they also have the unintended consequence of providing illegal criminal gangs with huge profit margins while risking the security of their citizens and the integrity of their democracies. As the OAS report argues:

> ...the main issue is not simply a matter of better policy implementation but the laws and policies themselves, some of which are seen on balance to be producing more costs than benefits... [T]he unintended consequences and costs of such policies include an increased burden on all sectors of the criminal justice and health systems, opportunity costs of enforcement spending, increased risks to individuals and communities associated with drug trade and use, the creation of profit opportunities for organized crime leading to money laundering, corruption, and undermining of democratic institutions, and many other costs. Others see the rigorous enforcement and militarization of drug control, the expansion of state security apparatuses, and other aspects of what used to be called the 'war on drugs' as not being in the best interests of the hemisphere.[62]

The cultural pluralist approach argues that there is no such thing as a universal solution to the drug problem, particularly at the level of formal framings of law, good government and institutional capacity. While drugs might be a problem, using the law to prohibit drug production, transportation and use is also a problem where the socio-cultural context militates against its effective operation or produces even more problematic unintended consequences in the increase of police and paramilitary power. It seems that the paradox of liberal approaches is that the unintended consequences of their adoption appear to be just as problematic as the problems they are intended to resolve. The paradoxes or contradictions of liberal interventionist approaches based on universalist assumptions have of course been well rehearsed in the international peacebuilding and state-building literatures.[63]

Pluralist approaches attempt to escape this paradox through either working to adapt local cultures to the rule of law or (using the same ontological framing, but privileging 'local' rather than 'international'

[61] *Ibid* at 41. [62] *Ibid* at 42.

[63] See, for example, Roland Paris & Timothy D Sisk, *The Dilemmas of Statebuilding: Confronting the Contradictions of Postwar Peace Operations* (Routledge, 2009).

voices) adapting law to the social context. The pluralist approach as portrayed in the OAS report appears to adopt the latter perspective, advocated by the more radical critics of liberal peace,[64] and outlined in the 'Pathways' scenario which rearticulates the drug problem in less universalist terms:

> Problematic drug use is analogous to a chronic condition, like diabetes, which the world has to learn to manage more effectively, while the current policy regime, as managed in too many countries, treats it like a cancer that needs to be surgically removed - even if that means damaging healthy tissue in the process.[65]

The reason for a pluralist approach, it is argued, is that the drug problem and the use of law enforcement to address it cannot be properly grasped outside of the specific cultural-socio-political context:

> ...the international drug control framework may operate well enough for some countries but generates serious problems for others. For example, harms and costs related to drug consumption in the region (loss of productivity, dependency, treatment costs, stress on families) and those related to drug control enforcement are unevenly distributed and do not affect every country in the hemisphere in the same way or to the same extent. Political leaders in some Central and South American countries where there is drug crop cultivation believe that problems of drug-related violence, high homicide rates, insecurity, overcrowded prisons, and human rights violations are made worse or are even largely caused by efforts to prevent the illicit production and trafficking of drugs.[66]

This argument to a certain extent reflects the discussion in the United States where the war on drugs has been seen to be a war on the poor and marginalised (both inside and outside America), and it is argued that the balance needs to be refocused in a more 'emancipatory' way to concerns of human rights, health provision and the development and protection of cultural and indigenous rights.[67]

The cultural pluralist understanding focuses much less on the institutional frameworks and more on the specific cultural context in which the law operates, and in this way seeks to mitigate the unintended

[64] However the challenge to liberal universalist understandings could also be seen as a less emancipatory lowering of expectations, analogous to Merilee S. Grindle's conception of 'good enough governance'. See further Merilee S Grindle, 'Good Enough Governance: Poverty Reduction and Reform in Developing Countries' (2004) 17:4 *Governance* 525 at 525–48; Merilee S Grindle, 'Good Enough Governance Revisited' (2007) 25:5 *Dev Policy Rev* 533 at 553–74.

[65] OAS, *supra* note 11 at 43. [66] *Ibid* at 45. [67] *Ibid* at 47.

consequences of universalist approaches which are understood to cause more harm than good in situations where law enforcement agencies and processes are as much part of the problem as the solution. The location of the solution is shifted downwards to experiment with alternative legal and regulatory frameworks. The most consensual regulatory shift in this regard is experimentation with the decriminalisation of softer drugs such as cannabis and focusing more resources on major criminal networks than on small-scale production and consumption. In this way, resources can be better distributed, lifting the burden on police, prisons and courts as well as reducing the drug market and enabling drugs, which are decriminalised, to be better regulated.

Of course, it should be noted that, in this framing, law is being adapted to the socio-cultural reality rather than making a 'culture of lawfulness' attempt to adapt socio-cultural reality to the law. However, the problems of privileging local culture and values and of adapting law to the reality of the 'local' – the paradox discussed earlier – becomes clear. In relation to the discussion in the US, regarding the decriminalisation of cannabis, the contradictions have been highlighted by critics, such as *Wire* creator David Simon, who have argued that such changes would be just as 'artificial', merely benefiting privileged middle class white adolescents and young adults, while intensifying the criminalisation of poor African-Americans in crack-infested communities.[68] There are clear limits to the capacity of adapting law to local reality, as removing the universal 'detachment' of law from reality leaves the law open to accusations of arbitrariness and cultural relativism. If law really was 'culture', then these accusations would be hard to avoid.

13.4.2 The Resilience Approach

The 'Resilience' approach is notable in that the focus is no longer upon law and its enforcement and instead is placed upon states' 'improved social capital to build community-based approaches, in which the underlying emphasis shifts from treating drug use and related violence as primarily a legal or security matter to responding to the drug problem by strengthening community resilience'.[69] The resilience approach

[68] Ed Vulliamy and Saptarshi Ray, 'David Simon, Creator of The Wire, Says New US drug Laws Help Only "white, middle-class kids"', *The Observer* (25 May 2013), online: www.guardian.co.uk/world/2013/may/25/the-wire-creator-us-drug-laws.

[69] OAS, *supra* note 11 at 20.

locates the problem of drugs as an outcome of complex societal practices, not as something which can be dealt with as a discrete problem to be tackled by law. Rather, 'the drug problem is a manifestation and magnifier of underlying social and economic dysfunctions that lead to violence and addiction'.[70]

It should be clear that not only is the drug problem not a discrete problem to be solved in isolation, resilience approaches, of necessity, construct the drug problem as a matter of community practices and amenable to community solutions. This is well summed up by a quote in the OAS report:

> When television flashed those images of Davis Inlet youth in the Canadian North – some as young as eleven and twelve, huffing gas out of paper bags with their vacant-looking eyes – across our urban TV screens in the 1990s, Canadians immediately understood the problem, and no one figured it to be the gasoline.[71]

In resilience approaches, drug-users and traffickers are less likely to be seen as criminals and as objects of the law and more likely to be understood as potential agents of transformation. The individuals most likely to be involved in the production, trafficking, and consumption of drugs, as well as the communities in which they live, would be subject to interventions designed to use cultural, communal, and informal networks to produce less problematic practices. Rather than intervene coercively to enforce the law or adapt law to the differentiated level of the 'local', resilience approaches seek to use the 'really existing' power of the local community as a transformative mechanism. It is this element of transformative agency that distinguishes resilience approaches from those of liberal top-down approaches which see individuals as objects of law and subject to social engineering, and those of cultural pluralism which understand local cultural-socio-political milieus as barriers to universal frameworks of law, and thereby seek to adapt the law to the circumstances.

As the OAS scenarios report suggests, the resilience approach works directly with – and not against – individuals and communities caught up in the drugs problem:

> The significantly expanded drug and alcohol treatment, harm reduction, screening and early intervention programs, and alternatives to

[70] *Ibid* at 23. [71] *Ibid* at 56.

> incarceration, decriminalization of possession for personal use in most regions, drug treatment courts, probation services, monitoring, and counselling, health services within prisons for drug-dependent users, and restorative justice initiatives involving victims and offenders – all lead to an increased number of people who benefit to such an extent that many of them manage to rebuild their families and work lives. These successes, in turn, impact levels of crime, family cohesion, and community health in a number of areas.[72]

Rather than a cultural pluralist or new institutionalist approach, which emphasises the hold of the past in terms of path dependencies and deep cultural values, resilience approaches argue that everyday settings can be enabling and transformative. As well as focusing on the 'roots' of the problem in terms of those directly involved in the practices of producing, trafficking and consuming drugs, there is also a great deal of attention to the community networks and relationships seen to provide the context for practices. Thereby, resilience responses are:

> . . .supported by the flowering of initiatives in other related fields as well: regional Responsible Fatherhood and Motherhood campaigns, values programs for schools, prison education programs, sports and cultural programs for underprivileged communities, vocational training programs, basic skills for a successful life programs for young, uneducated parents, and community-based policing programs for the region.[73]

The emphasis, as stated, moves away from drugs per se to a focus on resilient people and communities. As the OAS report states, in this framing 'citizens gradually become aware that they are fundamental part of the solution and not just victims of the problem'.[74] With this shift, the focus is no longer on the problem of community understandings and values – the problem is not understood to be 'in the heads' of local people, but in the context shaping the outcomes of their practices. Law is no longer the key framework for measuring success in dealing the with 'drug problem'. Instead, the metrics concern everyday practices from parenting to employment training: 'The paradigm change of focussing on building resilient societies forces people and governments to look inwards for solutions and to acknowledge the need for social reforms'.[75]

[72] *Ibid* at 58. [73] *Ibid.* [74] *Ibid* at 61. [75] *Ibid* at 62.

13.5 Conclusion

Liberal universalist frameworks of constitutionalism, rights protections and the rule of law depend on representational understandings of the universal rational subject, which today are increasingly understood to be too abstract and unreal to frame the governance of socio-cultural complexity, whether domestically or internationally. The formal framework of law, like governments themselves, is understood to be too distant and out of touch with the realities of everyday life. It appears that complexity and socio-cultural diversity makes governance through the rule of law an unwieldy and out-dated framework, too heavily reliant on modernist constructions of social and community cohesion, shared values, and high levels of public engagement. The problem with liberal formal understandings of law is that its ability to adapt to socio-cultural complexity and the perceived fluidity of a globalised and interconnected world is highly limited precisely because of its universalist basis in modern rationalist assumptions.

It could perhaps be argued that fluid conceptions of reflexive law, as articulated by the Stockholm Resilience Centre above, demonstrate that liberal framings can survive the end of universalist approaches to law. However, law loses its liberal moorings in universal understandings of the subject: it is precisely the 'rule' of law over social complexity that is rejected. Law becomes a diverse and plural set of administrative processes where the pragmatic approach of 'learning by doing' takes precedence over law as the product of shared norms and values or as a guide to action and understanding. Liberal modernist framings of law as a mechanism of societal regulation, above the conflicts and differences of the social and economic sphere, depended upon its formal abstraction from the 'reality' of everyday life. Law can rule *over* social complexity and contestation but it cannot rule *through* social complexity.

The shift away from liberal universalist formulations towards the pragmatic philosophy of resilience moves beyond the abstractions of formal frameworks to focus on the 'reality' of the everyday. However, there seems to be little evidence to suggest that reframing international legal interventions without the baggage of liberal universalist understandings will lead to the improved outcomes through 'practical learning', which pragmatist thought seems to promise. Jettisoning liberal concerns with constitutionalism and law does little to clarify accountability for policy failures. At least liberal universalist frameworks forced a discussion of policy accountability on to the agenda and thereby clarified whether failures would be addressed through universalism or cultural relativism: allocating agency and responsibility to either internationals or locals. Pragmatic approaches of resilience seek to blur this accountability, as the focus upon the practices of the 'everyday' allows the insinuation of international intervention into mechanisms of community development in ways which suggest that international-local synergies can be finally achieved through understanding international 'strategy' as dependent for its success upon the agency of local 'tactics'.

BIBLIOGRAPHY

Abdal-Rehim, Abdal-Rahman. "The Family and Gender Laws in Egypt during the Ottoman Period." In *Women, the Family, and Divorce Laws in Islamic History*, edited by Amira El Azhary Sonbol. Syracuse: Syracuse University Press, 1996.

Abel, Richard L. ed. *The Politics of Informal Justice*. 2 Vols. New York: Academic Press, 1982.

Abramowitz, Sharon Alane. *Searching for Normal in the Wake of the Liberian War*. Philadelphia: University of Pennsylvania Press, 2014.

Abu-Lughod, Lila. "Against Universals: The Dialects of (Women's) Human Rights and Human Capabilities." In *Rethinking the Human*, edited by Michelle Molina and Donald K. Swearer. Cambridge MA: Center for the Study of World Religions, Harvard Divinity School, Harvard University Press, 2010.

"Do Muslim Women Really Need Saving? Anthropological Reflections on Cultural Relativism and Its Others." *American Anthropologist* 104, no. 3 (2002): 783–90.

Abu-Odeh, Lama. "Modernizing Muslim Family Law: The Case of Egypt." *V and. J. Transnat'l L.* 37 (2004): 1043.

Acorn, Annalise. *Compulsory Compassion: A Critique of Restorative Justice*. Vancouver: UBC Press, 2004.

"Addresses Delivered at the National Conference on the Causes of Popular Dissatisfaction with the Administration of Justice," 70:79. F. R. D., 1976.

Adjovi, Roland. "Introduction - L'Afrique dans le développement de la justice pénale international." *Afr YB Int'l L* 14 (2006): 3.

Adler, Peter, Karen Lovaas, and Neal Milner. "The Ideologies of Mediation: The Movement's Own Story(1988)." *Law & Policy* 10 (n.d.): 317–39.

Ahmed, Farrah. "Personal Autonomy and the Option of Religious Law." *International Journal of Law, Policy and the Family* 24, no. 2 (2010): 222.

Ahmed, Leila. *Women and Gender in Islam: Historical Roots of a Modern Debate*. New Haven: Yale University Press, 1992.

AIATSIS. *Mediation, Negotiation & Facilitation*, 2013.

Alberstein, Michal. "Forms of Mediation and Law: Cultures of Dispute Resolution." *Ohio St. J. on Disp. Resol.* 22 (2007): 321.

Allen, Carleton Kemp. *Law in the Making*. 6th edn. Vol. 29. Oxford: Clarendon Press, 1958.

Allen, David. *Solid Work You Mob Are Doing: Case Studies in Indigenous Dispute Resolution & Conflict Management in Australia*. National Alternative Dispute Resolution Advisory Council, 2009.

Allen, Tim. "Ritual (Ab) Use? Problems with Traditional Justice in Northern Uganda." In *Courting Conflict? Justice, Peace, and the ICC in Africa*, edited by Nicolas Wadell and Phil Clark, 47–54. London: Royal African Society, 2008.

Alliot, Michel. "La Coutume Dans Les Droits Originellement Africains, Communication Au Congrès de La Société Jean Bodin Sur La Coutume, Bruxelles, 1er-6 Octobre 1984." *Bulletin de Liaison Du LAJP*, January 1985. www.dhdi.free.fr/recherches/theoriedroit/articles/alliotcoutume.doc.

"L'évolution de La Notion de Droit En Afrique." In *Dynamiques et Finalités Des Droits Africains*, edited by Gérard Conac. Paris: Economica, 1980.

Allott, Anthony N. "The People as Law Makers: Custom, Practice, and Public Opinion as Sources of Law in Africa and England." *Journal of African Law* 21, no. 1 (1977): 1–23.

Allott, A. N. "African Law." In *An Introduction to Legal Systems*, edited by J. Duncan and M. Derrett. London: Sweet & Maxwell, 1968.

"Methods of Legal Research into Customary Law." In *Folk Law: Essays in the Theory and Practice of Lex Non Scripta*, edited by A. Dundes Renteln and A. Dundes. University of Wisconsin Press, 1995.

Almog, Shulamit. "Images of Justice or Images of Dissonance: the Sissons-Morrow Collection," paper delivered at the McGill Faculty of Law, 7 October 2005.

Andersen, Chris. "Governing Aboriginal Justice in Canada: Constructing Responsible Individuals and Communities through 'Tradition'." *Crime, Law and Social Change* 31, no. 4 (1999): 303.

Andro, Armelle, and Marie Lesclingand. "Les Mutilations Sexuelles Féminines: Le Point Sur La Situation En Afrique et En France." *Population & Société* 438 (2007): 1.

Anker, Kirsten. *Declarations of Interdependence: A Legal Pluralist Approach to Indigenous Rights*. Farham, Surrey: Ashgate, 2014.

"The Law of the Other: Exploring the Paradox of Legal Pluralism in Australian Native Title," 2008. http://papers.ssrn.com/sol3/papers.cfm?abstract_id=1606967.

"The Law of the Other: Exploring the Paradox of Legal Pluralism in Australian Native Title." In *Dealing with the Other: Australia's Faces and Interfaces*, edited by Pierre Lagayette. Paris: Sorbonne University Press, 2008.

"The Truth in Painting: Cultural Artefacts as Proof of Native Title." *Law Text Culture* 9 (2005): 91.

"Translating Sui Generis Aboriginal Rights in the Civilian Imagination." In *Les Intraduisible En Droit Civil*, edited by Alexandra Popovici, Lionel Smith, and Régine Tremblay. Montreal: Editions Thémis, 2014.

Appadurai, Arjun. "Dead Certainty: Ethnic Violence in the Era of Globalization." *Public Cult* 10, no. 2 (1998): 225.

Appiah, Anthony. "Identity, Authenticity, Survival: Multicultural Societies and Social Reproduction." In *Multiculturalism: Examining The Politics of Recognition*, edited by Amy Gutmann. Princeton: Princeton University Press, 1994.

Arthurs, H. W. "Alternatives to the Formal Justice System: Reminiscing about the Future." In *The Cost of Justice: Papers Prepared for Presentation a the Canadian Institute for the Administration of Justice Conference on the Cost of Justice Held at Toronto on November 14 to 16, 1979*, 1–14. Toronto: Carswell, 1980.

Assier-Andrieu, L. "Coutume et Usage." In *Dictionnaire de La Culture Juridique*, edited by Denis Alland and Stéphane Rials. Paris: Presses universitaires de France, 2003

Astell, Ann W. *Eating Beauty: The Eucharist and the Spiritual Arts of the Middle Ages*. Cornell University Press, 2006.

Atran, Scott, and Douglas Medin. *The Native Mind and the Cultural Construction of Nature*. MIT Press, 2008.

Aubertie, S., et al. *Pertinence et Faisabilité de Dispositifs D'accès et de Partage Des Avantages En Outre-Mer, Portant Sur Les Ressources Génétiques et Les Connaissances Traditionnelles Associées*. Etudes et Documents Du Commissariat Général Au Développement Durable n 48, 2011.

Auerbach, Jerold S. *Justice without Law?* New York: Oxford University Press, 1983.

Augsburger, David W. *Conflict Mediation across Cultures: Pathways and Patterns*. Louisville: Westminster/John Knox, 1992.

Austin, John L. "1995." In *The Province of Jurisprudence Determined*, 1832.

Australian Law Reform Commission. *The Recognition of Aboriginal Customary Laws*, 1986.

Avruch, Kevin. "Culture as Context, Culture as Communication: Considerations for Humanitarian Negotiators." *Harv Negot L Rev* 9 (2004): 391.

Introduction: Culture and Conflict Resolution. Boulder, CO: Paradigm Publishers, 1991.

Avruch, Kevin and Peter W. Black. "ADR, Palau and the Contribution of Anthropology." In *Anthropological Contributions to Conflict Resolution*, edited by Alvin W. Wolfe and Honggang Yang, 47–63. Athens, GA: University of Georgia Press, 1996.

Badran, Margot. *Feminists, Islam, and Nation: Gender and the Making of Modern Egypt*. Princeton: Princeton University Press, 1996.

Bakht, Natasha. "Religious Arbitration in Canada: Protecting Women by Protecting Them from Religion." *Can. J. Women & L.* 19 (2007): 119–44.

Bakhtin, Mikhail M. *The Dialogic Imagination: Four Essays*. Edited by Michael Holquist. Austin: University of Texas Press, 1982.

Banakar, Reza. "Law and Regulation in Late Modernity." In *Law and Social Theory*, edited by Reza Banakar and M. Travers. Oxford: Hart Publishing, 2013.

Bano, Samia. "Muslim Family Justice and Human Rights: The Experience of British Muslim Women." *J. Comp. L.* 2, no. 2 (2007): 1–29.

Muslim Women and Shari'ah Councils: Transcending the Boundaries of Community and Law. New York: Palgrave Macmillan, 2012.

Barlas, Asma. *Believing Women in Islam: Unreading Patriarchal Interpretations of the Qur'an*. Austin: University of Texas Press, 2002.

Barnes, Karen, Peter Albrecht and Maria Olson. *Addressing Gender-based Violence in Sierra Leone: Mapping Challenges, Responses and Future Entry Points*. International Alert, 2007.

Baron, Jane B. "Resistance to Stories." *S. Cal. L. Rev* 67 (1994): 255.

Barrett, Jerome T., and Joseph Barrett. *A History of Alternative Dispute Resolution: The Story of a Political, Social, and Cultural Movement*. San Francisco: Jossey-Bass, 2004.

Barsh, Russel, and James Henderson. "The Supreme Court's Van Der Peet Trilogy: Naive Imperialism and Ropes of Sand (1997)." *McGill Law Journal* 42 (n.d.): 993–1009.

Barton, Roy Franklin. *The Kalingas: Their Institutions and Custom Law*. Chicago: University of Chicago Press, 1949.

Bassel, Leah. "Intersectional Politics at the Boundaries of the Nation State." *Ethnicities* 10, no. 2 (2010): 155–80.

Baxi, Pratiksha. "Access to Justice and Rule-of-[Good] Law: The Cunning of Judicial Reform in India." *Indian J. Hum. Dev.* 2 (2008): 279–302.

Beattie, J. H. M. "Informal Judicial Activity in Bunyoro." *Journal of African Administration* 4 (1957): 188–95.

Becker, Ted. "Conflict and Paradox in the New American Mediation Movement: Status Quo and Social Transformation." *Mo. J. Disp. Resol.*, (1986): 109.

Behrendt, Larissa. *Aboriginal Dispute Resolution*. Sydney: Federation Press, 1995.

Bélair, Karine. "Unearthing the Customary Law Foundations of Forced Marriages during Sierra Leone's Civil War: The Possible Impact of International Criminal Law on Customary Marriage and Women's Rights in Post-Conflict Sierra Leone." *Colum J Gender & L* 15 (2006): 551.

Bell, Catherine. "Indigenous Dispute Resolution Systems within Non-Indigenous Frameworks: Intercultural Dispute Resolution Initiatives in Canada." In *Intercultural Dispute Resolution in Aboriginal Contexts: Land Claims,*

Treaties, and Self-Government Agreements, edited by Catherine Bell and David Kahane, 241–79. Vancouver: UBC Press, 2004.

Bellin, Joshua David. *The Demon of the Continent: Indians and the Shaping of American Literature*. University of Pennsylvania Press, 2011.

Bellucci, Lucia. *Consuetudine, Diritti E Immigrazione. La Pratica Tradizionale Dell'escissione Nell'esperienza Francese*. Milano: Giuffrè, 2012. http://air.unimi.it/handle/2434/219742.

"Escissione e diritto nell'esperienza francese." *d/D il Diritto delle donne* 25 (1999): 20–1, Commissione Pari Opportunità della Regione Emilia-Romagna.

"Immigrazione, Escissione E Diritto in Francia." *Sociologia Del Diritto* 33, no. 3 (2006): 195–98.

"National Support for Film Production in the EU: An Analysis of the Commission Decision-Making Practice." *European Law Journal* 16, no. 2 (2010): 211–32.

Benda-Beckmann, Keebet von. "Folk, Indigenous, and Customary Law." In *International Encyclopedia of the Social and Behavioural Sciences*, edited by N. J. Smelser and P. B. Baltes, 5705–5708. Oxford, Pergamon Press, 2001.

Benhabib, Seyla. *The Claims of Culture: Equality and Diversity in the Global Era*. Princeton University Press, 2002.

Benham, Robert, and Ansley Boyd Barton. "Alternative Dispute Resolution: Ancient Models Provide Modern Inspiration." *Ga. St. UL Rev.* 12 (1996): 623.

Benjamin, Walter. "Critique of Violence." In *Walter Benjamin, Reflections, Essays, Aphorisms, Autobiographical Writings*, edited by Peter Demetz, 277–300. New York: Schocken Books, 1978.

Benveniste, Emile. "Indo-European Language and Society." In *Studies in General Linguistics*, edited by L. R. Palmer and G. C. Lepschy, translated by Elizabeth Palmer, Vol. 1, 368–371. London: Faber Faber, 1969.

Berger, Benjamin L "The Cultural Limits of Legal Tolerance." *Canadian Journal of Law and Jurisprudence* 21, no. 2 (2008): 245–277.

Bergner, Daniel. "The Most Unconventional Weapon." *The New York Times Mag* 26 (2003): 48.

Berman, Jesse. "The Cuban Popular Tribunals." *Columbia Law Review* 69 (1969): 1317–54.

Bhabha, Homi K. *The Location of Culture*. Psychology Press, 1994.

Bhandar, Brenna. "Plasticity and Post-Colonial Recognition: Owning, Knowing and Being." *Law and Critique* 22, no. 3 (2011): 227–49.

Bing, William. "Normative and Legal Pluralism: A Global Perspective." *Duke J. Comp. & Int'l L.* 20 (2009): 473.

Biquard, Anne. "Bouturage, L'initiation Des Femmes." *Nouvelle Revue d'Ethnopsychiatrie* 18 (1991): 153–71.

Black, Ann. "Alternative Dispute Resolution in Brunei Darussalam: The Blending of Imported and Traditional Processes." *Bond Law Review* 13, no. 2 (2001): Article 4.

Blau, Francine D., Marianne A. Ferber, and Anne E. Winkler. *The Economics of Women, Men, and Work*. 3rd edn., 1988.

Blecher-Prigat, Ayelet, and Benjamin Shmueli. "Interplay between Tort Law and Religious Family Law: The Israeli Case, The." *Ariz. J. Int'l & Comp. L.* 26 (2009): 279.

Bleich, David J. "Jewish Divorce: Judicial Misconceptions and Possible Means of Civil Enforcement." *Conn. L. Rev.* 16 (1983): 232.

Bobbio, Norberto. *La Consuetudine Come Fatto Normativo*. Padova: Cedam, 1942.

Bohannan, Paul. "Ethnography and Comparison in Legal Anthropology." In *Law in Culture and Society*, edited by Laura Nader, 401–18. Chicago: Aldine, 1969.

Justice and Judgment among the Tiv. London: Oxford University Press for International African Institute, 1957.

"Law and Legal Institutions." *International Encyclopedia of the Social Sciences* 9 (1968): 73–78.

"The Differing Realms of the Law." *American Anthropologist* 67, no. 6 (1965): 33–42.

Bohannan, P. and R. French. "Legal Anthropology." In *Encyclopedia of Cultural Anthropology*, edited by David Levinson and Melvin Ember, Vol. II. New York: Henry Holt, 1996.

Borrows, John. *Recovering Canada: The Resurgence of Indigenous Law*. Toronto: University of Toronto Press, 2002 at 64.

"Wampum at Niagara: The Royal Proclamation, Canadian Legal History, and Self-Government." In *Aboriginal and Treaty Rights in Canada: Essays on Law, Equality and Respect for Difference*, edited by Michael Asch, 155–72. Vancouver: University of British Columbia Press, 1997.

Borrows, John, and Leonard Rotman. "The Sui Generis Nature of Aboriginal Rights: Does It Make a Difference?" *Alta. L. Rev.* 36, no. 1 (1997): 9–45.

Bourdin, Marie-José. "Les Blancs Ont Dit C'est Pas Bon Pour Les Filles." *Acceuillir* 195 (1994): 34–37.

"'Tu Ne Me Couperas Point'. L'excision Ou L'impossible Compromis." *Migrations-Santé* 70 (1992): 5–7.

Bowen, John. "What Is True and False about UK Sharia Councils." Presented at the RELIGARE Expert Conference: Unregistered Marriages and Alternative Dispute Resolution in European Legal Systems, London: Queen Mary University of London, September 5, 2012.

Boyle, James. "The Politics of Reason: Critical Legal Theory and Local Social Thought." *University of Pennsylvania Law Review* 133 (1985): 685.

Brierley, John EC and Roderick A. Macdonald. *Quebec Civil Law*. Toronto: Emond Montgomery, 1993.

Brigg, Morgan. "Culture: Challenges and Possibilities." In *Palgrave Advances in Peacebuilding: Critical Developments and Approaches*, edited by Oliver Richmond, 329–346. Basingstoke: Palgrave, 2010.

"Governance and Susceptibility in Conflict Resolution: Possibilities beyond Control." *Social & Legal Studies* 16, no. 1 (2007): 27–47.

"Mediation, Power, and Cultural Difference." *Conflict Resolution Quarterly* 20, no. 3 (2003): 287–306.

The New Politics of Conflict Resolution: Responding to Difference. New York: Palgrave Macmillan, 2008.

Broyde, Michael J. *Marriage, Divorce, and the Abandoned Wife in Jewish Law: A Conceptual Understanding of the Agunah Problems in America*. Hoboken, NJ: KTAV Publishing House, Inc., 2001.

Buckley-Zistel, Susanne. "We Are Pretending Peace: Local Memory and the Absence of Social Transformation and Reconciliation in Rwanda." In *Transitional Justice. Post-Conflict Reconstruction and Reconciliation in Rwanda and Beyond*, edited by P. Clark and Z.D. Kaufman, 125–44. New York: Columbia University Press, 2008.

Bueger, Christian. "From Epistemology to Practice: A Sociology of Science for International Relations." *Journal of International Relations and Development* 15, no. 1 (2012): 97–109.

Bunting, Annie. "Theorizing Women's Cultural Diversity in Feminist International Human Rights Strategies." *Journal of Law and Society* 20, no. 1 (1993): 6.

Burelli, Thomas. "La Loi Du Pays Sur La Protection Des Savoirs Traditionnelsde Nouvelle-Calédonie." In *Peuple Premier et Cohésion Sociale En Nouvelle-Calédonie: Identités et Rééquilibrages: Actes Du Colloque Organisé À Nouméa Les 30 et 31 Août 2012 Par La Maison de La Mélanésie-Paul de Deckker*, edited by Jean-Yves Faberon, Thierry Mennesson, and Maison de la Mélanésie. Presses universitaires d'Aix-Marseille, 2012.

"La Nouvelle-Calédonie Face Au Défi de La Mise En Œuvre D'un Dispositif D'accès et de Partage Des Avantages (APA). Premiers Retours de L'expérience Tentée Par La Province Sud." *Revue de La Recherche Juridique: Droit Prospectif* 3 (2011). www.developpementdurable.gouv.fr/IMG/pdf/PPT4-LOUBERSAC-Ifremer-Nlle-Caledonie-etude-cas.pdf.

"La Reconnaissance et de La Protection Des Savoirs Traditionnels Associés À La Biodiversité Dans L'outre-Mer Français: Une Nécessité Jusqu'à Présent Négligée." *Les Cahiers D'anthropologie Du Droit* (2012): 137–62.

Burger, Warren E. "Agenda for 2000 A.D.: Need for Systematic Anticipation." 70:83. F. R. D., 1976.

Burnet, Jennie. "The Injustice of Local Justice: Truth, Reconciliation, and Revenge in Rwanda." In *Transitional Justice: Global Mechanisms and Local Realities after Genocide and Mass Violence*, edited by A. Hinton, 95–118. New Brunswick, NJ: Rutgers University Press, 2011.

Genocide Lives in Us: Women, Memory, and Silence in Rwanda. Madison, WI: University of Wisconsin Press, 2012.

Burchell, Graham et al. *Security, Territory, Population: Lectures at the College de France 1977–1978*. Macmillan, 2009.

Bush, Robert A. Baruch, and Joseph P. Folger. *The Promise of Mediation: Responding to Conflict through Empowerment and Recognition*. San Francisco: Jossey-Bass, 1994.

Butamire, Pan. "Rwanda Still Unfolding." *The New Times*, December 31, 2010.

Butler, Judith. *Gender Trouble*. London and New York: Routledge, 1990.

Caillé, A. "Breve Réponse À Olivier Mongin." *Revue Du MAUSS* 4 (1989): 149–50.

"Notes Sur Les Problèmes Soulevés Par L'excision." *Revue Du MAUSS* 4 (1989): 116–23.

Cammack, Diana, Dinah McLeod, A. Rocha Menocal, and Karin Christiansen. *Donors and the "fragile States" Agenda: A Survey of Current Thinking and Practice*. London: Overseas Development Institute, 2006.

Campbell, Angela. *Sister Wives, Surrogates and Sex Workers: Outlaws by Choice?* Farnham, UK: Ashgate, 2013.

"Wives' Tales: Reflecting on Research in Bountiful." *Canadian Journal of Law and Society* 23 (2008): 121–41.

Campbell, Susanna, David Chandler, and Meera Sabaratnam. *A Liberal Peace?: The Problems and Practices of Peacebuilding*. London: Zed Books, 2011.

Canada Royal Commission on Aboriginal Peoples, *Bridging the Cultural Divide: A Report on Aboriginal People and Criminal Justice in Canada*. The Commission, 1996.

Capdevila, Luc and Danièle Voldman, trans. by Richard Veasy. *War Dead: Western Societies and Casualties of War*. Edinburgh: Edinburgh University Press, 2006.

Carey, Susan. *The Origin of Concepts*. Oxford: Oxford University Press, 2009.

Carroll, Lucy. "Muslim Women and 'Islamic Divorce'in England." *Journal of Muslim Minority Affairs* 17, no. 1 (1997): 97–115.

Cesarini, Paola, and Katherine Hite. "Introducing the Concept of Authoritarian Legacies." In *Authoritarian Legacies and Democracy in Latin America and Southern Europe*, edited by Katherine Hite and Paola Cesarini, 1–24. Notre-Dame: University of Notre-Dame Press, 2004.

Chakravarty, Anuradha. "Surrendering Consent: The Politics of Transitional Justice in Post-Genocide Rwanda." Political Science, Cornell University, 2009.

Chandler, David. *International Statebuilding: The Rise of Post-Liberal Governance.* Vol. 1. London: Routledge, 2010.

"Promoting Democratic Norms? Social Constructivism and the 'subjective'limits to Liberalism." *Democratization* 20, no. 2 (2013): 215–39.

Chanock, Martin. "Customary Law, Sustainable Development and the Failing State." In *The Role of Customary Law in Sustainable Development*, edited by P. Ørebech, F. Bosselman, J. Bjarup, D. Callies, M. Chanock, and H. Petersen. Cambridge: Cambridge University Press, 2005.

Law, Custom and Social Order: The Colonial Experience in Malawi and Zambia. Portsmouth: Heinemann, 1998.

Charsley, Katharine, and Anika Liversage. "Transforming Polygamy: Migration, Transnationalism and Multiple Marriages among Muslim Minorities." *Global Networks* 13 (2013): 60–78.

Chase, Oscar G. *Law, Culture, and Ritual: Disputing Systems in Cross-Cultural Context.* New York: New York University Press, 2005.

Chatterjee, Partha. *The Politics of the Governed: Reflections on Popular Politics in Most of the World.* New York: Columbia University Press, 2004.

Cheng, Chilwin. "Touring the Museum: A Comment on R. v. Van Der Peet"(1997)." *UT Fac. L. Rev.* 55 (n.d.): 419.

Chicoine-Wilson, Charlotte. *La reconnaissance de l'autonomie judiciaire autochtone: regard sur l'expérience colombienne.* LL.M Thesis, University of Ottawa, 2015.

Christie, Gordon. "The Court's Exercise of Plenary Power: Rewriting The Two-Row Wampum." *Supreme Court Law Review* 16 (2002): 285.

Christie, Nils. "Conflicts as Property." *British Journal of Criminology* 17, no. 1 (1977): 1–15.

Clark, Philip. *The Gacaca Courts, Post-Genocide Justice and Reconciliation in Rwanda: Justice without Lawyers.* Cambridge: Cambridge University Press, 2010.

Clark, Philip and Zachary D Kaufman, eds. "After Genocide: Transitional Justice, Post-Conflict Reconstruction and Reconciliation in Rwanda and beyond." In *Rwanda and Beyond.* New York: New York University Press, 2009.

Clarke, Kamari Maxine. *Fictions of Justice: The International Criminal Court and the Challenge of Legal Pluralism in Sub-Saharan Africa.* Cambridge: Cambridge University Press, 2009.

Clemmer, Richard O. *Roads in the Sky: The Hopi Indians in a Century of Change.* Boulder, CO: Westview Press Boulder, 1995.

Clifford, James. "Rearticulating Anthropology." In *Unwrapping the Sacred Bundle Reflections on the Disciplining of Anthropology*, edited by Daniel Segal and Sylvia Yanagisako, 24. Durham: Duke University Press, 2005.

Cobin, David. "Jewish Divorce and the Recalcitrant Husband: Refusal to Give a'Get' as Intentional Infliction of Emotional Distress." *The Journal of Law and Religion* 4, no. 2 (1986): 405–30.

Cohen, Jerome Alan. "Chinese Mediation on the Eve of Modernization." *California Law Review* 54 (1966): 1201–26.

Cohen, Lloyd. "Marriage, Divorce, and Quasi Rents; Or,'I Gave Him the Best Years of My Life.'" *The Journal of Legal Studies* 16, no. 2 (1987): 267–304.

"Marriage: The Long-Term Contract." In *The Law and Economics of Marriage and Divorce*, edited by Antony W. Dnes and Robert Rowthorn, 10. Cambridge: Cambridge University Press, 2002.

Cohn, Margit. "Women, Religious Law and Religious Courts in Israel–The Jewish Case." *Retfaerd [Scandinavian Journal of Social Sciences]* 27 (2004): 57–76.

Coin v. *Mowa*, (Hopie Appellate Court 1996).

Coleman, Jules L. and Scott Shapiro. "The Oxford Handbook of Jurisprudence and Philosophy of Law," 2002. http://philpapers.org/rec/COLTOH.

Colson, Elizabeth. *Social Organization of the Gwembe Tonga*. Manchester: Manchester University Press, 1960.

Comaroff, John. "Colonialism, Culture, and the Law: A Foreword." *Law & Social Inquiry* 26 (2001): 305–14.

Comaroff, John, and Jean Comaroff. *Ethnicity, Inc.* Chicago: University of Chicago Press, 2009.

Commission Law in UK. "Cohabitation: The Financial Consequences of Relationship Breakdown." *Law Com*, no. 307 (2007). http://lawcommission.justice.gov.uk/docs/lc307_Cohabitation.pdf.

Conklin, Beth A. "'Thus are our bodies, thus was our custom': Mortuary Cannibalism in an Amazonian Society." *Am Ethnol* 22, no. 1 (1995): 75.

Connolly, Anthony J. "Cultural Difference on Trial: The Nature and Limits of Judicial Understanding-Introduction." In A. Connolly, *Cultural Difference on Trial: The Nature and Limits of Judicial Understanding*. New York: Ashgate Publishing, 2010, 1–24.

"Cultures, Disciplines, and Differences: Author's Response to Commentators." *Austl. J. Leg. Phil.* 37 (2012): 323.

Naturalised Jurisprudence as an Experimental Philosophy of Law: An Incursion into the Methodology Debate. Forthcoming 2017. "Naturalising Cultural Difference and Law: Author's Introduction." *Austl. J. Leg. Phil.* 37 (2012): 280.

Conseil d'État, Avis N° 385.945, January 24, 2012.

Constable, Marianne. "Law as Language." *Critical Analysis of Law* 1, no. 1 (2014): 63–74.

Coomaraswamy, Radhika. "Identity within: Cultural Relativism, Minority Rights and the Empowerment of Women." *Geo. Wash. Int'l L. Rev.* 34 (1964): 483.

Coons, John E. "Approaches to Court Imposed Compromise-The Uses of Doubt and Reason." *Nw. UL Rev.* 58 (1964): 750.

Cormack, Bradin. *A Power to Do Justice. Jurisdiction, English Literature, and the Rise of Common Law, 1509–1625.* Chicago: University of Chicago Press, 2008.

Cornell, Drucilla. *The Philosophy of the Limit.* London: Routledge, 1992.

Cornut, Étienne. "La Juridicité de La Coutume Kanak." *Droit et Cultures* 60 (2011): 151.

Correy, Simon. "The Reconstitution of Aboriginal Sociality through the Identification of Traditional Owners in New South Wales." *Australian Journal of Anthropology* 17, no. 3 (2006): 336.

Cotran, E. "African Law." In *International Encyclopedia of Comparative Law, Vol. II 'The Legal Systems of the World: Their Comparison and Unification'* edited by R. David. JCB Mohr (Paul Siebeck), 1974, 163.

Coulthard, Glen. "Subjects of Empire: Indigenous Peoples and the 'Politics of Recognition' in Canada." *Contemporary Political Theory* 6 (2007): 437–60.

Cover, Robert M. "Foreword: Nomos and Narrative." *Harv. L. Rev* 97 (1983).

Crampton, Alexandra. "Addressing Questions of Culture and Power in the Globalization of ADR: Lessons from African Influence on American Mediation." *Hamline J. Pub. L. & Pol'y* 27 (2006): 229.

Curtis, Polly. "Family Law Including Divorce and Child Residence Cases Would No Longer Be Eligible for Legal Aid Other than Where Domestic Violence, Forced Marriage or International Child Abduction Is Proven." *The Guardian*, n.d.

D'Almeida, L.D. and et. al., eds. *Reading HLA Hart's' The Concept of Law.* Oxford: Hart Publishing, n.d. Accessed June 25, 2014.

D'Andrade, Roy G. *The Development of Cognitive Anthropology.* Cambridge: Cambridge University Press, 1995.

Daly, Kathleen. "Revisiting the Relationship between Retributive and Restorative Justice." In *Restorative Justice: Philosophy to Practice*, edited by Heather Strang and John Braithwaite, 33–54. Aldershot: Ashgate, 2000.

Daniel, Atkilt, et. al. *Shimgelina (Under the Shade): Merging Ethiopian Wise-Counsel Mediation and Facilitative Mediation: A Training Manual.* Addis Ababa: House of Federation, 2013.

Danzig, Richard. "Toward the Creation of a Complementary, Decentralized System of Criminal Justice." *Stanford Law Review* 26 (1973): 1–54.

Danzig, Richard and Michael J. Lowy. "Everyday Disputes and Mediation in the United States: A Reply to Professor Felstiner." *Law and Society Review* 9 (1975): 675–94.

David, René ed. "Introduction." In *International Encyclopedia of Comparative Law*, Vol. 2. Brill Archive, 1986.

ed. "Introduction." In *The Legal Systems of the World: Their Comparison and Unification*. Tübingen, The Hague, Boston and London: JCB Mohr (Paul Siebeck) & Martinus Nijhoff, 1984.

Davidson, Donald. *Inquiries into Truth and Interpretation*. Oxford: Clarendon Press, 1984.

Davies, Margaret Jane. *Asking the Law Question*. Sydney: Lawbook Co, 1994.

Darian-Smith, E. "Ethnographies of Law." In *The Blackwell Companion to Law and Society*, edited by Austin Sarat. Oxford: Blackwell, 2004.

De Baets, Antoon. "A Declaration of the Responsibilities of Present Generations toward Past Generations." *Hist Theory* 43, no. 4 (2004): 130.

De Lame, Danielle. *A Hill among a Thousand: Transformations and Ruptures in Rural Rwanda*. Translated by H. Arnold. Madison, WI: University of Wisconsin Press, 2005.

De Rosny, Eric. "Justice et sorcellerie en Afrique." *Études – Rev Cult Contemp* 403, no. 9 (2005): 171–175.

De Sousa Santos, Boaventura. *Epistemologies of the South: Justice against Epistemicide*. Paradigm Publishers, 2014.

"Law: A Map of Misreading. Toward a Postmodern Conception of Law." *Journal of Law and Society* 14 (1987): 279.

Toward a New Common Sense: Law, Science and Politics in the Paradigmatic Transition. New York: Routledge, 1995.

Delgamuukw v. *British Columbia*, 3 Supreme Court Reporter 1010 (1997).

Dennett, D. C. *The Intentional Stance*. Cambridge: MIT Press, 1987.

Derrida, Jacques. "Before the Law." In *Acts of Literature*, edited by Derek Attridge, 181. London: Routledge, 1992.

"Force of Law: The Mystical Foundation of Authority." In *Deconstruction and the Possibility of Justice*, edited by M. Rosenfeld, D. G. Carlson, and D. Cornell, translated by M. Quaintance, 3–67. New York: Routledge, 1992.

Limited Inc. Edited by Gerald Graff. Evanston, IL: Northwestern University Press, 1988.

Devitt, Michael, and Kim Sterelny. *Language and Reality: An Introduction to the Philosophy of Language*. Cambridge: MIT Press, 1987.

Dewey, John. *The Later Works, 1925–1953, Volume 4: The Quest for Certainty*. Carbondale, IL: Southern Illinois University Press, 2008.

The Public and Its Problems: An Essay in Political Inquiry. Penn State Press, 2012.

The Quest for Certainty, The Later Works, 1925–1953, Vol. 4: 1929. Carbondale, IL: Southern Illinois University Press, 1984.

Diamond, Stanley. "The Rule of Law versus the Order of Custom." *Social Research* 38 (1971): 42–72.

Dick, Caroline. "Culture and the Courts' Revisited: Group-Rights Scholarship and the Evolution of S. 35 (1)." *Canadian Journal of Political Science* 42, no. 4 (2009): 957–79.

Dickson, Julie. *Evaluation and Legal Theory*. Oxford: Hart Publishing, 2001.

Dobriansky, Paula J. "Promoting a Culture of Lawfulness." Remarks at Georgetown University, Washington, DC, September 13, 2004. http://2001-2009.state.gov/g/rls/rm/2004/37196.htm.

Dodson, Michael. "Power and Cultural Difference in Native Title Mediation." *Aboriginal Law Bulletin* 3, no. 84 (1996): 8.

Dolman, Kevin. "Native Title Mediation: Is It fair?[Condensed Version of a Paper Submitted for Assessment at the University of NSW]." *Indigenous Law Bulletin* 4, no. 21 (1999): 8.

Domestic Proceedings and Magistrates' Court Act 1978, n.d.

Dorff, Elliot N., and Arthur Rossett. *A Living Tree: The Roots and Growth of Jewish Law*. Albany, NY: SUNY Press, 1988.

Dörmann, Knut. *Elements of War Crimes under the Rome Statute of the International Criminal Court: Sources and Commentary*. Cambridge University Press, 2003.

Douglas-Scott, Sionaidh. *Law after Modernity*. Oxford: Oxford University Press, 2013.

Douglas, Gillian "Religious Divorce in the Secular-State: A Case-Study Analysis." Presented at the RELIGARE Expert Conference: Unregistered Marriages and Alternative Dispute Resolution in European Legal Systems, London: Queen Mary University of London, September 5, 2012.

Douglas, Gillian Felicity, Christopher Norman Doe, Sophie Gilliat-Ray, Russell Sandberg, and Asma Khan. *Social Cohesion and Civil Law: Marriage, Divorce and Religious Courts*. Report of a Research Study Funded by the AHRC. Cardiff: Cardiff University, 2011.

Douglas, Mary. *How Institutions Think*. Syracuse University Press, 1986.

Natural Symbols: Explorations in Cosmology. Routledge, 2004.

Purity and Danger: An Analysis of Concepts of Pollution and Taboo. Routledge, 2013.

Douzinas, Costas. "The Metaphysics of Jurisdiction." In *Jurisprudence of Jurisdiction*, edited by Shaun McVeigh. New York: Routledge Cavendish Press, 2007.

Douzinas, Costas and Adam Gearey. *Critical Jurisprudence: The Political Philosophy of Justice*. Oxford: Hart, 2005.

Driberg, Jack Jerbert. "The African Conception of Law." *Journal of Comparative Legislation and International Law* 16 (1934): 230.

De Bouzet, E. *Déclaration Du Chef de Division, Gouverneur Des Établissements Français de l'Océanie, Relative À La Propriété et L'aliénation Des Terres, En Nouvelle-Calédonie et Dépendances.*, 1855.

Dubois, J. "Une Violence Sacralisée, La Judiciarisation de L'excision." In *La Violence et l'Etat. Formes et Évolution D'un Monopole*, edited by Etienne Le Roy and T. V. Trotha. Paris: Editions L'Harmattan, 1993.

Dugan, Emily. "Courts Becoming Clogged as Legal Aid Cuts Affect Separating Couples Seeking Mediation." *The Independent*, January 13, 2014.

Duffield, Mark. *Development, Security and Unending War: Governing the World of Peoples*. Cambridge: Polity Press, 2007.

Dworkin, Ronald. *Law's Empire, 1986*. Oxford: Hart Publishing, 1998.

E.C. "Excision: Un Crime Souvent Impuni." *L'Express*, November 8, 1991, 57.

Eades, Diana. *Language in Evidence: Issues Confronting Aboriginal and Multicultural Australia*. Sydney: UNSW Press, 1995.

Sociolinguistics and the Legal Process. Bristol: Multilingual Matters, 2010.

Eagleton, Terry. *The Idea of Culture*. Oxford: Blackwell, 2000.

Eberhard, Christoph. "Penser Le Pluralisme Juridique de Manière pluraliste–Défi Pour Une Théorie Interculturelle Du Droit." *Cahiers D'anthropologie Du Droit* 2 (2003).

Eggan, Frederick R. *Social Organization of the Western Pueblos*. Chicago: University of Chicago Press, 1950.

El Alami, Dawoud Sudqi, and Doreen Hinchcliffe. *Islamic Marriage and Divorce Laws of the Arab World*. London: Brill, 1996

Emmett, Isabel. *A North Wales Village: A Social Anthropological Study*. London: Routledge & Kegan Paul, 1964.

Encyclopaedia Universalis, 2000. infoscience.epfl.ch/record/3013.

Endicott, T. "The Generality of Law." In *Reading HLA Hart's The Concept of Law*, edited by L. Duarte D'Almeida and et. al. Oxford: Hart Publishing, 2013.

Englund, Harri. *Prisoners of Freedom: Human Rights and the African Poor*. Berkeley: University of California Press, 2006.

Epstein, Joe, and Darby Sais. "Native American Wisdom: Lessons Learned for Mediation." *Preventive L. Rep.* 22 (2003): 27.

Epstein, Louis M. *The Jewish Marriage Contract: A Study in the Status of the Woman in Jewish Law*. Clark, NJ: The Lawbook Exchange Ltd., 2005.

Erlich, Michael. "Notions de Mutilation et Criminalization de L'excision En France." *Droit et Cultures: Revue Semestrielle D'anthropologie et D'histoire* 20 (1990): 151–62.

Erlich, Michel. "Circoncision, Excision et Racisme." *Nouvelle Revue d'Ethnopsychiatrie* 18 (1991): 125–140.

La Femme Blessée: Essai Sur Les Mutilations Sexuelles Féminines. Editions L'Harmattan, 1986.

Esposito, John L., and Natana J. DeLong-Bas. *Women in Muslim Family Law*. Syracuse, NY: Syracuse University Press, 2001.

"Established Usage Having the Force of Law or Right." Accessed October 2, 2013. www.oxforddictionaries.com/definition/english/custom.

Estey, Willard. "Who Needs Courts." *Windsor YB Access Just.* 1 (1981): 263.

Estin, Ann Laquer. "Embracing Tradition: Pluralism in American Family Law." *Md. L. Rev.* 63 (2004): 540.

"Unofficial Family Law." *Iowa L. Rev.* 94 (2008): 449.

Evans, Brad, and Julian Reid. "Dangerously Exposed: The Life and Death of the Resilient Subject." *Resilience* 1, no. 2 (2013): 83–98.

Evans-Pritchard, E. E. *The Nuer: A Description of the Modes of Livelihood and Political Institutions of a Nilotic People.* Oxford: Oxford University Press, 1940.

Faberon, Jean-Yves. *Des Institutions Pour Un Pays: La Nouvelle-Calédonie En Devenir.* Aix : Presses universitaires d'Aix-Marseille, 2012.

Faberon, Jean-Yves, Viviane Fayaud, Jean-Marc Regnault, and R. Lafargue, eds. *Destins Des Collectivités Politiques d'Océanie: Peuples, Populations, Nations, États, Territoires, Pays, Patries, Communautés, Frontières: Actes Du Colloque International Organisé Du 7 Au 10 Mars 2011 À Nouméa*, Vol. 2. Singularités. Aix : Presses universitaires d'Aix-Marseille, 2011.

Faberon, Jean-Yves, and Jacques Ziller. *Droit Des Collectivités d'Outre-Mer.* LGDJ, 2007.

Facchi, Alessandra. *I Diritti nell'Europa Multiculturale: Pluralismo Normativo E Immigrazione.* Roma Bari: Laterza, 2001.

Immigrati, Diritti E Conflitti: Saggi Sul Pluralismo Normativo. Bologna: Clueb, 1999.

"L'escissione: Un Caso Giudiziario." In *Contributi in Tema Di Pluralismo Giuridico*, edited by M. Barisone, L. Graziano, and F. Prina, 36–53. Torino: Università degli Studi di Torino, 1992.

"L'escissione: Un Caso Giudiziario." *Sociologia Del Diritto* 19, no. 1 (1992): 111–19.

"Pratiche Culturali E Sfide Al Diritto: Il Caso Dell'escissione." In *Elementi Di Etica Pratica: Argomenti Normativi E Spazi Del Diritto*, edited by Gianfrancesco Zanetti, Vol. 223. Rome: Carocci, 2003.

Facchi, Alessandra, V. Ferrari, P. Ronfani, and S. Stabile. "Prospettive Attuali Del Pluralismo Normativo Nella Società Multietnica." In *Conflitti E Diritti Nella Società Transnazionale.* Milan: Franco Angeli, 2001.

Fainzang, Sylvie. "Circoncision, Excision et Rapports de Domination." *Anthropologie et Sociétés* 9, no. 1 (1985): 117–27.

"Excision et Ordre Social." *Droit et Cultures* 20 (1990): 177–82.

"L'excision, Ici et Maintenant. Étude Ethnologique." In *Les Mutilations Du Sexe Des Femmes Aujourd'hui En France.* Paris: Tierce, 1984.

Fairbairn, Catherine. *Polygamy.* Home Affairs Section. House of Commons Library: Parliament, July 19, 2012. www.parliament.uk/briefing-papers/sn05051.pdf.

Fanon, Franz. *Black Skin, White Masks.* Translated by Charles Markmann. New York: Grove Press, 1967 at 222.

Farrell, Ian P. "HLA Hart and the Methodology of Jurisprudence." *Tex. L. Rev.* 84 (2006): 983–2135.

Faulkes, Wendy. "The Modern Development of Alternative Dispute Resolution in Australia." *Australian Dispute Resolution Journal* 1 (1990): 61.

Favali, Lyda, and Roy Pateman. *Sangue, Terra E sesso. Pluralismo Giuridico E Politico in Eritrea.* Vol. 43. Milano: Giuffrè Editore, 2007.

Federal Court of Australia. *Solid Work You Mob Are Doing: Case Studies in Indigenous Dispute Resolution & Conflict Management in Australia.* Melbourne: Federal Court of Australia's Indigenous Dispute Resolution & Conflict Management Case Study Project, 2009.

Felstiner, William L.F. "Influences of Social Organization on Dispute Processing." *Law and Society Review* 9 (1974): 63–94.

Ferme, Mariane Conchita. *The Underneath of Things: Violence, History, and The Everyday in Sierra Leone.* University of California Press, 2001.

Ferme, Mariane Conchita and Danny Hoffman, "Hunter Militias and the International Human Rights Discourse in Sierra Leone and beyond." *Afr. Today* 50 (2004): 73.

Filoche, Geoffroy. "Les Connaissances, Innovations et Pratiques Traditionnelles En Matière de Biodiversité: Un Kaléidoscope Juridique." *Droit et Société* 72 (2009): 433–56.

Finnström, Sverker. "Reconciliation Grown Bitter? War, Retribution, and Ritual Action in Northern Uganda." In *Localizing Transitional Justice*, edited by R. Shaw, L. Waldorf, and P. Hazan, 135–56. Stanford: Stanford University Press, 2010.

Fishbayn, Lisa. "Gender, Multiculturalism and Dialogue: The Case of Jewish Divorce." *Can. JL & Jurisprudence* 21 (2008): 80.

Fisher, Eric A. "Community Courts: An Alternative to Conventional Criminal Adjudication." *Am. UL Rev.* 24 (1974): 1253.

Fiss, Owen M. "Against Settlement." *Yale LJ* 93 (1984): 1073.

Fitzpatrick, Peter. "The Impossibility of Popular Justice." *Social & Legal Studies* 1, no. 2 (1992): 199–215.

"The Rise and Rise of Informalism." *Informal Justice* (1988): 178–198.

Foblets, Marie-Claire. "Les délits culturels : de la répercussion des conflits de culture sur la conduite délinquante ; réflexions sur l'apport de l'anthropologie du droit à un débat contemporain." *Droit et cultures* 35, no. 1 (1998): 195–222.

Folger, Joseph. "Harmony and Transformative Mediation Practice: Sustaining Ideological Differences in Purpose and Practice." *NDL Rev.* 84 (2008): 823.

Forced Marriage. Marriage, Civil Partnership and Divorce. GOV.UK, November 8, 2013. www.gov.uk/stop-forced-marriage.

Forced Marriage (Civil Protection) Act 2007, n.d.

Ford, Richard T. "Law's Territory (A History of Jurisdiction)." *Michigan Law Review* 97, no. 4 (1999): 843–930.

Foucault, Michel. *Power/Knowledge: Selected Interviews and Other Writings, 1972–1977*. New York: Random House, 1980.

Security, Territory, Population: Lectures at the College de France 1977–1978. Vol. 4. Basingstoke: Palgrave, 2007.

"Society Must Be Defended": Lectures at the Collège de France, 1975–1976. London: Allen Lane, 2003.

The Essential Works of Foucault, 1954–1984. New York: New Press, 1997.

The History of Sexuality: An Introduction/Transl. from the French by Robert Hurley. New York: Penguin Books, 1984.

Foucault, Michel, Paul Rabinow, and Nikolas S. Rose. *The Essential Foucault: Selections from Essential Works of Foucault, 1954–1984*. New York: New Press, 2003.

Fournier, Pascale. "Calculating Claims: Jewish and Muslim Women Navigating Religion, Economics and Law in Canada." *International Journal of Law in Context* 8, no. 1 (2012): 47–72.

"Halacha, The 'Jewish State' and The Canadian Agunah: Comparative Law at the Intersection of Religious and Secular Orders." *The Journal of Legal Pluralism and Unofficial Law* 65 (2012): 165–204.

Muslim Marriage in Western Courts: Lost in Transplantation. Farnham: Ashgate Publishing Ltd., 2010.

"Secular Portraits and Religious Shadows: An Empirical Study of Religious Women in France." In *Secularism on the Edge: Contemporary Church-State Relations in the United States, France and Israel*, edited by Jacques Berlinerblau. New York: Palgrave Macmillan, 2014

Fournier, Pascale, and Pascal McDougall. "False Jurisdictions: A Revisionist Take on Customary (Religious) Law in Germany." *Texas Inter'l L.J.* 48, no. 3 (2013): 435–63.

Frank, Jerome. *Courts on Trial: Myth and Reality in American Justice*. Princeton: Princeton University Press, 1949.

Fraser, Nancy. *Justice Interruptus: Critical Reflections on the "postsocialist" Condition*. New York: Routledge, 1997.

"Recognition without Ethics?" *Theory, Culture & Society* 18, no. 2–3 (2001): 21–42.

"Rethinking Recognition." *New Left Review* 3 (2000): 107–20.

Frezet, Pierre. "Chronique D'un Jugement Qui Ne Sera Jamais Rendu." *Droit et Cultures. Revue Internationale Interdisciplinaire*, no. 51 (2006): 233–41.

Freeman, M. *Lloyd's Introduction to Jurisprudence*. 8th edn. London: Sweet & Maxwell, 2008.

Friedman, Lawrence M. "The Place of Legal Culture in the Sociology of Law." In *Law & Sociology: Current Legal Issues*, edited by L.M. Friedman, volume 8, chapter 11, 185–199 at 189. Oxford: Oxford University Press, 2006.

Friedrichs, Jörg, and Friedrich Kratochwil. "On Acting and Knowing: How Pragmatism Can Advance International Relations Research and Methodology." *International Organization* 63, no. 3 (2009): 701–31.

Fuchs, Esther. "Jewish Feminist Scholarship: A Critical Perspective." In *14 Studies in Jewish Civilization*, edited by Leonard J. Greenspoon, Ronald A. Simkins, Brian J. Horowitz, and others, 3, no. 225. Omaha, NE: Creighton University Press, 2003.

Fuller, Lon L. "Human Interaction and the Law." *Am J Juris* 14 (1969): 1.

"Mediation–its Forms and Functions." *S. Cal. L. Rev.* 44 (1970): 305.

"Positivism and Fidelity to Law: A Reply to Professor Hart." *Harv Law Rev* (1958): 630.

The Morality of Law. Revised Edition(Second Printing.). Yale University Press, 1969.

Gahamanyi, Bibane Mbaye. "Rwanda: Building Constitutional Order in the Aftermath of Genocide." In *Human Rights under African Constitutions: Realizing the Promise for Ourselves*, edited by A.A. An-Na'im, 252–94. Philadelphia: University of Pennsylvania Press, 2003.

Galanter, Marc. "Lawyers in the Mist: The Golden Age of Legal Nostalgia." *Dick. L. Rev.* 100 (1996): 549.

Garde, François. *Les autochtones et la République*. AJDA, 1999.

Geertz, Armin W. *The Invention of Prophecy: Continuity and Meaning in Hopi Indian Religion*. Berkeley and Los Angeles: University of California Press, 1994.

Geertz, Clifford. *Available Light: Anthropological Reflections on Philosophical Topics*. Princeton University Press, 2001.

Local Knowledge: Further Essays in Interpretive Anthropology. Vol. 5110. New York: Basic Books, 1983.

The Interpretation of Cultures. New York: Basic Books, 1973.

"Thick Description: Toward an Interpretive Theory of Culture." In *The Interpretation of Cultures: Selected Essays*. New York: Basic Books, 1973.

Gephart, Werner. *Law as Culture. For a Study of Law in the Process of Globalization from the Perspective of the Humanities*. Frankfurt am Main: Klostermann, 2010.

Geschiere, Peter and Janet Roitman. *The Modernity of Witchcraft: Politics and the Occult in Postcolonial Africa*. University of Virginia Press, 1997.

Ghislain, Otis. "Les Figures de La Théorie Pluraliste Dans La Recherche Juridique." In *Méthodologie Du Pluralisme Juridique*, 9 (2012), Karthala.

"Opposing Aboriginality to Modernity: The Doctrine of Aboriginal Rights in Canada." *Br J Can Stud* 12, no. 2 (1997): 182.

Gibbs Jr., James L. *Some Judicial Implications of Marital Instability among the Kpelle*. Harvard University, 1960.

Giddens, Anthony. *The Consequences of Modernity*. Cambridge: Polity Press, 1990.

Gilissen, J. ed. "Essai de Synthèse Générale." In *La Coutume-Costume*, 1990.

"La Coutume. Présentation Du Thème et Note Introductive." In *La Coutume-Costume*, edited by J. Gilissen, Vol. LI. Recueils de La Société Jean Bodin Pour L'histoire Comparative Des institutions/Transactions of the Jean Bodin Society for Comparative Institutional Law. Brussels: De Boeck université, 1990.

Gillette, Isabelle. *La Polygamie et L'excision Dans L'immigration Africaine En France Analysées Sous L'angle de La Souffrance Sociale Des Femmes*. Lille: Presses Universitaires Du Septentrion, 1998.

Gillette-Frenoy, Isabelle. "L'excision et Sa Présence En France." *L'Ethnographie* 88, no. 2 (1992): 21–50.

L'excision et Sa Présence En France: Étude Ethno-Sociologique. Paris: Ed. GAMS, 1992.

Giudicelli-Delage, Geneviève. "Excision et Droit Pénal." *Droit et Cultures* 20 (1990): 201–11.

Gluckman, Max. "Concepts in the Comparative Study of Tribal Law." In *Law in Culture and Society*, edited by Laura Nader, 349–73. Chicago: Aldine, 1969.

Custom and Conflict in Africa. Oxford: Basil Blackwell, 1963.

Ideas and Procedures in African Customary Law: Studies Presented and Discussed at the Eighth International African Seminar at the Haile Sellassie I University, Addis Ababa, January 1966. Vol. 8. London: International African Institute, 1969.

Politics, Law and Ritual in Tribal Society. New York: Basil Blackwell, 1965.

The Ideas in Barotse Jurisprudence. Manchester: Manchester University Press, 1965.

The Judicial Process among the Barotse of Northern Rhodesia. Manchester: Manchester University Press for Rhodes-Livingstone Institute, 1955.

Goldberg, Carole E. "Overextended Borrowing: Tribal Peacemaking Applied in Non-Indian Disputes." *Wash. L. Rev.* 72 (1997): 1003.

Goodrich, Peter. "Interstitium and Non-Law." In *Methods of Comparative Law*, edited by Pier Giuseppe Monateri. Cheltenham: Edward Elgar, 2013.

Gopnik, Alison, and Andrew N. Meltzoff. *Words, Thoughts, and Theories*. Cambridge MA: MIT Press, 1997.

Gordon Green, Ross. *Justice in Aboriginal Communities: Sentencing Alternatives*. Saskatoon, SK: Purich Pub., 1998.

"Government's Legal Aid Cuts Will Harm Women and Children, Say National Meeting of Family Barristers." *Family Law Week*, September 19, 2011. www.familylawweek.co.uk/site.aspx?i=ed86242.

Graetz, Naomi. *Unlocking the Garden: A Feminist Jewish Look at the Bible, Midrash and God*. Piscataway, NJ: Gorgias Press LLC, 2005.

Grammond, Sébastien. "L'appartenance Aux Communautés Inuit Du Nunavik: Un Cas de Réception de L'ordre Juridique Inuit?" *Canadian Journal of Law and Society* 23, no. 1–2 (2008): 93–119.

Gray, John Chipman. *The Rule against Perpetuities*. 4th edn. Boston: Little Brown & Co., 1942.

Gray, S. "Monsters Round the Stomping-Ground: An Alternative Dispute Resolution Proposal for Indigenous Communities in the Northern Territory." *Alternative Law Journal* 5, no. 24 (1999): 216–20.

Greenawalt, Kent. "The Rule of Recognition and the Constitution." *Michigan L. Rev.* 85 (1987): 621.

Greenberg-Kobrin, Michelle. "Civil Enforceability of Religious Prenuptial Agreements." *Colum. JL & Soc. Probs.* 32 (1999, 1998): 359.

Griffiths, Anne MO. *In the Shadow of Marriage: Gender and Justice in an African Community*. University of Chicago Press, 1997.

Griffiths, John. "What Is Legal Pluralism?" *The Journal of Legal Pluralism* 24 (1986): 1–55.

Grindle, Merilee S. "Good Enough Governance Revisited." *Development Policy Review* 25, no. 5 (2007): 553–74.

"Good Enough Governance: Poverty Reduction and Reform in Developing Countries." *Governance: An International Journal of Policy, Administration and Institutions* 17, no. 4 (2004): 525–48.

Grose, Peter R. "An Indigenous Imperative: The Rationale for the Recognition of Aboriginal Dispute Resolution Mechanisms." *Mediation Quarterly* 12, no. 4 (1995): 327–38.

"Grotte d'Ouvéa : La République a Été Dévoyée Pour Des Raisons de Basse Politique." *Journal Le Monde*, November 2, 2011.

Guille-Escuret, G. "Le corps du délit et l'exoticisme artificiel: à propos de l'anthropophagie guerrière en forêt centrafricaine." In *Le Corps Humain Supplicié, Possédé, Cannibalisé (Eds)*, edited by Maurice Godelier and Michel Panoff, 109–35. Amsterdam: Editions des archives contemporaines, 1998.

Gulliver, P.H. "Dispute Settlement Without Courts: The Ndendeuli of Southern Tanzania." In *Law in Culture and Society*, edited by Laura Nader, 24–68. Chicago: Aldine, 1969.

"Negotiations as a Mode of Dispute Settlement: Towards a General Model." *Law & Society Review* 7 (1973): 667–91.

Gutmann, Amy ed. *Multiculturalism And "The Politics Of Recognition": An Essay*. Princeton, NJ: Princeton University Press, 1994.

Habermas, Jurgen. *Between Facts and Norms: Contributions to a Discourse Theory of Law and Democracy*. Cambridge: MIT Press, 1998.

"Lifeworld and System: A Critique of Functionalist Reason." In *The Theory of Communicative Action*, translated by T. McCarthy, Vol. 2. Boston: Beacon Press, 1987.

"Reason and the Rationalization of Society." In *The Theory of Communicative Action*, translated by T. McCarthy, Vol. 1. Cambridge: Polity Press, 1984.

Hacohen, Aviad. *Tears of the Oppressed: An Examination of the Agunah Problem: Background and Halakhic Sources*. Edited by Blu Greenberg. Jersey City, NJ: KTAV Publishing House, Inc., 2004.

"Halakhah." *Encyclopaedia Judaica*. New York: Macmillan Co., 1971.

Hahm, Pyong-Choon. "The Decision Process in Korea." In *Comparative Judicial Behavior: Cross-Cultural Studies of Political Decision-Making in the East and West*, edited by Glendon A. Schubert and David Joseph Danelski. New York: Oxford University Press, 1969.

Hale, Robert L. "Coercion and Distribution in a Supposedly Non-Coercive State." *Political Science Quarterly* 38, no. 3 (1923): 470–94.

Halley, Janet, and Kerry Rittich. "Critical Directions in Comparative Family Law: Genealogies and Contemporary Studies of Family Law Exceptionalism." *American Journal of Comparative Law* 58, no. 4 (2010): 753–76.

Halperin-Kaddari, Ruth. *Women in Israel: A State of Their Own*. Philadelphia: University of Pennsylvania Press, 2004.

Hansen, John George. *Cree Restorative Justice: From the Ancient to the Present*. Kanata, Ont.: J. Charlton, 2009.

Harrington, Christine B. "Delegalization Reform Movements: A Historical Analysis." In *The Politics of Informal Justice*, edited by Richard L. Abel, 1:35–71. New York: Academic Press, 1982.

Harrington, Christine B., and Sally Engle Merry. "Ideological Production: The Making of Community Mediation." *Law and Society Review* 22 (1988): 709–35.

Hart, Herbert LA. *The Concept of Law*. 2nd ed. Oxford: Oxford University Press, 1994.

Hartland, Edwin Sidney. *Primitive Law*. London: Methuen, 1924.

Hasan, Khola. Interview, January 23, 2012.

Hauptman, Judith. "Feminist Perspectives on Rabbinic Texts." In *Feminist Perspectives on Jewish Studies*, edited by Lynn Davidman and Shelly Tenenbaum, 40–61. New Haven: Yale University Press, 1994.

Haut, Irwin H. *Divorce in Jewish Law and Life (Studies in Jewish Jurisprudence Volume 5)*. New York: Sepher-Hermon Press, 1983.

Hayek, Friedrich A. *The Constitution of Liberty*. London: Routledge, 1960.

Hegel, G. W. F. *Phenomenology of Spirit (1807)*. Translated by A. V. Miller. Oxford: Oxford University Press, 1977.

Hellum, Anne. "Actor Perspectives on Gender and Legal Pluralism in Africa." In *Legal Polycentricity: Consequences of Pluralism in Law*, edited by H. Petersen and H. Zahle, 1. Dartmouth: Aldershot and Brookfield, 1995.

Henderson, David K. *Interpretation and Explanation in the Human Sciences*. Albany: State University of New York Press, 1993.

Henderson, James (Sakej) Youngblood. "First Nations Legal Inheritances in Canada: The Mikmaq Model." *Man. LJ* 23 (1995): 1–31.

Hendry, Jennifer. "Legal Pluralism and Normative Transfer." In *Order from Transfer: Comparative Constitutional Design and Legal Culture*, edited by Günter Frankenberg. Cheltenham: Edward Elgar, 2013.

Hinton, Alexander Laban ed. *Transitional Justice: Global Mechanisms and Local Realities after Genocide and Mass Violence*. New Brunswick, NJ: Rutgers University Press, 2010.

Hobbes, Thomas. *Leviathan, or the Matter, Forme and Power of a Commonwealth Ecclesiasticall and Civil*. Yale University Press, 1928.

Hobsbawm, Eric. "Introduction: Inventing Traditions." In *The Invention of Tradition*, edited by Eric Hobsbawm and Terrence Ranger, 1–14. Cambridge: Cambridge University Press, 1983.

Hoebel, Edward Adamson. "Law and Anthropology." *Virginia Law Review* 32 (1946): 835–54.

The Law of Primitive Man: A Study in Comparative Legal Dynamics. Cambridge: Harvard University Press, 1954.

Hoffman, Danny. *The War Machines: Young Men and Violence in Sierra Leone and Liberia*. Durham, NC: Duke University Press, 2011.

Honie v. *Hopi Tribal Housing Authority* (Hopi Appellate Court 1998).

Honneth, Axel. *The Struggle for Recognition: The Moral Grammar of Social Conflicts*. Cambridge: Polity Press, 1995.

Honwana, Alcinda. "Healing and Social Reintegration in Mozambique and Angola." In *Roads to Reconciliation*, edited by E. Skaar, S. Gloppen, and A. Suhrke, 83–100. New York: Lexington Books, 2005.

Hoodfar, Homa. "Circumventing Legal Limitation: Mahr and Marriage Negotiation in Egyptian Low-Income Communities." In *Shifting Boundaries in Marriage and Divorce in Muslim Communities*, edited by Homa Hoodfar, Vol. Special Dossier, Volume 1. Gabels, France: Women Living Under Muslim Laws, 1996.

hooks, bell. "Postmodern Blackness." *Postmodern Culture* 1, no. 1 (1990).

Hoque, Ashraf-ul, and Prakash Shah. *Challenges of Religious Accommodation in Family Law, Labour Law and Legal Regulation of Public Space and Public Funding: United Kingdom Socio-Legal Research Report*. Leuven, Belgium: RELIGARE Project, 2012. www.religareproject.eu/system/files/UK%20Report%20on%20fieldwork.pdf.

Horrocks, Russell L. "Alternatives to the Courts in Canada." *Alta. L. Rev.* 20 (1982): 326.

Hosmanek, Andrew J. "Cutting the Cord: Ho'oponopono and Hawaiian Restorative Justice in the Criminal Law Context." *Pepp. Disp. Resol. LJ* 5 (2005): 359.

Howard, George E. *An Introduction to the Local Constitutional History of the United States*. Vol. 1. Baltimore: Publication agency of the Johns Hopkins University, 1889.

Howell, Paul Philip. *A Manual of Nuer Law: Being an Account of Customary Law, Its Evolution and Development in the Courts Established by the Sudan Government*. London: Oxford University Press for International African Institute, 1954.

Howes, David. "Introduction: Culture in the Domains of Law." *Canadian Journal of Law and Society* 20, no. 1 (2005): 9.

Igreja, Victor, and Beatrice Dias-Lambranca. "Restorative Justice and the Role of Magamba Spirits in Post-Civil War Gorongosa, Central Mozambique." In *Traditional Justice and Reconciliation after Violent Conflict: Lessons from African Experiences*, edited by L. Huyse and M. Salter. Stockholm: International IDEA, 2008.

In The Matter of the Estate of Neomi Komaquaptewa (Hopi Appellate Court 2002).

Ingelaere, Bert. "Do We Understand Life after Genocide? Center and Periphery in the Construction of Knowledge in Postgenocide Rwanda." *African Studies Review* 53, no. 1 (2010): 41–59.

"'Does the Truth Pass across the Fire without Burning?' Locating the Short Circuit in Rwanda's Gacaca Courts." *The Journal of Modern African Studies* 47, no. 04 (2009): 507–28.

"Peasants, Power and Ethnicity: A Bottom-up Perspective on Rwanda's Political Transition." *African Affairs* 109, no. 435 (2010): 273–92.

Ingelaere, Bert, L. Huyse, and M. Salter. "The Gacaca Courts in Rwanda." In *Traditional Justice and Reconciliation after Violent Conflict: Learning from African Experiences, Stockholm, Sweden: International Institute for Democracy and Electoral Assistance*, 25–59. IDEA, 2008.

Isabelle, Gillette-Frenoy. "*L'excision et Sa Présence En France.*" Paris: Ed. GAMS, 1992.

Ito, Karen L. "Ho'oponopono,'to Make Right': Hawaiian Conflict Resolution and Metaphor in the Construction of a Family Therapy." *Culture, Medicine and Psychiatry* 9 (1985): 201–17.

Jabri, Vivienne. *War and the Transformation of Global Politics*. Basingstoke: Palgrave Macmillan, 2007.

Jackson, Bernard S. *Making Sense in Law: Linguistic, Psychological and Semiotic Perspectives*. Legal Semiotics Monographs. Liverpool, UK: Deborah Charles Liverpool, 1995.

Jackson, Robert H. *Quasi-States: Sovereignty, International Relations and the Third World*. Cambridge: Cambridge University Press, 1960.

Jackson, Sherman. "Legal Pluralism Between Islam and the Nation-State: Romantic Medievalism or Pragmatic Modernity." *Fordham LJ* 30 (2006): 158–76.

Jacobs, Wilbur. "Wampum: The Protocol of Indian Diplomacy." *William and Mary Quarterly* 6, no. 4 (1949): 596–604.

"James Bay and Northern Quebec Agreement, Complementary Agreement No.18," n.d.

James L., Gibbs. "The Kpelle Moot: A Therapeutic Model for the Informal Settlement of Disputes." *Africa* 33, no. 01 (1963): 1–11.

Jenkins, Morris. "Gullah Island Dispute Resolution An Example of Afrocentric Restorative Justice." *Journal of Black Studies* 37, no. 2 (2006): 299–319.

Johnston, Darlene. "Connecting People to Place: Great Lakes Aboriginal History in Cultural Context." *Ipperwash Inquiry* (2006), online: http://papers.ssrn.com/sol3/papers.cfm?abstract_id=1864900;

Johnstone, Gerry. *Restorative Justice: Ideas, Values, Debates*. 2nd edn. New York: Routledge, 2011.

Jones, Mark L. "The Legal Nature of the European Community: A Jurisprudential Analysis Using HLA Hart's Model of Law and a Legal System." *Cornell Int'l L. J.* 17, no. 1 (1984): 1.

Jones, P. R., and S. Shah. "Arranged Marriages: A Sample Survey of the Asian Case." *Journal of Ethnic and Migration Studies* 8, no. 3 (1980): 339–43.

Jong, De, JPB de Josselin, and Koninklijke Vereeniging. *Customary Law: (a Confusing Fiction)*. Amsterdam: Indisch Instituut, 1948.

Joseph, N. "Jewish Law and Gender." In *2 Encyclopedia of Women and Religion*, edited by Rosemary Skinner Keller and Rosemary Radford Ruether, 576. Bloomington, IN: Indiana University Press, 2005.

Jutras, Daniel. "Legal Dimensions of Everyday Life, The." *Can JL Soc* 16 (2001): 45.

Joyce James, et. al. v. *Ruth Smith* (1998).

Kafka, Franz. *The Trial*. New York: Knopf, 1992.

Kahan, Linda S. "Note, Jewish Divorce and Secular Courts: The Promise of Avitzur." *Geo. LJ* 73 (1984): 193.

Kahn, Paul. *The Cultural Study of Law: Reconstructing Legal Scholarship*. Chicago: University of Chicago Press, 1999.

Kairys, David. *The Politics of Law: A Progressive Critique*. New York: Pantheon Books, 1998.

Kallinen, Timo. "Law Versus Tradition : Human Rights and Witchcraft in Sub-Saharan Africa." In *Normative Pluralism and International Law: Exploring Global Governance*, edited by Jan Klabbers and Touko Piiparinen, 248. Cambridge University Press, 2013.

Kalous, Milan. *Cannibals and Tongo Players of Sierra Leone*. Auckland, 1974.

Kandiyoti, Deniz. "Bargaining with Patriarchy." *Gender & Society* 2, no. 3 (1988): 274–90.

Kaplan, Robert D. "The Coming Anarchy." *The Atlantic* (February 1994), online: www.theatlantic.com/magazine/archive/1994/02/the-coming-anarchy/304670/?single_page=true.

Kaplan, Yehiel S. "Enforcement of Divorce Judgments by Imprisonment: Principles of Jewish Law." *Jewish L. Annual* 15 (2004): 57.

Kasirer, Nicholas. "Legal Education as métissage." *Tul L Rev* 78 (2003): 481.

Kayaoglu, Turan. *Legal Imperialism: Sovereignty and Extraterritoriality in Japan, the Ottoman Empire, and China.* Cambridge: Cambridge University Press, 2010.

Keil, F. C. *Concepts, Kinds, and Cognitive Development, 1989.* Cambridge, MA: MIT Press, 1989.

Kelsall, Tim. *Culture under Cross-Examination: International Justice and the Special Court for Sierra Leone.* Cambridge: Cambridge University Press, 2013.

"Truth, Lies, Ritual: Preliminary Reflections on the Truth and Reconciliation Commmission in Sierra Leone." *Human Rights Quarterly* 27, no. 2 (2005): 361–91.

Kemp, Graham and Douglas P. Fry, eds. *Keeping the Peace: Conflict Resolution and Peaceful Societies around the World.* London: Routledge, 2004.

Kennedy, D. *Critique of Adjudication (fin de Siecle).* Harvard: Harvard University Press, 1997.

Kennedy, Duncan. "Distributive and Paternalistic Motives in Contract and Tort Law, with Special Reference to Compulsory Terms and Unequal Bargaining Power." *Maryland Law Review* 41 (1982): 626.

"Legal Economics of US Low Income Housing Markets in Light of Informality Analysis." *JL Soc'y* 4 (2002): 71.

"The Stakes of Law, or Hale and Foucault." *Legal Stud. F.* 15 (1991): 327.

Kerruish, V. *Jurisprudence as Ideology.* Reason and the Rationalization of Society: Routledge, 1991.

Kessler, Oliver, and Xavier Guillaume. "Everyday Practices of International Relations: People in Organizations." *Journal of International Relations and Development* 15, no. 1 (2012): 110–20.

Khan, Aina. "Aina Khan and Baroness Warsi Kickstart Muslim Marriage Project." *Online: Duncan Lewis Solicitors*, January 13, 2014. www.duncanlewis.co.uk/news/Aina_Khan_and_Baroness_Warsi_kickstart_Muslim_Marriage_Project_(13_January_2014).html#sthash.Ax5r7HgD.I2JzoNKf.dpuf.

"The Way Forward for Islam and English Law." Russell Jones & Walker, London, UK., December 13, 2011.

Kilgour, Maggie. *From Communion to Cannibalism: An Anatomy of Metaphors of Incorporation.* Princeton University Press, 1990.

"Introduction." In *Eating Their Words: Cannibalism and the Boundaries of Cultural Identity*, edited by Kristen Guest. SUNY Press, 2001.

"Review of Cannibals: The Discovery and Representation of the Cannibal from Columbus to Jules Verne by Frank Lestringant." *Coll Lit* 26, no. 1 (1999): 209–11.

Kim Lecoyer, and Barbara Truffin. “Pathways to Family Dispute Resolution within Migrant Families in Belgium.” Presented at the RELIGARE Expert Conference: Unregistered Marriages and Alternative Dispute Resolution in European Legal Systems, London: Queen Mary University of London, September 5, 2012.

Kingsley, Mary H. *West African Studies*. 2nd edn. London: Macmillan, 1901.

Kleinhans, Martha-Marie, and Roderick A. Macdonald. “What Is a Critical Legal Pluralism?” *Can. JL & Soc.* 12, no. 2 (1997): 25.

Korteweg, Anna C. “The Sharia Debate in Ontario Gender, Islam, and Representations of Muslim Women’s Agency.” *Gender & Society* 22 (2008): 434–54.

Kotiswaran, Prabha. *Dangerous Sex, Invisible Labor: Sex Work and the Law in India*. Princeton: Princeton University Press, 2011.

Kottler, C. “‘L’excision En France Est-Elle Une Affaire Judiciaire?’” *Nouvelle Revue d’Ethnopsychiatrie* 18 (1991): 51–56.

Kramer, Xandra Ellen. “Harmonisation of Civil Procedure and the Interaction with Private International Law.” In *Civil Litigation in a Globalising World*, edited by Cornelis H. van Rhee and X. E. Kramer. The Hague: T.M.C. Asser Press, 2012.

Kripke, Saul A. *Naming and Necessity*. Cambridge: Harvard University Press, 1972.

Kroskrity, Paul V. *Language, History, and Identity: Ethnolinguistic Studies of the Arizona Tewa*. Tucson: University of Arizona Press, 1993.

Kuper, Adam. *Culture: The Anthropologists’ Account*. Harvard University Press, 2009.

“Culture, Identity and the Project of a Cosmopolitan Anthropology.” *Man* 29 (1994): 537.

Kuttner, Ran. “From Adversity to Relationality: A Buddhist-Oriented View of Integrative Negotiation and Mediation.” *Ohio St. J. on Disp. Resol.* 25 (2010): 931.

Kuyu, C. “Les Réformes Des Droits Africains de La Famille: Un Projet Juridique Visant Une Hégémonie Culturelle.” In *À La Recherche Du Droit Africain Du XXIe Siècle*, edited by C. Kuyu. Paris: Éditions Connaissances et Savoirs, 2005.

Kymlicka, Will. *Liberalism, Community and Culture*. Oxford: Oxford University Press, 1989 at 163–5.

Multicultural Citizenship: A Liberal Theory of Minority Rights. New York: Oxford University Press, 1995.

Lafargue, Régis. “Dire Le Droit de L’autre : Contribution À Une Approche Réaliste Du Pluralisme Juridique.” In *Les Collectivités Françaises d’Amérique Au Carrefour Des Institutions*, edited by J.-Y. Faberon. Paris: la Documentation française, 2006.

“La ‘voie’ Néo-Calédonienne Pour Sortir de ‘l’enchevêtrement Normatif’: Jeu D’ombres et de Lumières Sur La Coutume.” In *Mondes Océaniens: Etudes En*

L'honneur de Paul de Deckker, edited by J.-Y. Faberon and Hage, A., 57. Paris: L'Harmattan, 2010.

La Coutume Face À Son Destin: Réflexions Sur La Coutume Judiciaire En Nouvelle-Calédonie et La Résilience Des Ordres Juridiques Infra-Étatiques. LGDJ, 2010.

La Coutume Judiciaire En Nouvelle-Calédonie. Aix: Presses universitaires d'Aix-Marseille, 2003.

"Le Préjudice Civilisationnel Pour Atteinte À L'environnement. Droit Au Cadre Naturel et Réalités Socioculturelles: Interdépendances et Interdisciplinarité." *Droit et Société* 1 (2010): 151–169.

"Le Préjudice Collectif Né Du Dommage Environnemental." In *Nomenclature Des Préjudices Environnementaux*, edited by Laurent Neyret and Gilles J. Martin, 193–218. Paris: LGDJ, 2012.

"Les Kanak et La Justice de l'État Aujourd'hui: Du Juge Serviteur de La Loi, Au Juge Gardien Des Promesses." In *Figures de l'État Dans Le Pacifique*, edited by Paul de Deckker. Paris: L'Harmattan, 2006.

Lauterpacht, Hersch. "Law of Nations and the Punishment of War Crimes, The." *Brit YB Intl L* 21 (1944): 58–78.

Lawrence, Sonia. "Cultural (in) Sensitivity: The Dangers of a Simplistic Approach to Culture in the Courtroom." *Can. J. Women & L.* 13 (2001): 107.

Le Roy, É. "L'esprit de La Coutume et L'idéologie de La loi.(Contribution À Une Rupture Épistémologique Dans La Connaissance Du Droit Africain À Partir D'exemples Sénégalais Contemporains)." Presented at the La Connaissance Du Droit En Afrique, Bruxelles, December 2, 1983.

"L'esprit de La Coutume et L'idéologie de La Loi À Travers Quelques Exemples Sénégalais Contemporains." In *La Connaissance Du Droit En Afrique*, edited by J. Vanderlinden. Brussels: Arsom, 1984.

"La Coutume et La Réception Des Droits Romanistes En Afrique Noire." In *La Coutume-Costume*, edited by J. Gilissen, Vol. LI, 1990.

"Norme (en Anthropologie Du Droit)." In *Dictionnaire Encyclopédique de Théorie et de Sociologie Du Droit*, edited by André Jean Arnaud. Paris: Libr. générale de droit et de jurisprudence, 1993.

Le Roy, Étienne and Mamadou Wane. "La Formation Des Droits 'Non-Étatiques.'" In *Encyclopédie Juridique de l'Afrique*, edited by P. F. Gonidec and M. A. Glele, Vol. 1. Dakar: Les Nouvelles Editions Africaines, 1982.

Leach, Edmund Ronald. *Sistemi Politici Birmani: La Struttura Sociale Dei Kachin.* Translated by L. Trevisan. Milano: Franco Angeli, 1979.

Leckey, Robert. "Relational Contract and Other Models of Marriage." *Osgoode Hall Law Journal* 40 (2002): 1–47.

"What Is Left of Pelech?" *Supreme Court Law Review* 41 (2008): 103–29.

Lefeuvre, M. "Le Devoir D'excision." *Revue Du MAUSS* 1 (1988): 65–95.

Legrand, Pierre. "Comparative Legal Studies and the Matter of Authenticity." *J. Comp. L.* 1 (2006): 365.

"Econocentrism." *Univ Tor Law J* 59, no. 2 (2009): 215.

"European Legal Systems Are Not Converging." *Int Comp Law Q* 45 (1996): 52.

"How to Compare Now." *Legal Studies* 16, no. 2 (1996): 232.

"The Impossibility of 'Legal Transplants.'" *Maastricht J. Eur. & Comp. L.* 4 (1997): 111.

Legrand, Pierre and Roderick Munday, eds., *Comparative Legal Studies: Traditions and Transitions*. Cambridge: Cambridge University Press, 2003.

Leiter, Brian. *Naturalizing Jurisprudence: Essays on American Legal Realism and Naturalism in Legal Philosophy*. Oxford: Oxford University Press, 2007.

Lemarchand, René. *Rwanda and Burundi*. New York: Praegar Publishers, 1970.

Lestringant, Frank. *Cannibals: the Discovery and Representation of the Cannibal from Columbus to Jules Verne*. Berkeley: University of California Press, 1997.

Lévi-Strauss, Claude. *Tristes tropiques*. New York: Atheneum, 1974.

Levitt, Laura. *Jews and Feminism: The Ambivalent Search for Home*. New York: Routledge, 1997.

Levy, Yael. "The Agunah and the Missing Husband: An American Solution to a Jewish Problem." *The Journal of Law and Religion* 10, no. 1 (1993): 49–71.

Little Bear, Leroy. "Aboriginal Paradigms: Implications for Relationships in Land and Treaty Making." In *Advancing Aboriginal Claims: Visions/Strategies/Directions*, edited by K. Wilkins, 26–38. Saskatoon, SK: Purich Publishing, 2004.

Liversage, Anika. "Unregistered Marriages in Denmark." Presented at the RELIGARE Expert Conference: Unregistered Marriages and Alternative Dispute Resolution in European Legal Systems, London: Queen Mary University of London, September 5, 2012.

Llewellyn, Jennifer, and Robert L. Howse. "Restorative Justice: A Conceptual Framework." *Law Commission of Canada*, 1998.

Llewellyn, K. N., and E. Adamson Hoebel. *The Cheyenne Way: Conflict and Case Law in Primitive Jurisprudence*. Oklahoma: The University of Oklahoma Press, 1941.

Longman, Timothy. *Christianity and Genocide in Rwanda*. Cambridge: Cambridge University Press, 2010.

"Justice at the Grassroots? Gacaca Trials in Rwanda." In *Transitional Justice in the Twenty-First Century*, edited by N. Roht-Arriaza and J. Mariezcurrena, 206–28. Cambridge: Cambridge University Press, 2006.

Lowy, Michael J. "Modernizing the American Legal System: An Example of the Peaceful Use of Anthropology." *Human Org* 32 (1973): 205–9.

Lubman, Stanley. "Mao and Mediation: Politics and Dispute Resolution in Communist China." *California Law Review* 55 (1967): 1284–1359.

Lucas v. *Hamm* (California Supreme Court 1963).

Lucy, William. *Understanding and Explaining Adjudication*. Oxford: Oxford University Press, 1999.

Luhmann, Niklas. *Social Systems*. Stanford University Press, 1995.

Mac Ginty, Roger. "Indigenous Peace-Making versus the Liberal Peace." *Cooperation and Conflict* 43, no. 2 (2008): 139–63.

International Peacebuilding and Local Resistance: Hybrid Forms of Peace. New York: Palgrave Macmillan, 2011.

Macdonald, Roderick A. "Custom Made—For a Non-Chirographic Critical Legal Pluralism." *Canadian Journal of Law and Society* 26 (2011): 301–27.

"Here, There... and Everywhere. Theorizing Legal Pluralism; Theorizing Jacques Vanderlinden." In *Mélanges Jacques Vanderlinden*, 381. Montreal: Yvon Blais, 2006.

"L'Hypothese Du Pluralisme Juridique Dans Les Societes Democratiques Avancees." *RDUS* 33, no. 1–2 (2002): 133–399.

Lessons of Everyday Law. Montreal: Mcgill-Queen's Press for the School of Policy Studies, Queen's University and the Law Commission of Canada, 2002.

Macdonald, Roderick A. and David Sandomierski, "Against Nomopolies." *N Ir Leg Q* 57 (2006): 610.

MacKinnon, Catharine A. *Feminism Unmodified: Discourses on Life and Law*. Cambridge: Harvard University Press, 1987.

Macklem, Patrick. *Indigenous Difference and the Constitution of Canada*. Toronto: University of Toronto Press, 2001.

Maclean, Mavis and John Eekelaar, eds. *Managing Family Justice in Diverse Societies*. Oñati International Series in Law and Society. Oxford: Hart Publishing, 2013.

Maertens, Jean-Thierry. "Les Mutilations Rituelles En Corps et Toujours." *Droit et Cultures: Revue Semestrielle D'anthropologie et D'histoire* 20 (1990): 163–76.

Majorelle, Michelle. "L'excision des six filles Coulibaly." *Libération* April 15 (1986): 26–7.

Maligne, Pierre. "L'Excision Des Enfants Africains: Politique Du Parquet Général de Paris." *Droit et Cultures* 25 (1993): 139–40.

Malik, Maleiha. *Minority Legal Orders in the UK: Minorities, Pluralism and the Law*. London: The British Academy, 2012.

Malinowski, Bronislaw. "A New Instrument for the Interpretation of Law. Especially Primitive." *Yale Law Journal* 51 (1942): 1237–54.

Argonauts of the Western Pacific: An Account of Native Enterprise and Adventure in the Archipelagoes of Melanesian New Guinea. New York: EP Dutton, 1961.

Crime and Custom in Savage Society. New York: Harcourt Brace, 1926.

"Introduction." In *Law and Order in Polynesia. A Study of Primitive Legal Institutions*, edited by Herbert I. Hogbin. New York: Shoe String Press, 1961.

Manchec, K., A. Somat, and M.-A. Vazel. "L'affaire MC Ruby: L'influence Des Médias Dans Le Déroulement D'un Procès Exemplaire: Un Procès Au Crible Des Sciences Humaines: L'affaire MC Ruby." *Droit et Cultures*, no. 36 (1998): 65–86.

Manderson, Desmond. "From Hunger to Love: Myths of the Source, Interpretation, and Constitution of Law in Children's Literature." *Law Lit* 15, no. 1 (2003): 87–122.

Margolis, Eric and Stephen Laurence, eds. *Concepts: Core Readings*. Cambridge: MIT Press, 1999.

Markell, Patchen. *Bound by Recognition*. Princeton: Princeton University Press, 2003.

Massey, Doreen. *For Space*. London: Sage, 2005.

Mathias, Chauchat. *Les Institutions En Nouvelle-Calédonie*. Centre de Documentation Pédagogique de Nouvelle-Calédonie, 2011.

Mattei, Ugo, and Laura Nader. *Plunder: When the Rule of Law Is Illegal*. Malden, MA: Blackwell, 2008.

May, Thomas Erskine. "Parliament." In *The Encyclopædia Britannica: A Dictionary of Arts, Sciences, and General Literature*. Philadelphia: J.M. Stoddart, 1885.

Mazzeo, I. "Les Aires Marines Protégées de Nouvelle-Calédonie," 1er Colloque Sur Les Aires Marines Protégées : Quelle Stratégie Pour Quels Objectifs?" 2007. www.uicn.fr/IMG/pdf/Les_aires_marines_protegees_de_Nouvelle_Caledonie.pdf.

Mbembe, Achille. "Provisional Notes on the Postcolony." *Africa* 62, no. 01 (1992): 3–8.

McCaslin, Wanda D. *Justice as Healing: Indigenous Ways*. St Paul MN: Living Justice Press, 2005.

McClintock, Anne. *Imperial Leather: Race, Gender, and Sexuality in the Colonial Contest*. New York: Routledge, 1995.

McNay, Lois. *Against Recognition*. Cambridge: Polity Press, 2008 at 10.

McNeil, Kent. "The Onus of Proof of Aboriginal Title." *Osgoode Hall LJ* 37, no. 4 (1999): 775.

McVeigh, Shaun ed. *Jurisprudence of Jurisdiction*. New York: Routledge Cavendish Press, 2007.

Melissaris, Emmanuel. *Ubiquitous Law: Legal Theory and the Space for Legal Pluralism*. Farham, Surrey: Ashgate, 2009.

Melnyk, Andrew. *A Physicalist Manifesto: Thoroughly Modern Materialism*. Cambridge: Cambridge University Press, 2003.

Menkel-Meadow, Carrie. "Exporting and Importing ADR." *Disp. Resol. Mag.* 12 (2005): 5.

"Exporting and Importing ADR: 'I've Looked at Life from Both Sides Now.'" *Disp. Resol. Mag* 12 (2006): 5–8.

"From Legal Disputes to Conflict Resolution and Human Problem Solving: Legal Dispute Resolution in a Multidisciplinary Context." *J Legal Educ* 54 (2004): 7.

"Introduction: What Will We Do When Adjudication Ends? A Brief Intellectual History of ADR." *UCLA L. Rev.* 44 (n.d.): 1613.

"Mothers and Fathers of Invention: The Intellectual Founders of ADR." *Ohio St. J. Disp. Resol.* 16 (2000): 1.

Menski, Werner. "Governance and Governability in South Asian Family Laws and in Diaspora." *The Journal of Legal Pluralism and Unofficial Law* 45, no. 1 (2013): 42–57.

"Angrezi Shariat: Glocalised Plural Arrangements by Migrants in Britain." *Law Vision*, no. 10 (2008): 10–12.

Mernissi, Fatima. *Beyond the Veil: Male-Female Dynamics in Modern Muslim Society*. Bloomington, IN: Indiana University Press, 1985.

Merry, Sally Engle. "Book Review: Disputing Without Culture." *Harvard Law Review* 100 (1987): 2057–63.

"Colonial and Postcolonial Law." In *The Blackwell Companion to Law and Society*, edited by Austin Sarat. Malden, Oxford and Carlton: Blackwell, 2004.

"Everyday Understandings of the Law in Working-Class America." *American Ethnologist* 13 (1986): 253–70.

Human Rights and Gender Violence: Translating International Law into Local Justice. Chicago: University of Chicago Press, 2006.

"Human Rights Law and the Demonization of Culture (and Anthropology along the Way)." *Polar: Political and Legal Anthropology Review* 26, no. 1 (2003): 55.

"Law: Anthropological Aspects." In *International Encyclopedia of the Social & Behavioral Sciences*, edited by Neil J. Smelser and Paul B. Baltes, Vol. 11. Amsterdam: Pergamon, 2001.

"Legal Pluralism." *Law and Society Review* 22 (1988): 869–96.

"Sorting Out Popular Justice." In *The Possibility of Popular Justice: A Case Study of Community Mediation in the United States*, edited by Neal Milner and Sally Engle Merry, 31–66. Ann Arbor: University of Michigan Press, 1995.

"The Social Organization of Mediation in Nonindustrial Societies: Implications for Informal Community Justice in America." *The Politics of Informal Justice* 2 (1982): 17–45.

Meschievitz, Catherine S., and Marc Galanter. "In Search of Nyaya Panchayats: The Politics of a Moribund Institution." In *The Politics of Informal Justice*, edited by Richard L. Abel, 2:47–77. New York: Academic Press, 1982.

Meyer, Jon'a F. "'It Is a Gift from the Creator to Keep Us in Harmony:' Original (vs. Alternative) Dispute Resolution on the Navajo Nation." *International Journal of Public Administration* 25 (2002): 1379–1401.

Mezey, Naomi. In *Cultural Analysis, Cultural Studies, and the Law: Moving Beyond Legal Realism*, edited by Austin Sarat and Jonathan Simon. Durham, NC: Duke University Press, 2003.

Michaels, Ralf. "The Re-State-Ment of Non-State Law: The State, Choice of Law, and the Challenge from Global Legal Pluralism." *Wayne L. Rev.* 51 (2005): 1209.

Miller, Kathleen. "Who Says Muslim Women Don't Have the Right to Divorce?–A Comparison Between Anglo-American Law and Islamic Law." *New York International Law Review* 22 (2009): 201.

Ministère Public v. *Fisdiepas* (Cour d'appel de Nouméa 2009).

Ministry of Justice (UK). *Muslim Marriage: Report of Working Group – Submission*. London: Ministry of Justice, October 11, 2012.

Ministry of Local Government, Good Governance, Community Development, and Social Affairs. Government of Rwanda. *Community Development Policy*, 2008.

Minow, Martha. *Between Vengeance and Forgiveness: Facing History after Genocide and Mass Violence*. Boston: Beacon Press, 1998.

Making All the Difference: Inclusion, Exclusion, and American Law. Ithaca: Cornell University Press, 1990.

Miraglia, Paula, Rolando Ochoa, and Ivan Briscoe. *OECD Development Cooperation Working Paper* 3 (2012).

Mitchell v. *MNR*, 1 Supreme Court Reporter 911 (2001).

Mnookin, Robert H., and Lewis Kornhauser. "Bargaining in the Shadow of the Law: The Case of Divorce." *Yale Law Journal* 88 (1979): 950–97.

Moghissi, Hiadeh. *Feminism and Islamic Fundamentalism: The Limits of Postmodern Analysis*. New York: Zed Books, 1999.

Mohr, Richard D. "Some Conditions for Culturally Diverse Deliberation." *Canadian Journal of Law and Society* 20, no. 1 (2005): 87.

Mongin, O. "L'excision En Procès." *Revue Du MAUSS* 4 (1989): 137–43.

Moore, C. M. "'Why Do We Mediate.' New Directions in Mediation." *Communication Research and Perspectives*, 1994, 265–75.

Moore, Sally Falk. "Certainties Undone: Fifty Turbulent Years of Legal Anthropology, 1949–1999." *Journal of the Royal Anthropological Institute* 7 (2001): 95–116.

Law as Process: An Anthropological Approach. London: Routledge, 1978.

"Law and Social Change: The Semi-Autonomous Social Field as an Appropriate Subject of Study." *Law and Society Review* 7, no. 4 (1973): 719.

Social Facts and Fabrications "Customary" Law on Kilimanjaro, 1880–1980. Cambridge: Cambridge University Press, 1986.

Morrill, Constance. "Show Business and 'Lawfare' in Rwanda: Twelve Years After the Genocide." *Dissent* 53, no. 3 (2006): 14–20.

Morse, Bradford W., and Gordon R. Woodman. "Introductory Essay: The State's Options." In *Indigenous Law and the State*, edited by B. Morse W. and G. R. Woodman, 5–26. Dordrecht: Foris Publications, 1988.

Morse, Bradford W., Gordon R. Woodman, and G. R. Woodman, eds. "How State Courts Create Customary Law in Ghana and Nigeria." In *Indigenous Law and the State*. Dordrecht: Foris Publications, 1987.

Morton, Adam David. "Failed-State Status and the War on Drugs in Mexico." *Glob Dialogue* 13, no. 1 (2011).

"The War on Drugs in Mexico: A Failed State?" *Third World Quarterly* 33, no. 9 (2012): 1631–45.

Motha, Stewart. "MABO-Encountering the Epistemic Limit of the Recognition of Difference." *Griffith L. Rev.* 7, no. 1 (1998): 79–96.

Muller, Sam. "The Triple Helix of Culture, International Law, and the Development of International Law." In *Culture and International Law*, edited by Paul Meerts. Cambridge: Cambridge University Press, 2008.

Murphy, G. L. *The Big Book of Concepts*. Cambridge MA: MIT Press, 2002.

Murphy, Michael. "Culture and the Courts: A New Direction in Canadian Jurisprudence on Aboriginal Rights?" *Canadian Journal of Political Science/ Revue Canadienne de Science Politique* 34, no. 1 (2001): 109–29.

MWA VEE. "À La Recherche Des Savoirs Kanak." *Revue Culturelle Kanak* 40 (2003): 1–68.

Nadasdy, Paul. *Hunters and Bureaucrats. Power, Knowledge, and Aboriginal-State Relations in the Southwest Yukon*. UBC Press, 2003.

Nader, Laura. "A Wide-Angle on Dispute Management." *Willamette Journal of International Law & Dispute Resolution* 10, no. 37 (2002): 37–46.

"An Analysis of Zapotec Law Cases." *Ethnology* 3 (1964): 404–19.

"Civilization and Its Negotiations." In *Understanding Disputes: The Politics of Argument*, edited by Gino Bedani and Pat Caplan, 39–64. London: Bloomsbury Academic, 1995.

"Controlling Processes in the Practice of Law: Hierarchy and Pacification in the Movement to Re-Form Dispute Ideology." *Ohio St. J. on Disp. Resol.* 9 (1993): 1.

Harmony Ideology: Justice and Control in a Zapotec Mountain Village. Stanford: Stanford University Press, 1990.

"Harmony Models and the Construction of Law." In *Conflict Resolution: Cross-Cultural Perspectives*, edited by Kevin Avruch, Peter W. Black, and Joseph A. Scimecca, 41–59. New York: Greenwood Press, 1991.

"Introduction." In *Law in Culture and Society*, edited by Laura Nader. Chicago: Aldine, 1969.

"Pushing the Limits: Eclecticism on Purpose." *Political and Legal Anthropology Review* 22, no. 1 (1999): 106–9.

"The ADR Explosion-The Implications of Rhetoric in Legal Reform." *Windsor Yearbook of Access to Justice* 8 (1988): 269.

"The Anthropological Study of Law." *American Anthropologist* 67, no. 6 (1965): 3–32.

"The Globalization of Law: ADR as Soft Technology," *Am. Soc'y Int'l L. Proc.* 93 (1999): 304.

The Life of the Law: Anthropological Projects. Berkeley: University of California Press, 2002.

Nader, Laura, and Duane Metzger. "Conflict Resolution in Two Mexican Communities." *American Anthropologist* 65 (1963): 584–92.

Nader, Laura, Klaus F., Koch, and Bruce Cox. "The Ethnography of Law: A Bibliographical Survey." *Current Anthropology* 7 (1966): 267–94.

NADRAC. *A Fair Say: Managing Differences in Mediation and Conciliation, a Guide for All Involved.* Canberra, Australia: National Alternative Dispute Resolution Advisory Council, 1999.

Nasir, Jamal J. *The Islamic Law of Personal Status.* 3rd edn. New York: Springer, Arab and Islamic Law Series, 2002.

National Strategy Information Center. *Fostering a Culture of Lawfulness: Multi-Sector Success in Pereira, Columbia 2008–2010*, April 2011.: http://pdf.usaid.gov/pdf_docs/PDACT131.pdf.

Nedelsky, Jennifer. "Embodied Diversity and the Challenges to Law." *McGill LJ* 42, no. 1 (1997): 91.

Law's Relations: A Relational Theory of Self, Autonomy, and Law. New York: Oxford University Press, 2011.

Nee, Ann, and Peter Uvin. "Silence and Dialogue: Burundians' Alternatives to Transitional Justice." In *Localizing Transitional Justice*, edited by R. Shaw, L. Waldorf, and P. Hazan, 157–82. Stanford: Stanford University Press, 2010.

Nelken, David. "Comparative Sociology of Law." In *Introduction to Law and Social Theory*, edited by Reza Banakar and Max Travers. Oxford: Hart, 2002.

"Defining and Using the Concept of Legal Culture." In *Comparative Law: A Handbook*, edited by David Nelken and Esin Örücü, 109, 117–22. Oxford: Hart, 2007.

"Using the Concept of Legal Culture." *Austl J Leg Phil* 29 (2004): 1.

Nelkin, Dorothy and Lori Andrews. "Do the Dead Have Interests? Policy Issues for Research after Life." *American Journal of Law and Medicine* 24, no. 2–3 (1998): 261.

Neocleous, Mark. "Commentary: Resisting Resilience." *Radical Philosophy* 178 (2013): 2–7.

Neumann, Iver B. "Returning Practice to the Linguistic Turn: The Case of Diplomacy." *Millennium-Journal of International Studies* 31, no. 3 (2002): 627–51.

Neves, Marcelo. *Transconstitutionalism.* Oxford: Hart Publishing, 2013.

Newbury, Catharine. "Ethnicity in Rwanda: The Case of Kinyaga." *Africa* 48, no. 1 (1978): 17–29.

Newman, Dwight. "You Still Know Nothin' Bout Me: Toward Cross-Cultural Theorizing of Aboriginal Rights." *McGill LJ* 52 (2007): 725.

Newman Edward, Roland Paris, and Oliver Richmond, eds. *New Perspectives on Liberal Peacebuilding*. New York: United Nations University, 2009.

Nichols, Joel A. "Multi-Tiered Marriage: Ideas and Influences from New York and Louisiana to the International Community." *Vand. J. Transnat'l L.* 40 (2007): 135.

Nicolau, Gilda, Geneviève Pignarre and Régis Lafargue. *Ethnologie juridique: autour de trois exercices*. Paris: Dalloz, 2007.

Nielsen, J. "Islam and Secular Values in Europe: From Canon to Chaos?" In *Religion, Rights and Secular Society: European Perspectives*, edited by Peter Cumper and Tom Lewis. Northampton, MA: Edward Elgar Publishing, 2012.

Niezen, Ronald. "Culture and the Judiciary: The Meaning of the Culture Concept as a Source of Aboriginal Rights in Canada." *Can. JL & Soc.* 18, no. 2 (2003): 1.

Truth and Indignation: Canada's Truth and Reconciliation Commission on Indian Residential Schools. University of Toronto Press, 2013.

Nisak, Catherine. "L'excision une pratique en recul?" *Enfant d'abord* June (1986): 33–44.

North, Douglass C. *Institutions, Institutional Change and Economic Performance*. Cambridge: Cambridge University Press, 1990.

Ntampaka, C. "La Coutume Dans Les Droits Africains Après La Réception Des Droits Romanistes: L'exemple Des Pays d'Afrique Centrale, Le Rwanda et Le Zaïre." In *La Coutume-Costume*, edited by J. Gilissen, Vol. LI, 1990.

Nunn, Kenneth B. "Law as a Eurocentric Enterprise." *Law and Inequality* 15 (1997): 323–71.

Nussbaum, Martha C. *Women and Human Development: The Capabilities Approach*. Vol. 3. Cambridge: Cambridge University Press, 2001.

Nutongla-Sanchez v. *Garcia et al.* (Hopi Appellate Court 1999).

O'Donnell, Marg. "Mediation within Aboriginal Communities: Issues and Challenges." In *Popular Justice and Community Regeneration. Pathways of Indigenous Reform*, edited by Kayleen Hazelhurst, 89–102. Westport, CT: Praeger, 1995.

O'Hear, Anthony. "Culture." In *Routledge Encyclopedia of Philosophy*, edited by Edward Craig. London: Routledge, 1998.

OAS. *Scenarios for the Drug Problem in the Americas 2013–2025*. Washington, DC: OAS, 2013.

Obeyesekere, Gananath. *Cannibal Talk: The Man-Eating Myth and Human Sacrifice in the South Seas*. University of California Press, 2005.

Obrou, Tarek. "Mutilations Sexuelles Ou Mutilations de L'information." *Migrations-Santé* special no. (January 1984): 102–5.

Office for National Statistics (ONS). *Focus on Religion*, October 2004.

Okin, Susan Moller. *Is Multiculturalism Bad for Women?* Edited by Joshua Cohen, Matthew Howard, and Martha C. Nussbaum. Princeton: Princeton University Press, 1999.

Oliver, Kelly. *Witnessing: Beyond Recognition*. Minneapolis: University of Minnesota Press, 2001, 2.

Olsen, Frances E. "The Family and the Market: A Study of Ideology and Legal Reform." *Harvard Law Review* 96 (1983): 1497–578.

ONS. *Table 3.4: Marriages (numbers and Percentages): Type of Ceremony, Denomination and Day of Occurrence*. Marriages Series FM2 No. 29. England and Wales, 2001.

Ørebech, P. "The Linkage between Sustainable Development and Customary Law." In *The Role of Customary Law in Sustainable Development*, edited by Peter Ørebech, Fred Bosselman, Jes Bjarup, David Callies, Martin Chanock, and Hanne Petersen. Cambridge University Press, 2005.

Organization of American States (OAS). *The Drug Problem in the Americas*. Washington, DC: OAS, 2013.

Ortiz, Alfonso. *The Tewa World: Space, Time, Being, and Becoming in a Pueblo Society*. Chicago: University of Chicago Press, 1972.

Osi, Carlo. "Understanding Indigenous Dispute Resolution Processes and Western Alternative Dispute Resolution: Cultivating Culturally Appropriate Methods in Lieu of Litigation." *Cardozo J. Conflict Resol.* 10 (2008): 163.

Otis, Ghislain. "Custom and Indigenous Self-Determination: Reflections on Post-Territoriality." In *Recognition versus Self-Determination: Dilemmas of Emancipatory Politics*, edited by Avigail Eisenberg, Jeremy Webber, Glen Coulthard, Andrée Boisselle, 253. UBC Press, 2014.

"Opposing Aboriginality to Modernity: The Doctrine of Aboriginal Rights in Canada." *British Journal of Canadian Studies* 12, no. 2 (1997): 182–94.

Pageard, R. "A Propos Des Procès D'excision En France." *Droit et Cultures* 25 (1993): 141–42.

Pappas, Caroline. *Law and Politics: Australia's War Crimes Trials in the Pacific, 1943–1961*. University of New South Wales, Australian Defence Force Academy, 1998.

Paris, Roland. *At War's End: Building Peace after Civil Conflict*. Cambridge: Cambridge University Press, 2004.

Paris, Roland and Timothy D. Sisk, eds. *The Dilemmas of Statebuilding: Confronting the Contradictions of Postwar Peace Operations*. London: Routledge, 2008.

Park, Augustine SJ. "Consolidating Peace: Rule of Law Institutions and Local Justice Practices in Sierra Leone." *South African Journal on Human Rights* 24, no. 3 (2008): 536.

Patterson, Dennis ed. *A Companion to Philosophy of Law and Legal Theory*. Oxford: Blackwell Publishing, 1996.

Pavlich, George. *Justice Fragmented: Mediating Community Disputes under Postmodern Conditions*. Psychology Press, 1996.

"The Power of Community Mediation: Government and Formation of Self-Identity." *Law and Society Review* 30 (1996): 707–33.

Pearce, Roy Harvey. *Savagism and Civilization: A Study of the Indian and the American Mind.* University of California Press, 1988.

Pearl, David, and Werner Menski. *Muslim Family Law.* 3rd edn. London: Sweet & Maxwell, 1998.

Peirce, Charles S. *The Collected Papers of Charles Sanders Peirce Vol. 1 Principles of Philosophy*, 1931.

Peller, Gary. "The Metaphysics of American Law." *California Law Review* 73 (1985): 1151–290.

Pether, Penny. "Principles or Skeletons-Mabo and the Discursive Constitution of the Australian Nation." *Law Text Culture* 4, no. 1 (1998): 115–45.

Petrig, Anna. "The War Dead and their Gravesites." *Int Rev Red Cross* 91, no. 874 (2009): 341–3.

Phillips, Anne, and Moira Dustin. "UK Initiatives on Forced Marriage: Regulation, Dialogue and Exit." *Political Studies* 52, no. 3 (2004): 531–51.

Piamenta, Moshe. *Islam in Everyday Arabic Speech.* Leiden: Brill Academic Pub, 1997.

Piccigallo, Philip R. *The Japanese on Trial: Allied War Crimes Operations in the East, 1945–1951.* Austin: University of Texas Press, 1979.

Piet, E. and B. Topuz. *Note À L'attention Des Médecins de Protection Maternelle Infantile et de Planification Familiale. Objet: Conduite À Tenir Pour Lutter Contre Les Mutilations Sexuelles Féminines.* Bobigny: Seine-Saint-Denis. Conseil Général. Direction de l'Enfance et de la Famille. Service de la Protection Maternelle et Infantile, June 20, 2006.

Poland, Jeffrey Stephen. *Physicalism, the Philosophical Foundations.* New York: Oxford University Press, 1994.

Pollak, Robert A. "Gary Becker's Contributions to Family and Household Economics." *Review of Economics of the Household* 1 (2003): 111–41.

"Legal Aid Cuts Will Hit Women the Hardest, Says Justice Department." *The Guardian*, December 26, 2010. www.theguardian.com/law/2010/dec/26/legal-aid-cuts-hit-women-justice.

Poole, Fitz John Porter. "Cannibals, Tricksters, and Witches: Anthropophagic Images among Bimin-Kuskusmin." In *The Ethnography of Cannibalism*, edited by Paula Brown and Donald Tuzin, 6. Washington, DC: Society for Psychological Anthropology, 1983.

Pospisil, Leonard. "Comment." *Human Org* 32 (1973): 211–12.

Pospisil, Leopold J. *Anthropology of Law: A Comparative Theory.* Harper & Row New York, 1971.

Poulter, Sebastian. "Chapter 6: Muslims: The Claim to a Separate System of Personal Law." In *Ethnicity, Law and Human Rights: The English Experience.* Oxford: Oxford University Press, 1999.

English Law and Ethnic Minority Customs. London: Butterworth, 1986.

Pound, Roscoe. "The Causes of Popular Dissatisfaction with the Administration of Justice." *Am. Law* 14 (1906): 445–51.

Postema, Gerald J. "Implicit Law." *Law and Philosophy* 13, no. 3 (1994): 361.

Prinz, Jesse J. *Furnishing the Mind: Concepts and Their Perceptual Basis*. Cambridge, Mass: MIT Press, 2002.

Protocole D'accord Portant Pacte Pour Un Développement Durable Du Grand Sud, 2008.

Provost, R. "Judging in Splendid Isolation." *American Journal of Comparative Law* 56, no. 1 (2008): 125.

"Magic and Modernity in Tintin au Congo (1930) and the Sierra Leone Special Court." *Law Text Culture* 16, no. 1 (2012): 183.

"The International Committee of the Red Widget? The Diversity Debate and International Humanitarian Law." *Israel Law Review* 40, no. 2 (2007): 614.

The Pulitzer Centre Project. Fragile States: The Drug War in Central America, n.d. http://pulitzercenter.org/node/10031/all.

Quiminal, Q. "Les Soninké En France et Au Mali: Le Débat Sur Les Mutilations Sexuelles." *Droit et Cultures* 20 (1990): 183–92.

Quiminal, Catherine. *Gens D'ici, Gens D'ailleurs. Migrations Soninké et Transformations Villageoises*. Paris: C. Bourgois, 1991.

R v. *Bernard Transcripts*, 1999.

R v. *Marshall*; *R* v. *Bernard*, 2 Supreme Court Reporter 220 (2006).

R v. *Sappier*; *R* v. *Gray*, 2 Supreme Court Reporter 686 (2006).

R v. *Van Der Peet*, 2 Supreme Court Reporter 507 (1996).

Rabain, Jacqueline. *L'enfant Du Lignage: Du Sevrage À La Classe D'âge Chez Les Wolof Du Sénégal*. Vol. 50. Paris: Payot, 1979.

Radcliffe-Brown, A. R. "Sanction, Social." In *Encyclopedia of the Social Sciences*. New York: The Macmillan Company, 1934.

Rattray, R. S. *Ashanti Law and Constitution*. Oxford: Clarendon Press, 1929.

Rau, Eric. *Institutions et Coutumes Canaques*. Paris: L'Harmattan rééditions, 2006.

Raulin, Anne. *Femme En Cause: Mutilations Sexuelles Des Fillettes Africaines En France Aujourd'hui. Centre Fédéral (FEN)*, 1987.

"Problemes Éthiques D'une Récherche En Sciences Sociales: L'excision et Sa Présence En France." *Cahiers Internationaux de Sociologie* 88 (1990): 157–71.

Ray, Arthur J. "Native History on Trial: Confessions of an Expert Witness." *Canadian Historical Review* 84, no. 2 (2003): 253.

Raz, Joseph. "Can There Be a Theory of Law." In *Between Theory and Interpretation*. Oxford: Oxford University Press, 2009.

Two Views of the Nature of the Theory of Law: A Partial Comparison." In *Hart's Postscript: Essays on the Postscript to The Concept of Law*, edited by J. Coleman, 249–82. Oxford: Oxford University Press, 2001.

Razack, Sherene. *Casting out: The Eviction of Muslims from Western Law and Politics*. Toronto: University of Toronto Press, 2007.

"The 'Sharia Law Debate'in Ontario: The Modernity/premodernity Distinction in Legal Efforts to Protect Women from Culture." *Feminist Legal Studies* 15, no. 1 (2007): 3–32.

Académie Nationale de Médecine, "Recommandations de l'Académie Nationale de Médecine Visant À L'éradication Des Mutilations Sexuelles Féminines (MSF)." *Supplement Au Bulletin de l'Académie Nationale de Médicine* 188, no. 6 (2004): 122.

Regan, Paulette. *Unsettling the Settler within: Indian Residential Schools, Truth Telling, and Reconciliation in Canada*. Vancouver: UBC Press, 2010.

Reisman, W. Michael. *Law in Brief Encounters*. Yale University Press, 1999.

Reiss, Jonathan and Michael J. Broyde. "Prenuptial Agreements in Talmudic, Medieval, and Modern Jewish Thought." In *Marriage, Sex and Family in Judaism*, edited by Michael J. Broyde and Michael Ausubel, 192. Oxford: Rowman & Littlefield Publishers, 2005.

Reiter, Eric H. "Fact, Narrative, and the Judicial Uses of History: Delgamuukw and beyond." *Indigenous LJ* 8 (2010): 55.

Renteln, Alison Dundes. *The Cultural Defense*. Oxford: Oxford University Press, 2005.

Renteln, Alison Dundes and Alan Dundes. *Folk Law: Essays in the Theory and Practice of Lex Non Scripta*. Madison: University of Wisconsin Press, 1995.

Renteln, Alison Dundes and Marie-Claire Foblets. *Multicultural Jurisprudence: Comparative Perspectives on the Cultural Defense*. Oxford and Portland, Oregon: Hart Publishing, 2009.

Resolution H-12–76 (Hopi Tribe 1976).

Rettig, Max. "Gacaca: Truth, Justice, and Reconciliation in Postconflict Rwanda?" *African Studies Review* 51, no. 3 (2008): 25–50.

Reyntjens, Filip. "Le Gacaca Ou La Justice Du Gazon Au Rwanda." *Politique Africaine* 31 (1990): 31–41.

Pouvoir et Droit Au Rwanda: Droit Public et Évolution Politique, 1916–1973. Tervuren, Belgique: Musée royal de l'Afrique centrale, 1985.

Reyntjens, Filip, and Stef Vandeginste. "Rwanda: An Atypical Transition." In *Roads to Reconciliation*, edited by E. Skaar, S. Gloppen, and A. Suhrke, 101:101–27. New York: Lexington Books, 2005.

Richards, Paul. "Chimpanzees, Diamonds and War: The Discourses of Global Environmental Change and Local Violence on the Liberia-Sierra Leone Border." In *The Future of Anthropological Knowledge*, edited by Henrietta L. Moore, 139. London: Routledge, 1996.

Fighting for the Rain Forest: War, Youth & Resources in Sierra Leone. International African Institute, 1996.

Richland, Justin B. *Arguing with Tradition: The Language of Law in Hopi Tribal Court*. Chicago: University of Chicago Press, 2008.

"Hopi Tradition as Jurisdiction: On the Potentializing Limits of Hopi Sovereignty." *Law & Social Inquiry* 36, no. 1 (2011): 201–34.

"Jurisdiction: Grounding Law in Language." *Annual Review of Anthropology* 42 (2013): 209–26.

"Pragmatic Paradoxes and Ironies of Indigeneity." *American Ethnologist* 34, no. 3 (2007): 540–58.

"The Multiple Calculi of Meaning." *Discourse & Society* 17, no. 1 (2006): 65–97.

"The State of Hopi Exception: When Inheritance Is What You Have." *Law & Literature* 20, no. 2 (2008): 261–78.

"'What Are You Going to Do with the Village's Knowledge?' Talking Tradition, Talking Law in Hopi Tribal Court." *Law and Society Review* 39 (2005): 235–71.

Richmond, Oliver. *A Post-Liberal Peace*. London: Routledge, 2011.

"A Post-Liberal Peace: Eirenism and the Everyday." *Review of International Studies* 35, no. 03 (2009): 557–80.

"Becoming Liberal, Unbecoming Liberalism: Liberal-Local Hybridity via the Everyday as a Response to the Paradoxes of Liberal Peacebuilding." *Journal of Intervention and Statebuilding* 3, no. 3 (2009): 324–44.

"Resistance and the Post-Liberal Peace." *Millennium-Journal of International Studies* 38 (2010): 665–692.

Richmond, Oliver and Audra Mitchell. *Hybrid Forms of Peace: From Everyday Agency to Post-Liberalism*. Basingstoke: Palgrave Macmillan, 2011.

Richstone, J. "The Inuit and Customary Law: Constitutional Perspectives." In *Indigenous Law and the State*, edited by B. W. Morse and G. R. Woodman. Dordrecht: Foris, 1987.

Ricoeur, Paul. *Freud and Philosophy; an Essay on Interpretation*. Translated by Denis Savage. New Haven: Yale University Press, 1970.

The Course of Recognition. Translated by David Pellauer. Harvard: Harvard University Press, 2005.

Riles, Annelise. "Anthropology, Human Rights, and Legal Knowledge." *American Anthropologist* 108, no. 1 (2006): 52–65.

"Anthropology, Human Rights, and Legal Knowledge: Culture in the Iron Cage." *American Anthropologist* 108 (2006): 108.

"Representing in-between: Law, Anthropology, and the Rhetoric of Interdisciplinary." *U Ill L Rev* (1994): 597.

Riskin, Leonard L. "Mediation and Lawyers." *Ohio St. LJ* 43 (1982): 29–60.

Roberts, David. "Hybrid Polities and Indigenous Pluralities: Advanced Lessons in Statebuilding from Cambodia." *Journal of Intervention and Statebuilding* 1, no. 3 (2007): 379–402.

Roberts, S. "Culture Juridique Africain. I. Nature de L'ordre Juridique En Afrique." In *Dictionnaire Encyclopédique de Théorie et de Sociologie Du Droit*, edited by André Jean Arnaud. Paris: Libr. générale de droit et de jurisprudence, 1993.

"The Recording of Customary Law. Some Problems of Method." In *Folk Law: Essays in the Theory and Practice of Lex Non Scripta*, edited by A. Dundes Renteln and A. Dundes, Vol. 1. New York and London: Garland, 1994.

Rodon, Thierry. *En partenariat avec l'État: les expériences de co-gestion des Autochtones du Canada*. Presses Universitaires de Laval, 2003.

Rohe, Mathias. "On the Applicability of Islamic Rules in Germany and Europe." *European Yearbook of Minority Issues* 3 (April 2003): 181.

Röling, Bernard Victor Aloysius and C. F. Rüter, eds., *The Tokyo Judgment: The International Military Tribunal for the Far East Majority Judgment* (IMTFE), 29 April 1946–12 November 1948, Volume I. Amsterdam: APA-University Press Amsterdam, 1977.

Romano, Cesare P. R., P. A. Nollkaemper and Jann K. Kleffner, *Internationalized Criminal Courts and Tribunals. Sierra Leone, East-Timor, Kosovo and Cambodia*. Oxford University Press, 2004.

Rose, Laurel. "Are Alternative Dispute Resolution (ADR) Programs Suitable for Africa." *Africa Notes* September (1996): 5–7.

Rosen, Lawrence. *Law as Culture: An Invitation*. Princeton: Princeton University Press, 2006.

Rosenberg, Maurice. "Devising Procedures That Are Civil to Promote Justice That Is Civilized." *Michigan Law Review* 69 (1971): 797–820.

Rosenblatt, Adam. "International Forensic Investigations and the Human Rights of the Dead." *Hum Rights Q* 32, no. 4 (2010): 921–941.

Rosenfeld, Esther. "Jewish Divorce Law." *U.C.Davis J.Int'l L. & Pol'y* 1 (1995): 147.

Ross, Tamar. *Expanding the Palace of Torah: Orthodoxy and Feminism*. Lebanon, NH: Brandeis University Press, 2004.

Ross v. *Sulu* (Hopi Appellate Court 1991).

Rouhette, A. "Coutumier (Droit)." *Encyclopedia Universalis*. Paris: Encyclopedia Universalis France, 2008.

"Dot." *Encyclopédie Universalis* 4 (1995): 656.

Rouland, Norbert. "La coutume et la pensée juridique sauvage: L'apport des sociétés Inuit." In *Coutume-Costume*, edited by J Gilissen, 316. Brussels: De Boeck université, 1990.

Roy, Etienne Le. "L'accès à l'universalisme par le dialogue interculturel." *Revue générale de droit* 26 (1995): 5.

Rude-Antoine, Edwige, ed. "Les Impensables de La Judiciarisation de L'excision." In *L'immigration Face Aux Lois de La République*. Paris: Karthala Editions, 1992.

Rundle, Kristen. *Forms Liberate: Reclaiming the Jurisprudence of Lon L. Fuller*. Hart Publishing, 2012.

Runyange, Médard. "Défis de La Justice Communautaire Comme Instrument de Résolution Des Conflicts: Cas de Gacaca Traditionnel Au Rwanda." *Cahiers de Centre de Gestion Des Conflicts* 8 (2003): 48–74.

Ryan, Erin. "The Discourse Beneath: Emotional Epistemology in Legal Deliberation and Negotiation." *Harvard Negotiation Law Review* 10 (n.d.): 231.

Sacco, Rodolfo. "Antropologia Giuridica." *Il Mulino, Bologna*, 2007.

Salem, Peter, Debra Kulak, and Robin M. Deutsch. "Triaging Family Court Services: The Connecticut Judicial Branch's Family Civil Intake Screen." *Pace L. Rev.* 27 (2007): 741.

Sander, Frank E.A. "Varieties of Dispute Processing," 70:111. F. R. D., 1976.

Sarat, Austin. "Law Is All Over: Power, Resistance and the Legal Consciousness of the Welfare Poor, The." *Yale JL & Human.* 2 (1990): 343.

Sarat, Austin, and Thomas R. Kearns. "Beyond the Great Divide: Forms of Legal Scholarship and Everyday Life." In *Law in Everyday Life*, edited by Austin Sarat and Thomas R. Kearns. Ann Arbor, MI: University of Michigan Press, 1993.

"The Cultural Lives of Law." In *Law in the Domains of Culture*, edited by Austin Sarat and Thomas R Kearns, 1–7. Ann Arbor: University of Michigan Press, 2000.

Sassoon, Isaac. *The Status of Women in Jewish Tradition*. New York: Cambridge University Press, 2011.

Sauvé, Madeleine. "Mediation: Towards an Aboriginal Conceptualisation." *Aboriginal Law Bulletin* 3, no. 81 (1996): 10.

Schauer, Frederick. "Was Austin Right After All? On the Role of Sanctions in a Theory of Law." *Ratio Juris* 23, no. 1 (2010): 1–6.

Scott, David. "Culture in Political Theory." *Political Theory* 31, no. 1 (2003): 92–115.

Seagle, William. "Primitive Law and Professor Malinowski." *American Anthropologist* 39, no. 2 (1937): 275–90.

Searle, John. "PROPER NAMES." *Mind* 67 (1958): 166–73.

Sen, Amartya Kumar. *The Idea of Justice*. London: Allen Lane, 2009.

Sermet, Laurent. "Le Pluralisme Juridique : Une Approche Française ?" *Revue Juridique, Politique et Économique de La Nouvelle-Calédonie* 22 (2013).

Seron, Carroll and Susan Silbey. "Profession, Science and Culture: An Emergent Canon of Law and Society Research." In *Blackwell Companion to Law and Society*, edited by Austin Sarat, 30–60. Oxford: Blackwell Publishing, 2004.

Sewell Jr, William H. "The Concept(s) of Culture." In *Beyond the Cultural Turn: New Directions in the Study of Society and Culture*, edited by Victoria Bonneil and Lynn Hunt, 35–61. California: University of California Press, 1999.

Shachar, Ayelet. *Multicultural Jurisdictions: Cultural Differences and Women's Rights*. Cambridge: Cambridge University Press, 2001.

"Privatizing Diversity: A Cautionary Tale from Religious Arbitration in Family Law." *Theoretical Inquiries in Law* 9 (2008): 573–607.

"Religion, State, and the Problem of Gender: New Modes of Citizenship and Governance in Diverse Societies." *McGill LJ* 50 (2005): 49.

Shah, Prakash. "A Reflection on the Shari'a Debate in Britain." *Studia Z Prawa Wyznaniowego"("Studies of Ecclesiastical Law")* 13 (2010): 71–98.

"Inconvenient Marriages, or What Happens When Ethnic Minorities Marry Trans-Jurisdictionally according to Their Self-Chosen Norms." *Utrecht L. Rev.* 6, no. 2 (2010).

"Transforming to Accommodate? Reflections on the Shari'a Debate in Britain." In *Legal Practice and Cultural Diversity*, edited by Ballard Grillo, and et al., 1:73–91. Aldershot: Ashgate, 2009.

"Unregistered Marriages in the English Courts." Presented at the RELIGARE Expert Conference: Unregistered Marriages and Alternative Dispute Resolution in European Legal Systems, London: Queen Mary University of London, September 5, 2012.

Shah-Kazemi, Sonia Nourin. "Cross-Cultural Mediation: A Critical View of the Dynamics of Culture in Family Disputes." *International Journal of Law, Policy and the Family* 14, no. 3 (2000): 302–25.

Shalev, Carmel. "Women in Israel: Fighting Tradition." In *Women's Rights, Human Rights: International Feminist Perspectives*, edited by Julie Peters and Andrea Wolper. New York: Routledge, 1995.

Shankman, Paul. "Le Rôti et le Bouilli: Lévi-Strauss Theory of Cannibalism." *Am Anthropol* 71, no. 1 (1969): 59–60.

Shapiro, Barbara J. *A Culture of Fact: England, 1550–1720*. Cornell University Press, 2003.

Shapiro, Daniel L. "Emotions in Negotiation: Peril or Promise." *Marq. L. Rev.* 87 (2004): 737.

Shaw, Rosalind. "Memory Frictions: Localizing the Truth and Reconciliation Commission in Sierra Leone." *International Journal of Transitional Justice* 1 (2007): 183–207.

"Rethinking Truth and Reconciliation Commissions: Lessons from Sierra Leone." *USIP Special Report* 130 (2005): 1–12.

Shaw, Rosalind, and Lars Waldorf. "Introduction: Localizing Transitional Justice." In *Localizing Transitional Justice*, edited by R. Shaw, L. Waldorf, and P. Hazan, 3–26. Stanford: Stanford University Press, 2010.

Shaw, Rosalind, Lars Waldorf, and Pierre Hazan, eds. *Localizing Transitional Justice: Interventions and Priorities after Mass Violence*. Stanford: Stanford University Press, 2010.

Sheehan, Bernard. *Savagism and Civility: Indians and Englishmen in Colonial Virginia*. Cambridge University Press Archive, 1980.

Shepler, Susan. *Childhood Deployed: Remaking Child Soldiers in Sierra Leone.* NYU Press, 2014.

Shook, E. Victoria. *Ho'oponopono: Contemporary Uses of a Hawaiian Problem-Solving Process.* Honolulu: University of Hawaii Press, Press for East-West Center, 1985.

Shook, E. Victoria, and Leonard Ke'ala Kwan. "Straightening Relationships and Settling Disputes in Hawai'i: Ho'oponopono and Mediation." In *Matsunada Institute for Peace, University of Hawai'I,* 1–56. Manoa, Program on Conflict Resolution, PCR Working Paper Series 1987–10. Manoa, Hawaii: n.p., 1987. www.peaceinstitute.hawaii.edu/resources/_epubs/Straightening-Relationships-and-Settling-Disputes-in-Hawaii.pdf.

Silbey, Susan S., and Patricia Ewick. *The Common Place of Law: Stories from Everyday Life.* Chicago: University of Chicago Press, 1998.

Silliman, G. Sidney. "A Political Analysis of the Philippines' Katarungang Pambarangay System of Informal Justice through Mediation." *Law and Society Review* 19 (1985): 279–301.

Sills, David L., ed. "Law and Legal Institutions." In *International Encyclopedia of the Social Sciences,* Vol. IX. New York: Macmillan, 1968.

Smith, David N. "A Warmer Way of Disputing: Mediation and Conciliation." *Am. J. Comp. L. Sup.* 26 (1977): 205.

Smith v. *James* (1999).

Snyder, Francis G. "Colonialism and Legal Form: The Creation of 'customary Law' in Senegal." In *Crime, Justice and Underdevelopment,* edited by Colin Sumner. London: Heinemann, 1982.

"Colonialism and Legal Form: The Creation of 'customary Law' in Senegal." *The Journal of Legal Pluralism and Unofficial Law* 13, no. 19 (1981): 49–90.

Sogge, David. *Repairing the Weakest Links: A New Agenda for Fragile States.* Madrid: Fride, 2009.

Solis, Gary D. *The Law of Armed Conflict: International Humanitarian Law in War.* Cambridge University Press, 2010.

Solovy, Jodi M. "Comment, Civil Enforcement of Jewish Marriage and Divorce: Constitutional Accommodation of a Religious Mandate." *DePaul L. Rev.* 45 (1996): 493.

Sona, Federica. "Polygamy in Britain." *Osservatorio Delle Libertà Ed Istituzioni Religiose, Online,* July 2005. www.Sona_Polygamy_in_Britain.pdf.

Stahl, Lucile. "Le Droit de La Protection de La Nature et de La Diversité Biologique Dans Les Collectivités Françaises d'Outre-Mer." *Lyon* 3 (2009). www.theses.fr/2008LYO31022.

Stanner, W. E. H., Diane Barwick, Jeremy Beckett, and Marie Reay. *Metaphors of Interpretation: Essays in Honour of WEH Stanner.* Australian National University Press, 1985.

Starr, June. "Mediation: Anthropological Perspectives." *ALSA Forum* 6 (1982): 221.

Starr, June and Jane Fishburne Collier. "Introduction: Dialogues in Legal Anthropology." In *History and Power in the Study of Law: New Directions in Legal Anthropology*, edited by June Starr and Jane Fishburne Collier. Ithaca: Cornell University Press, 1989.

Starr, June and Barbara Yngvesson. "Scarcity and Disputing: Zero-Ing in on Compromise Decisions." *American Ethnologist* 2 (1975): 553–66.

Stavrevska, Elena. "Ensuring Political Represen-Tation in a Restructured Bosnia and Herzegovina." In *CORE Policy Brief*. Oslo: Peace Research Institute Oslo, 2013. www.francescoragazzi.com/files/CORE_Policy_Brief_1-2013.pdf.

Stockholm Resilience Centre. *What Is Resilience: An Introduction to Social-Ecological Research*, n.d. www.stockholmresilience.org/download/18.5ea7abe0139d0dada521ac/resilience_summary_lowX.pdf.

Stopler, Gila. "The Free Exercise of Discrimination: Religious Liberty, Civic Community and Women's Equality." *William and Mary Journal of Women and Law* 10 (2004): 459.

Stowasser, Barbara "Gender Issues and Contemporary Qur'an Interpretations." In *Islam, Gender, & Social Change*, edited by Yvonne Yazbeck Haddad and John L. Esposito. Oxford: Oxford University Press, 1998.

Straus, Scott and Lars Waldorf, eds. *Remaking Rwanda: State Building and Human Rights after Mass Violence*. Madison: University of Wisconsin Press, 2011.

Strawson, P. F. *Individuals: An Essay in Descriptive Metaphysics*. London: Methuen, 1959.

Strum, Philippa. "Women and the Politics of Religion in Israel." *Hum. Rts. Q.* 11, no. 4 (1989): 483.

Strickland, Pat. *Forced Marriage*. Home Affairs Section. House of Commons Library, September 16, 2013. Parliament www.parliament.uk/briefing-papers/sn01003.pdf.

Stubbs, William. *The Constitutional History of England in Its Origin and Development*. Vol. 1. Oxford: Clarendon Press, 1880.

Sundari, Anitha, and Aisha Gill. "Coercion, Consent and the Forced Marriage Debate in the UK." *Feminist Legal Studies* 17, no. 2 (2009): 165–84.

Sunstein, Cass R. "Social Norms and Social Roles." *Columbia Law Rev* 96 (1996): 903.

Swindler, Ann. "Culture in Action: Symbols and Strategies." *American Sociological Review* 51, no. 2 (1986): 273–86.

Tadjbakhsh, Shahrbanou. *Rethinking the Liberal Peace: External Models and Local Alternatives*. London: Taylor & Francis, 2011.

Tamanaha, Brian. *A General Jurisprudence of Law and Society*. New York: Oxford University Press, 2001.

"A Non-Essentialist Version of Legal Pluralism." *Journal of Law and Society* 27, no. 2 (2000): 296–321.

On the Rule of Law: History, Politics, Theory. Vol. 1. Cambridge: Cambridge University Press, 2004.

"The Folly of the 'Social Scientific' Concept of Legal Pluralism." *Law and Society* 20 (1993): 192–217.

"Understanding Legal Pluralism: Past to Present, Local to Global." *Sydney L Rev* 30 (2008): 375–411.

Tanaka, Yuki. *Hidden Horrors–Japanese War Crimes in World War 2.* Boulder, CO: Westview Press, 1996.

Taylor, Charles. *Sources of the Self: The Making of the Modern Identity.* Cambridge, Mass: Harvard University Press, 1989.

"The Politics of Recognition." In *Multiculturalism and The Politics of Recognition,* edited by A. Gutmann. Princeton: Princeton University Press, 1992.

Teubner, Gunther. "The Two Faces of Janus: Rethinking Legal Pluralism." *Cardozo L. Rev.* 13 (1992): 1443.

Theidon, Kimberly. *Intimate Enemies: Violence and Reconciliation in Peru.* Philadelphia: University of Pennsylvania Press, 2012.

Thomas, Nicholas. *Possessions: Indigenous Art, Colonial Culture.* London: Thames and Hudson, 1999.

Thomson, Susan. "After Genocide: Transitional Justice, Post-Conflict Reconstruction." *The International Journal of African Historical Studies* 43, no. 1 (2010): 192–95.

"The Darker Side of Transitional Justice: The Power Dynamics behind Rwanda's Gacaca Courts." *Africa* 81, no. 3 (2011): 373–90.

Whispering Truth to Power: Everyday Resistance to Reconciliation in Postgenocide Rwanda. Madison: University of Wisconsin Press, 2013.

"Whispering Truth to Power: The Everyday Resistance of Rwandan Peasants to Post-Genocide Reconciliation." *African Affairs* 110, no. 440 (2011): 439–56.

Thomson, Susan, and Rosemary Nagy. "Law, Power and Justice: What Legalism Fails to Address in the Functioning of Rwanda's Gacaca Courts." *International Journal of Transitional Justice* 5, no. 1 (2011): 11–30.

Titiev, Mischa. *Old Oraibi: A Study of the Hopi Indians of Third Mesa.* Harvard University Peabody Museum of American Archaeology and Ethnology Papers. Cambridge, MA: Harvard University Press, 1944.

Tsilqot'in Nation v. *BC,* (SCC 14 2014).

Tokatlián, Juan Gabriel. *Organised Crime, Illicit Drugs and State Vulnerability.* Oslo: Norwegian Peacebuilding Centre, 2011.

Tully, James. *Strange Multiplicity: Constitutionalism in an Age of Diversity.* Cambridge: Cambridge University Press, 1995.

Turner, Dale. *This Is Not a Peace Pipe.* Toronto: University of Toronto Press, 2006 at 83.

Twining, William. "Narrative and Generalizations in Argumentation about Questions of Fact." *S Tex L Rev* 40 (1999): 351.

Rethinking Evidence: Exploratory Essays. Northwestern University Press, 1990.

Ulrich, Gretchen. “Widening the Circle: Adapting Traditional Indian Dispute Resolution Methods to Implement Alternative Dispute Resolution and Restorative Justice in Modern Communities.” *Hamline J. Pub. L. & Pol’y* 20 (1999): 419.

Umbreit, Mark S. “Humanistic Mediation: A Transformative Journey of Peacemaking.” *Mediation Quarterly* 14 (1997): 201–13.

Umbreit, Mark S., and Robert B. Coates. “Multicultural Implications of Restorative Justice:” *Fed. Probation* 63, no. 2 (1999): 44–51.

Unger, Roberto. *The Critical Legal Studies Movement.* Harvard: Harvard University Press, 1986. www.jstor.org/stable/1341032.

Uniform Law Commission. *The Uniform Statutory Rule Against Perpetuities, with 1990 Amendments, Prefatory Note.* Chicago: The National Conference of Commissioners on Uniform State Laws, 1990.

United States Census. *American Indian and Alaska Native Summary File (AIANSF),* 2000. www.census.gov/census2000/AIANSF.html (accessed December 28, 2012).

Van Den Bergh, G. C. J. J. “The Concept of Folk Law in Historical Context: A Brief Outline.” In *Folk Law: Essays in the Theory and Practice of Lex Non Scripta,* edited by A. Dundes Renteln and A. Dundes, Vol. 1. New York and London: Garland, 1994.

Van Praagh, Shauna. “Education of Religious Children: Families, Communities and Constitutions, The.” *Buff. L. Rev.* 47 (1999): 1343.

“Faith, Belonging, and the Protection of Our Children.” *Windsor YB Access Just.* 17 (1999): 154.

Van Veen, J. Benjamin. “Moot Courts and the Law School.” *NYUL Rev.* 1 (1924): 37.

Vanderlinden, Jacques. *Anthropologie Juridique.* Paris: Dalloz, 1996.

Vansina, Jan. *Antecedents to Modern Rwanda: The Nyiginya Kingdom.* Madison: University of Wisconsin Press, 2004.

Vanuxem, Sarah. “Le Devenir Des Régimes d’Accès Aux Ressources Génétiques et de Partage Des Avantages (APA). Etude Comparée Des Projets Calédonien et Européen.” *Droit de L’environnement* 214 (juillet/août 2013): 256–64.

Venables , Philip. *Mornington Island Restorative Justice (MIRJ) Project: Report on Its Development, Implementation and Transition to Community Management 2012.* Brisbane, Australia: Queensland Government Department of Justice and Attorney General, Dispute Resolution Branch., 2012.

Venter, Elise. “Eliminating Fear through Recreating Community in Rwanda: The Role of the Gacaca Courts.” *Texas Wesleyan Law Review* 13 (2006): 577–98.

Verdier, R. “Chercher Remède À L’excision: Une Nécessaire Concertation.” *Droit et Cultures* 20 (1990): 147–50.

"Le Double Procès de Mme Kéita (Paris-Bobigny, Mars-Juin 1991)." In *L'immigration Face Aux Lois de La République*, edited by E. Rude-Antoine. Karthala Editions, 1992.

"Une Exciseuse En Cour d'Assises, Le Procès de Soko Aramata Keita." *Droit et Cultures* 21 (1991): 184–87.

Vinogradoff, Paul. *Custom and Right*. Vol. 3. Oslo and Cambridge: The Lawbook Exchange Ltd., 1925.

Volpp, Leti. "Feminism versus Multiculturalism." *Columbia Law Review* 101 (2001): 1181–218.

Von Benda-Beckmann, Franz. "Law out of Context: A Comment on the Creation of Traditional Law Discussion." *J. Afr. Law* 28, no. 1/2 (1984): 28–33.

"Riding or Killing the Centaur: Reflections on the Identities of Legal Anthropology." In *Law and Anthropology*, edited by Michael Freeman and David Napier, 13–46. Oxford: Oxford University Press, 2009

Von Benda-Beckmann, Franz and Keebet von Benda-Beckmannn. "The Dynamics of Change and Continuity in Plural Legal Orders." *The Journal of Legal Pluralism and Unofficial Law*, no. 53 (2006): 1–44.

Von Benda-Beckmann, Franz, Keebet von Benda-Beckmann and Anne Griffiths, eds. *Spatializing Law*. Surrey: Ashgate, 2009.

Von Benda-Beckmann, Keebet. "Dispute sans Fin Sur La Méthode de L'anthropologie Juridique." *Droit et Culture* 21 (1991): 82.

Vulliamy, Ed and Saptarshi Ray. "David Simon, Creator of The Wire, Says New US Drug Laws Help Only 'white, Middle-Class Kids.'" *The Observer*, May 25, 2013. www.guardian.co.uk/world/2013/may/25/the-wire-creator-us-drug-laws.

Wadud, Amina. *Qur'an and Woman: Rereading the Sacred Text from a Woman's Perspective*. Oxford: Oxford University Press, 1999.

Wahrhaftig, Paul. "An Overview of Community-Oriented Citizen Dispute Resolution Programs in the United States." *The Politics of Informal Justice* 1 (1982): 75–97.

Waldorf, Lars. "Instrumentalizing Genocide: The RPF's Campaign against 'genocide Ideology.'" In *Remaking Genocide*, edited by S. Strauss and L. Waldorf, 48–66. Madison: University of Wisconsin Press, 2011.

"'Like Jews Waiting for Jesus': Posthumous Justice in Post-Genocide Rwanda." In *Localizing Transitional Justice: Interventions and Priorities after Mass Violence*, edited by R. Shaw, L. Waldorf, and P. Hazan, 183–202. Stanford: Stanford University Press, 2010.

"Mass Justice for Mass Atrocity: Rethinking Local Justice as Transitional Justice." *Temple Law Review* 79, no. 1 (2006): 1–87.

Waldron, Jane A., Colleen P. Roth, Patricia H. Fair, Eberhard M. Mann, and John F. McDermott. "A Therapeutic Mediation Model for Child Custody Dispute Resolution." *Mediation Quarterly*, no. 3 (1984): 5–20.

Waldron, Jeremy. "All We Like Sheep." *Can. JL & Jurisprudence* 12 (1999): 169–86.

Walker, Jeremy, and Melinda Cooper. "Genealogies of Resilience From Systems Ecology to the Political Economy of Crisis Adaptation." *Security Dialogue* 42, no. 2 (2011): 143–60.

Wall, James A., and Ronda Roberts Callister. "Ho'oponopono: Some Lessons from Hawaiian Mediation." *Negotiation Journal* 11 (1995): 45–54.

Walsh, Michael. "Interactional Styles in the Courtroom: An Example from Northern Australia." In *Language and the Law*, edited by J. Gibbons. London: Longman, 1994.

Walzer, Michael. *Spheres of Justice*. New York: Basic Books, 1983.

Wani, Mohammad Afzal. *The Islamic Law on Maintenance of Women, Children, Parents & Other Relatives: Classical Principles and Modern Legislations in India and Muslim Countries*. New Delhi: Upright Study Home, 1995.

Wastell, Sari. "When Is Law and Custom Not Customary Law?" *Journal of the Finnish Anthropological Society* 32, no. 2 (2007): 71–84.

Waterman, Adam John. The Price of the Purchase: Black Hawk's War and the Colonization of the Upper Mississippi River Valley. New York University, 2007. Unpublished PhD thesis.

Watson, A. "An Approach to Customary Law." In *Folk Law: Essays in the Theory and Practice of Lex Non Scripta*, edited by A. Dundes Renteln and A. Dundes. Madison: University of Wisconsin Press, 1995.

Legal Transplants: An Approach to Comparative Law. 2nd edn. Athens, GA: University of Georgia Press, 1993. "

"Legal Transplants and Law Reform." *Law Quarterly Review* 92 (1976): 79–84.

Waute v. *Pujapujane*, RG (Nouméa Court of Appeals 2013).

Webber, Jeremy. "Culture, Legal Culture, and Legal Reasoning: A Comment on Nelken." *Austl J Leg Phil* 29 (2004): 27.

"Legal Pluralism and Human Agency." *Osgoode Hall LJ* 1 (2006): 44.

Weber, Max. *The Religion of China. Confucianism and Taoism... Translated and Edited by Hans H. Gerth. With an Introduction by CK Yang*. Glencoe, Illinois: Free Press, 1951.

Wegner, Judith Romney. "The Status of Women in Jewish and Islamic Marriage and Divorce Law." *Harv. Women's LJ* 5 (1982): 32.

Weiner, James. "Culture in a Sealed Envelope: The Concealment of Australian Aboriginal Heritage and Tradition in the Hindmarsh Island Bridge Affair." *Journal of the Royal Anthropological Institute* 5, no. 2 (1999): 193–210.

Weiss, Susan. "Israeli Divorce Law: The Maldistribution of Power, Its Abuses, and the 'Status' of Jewish Women." In *Men and Women: Gender, Judaism and Democracy*, edited by Rachel Elior, 53. Van Leer Jerusalem Institute: Urim Publications, 2004.

Weiss, Susan Metzger. "Sign at Your Own Risk: The RCA Prenuptial May Prejudice the Fairness of Your Future Divorce Settlement." *Cardozo Women's LJ* 6 (1999): 49.

Wellman, Henry M., and Susan Gelman. "Cognitive Development: Foundational Theories of Core Domains." *Annual Review of Psychology* 43 (1992): 337–75.

White, Graham. "Cultures in Collision: Traditional Knowledge and Euro-Canadian Governance Processes in Northern Land-Claim Board." *Arctic* 59, no. 4 (2006): 401–14.

White, James Boyd. *Justice as Translation: An Essay in Cultural and Legal Criticism*. University of Chicago Press, 1994.

"Law as Rhetoric, Rhetoric as Law: The Arts of Cultural and Communal Life." *The University of Chicago Law Review* 52, no. 3 (1985): 684–702.

White, Lucie E. "Subordination, Rhetorical Survival Skills, and Sunday Shoes: Notes on the Hearing of Mrs. G." *Buff. L. Rev.* 38, no. 1 (1990): 33 n.96.

Whiteley, Peter. *Rethinking Hopi Ethnography*. Washington, DC: Smithsonian Institution Press Washington DC, 1998.

The Orayvi Split: A Hopi Transformation. New York: American Museum of Natural History, 2008.

Wilke, Christiane. "Reconsecrating the Temple of Justice: Invocations of Civilization and Humanity in the Nuremberg Justice Case." *Can J Law Soc* 24, no. 2 (2009): 181.

Williams, Nancy M., and M. Williams Nancy. *Two Laws: Managing Disputes in a Contemporary Aboriginal Community*. Canberra: Australian Institute of Aboriginal Studies, 1987.

Willis, John. "Foreign Borrowings." *UTLJ* 20 (1970): 274–82.

Wilson, Richard. *The Politics of Truth and Reconciliation in South Africa: Legitimizing the Post-Apartheid State*. Cambridge: Cambridge University Press, 2001.

Woodman, G. R. "African Legal Systems." In *International Encyclopedia of the Social & Behavioural Sciences*, edited by N. J. Smelser and P. B. Baltes. Amsterdam: Elsevier, 2004.

"Custom in African Laws After the Introduction of the Common Law." In *La Coutume-Costume*, edited by J. Glissen, Vol. LI, 1990.

"Customary Law, State Courts and The Notion of Institutionalization of Norms in Ghana and Nigeria." In *People's Law and State Law: The Bellagio Papers*, edited by Antony Allott and Gordon R. Woodman, 143–166. Dordrecht and Cinnaminson: Foris Publications, 1985.

"Some Realism About Customary Law–The West African Experience." In *Folk Law: Essays in the Theory and Practice of Lex Non Scripta*, edited by Allison Dundes Renteln, Vol. 1. Madison, WI: University of Wisconsin Press, 1995.

Woodman, Gordon R., and Akintunde Olusegun Obilade. *African Law and Legal Theory*. Dartmouth, 1995.

Yar, Majid. "Recognition and the Politics of Human (e) Desire." *Theory, Culture & Society* 18, no. 2–3 (2001): 57–76.

Yefet, Karin Carmit. "Unchaining the Agunot: Enlisting the Israeli Constitutional in the Service of Women's Marital Freedom." *Yale JL & Feminism* 20 (2008): 441.

Young, Iris Marion. *Justice and the Politics of Difference.* Princeton: Princeton University Press, 1990.

Zimmermann, Augusto. "The Rule of Law as a Culture of Legality: Legal and Extra-Legal Elements for the Realization of the Rule of Law in Society, The." *ELaw - Murdoch University Electronic Journal of Law* 14(1) (2007): 10–31.

Zorzetto, Silvia. *La Consuetudine Giuridica: Teoria, Storia, Ambiti Disciplinari.* Pisa: ETS, 2008.

INDEX

CAMBRIDGE STUDIES IN LAW AND SOCIETY

Books in the Series

Diseases of the Will Mariana Valverde

The Politics of Truth and Reconciliation in South Africa: Legitimizing the Post-Apartheid State Richard A. Wilson

Modernism and the Grounds of Law Peter Fitzpatrick

Unemployment and Government: Genealogies of the Social William Walters

Autonomy and Ethnicity: Negotiating Competing Claims in Multi-Ethnic States Yash Ghai

Constituting Democracy: Law, Globalism and South Africa's Political Reconstruction Heinz Klug

The Ritual of Rights in Japan: Law, Society, and Health Policy Eric A. Feldman

The Invention of the Passport: Surveillance, Citizenship and the State John Torpey

Governing Morals: A Social History of Moral Regulation Alan Hunt

The Colonies of Law: Colonialism, Zionism and Law in Early Mandate Palestine Ronen Shamir

Law and Nature David Delaney

Social Citizenship and Workfare in the United States and Western Europe: The Paradox of Inclusion Joel F. Handler

Law, Anthropology and the Constitution of the Social: Making Persons and Things Edited by Alain Pottage and Martha Mundy

Judicial Review and Bureaucratic Impact: International and Interdisciplinary Perspectives Edited by Marc Hertogh and Simon Halliday

Immigrants at the Margins: Law, Race, and Exclusion in Southern Europe Kitty Calavita

Lawyers and Regulation: The Politics of the Administrative Process Patrick Schmidt

Law and Globalization from Below: Toward a Cosmopolitan Legality Edited by Boaventura de Sousa Santos and Cesar A. Rodriguez-Garavito

Public Accountability: Designs, Dilemmas and Experiences Edited by Michael W. Dowdle

Law, Violence and Sovereignty among West Bank Palestinians Tobias Kelly

Legal Reform and Administrative Detention Powers in China Sarah Biddulph

The Practice of Human Rights: Tracking Law between the Global and the Local Edited by Mark Goodale and Sally Engle Merry

Judges beyond Politics in Democracy and Dictatorship: Lessons from Chile Lisa Hilbink

Paths to International Justice: Social and Legal Perspectives Edited by Marie-Bénédicte Dembour and Tobias Kelly

Law and Society in Vietnam: The Transition from Socialism in Comparative Perspective Mark Sidel

Constitutionalizing Economic Globalization: Investment Rules and Democracy's Promise David Schneiderman

The New World Trade Organization Knowledge Agreements: 2nd Edition Christopher Arup

Justice and Reconciliation in Post-Apartheid South Africa Edited by François du Bois and Antje du Bois-Pedain

Militarization and Violence against Women in Conflict Zones in the Middle East: A Palestinian Case-Study Nadera Shalhoub-Kevorkian

Child Pornography and Sexual Grooming: Legal and Societal Responses Suzanne Ost

Darfur and the Crime of Genocide John Hagan and Wenona Rymond-Richmond

Fictions of Justice: The International Criminal Court and the Challenge of Legal Pluralism in Sub-Saharan Africa Kamari Maxine Clarke

Conducting Law and Society Research: Reflections on Methods and Practices Simon Halliday and Patrick Schmidt

Planted Flags: Trees, Land, and Law in Israel/Palestine Irus Braverman

Culture under Cross-Examination: International Justice and the Special Court for Sierra Leone Tim Kelsall

Cultures of Legality: Judicialization and Political Activism in Latin America Edited by Javier Couso, Alexandra Huneeus and Rachel Sieder

Courting Democracy in Bosnia and Herzegovina: The Hague Tribunal's Impact in a Postwar State Lara J. Nettelfield

The Gacaca Courts and Post-Genocide Justice and Reconciliation in Rwanda: Justice without Lawyers Phil Clark

Law, Society, and History: Themes in the Legal Sociology and Legal History of Lawrence M. Friedman Robert W. Gordon and Morton J. Horwitz

After Abu Ghraib: Exploring Human Rights in America and the Middle East Shadi Mokhtari

Adjudication in Religious Family Laws: Cultural Accommodation: Legal Pluralism, and Gender Equality in India Gopika Solanki

Water on Tap: Rights and Regulation in the Transnational Governance of Urban Water Services Bronwen Morgan

Elements of Moral Cognition: Rawls' Linguistic Analogy and the Cognitive Science of Moral and Legal Judgment John Mikhail

A Sociology of Transnational Constitutions: Social Foundations of the Post-National Legal Structure Chris Thornhill

Mitigation and Aggravation at Sentencing Edited by Julian Roberts

Institutional Inequality and the Mobilization of the Family and Medical Leave Act: Rights on Leave Catherine R. Albiston

Authoritarian Rule of Law: Legislation, Discourse and Legitimacy in Singapore Jothie Rajah

Law and Development and the Global Discourses of Legal Transfers Edited by John Gillespie and Pip Nicholson

Law against the State: Ethnographic Forays into Law's Transformations Edited by Julia Eckert, Brian Donahoe, Christian Strümpell and Zerrin Özlem Biner

Transnational Legal Process and State Change Edited by Gregory C. Shaffer

Legal Mobilization under Authoritarianism: The Case of Post-Colonial Hong Kong Edited by Waikeung Tam

Complementarity in the Line of Fire: The Catalysing Effect of the International Criminal Court in Uganda and Sudan Sarah M. H. Nouwen

Political and Legal Transformations of an Indonesian Polity: The Nagari from Colonisation to Decentralisation Franz von Benda-Beckmann and Keebet von Benda-Beckmann

Pakistan's Experience with Formal Law: An Alien Justice Osama Siddique

Human Rights under State-Enforced Religious Family Laws in Israel, Egypt, and India Yüksel Sezgin

Why Prison? Edited by David Scott

Law's Fragile State: Colonial, Authoritarian, and Humanitarian Legacies in Sudan Mark Fathi Massoud

Rights for Others: The Slow Home-Coming of Human Rights in the Netherlands Barbara Oomen

European States and their Muslim Citizens: The Impact of Institutions on Perceptions and Boundaries Edited by John R. Bowen, Christophe Bertossi, Jan Willem Duyvendak and Mona Lena Krook

Environmental Litigation in China Rachel E. Stern

Indigeneity and Legal Pluralism in India: Claims, Histories, Meanings Pooja Parmar

Paper Tiger: Law, Bureaucracy and the Developmental State in Himalayan India Nayanika Mathur

Religion, Law and Society Russell Sandberg

The Experiences of Face Veil Wearers in Europe and the Law Edited by Eva Brems

The Contentious History of the International Bill of Human Rights Christopher N. J. Roberts

Transnational Legal Orders Edited by Terence C. Halliday and Gregory Shaffer

Lost in China?: Law, Culture and Society in Post-1997 Hong Kong Carol A. G. Jones

Security Theology, Surveillance and the Politics of Fear Nadera Shalhoub-Kevorkian

Opposing the Rule of Law: How Myanmar's Courts Make Law and Order Nick Cheesman

The Ironies of Colonial Governance: Law, Custom and Justice in Colonial India James Jaffe

The Clinic and the Court: Law, Medicine and Anthropology Edited by Tobias Kelly, Ian Harper and Akshay Khanna

A World of Indicators: The Making of Government Knowledge through Quantification Edited by Richard Rottenburg, Sally E. Merry, Sung-Joon Park and Johanna Mugler

Contesting Immigration Policy in Court: Legal Activism and its Radiating Effects in the United States and France Leila Kawar

The Quiet Power of Indicators: Measuring Governance, Corruption, and Rule of Law Edited by Sally Engle Merry, Kevin Davis and Benedict Kingsbury

Investing in Authoritarian Rule: Punishment and Patronage in Rwanda's Gacaca Courts for Genocide Crimes Anuradha Chakravarty

Contractual Knowledge: One Hundred Years of Legal Experimentation in Global Markets Edited by Grégoire Mallard and Jérôme Sgard

Iraq and the Crimes of Aggressive War: The Legal Cynicism of Criminal Militarism John Hagan, Joshua Kaiser, and Anna Hanson

Culture in the Domains of Law Edited by René Provost

China and Islam: The Prophet, the Party, and Law Matthew S. Erie

Diversity in Practice: Race, Gender, and Class in Legal and Professional Careers Edited by Spencer Headworth and Robert Nelson

A Sociology of Transnational Constitutions: Social Foundations of the Post-National Legal Structure Chris Thornhill

Shifting Legal Visions: Judicial Change and Human Rights Trials in Latin America Ezequiel A. González Ocantos

The Demographic Transformations of Citizenship Heli Askola

Criminal Defense in China: The Politics of Lawyers at Work Sida Liu and Terence C. Halliday

Contesting Economic and Social Rights in Ireland: Constitution, State and Society, 1848–2016 Thomas Murray

Buried in the Heart: Women, Complex Victimhood and the War in Northern Uganda Erin Baines

Palaces of Hope: The Anthropology of Global Organizations Edited by Ronald Niezen and Maria Sapignoli

The Politics of Bureaucratic Corruption in Post-Transitional Eastern Europe Marina Zaloznaya

Revisiting the Law and Governance of Trafficking, Forced Labor and Modern Slavery Prabha Kotiswaran

CPSIA information can be obtained
at www.ICGtesting.com
Printed in the USA
LVOW01*1037090217
523738LV00008B/26/P

9 781107 163331